STOP!

This is the back of the book.
You wouldn't want to spoil a great ending!

This book is printed "manga-style," in the authentic Japanese right-to-left format. Since none of the artwork has been flipped or altered, readers get to experience the story just as the creator intended. You've been asking for it, so TOKYOPOP® delivered: authentic, hot-off-the-press, and far more fun!

DIRECTIONS

If this is your first time reading manga-style, here's a quick guide to help you understand how it works.

It's easy... just start in the top right panel and follow the numbers. Have fun, and look for more 100% authentic manga from TOKYOPOP®!

Maid Sama!™

The class president has a little secret she's keeping from the sexy bad boy in school...

'It's hard to deny this guilty
oleasure when it looks like
t's having so much fun."
-About.com

Maid Sama!
Hiro Fujiwara
TOKYOPOP
2

1isaki's troubles with Usui are
ar from over! His apparent
eelings for her only confuse
1isaki right when she most
ıeeds to be clear-headed.
Two (male) distractions from a
ıigh-ranked prep school show up
o complicate matters, and the
chool sports festival is just
round the corner, too!
Vhat's a tough maid to do?

MANCE

T
TEEN
AGE 13+

BE SURE TO VISIT WWW.TOKYOPOP.COM/SHOP FOR EVERYTHING YOU COULD EVER WANT!

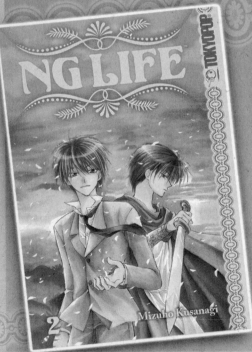

KARAKURI ODETTE

カラクリ オデット

SHE'S A HOT ROBOT IN HIGH SCHOOL WHAT'S THE WORST THAT COULD HAPPEN?

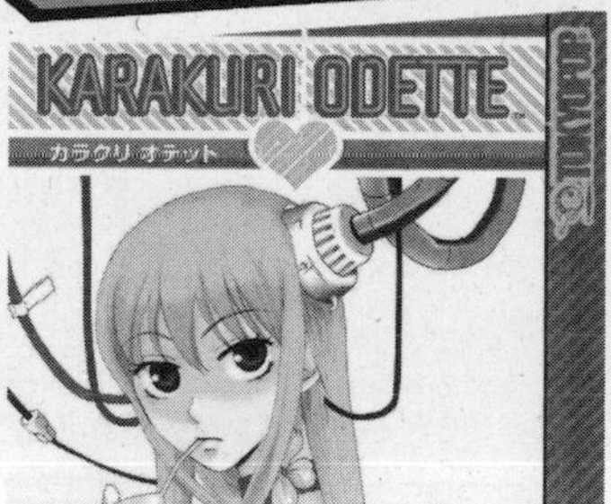
KARAKURI ODETTE
カラクリ オデット
TOKYOPOP
1
JULIETTA SUZUKI

From the creator of *Akuma to Dolce*

Odette is an android created by the young, talented Dr. Yoshizawa. Wanting to find the ultimate difference between humans and androids, she decides to enroll in high school. Follow Odette's adventures, as she ventures through her school's hallowed halls, in search of the true meaning of being a human!

BE SURE TO VISIT WWW.TOKYOPOP.COM/SHOP FOR EVERYTHING YOU COULD EVER WANT!

A dark, Gothic tale from the artist of *Trinity Blood*

A mysterious drug, known only as "Zone-00," seems to be causing demons all over Tokyo to lose control and revert to their old, violent ways. Enter two young students who stand on opposite sides of an ageless conflict. One a demon, the other an exorcist, they must now join forces to uncover the secret of "Zone-00" before it's too late!

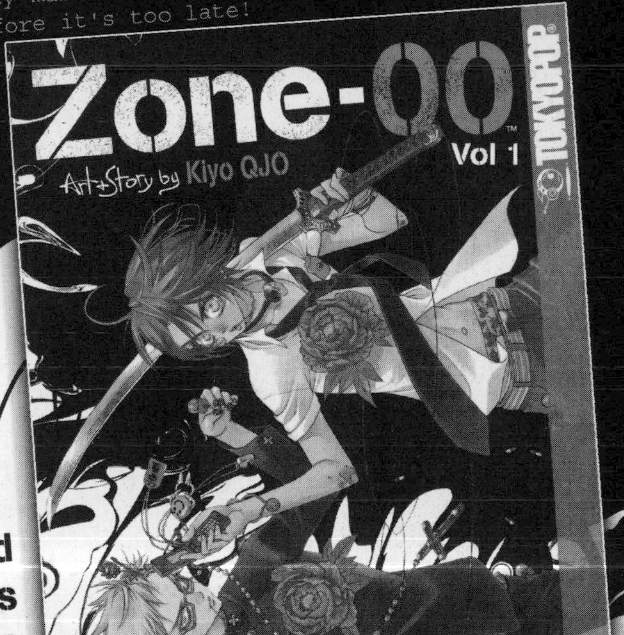
Zone-00™
Vol 1
Art+Story by Kiyo QJO
TOKYOPOP
From the artist of TRINITY BLOOD

In a world here humans and demons coexist under a fragile eace, change is coming...

BE SURE TO VISIT WWW.TOKYOPOP.COM/SHOP FOR EVERYTHING YOU COULD EVER WANT!

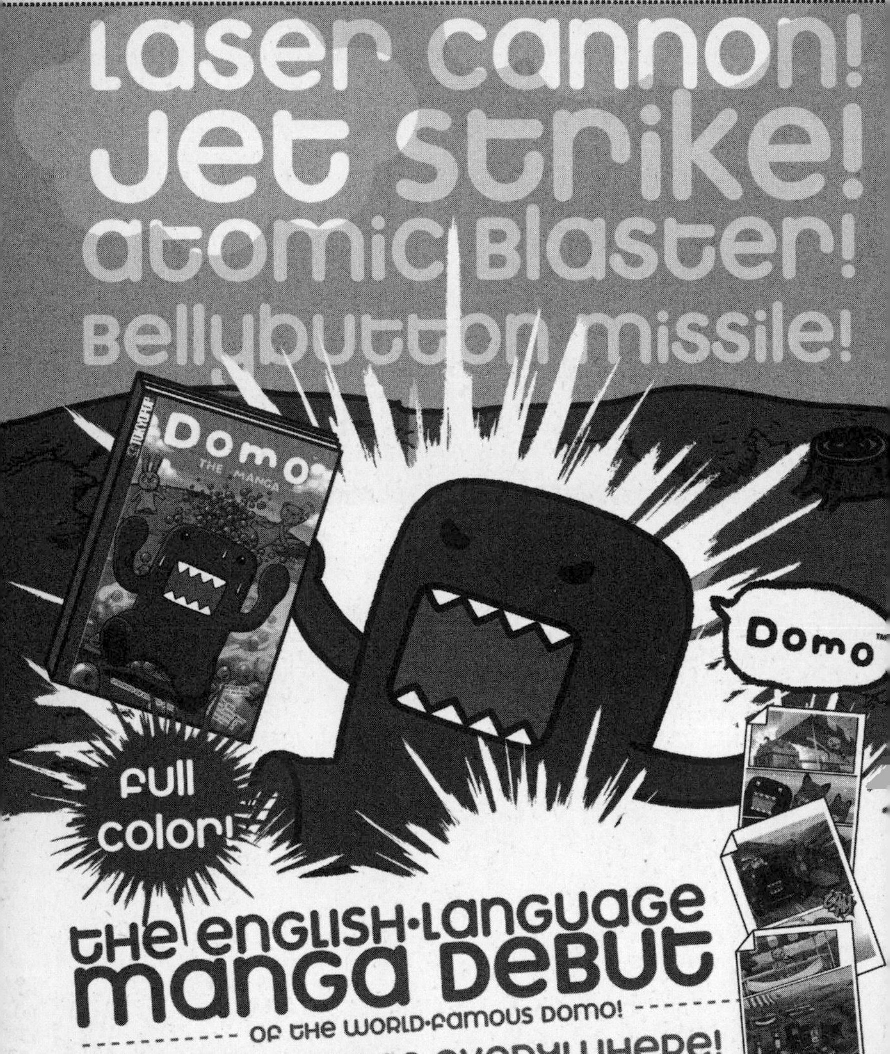
Laser Cannon!
Jet Strike!
Atomic Blaster!
Bellybutton Missile!
Domo
THE MANGA
Domo™
full color!
The English-Language
Manga Debut
of the World-Famous Domo!
Invading Stores Everywhere!
PREVIEWS, CONTESTS, AND MORE AT WWW.TOKYOPOP.COM/DOMO_MANGA
DOMO © NHK-TYO 1998-2009. DOMO ANIMATION © DOMO PRODUCTION COMMITTEE. ALL RIGHTS RESERVED. WWW.DOMONATION.COM

MIKANSEI NO.1

Majiko!

Disc

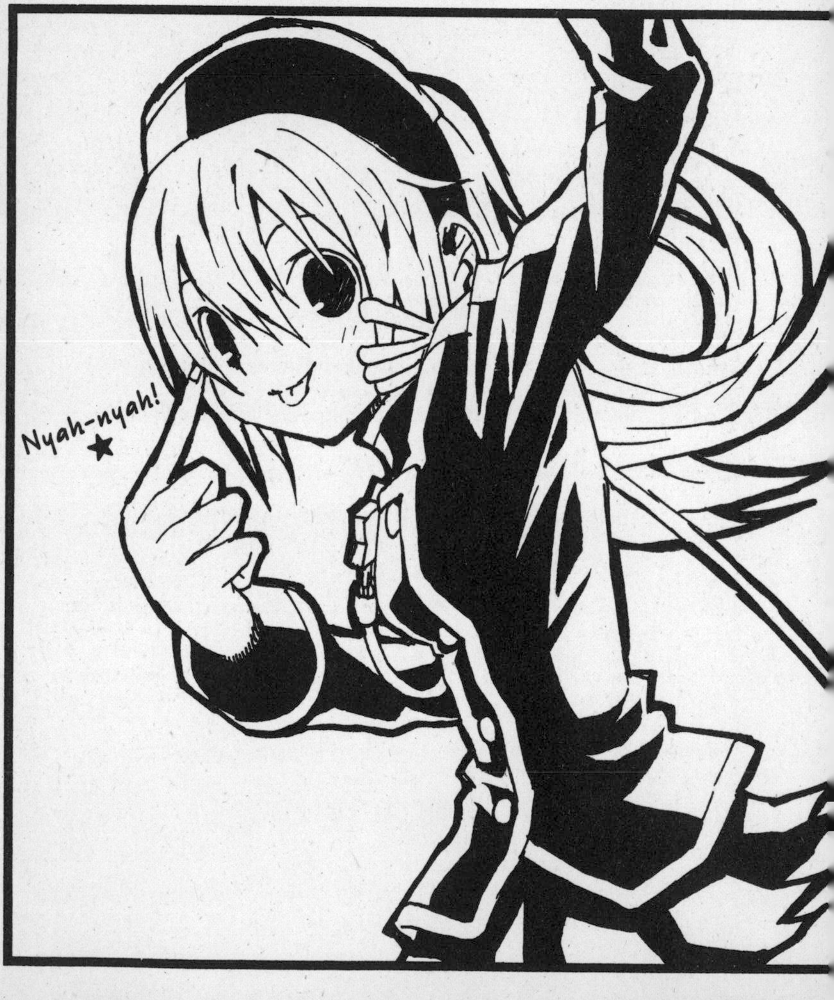
Nyah-nyah! ★

Mikansei No. 1 Volume 1
Created by MAJIKO!

Translation - Ray Yoshimoto
English Adaptation - Hope Donovan
Retouch and Lettering - Star Print Brokers
Production Artist - Michael Paolilli
Graphic Designer - Al-Insan Lashley

Editor - Cindy Suzuki
Print Production Manager - Lucas Rivera
Managing Editor - Vy Nguyen
Senior Designer - Louis Csontos
Director of Sales and Manufacturing - Allyson De Simone
Associate Publisher - Marco F. Pavia
President and C.O.O. - John Parker
C.E.O. and Chief Creative Officer - Stu Levy

A  Manga

TOKYOPOP and  are trademarks or registered trademarks of TOKYOPOP Inc.

TOKYOPOP Inc.
5900 Wilshire Blvd. Suite 2000
Los Angeles, CA 90036

E-mail: info@TOKYOPOP.com
Come visit us online at www.TOKYOPOP.com

ISBN: 978-1-4278-1602-3

First TOKYOPOP printing: November 2009
10 9 8 7 6 5 4 3 2 1
Printed in the USA

VOLUME 1
Created by Majiko!

HAMBURG // LONDON // LOS ANGELES // TOKYO

CONTENTS

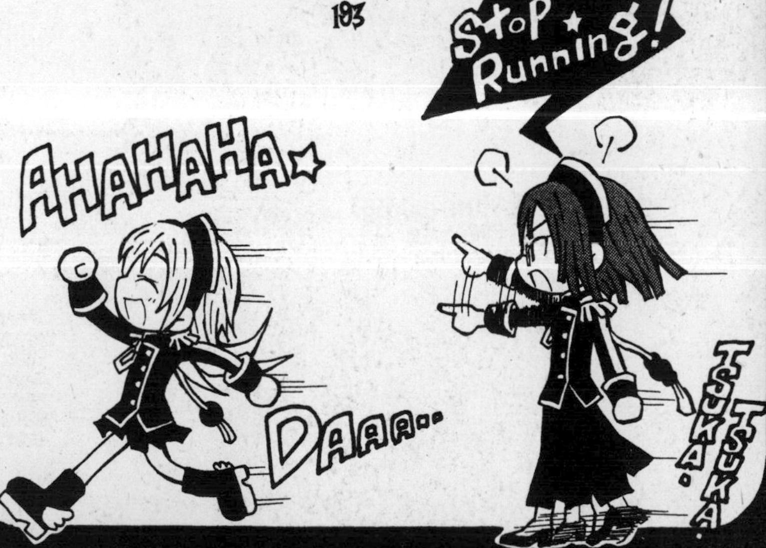

Stop ★ Running!
TSUKA TSUKA...
AHAHAHA★
DAAAA..

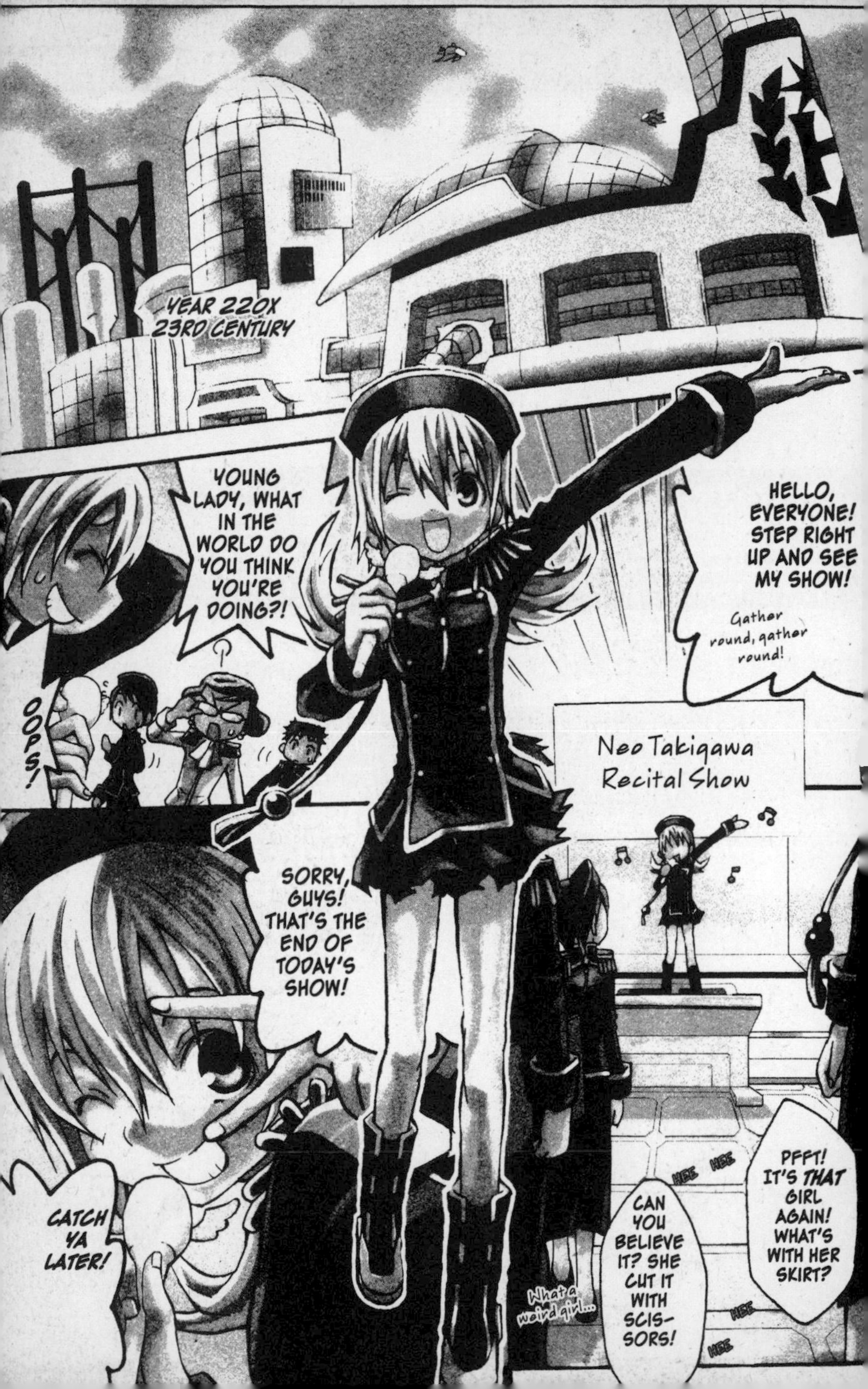

YEAR 220X 23RD CENTURY
HELLO, EVERYONE! STEP RIGHT UP AND SEE MY SHOW!
Gather round, gather round!
Neo Takigawa Recital Show
YOUNG LADY, WHAT IN THE WORLD DO YOU THINK YOU'RE DOING?!
OOPS!
PFFT! IT'S THAT GIRL AGAIN! WHAT'S WITH HER SKIRT?
HEE HEE
CAN YOU BELIEVE IT? SHE CUT IT WITH SCIS-SORS!
HEE HEE
What a weird girl...
SORRY, GUYS! THAT'S THE END OF TODAY'S SHOW!
CATCH YA LATER!

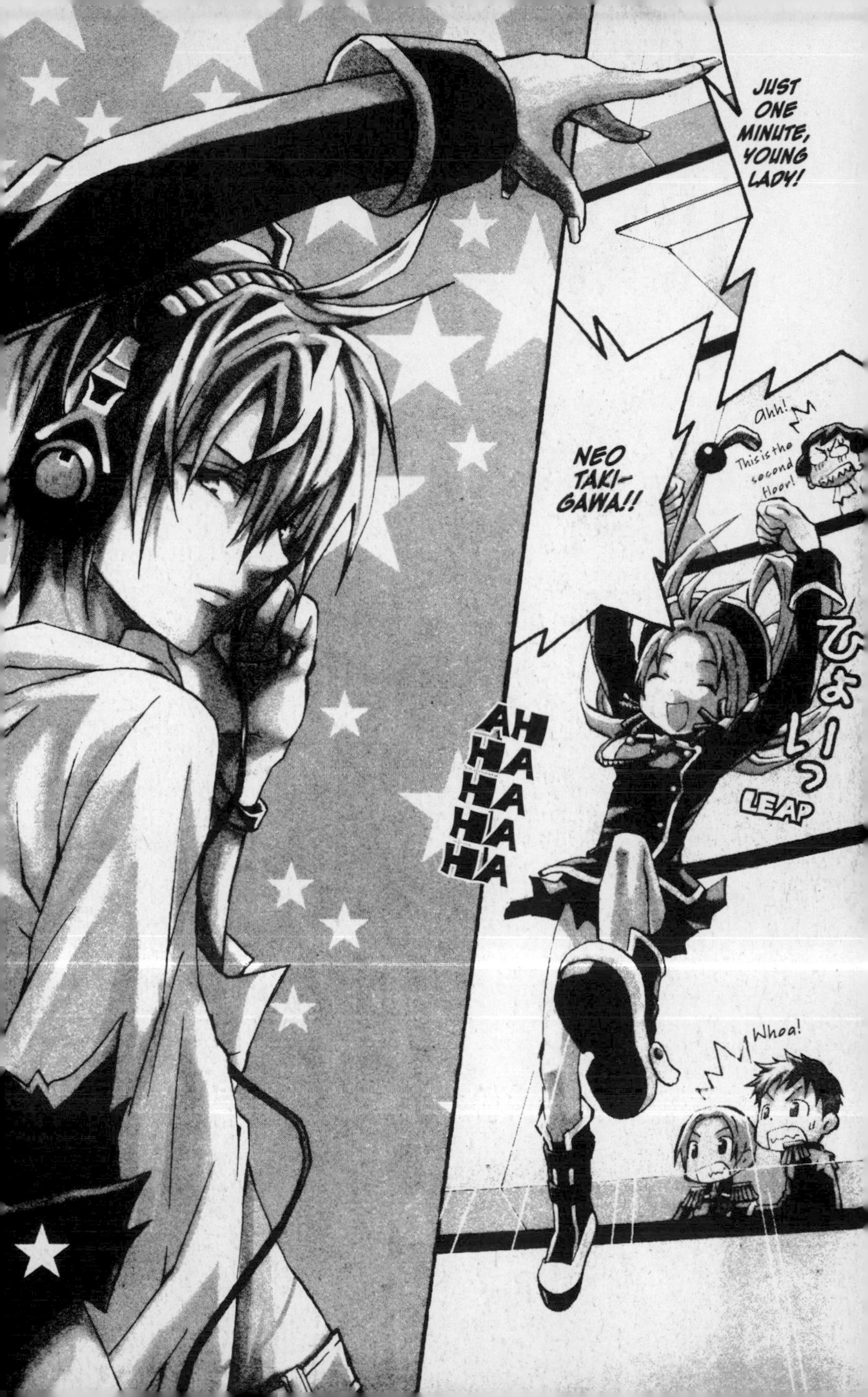

JUST ONE MINUTE, YOUNG LADY!
Ahh! This is the second floor!
NEO TAKI-GAWA!!
ひょーしっ
LEAP
AHAHAHAHAHA
Whoa!

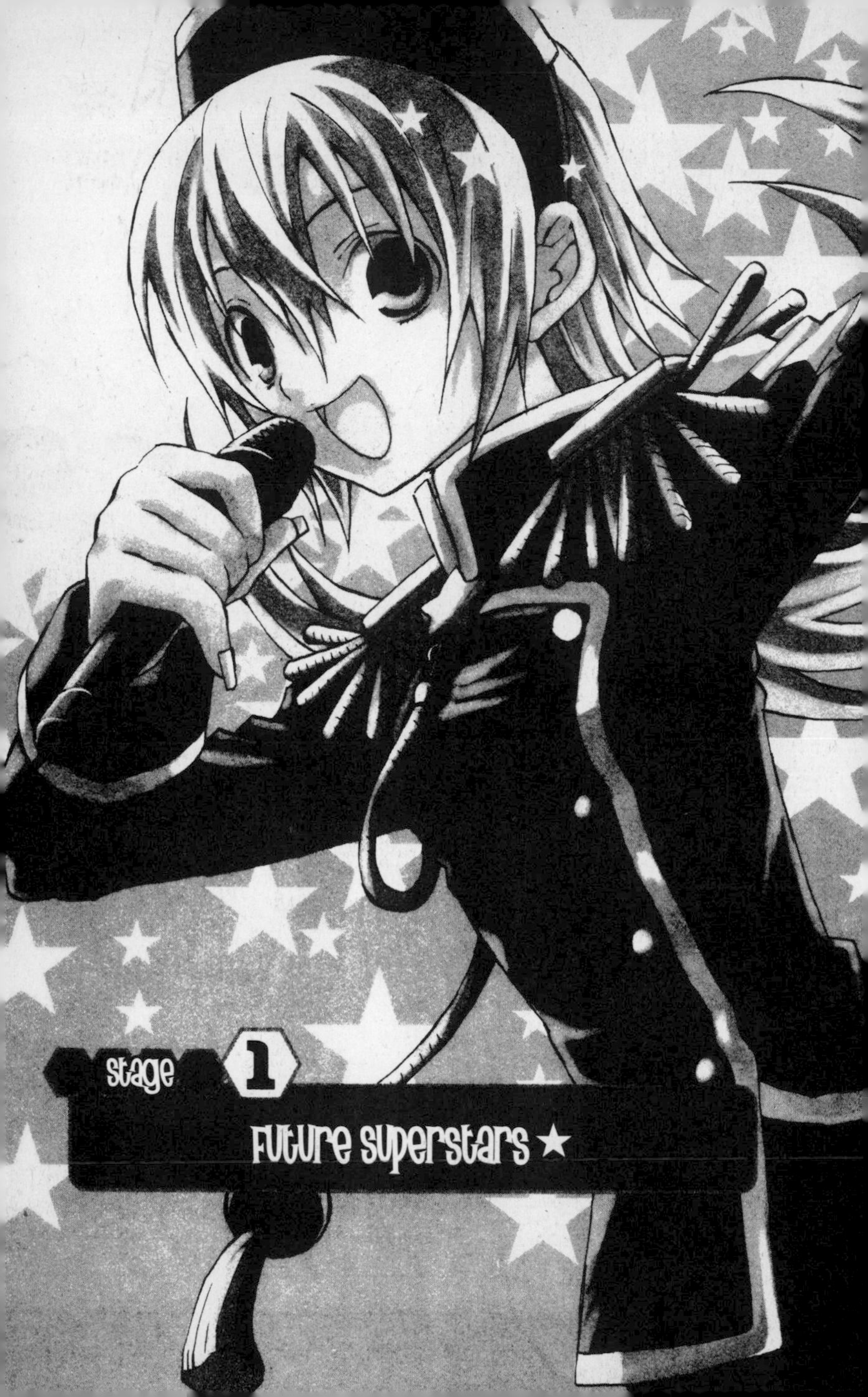
stage 1
Future superstars ★

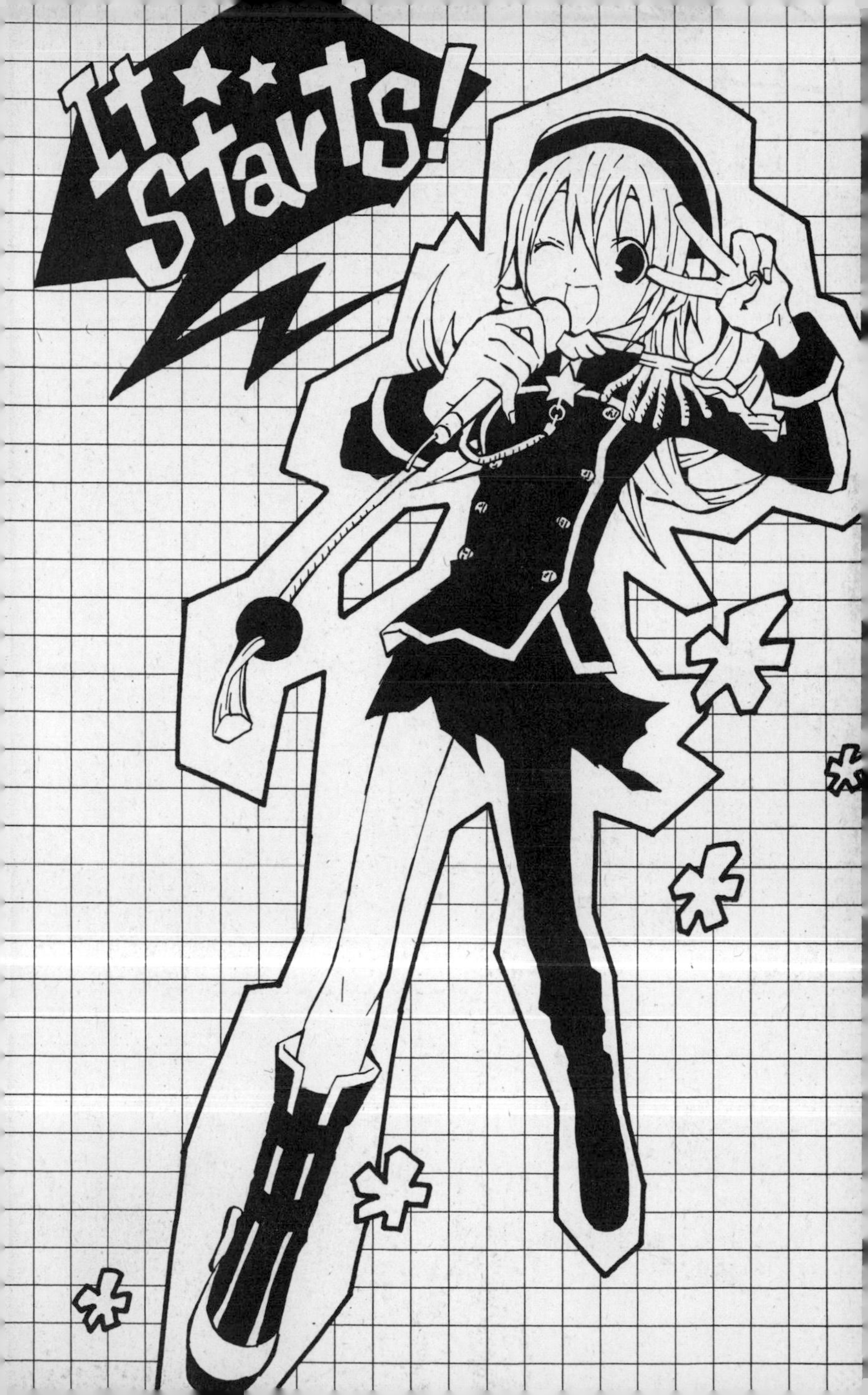
It ★★ Starts!

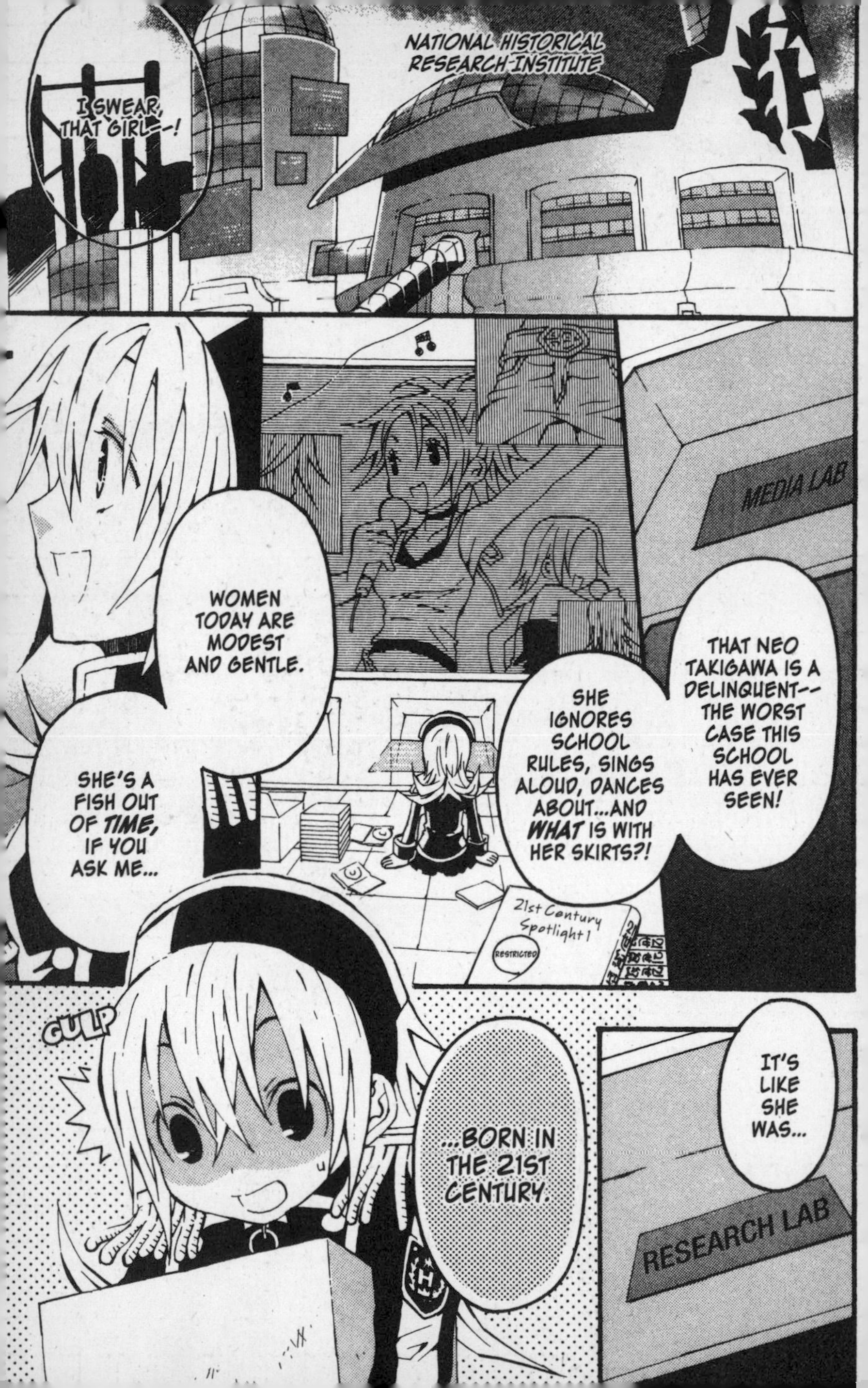
NATIONAL HISTORICAL RESEARCH INSTITUTE
I SWEAR, THAT GIRL--!
MEDIA LAB
THAT NEO TAKIGAWA IS A DELINQUENT-- THE WORST CASE THIS SCHOOL HAS EVER SEEN!
SHE IGNORES SCHOOL RULES, SINGS ALOUD, DANCES ABOUT...AND *WHAT* IS WITH HER SKIRTS?!
21st Century Spotlight 1
RESTRICTED
WOMEN TODAY ARE MODEST AND GENTLE.
SHE'S A FISH OUT OF *TIME*, IF YOU ASK ME...
IT'S LIKE SHE WAS...
RESEARCH LAB
...BORN IN THE 21ST CENTURY.
GULP

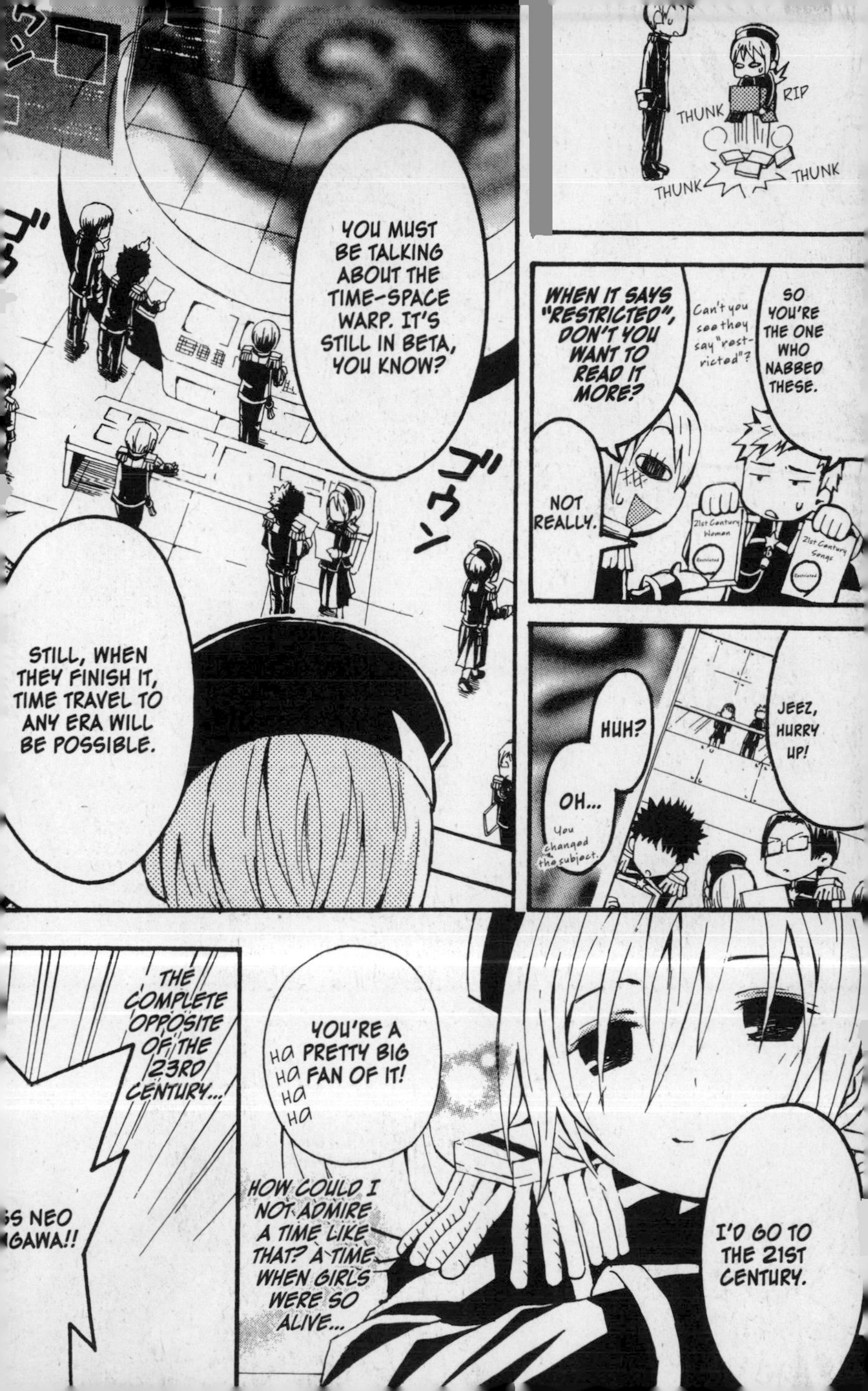
THUNK
RIP
THUNK
THUNK
SO YOU'RE THE ONE WHO NABBED THESE.
21st Century Woman
Restricted
21st Century Songs
Restricted
WHEN IT SAYS "RESTRICTED", DON'T YOU WANT TO READ IT MORE?
Can't you see they say "restricted"?
NOT REALLY.
JEEZ, HURRY UP!
HUH?
OH...
You changed the subject.
YOU MUST BE TALKING ABOUT THE TIME-SPACE WARP. IT'S STILL IN BETA, YOU KNOW?
ゴウン
STILL, WHEN THEY FINISH IT, TIME TRAVEL TO ANY ERA WILL BE POSSIBLE.
I'D GO TO THE 21ST CENTURY.
YOU'RE A PRETTY BIG FAN OF IT!
HA HA HA HA
HOW COULD I NOT ADMIRE A TIME LIKE THAT? A TIME WHEN GIRLS WERE SO ALIVE...
THE COMPLETE OPPOSITE OF THE 23RD CENTURY...
SS NEO GAWA!!

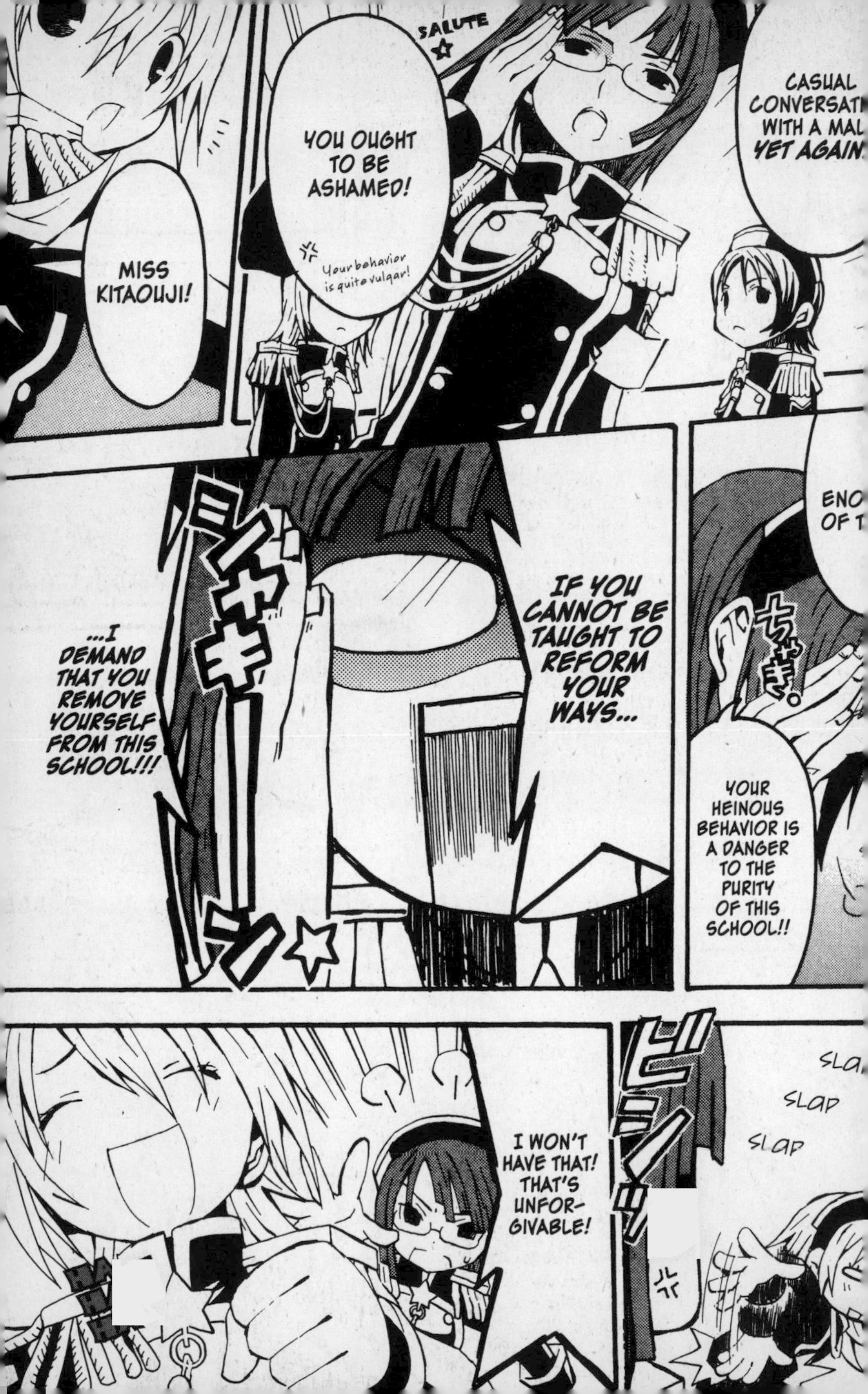
CASUAL CONVERSATI
WITH A MAL
YET AGAIN
SALUTE
YOU OUGHT TO BE ASHAMED!
Your behavior is quite vulgar!
MISS KITAOUJI!
ENO
OF T
ちゃき。
YOUR HEINOUS BEHAVIOR IS A DANGER TO THE PURITY OF THIS SCHOOL!!
IF YOU CANNOT BE TAUGHT TO REFORM YOUR WAYS...
...I DEMAND THAT YOU REMOVE YOURSELF FROM THIS SCHOOL!!!
slap
slap
slap
I WON'T HAVE THAT! THAT'S UNFOR-GIVABLE!

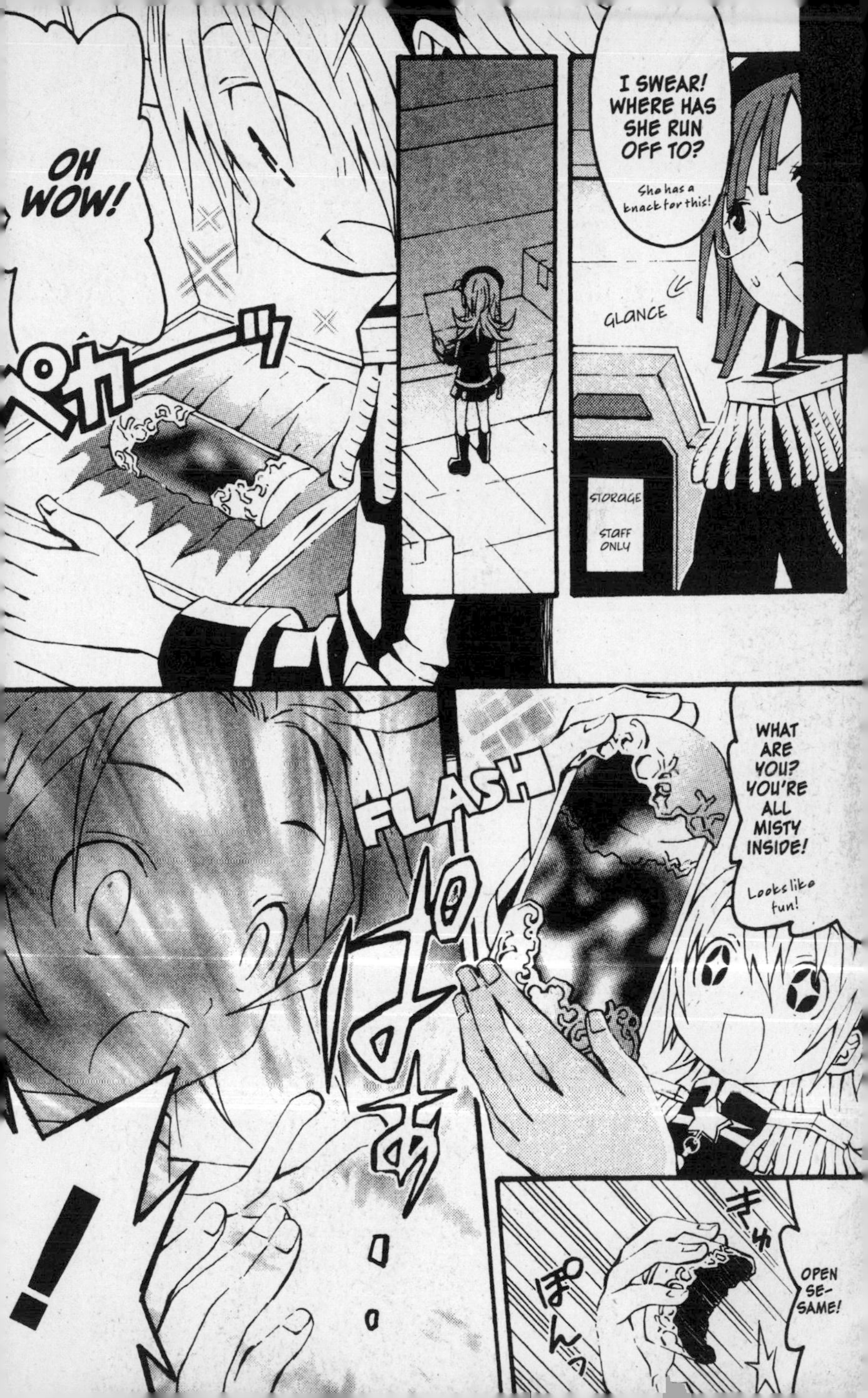
I SWEAR! WHERE HAS SHE RUN OFF TO?
She has a knack for this!
GLANCE
STORAGE
STAFF ONLY
OH WOW!
WHAT ARE YOU? YOU'RE ALL MISTY INSIDE!
Looks like fun!
FLASH
!
OPEN SE-SAME!

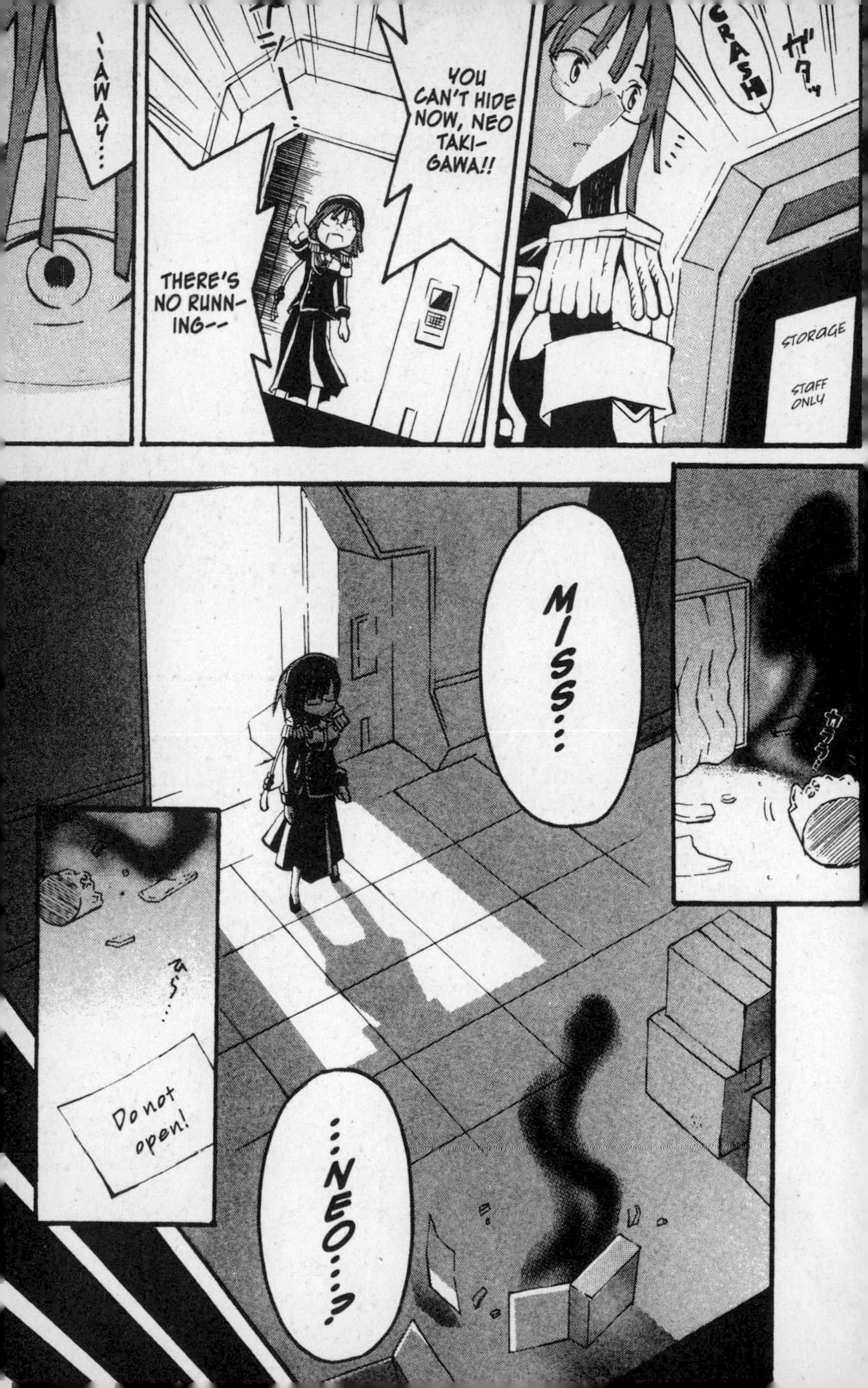
ガタッ
CRASH
YOU CAN'T HIDE NOW, NEO TAKI-GAWA!!
THERE'S NO RUNN-ING--
!!AWAY...
STORAGE
STAFF ONLY
MISS...
...NEO...?
Do not open!

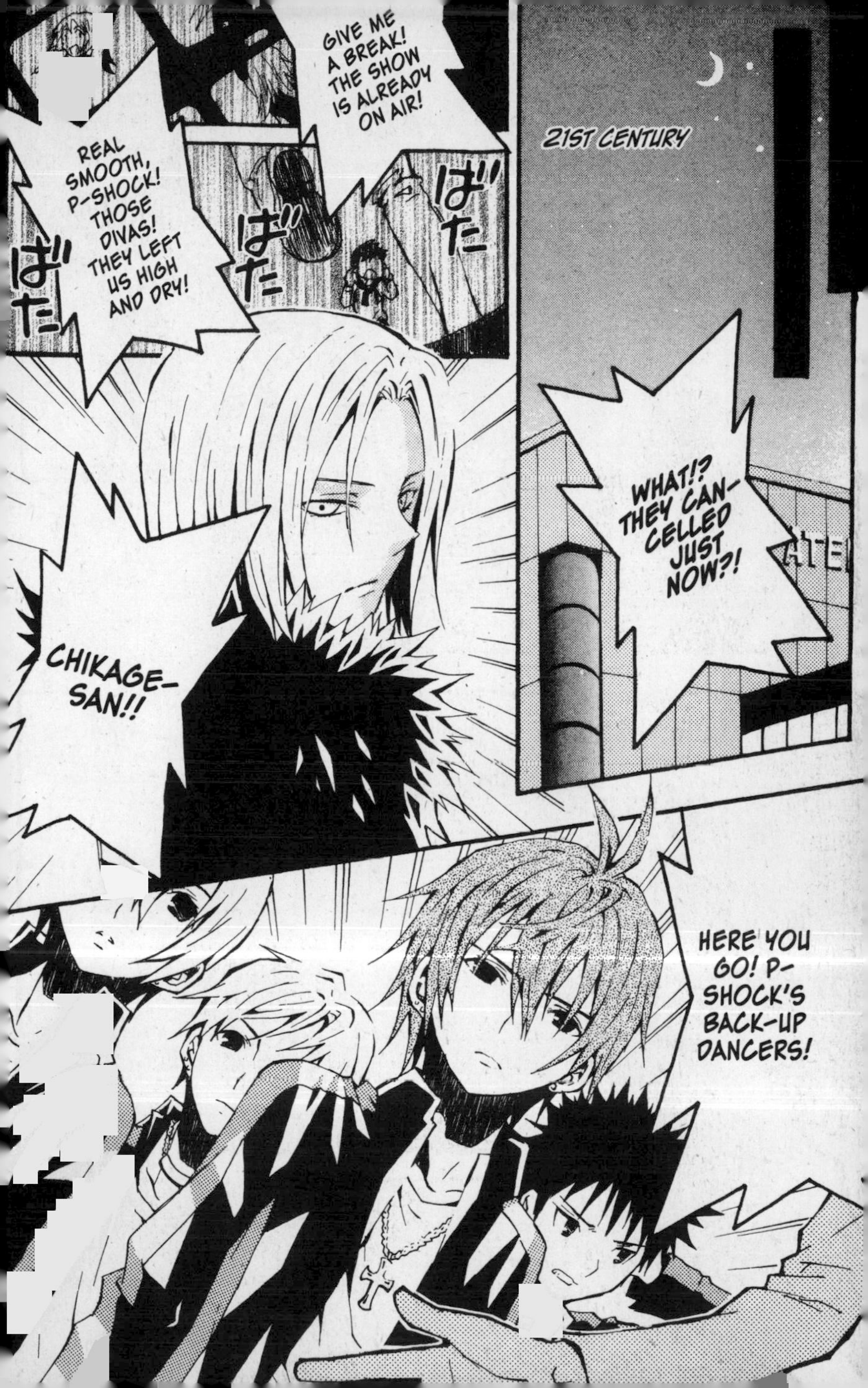
21ST CENTURY
WHAT!? THEY CAN-CELLED JUST NOW?!
GIVE ME A BREAK! THE SHOW IS ALREADY ON AIR!
ばた
ばた
REAL SMOOTH, P-SHOCK! THOSE DIVAS! THEY LEFT US HIGH AND DRY!
ばた
CHIKAGE-SAN!!
HERE YOU GO! P-SHOCK'S BACK-UP DANCERS!

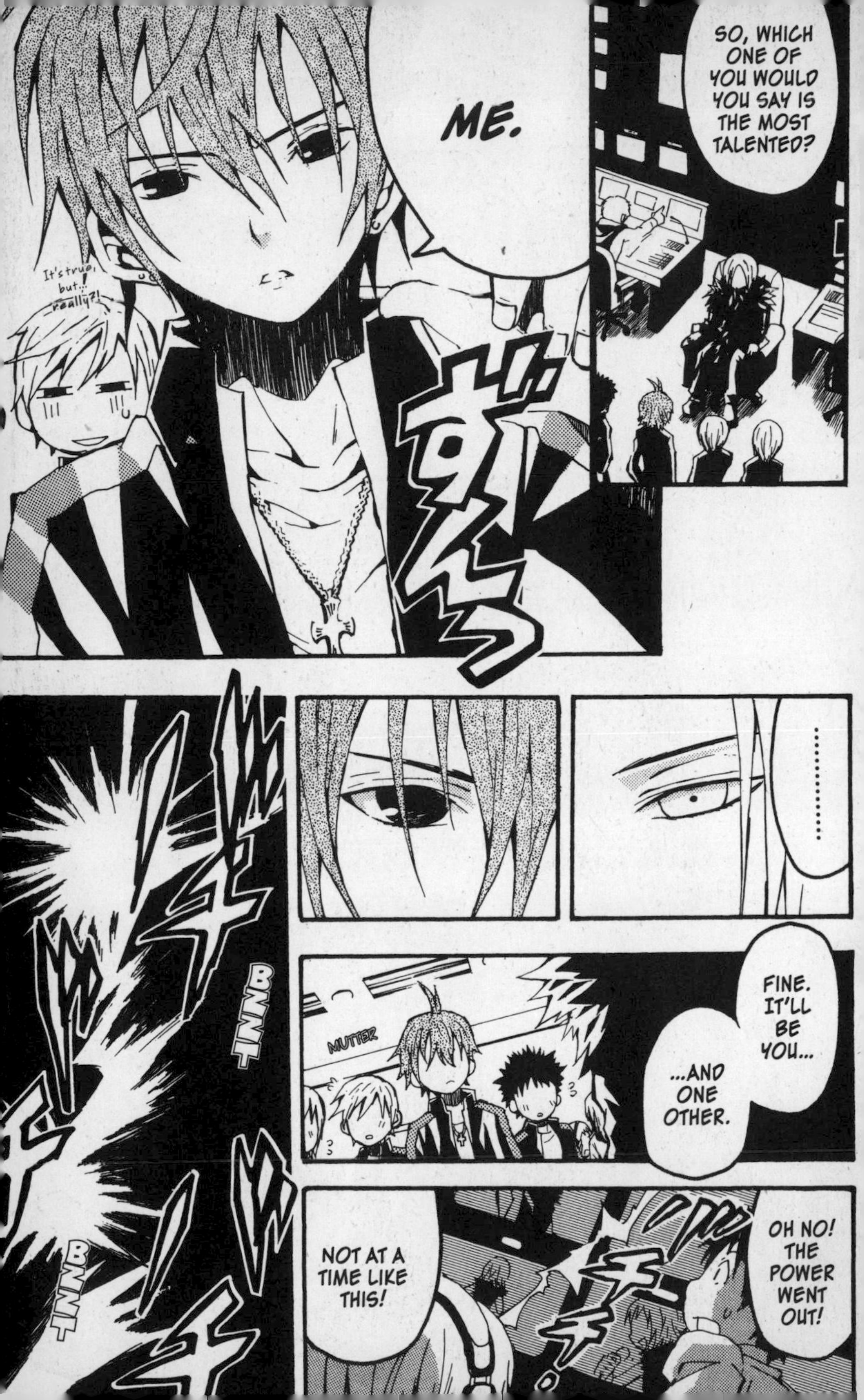
SO, WHICH ONE OF YOU WOULD YOU SAY IS THE MOST TALENTED?
ME.
It's true, but... really?!
....
FINE. IT'LL BE YOU...
...AND ONE OTHER.
MUTTER
OH NO! THE POWER WENT OUT!
NOT AT A TIME LIKE THIS!
BNNT
BNNT

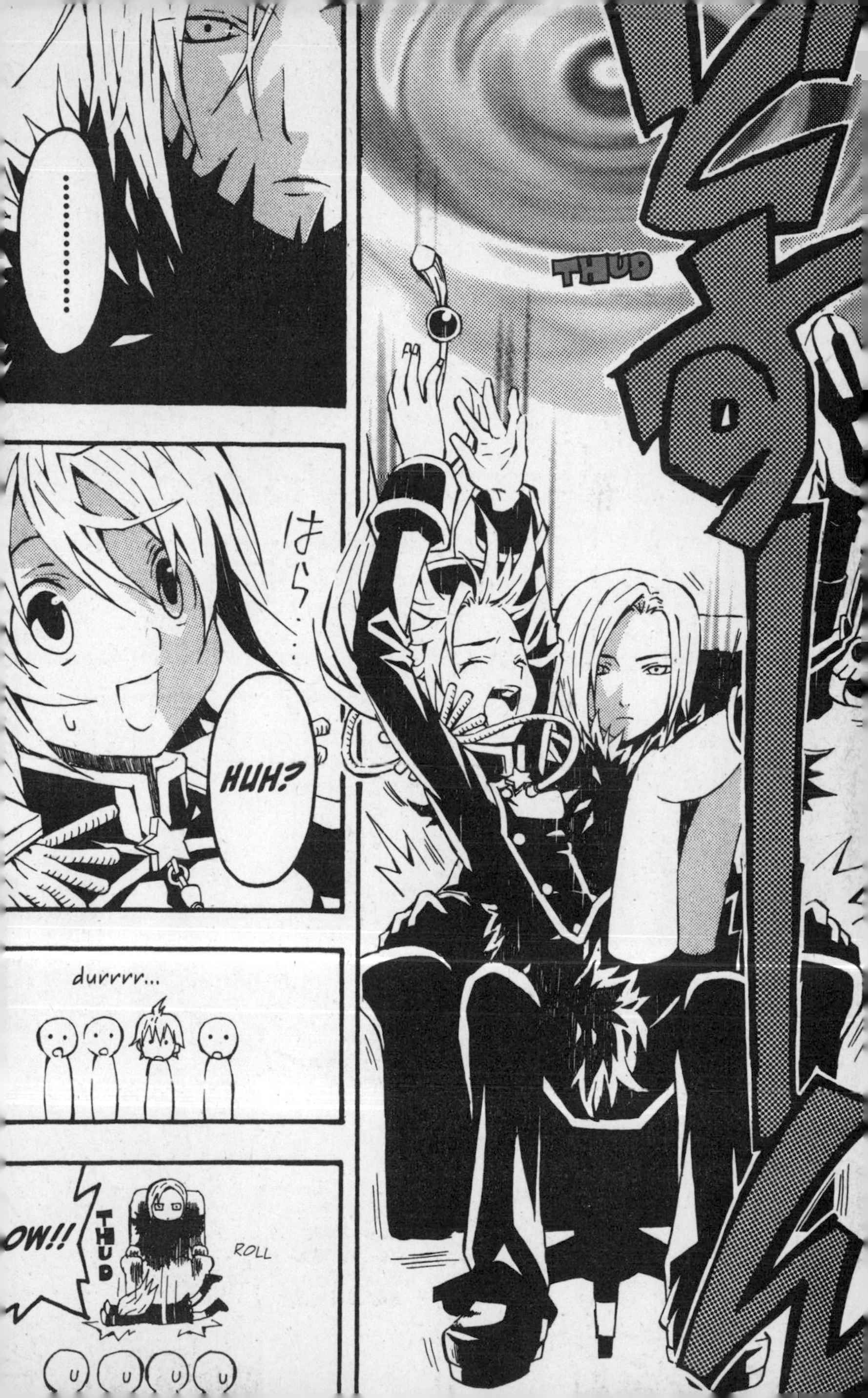
THUD
……
はら…
HUH?
durrrr...
OW!!
THUD
ROLL

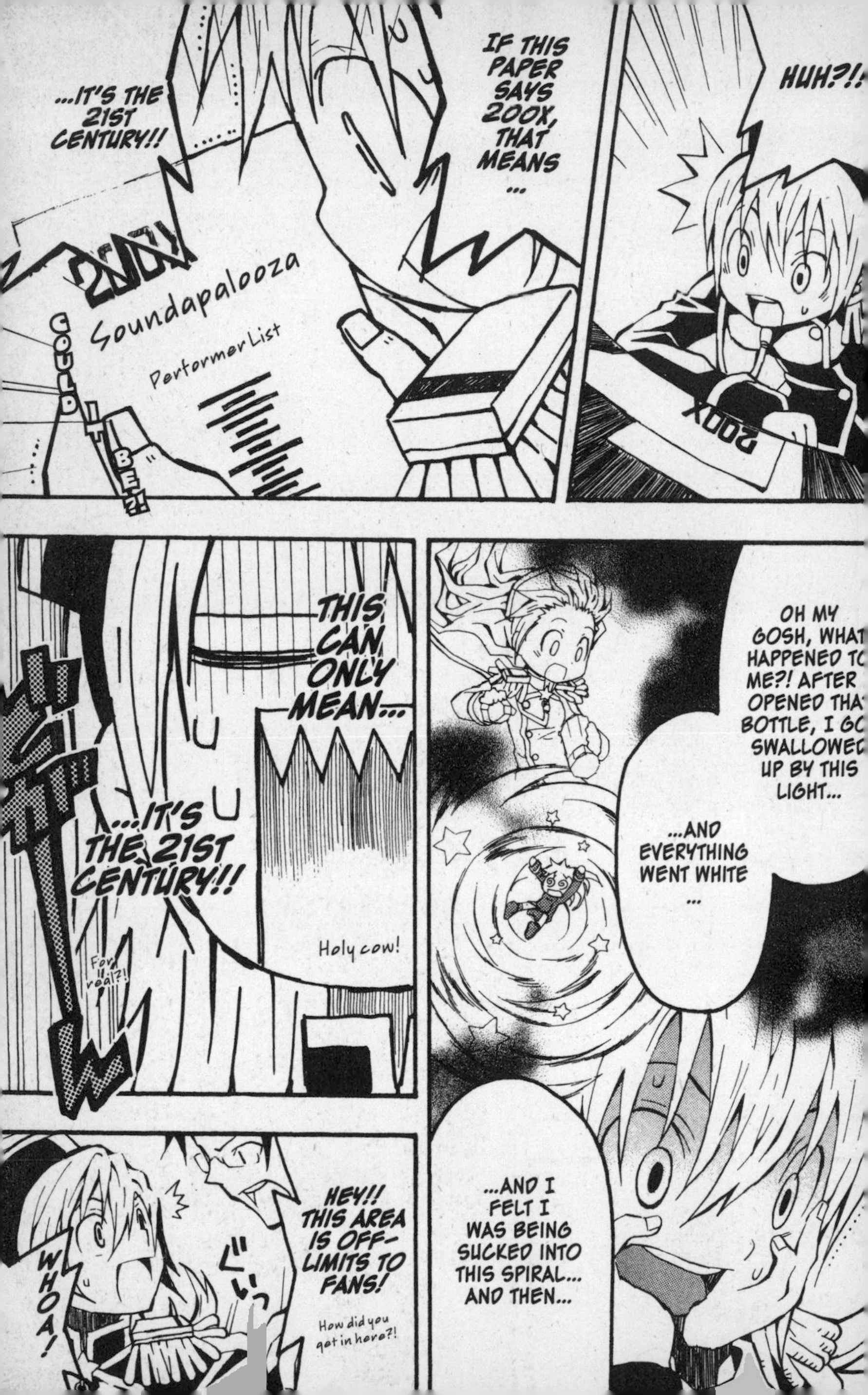
HUH?!
200X
IF THIS PAPER SAYS 200X, THAT MEANS...
...IT'S THE 21ST CENTURY!!
200X
Soundapalooza
Performer List
COULD IT BE?!
OH MY GOSH, WHAT HAPPENED TO ME?! AFTER OPENED THA BOTTLE, I GO SWALLOWED UP BY THIS LIGHT...
...AND EVERYTHING WENT WHITE...
...AND I FELT I WAS BEING SUCKED INTO THIS SPIRAL... AND THEN...
THIS CAN ONLY MEAN...
...IT'S THE 21ST CENTURY!!
Holy cow!
For real?!
HEY!! THIS AREA IS OFF-LIMITS TO FANS!
How did you get in here?!
ぐいっ
WHOA!

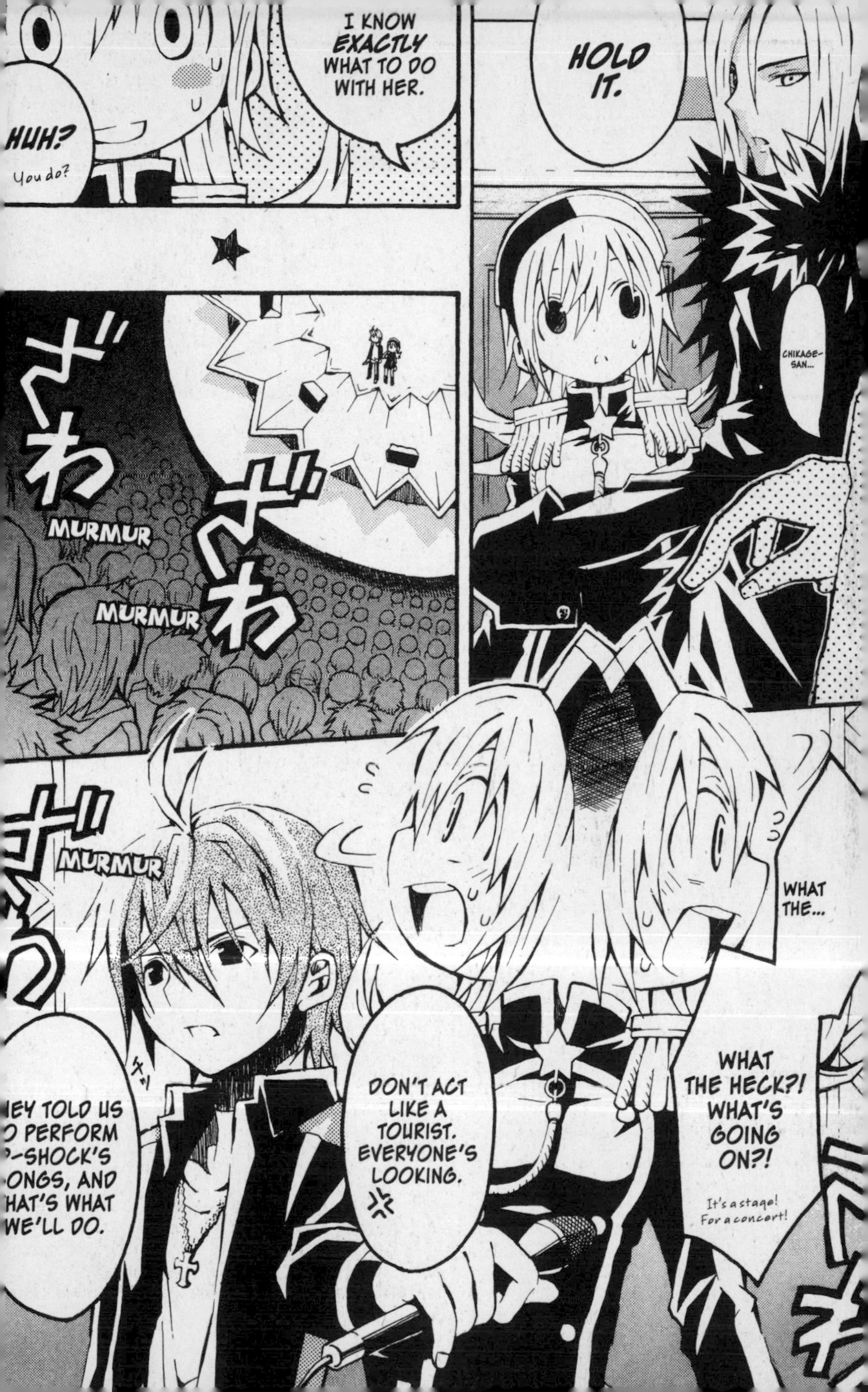
HOLD IT.
CHIKAGE-SAN...
I KNOW EXACTLY WHAT TO DO WITH HER.
HUH?
You do?
ざわ
ざわ
MURMUR
MURMUR
WHAT THE...
WHAT THE HECK?! WHAT'S GOING ON?!
It's a stage! For a concert!
DON'T ACT LIKE A TOURIST. EVERYONE'S LOOKING.
MURMUR
EY TOLD US O PERFORM -SHOCK'S ONGS, AND HAT'S WHAT WE'LL DO.

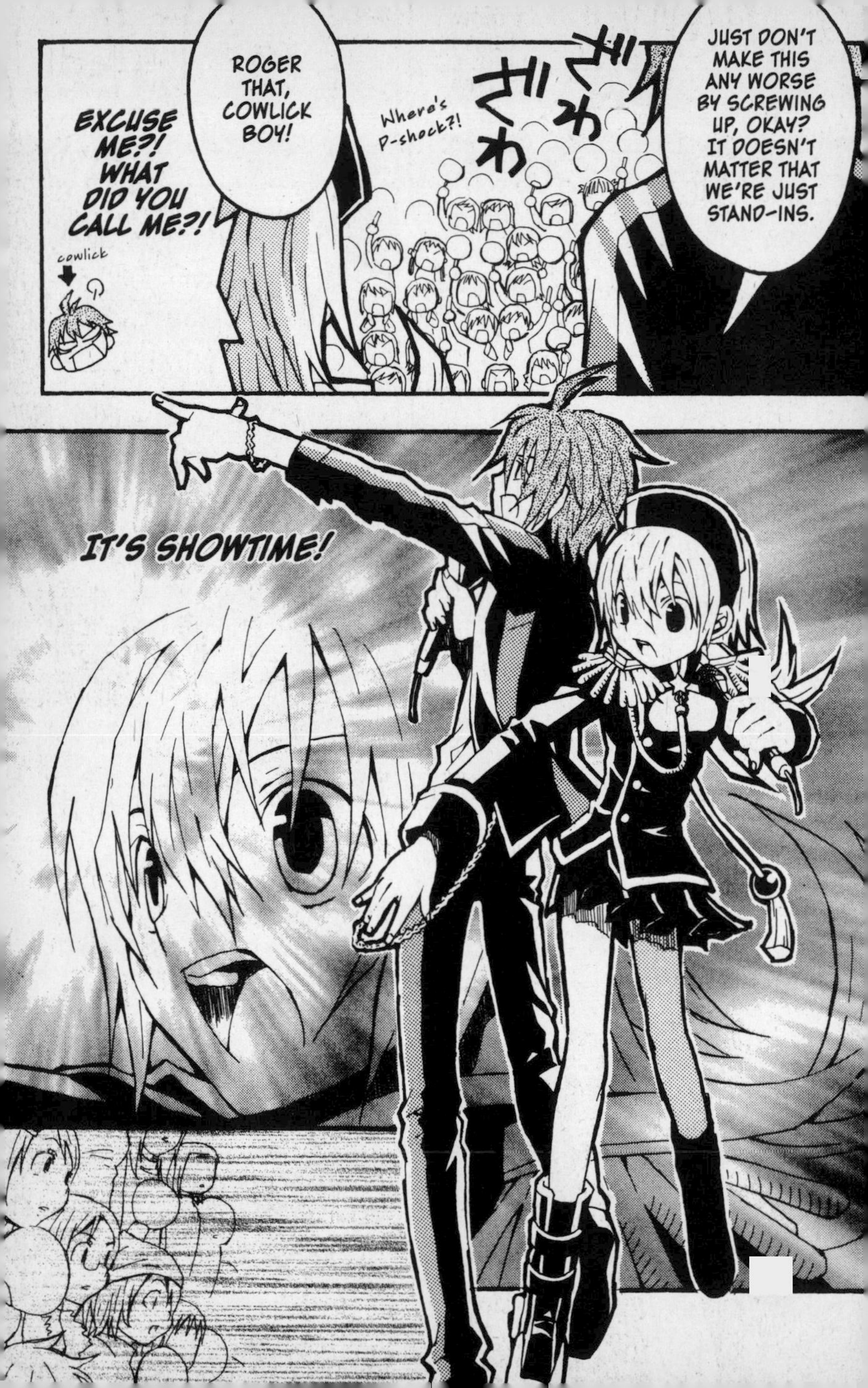
JUST DON'T MAKE THIS ANY WORSE BY SCREWING UP, OKAY? IT DOESN'T MATTER THAT WE'RE JUST STAND-INS.
ざわ
ざわ
Where's P-shock?!
ROGER THAT, COWLICK BOY!
EXCUSE ME?! WHAT DID YOU CALL ME?!
cowlick
IT'S SHOWTIME!

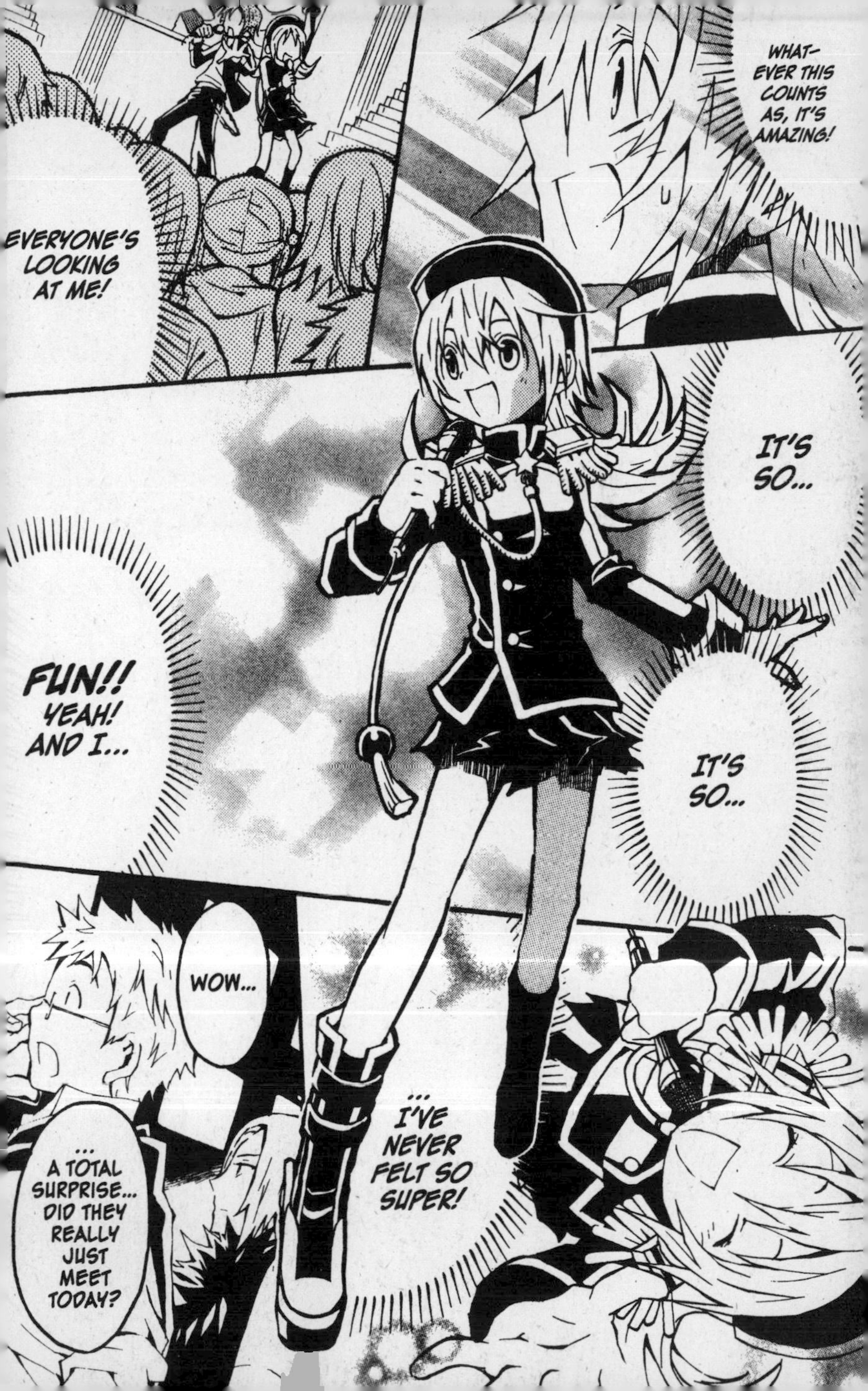
WHATEVER THIS COUNTS AS, IT'S AMAZING!
EVERYONE'S LOOKING AT ME!
IT'S SO...
IT'S SO...
FUN!! YEAH! AND I...
...I'VE NEVER FELT SO SUPER!
WOW...
...A TOTAL SURPRISE... DID THEY REALLY JUST MEET TODAY?

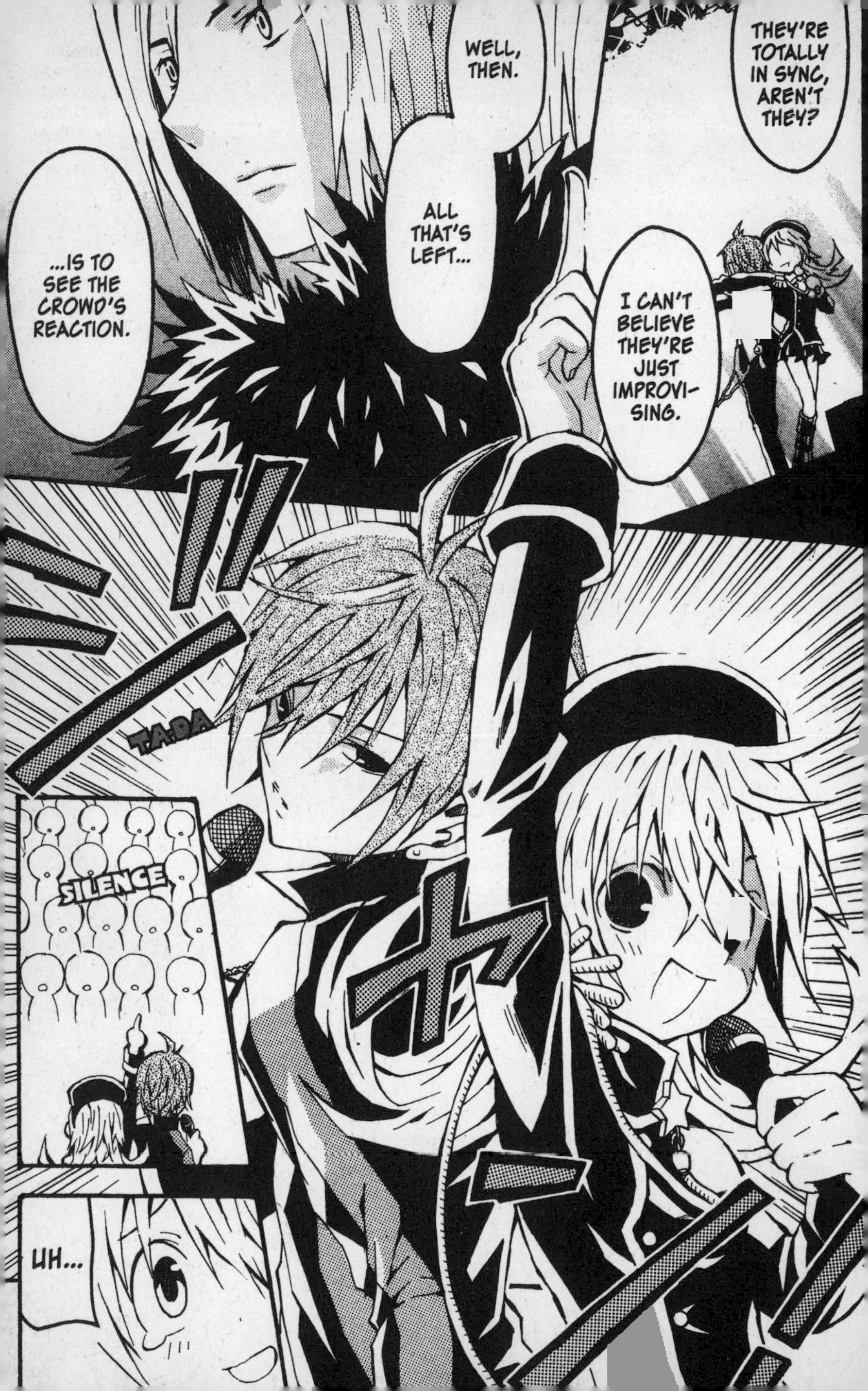
THEY'RE TOTALLY IN SYNC, AREN'T THEY?
I CAN'T BELIEVE THEY'RE JUST IMPROVISING.
WELL, THEN.
ALL THAT'S LEFT...
...IS TO SEE THE CROWD'S REACTION.
TA-DA
SILENCE
UH...

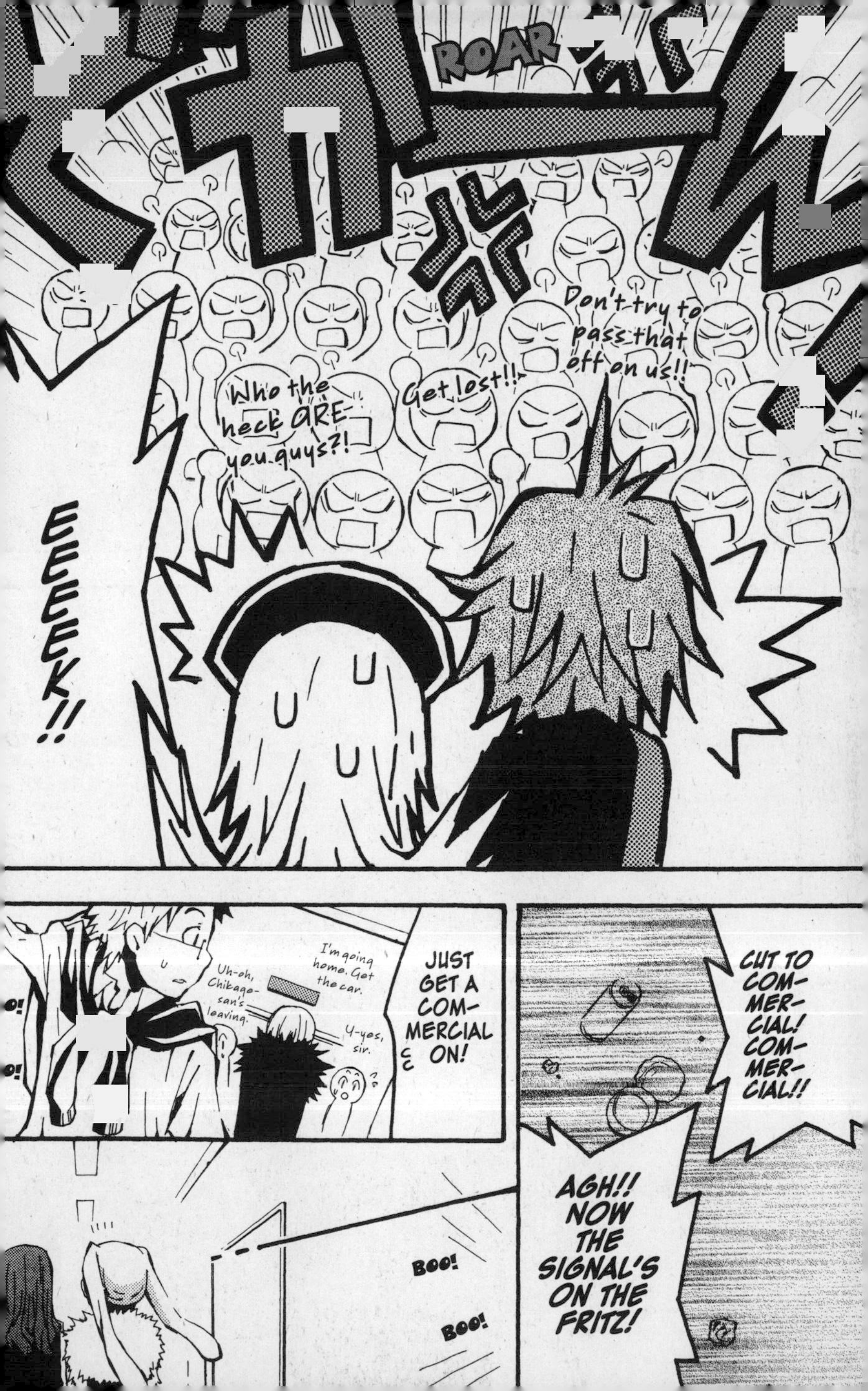
ROAR
Don't try to pass that off on us!!
Get lost!!
Who the heck ARE you guys?!
EEEEEK!!
CUT TO COM-MER-CIAL! COM-MER-CIAL!!
AGH!! NOW THE SIGNAL'S ON THE FRITZ!
JUST GET A COM-MERCIAL ON!
I'm going home. Get the car.
U-yes, sir.
Uh-oh, Chikage-san's leaving.
O!
O!
BOO!
BOO!

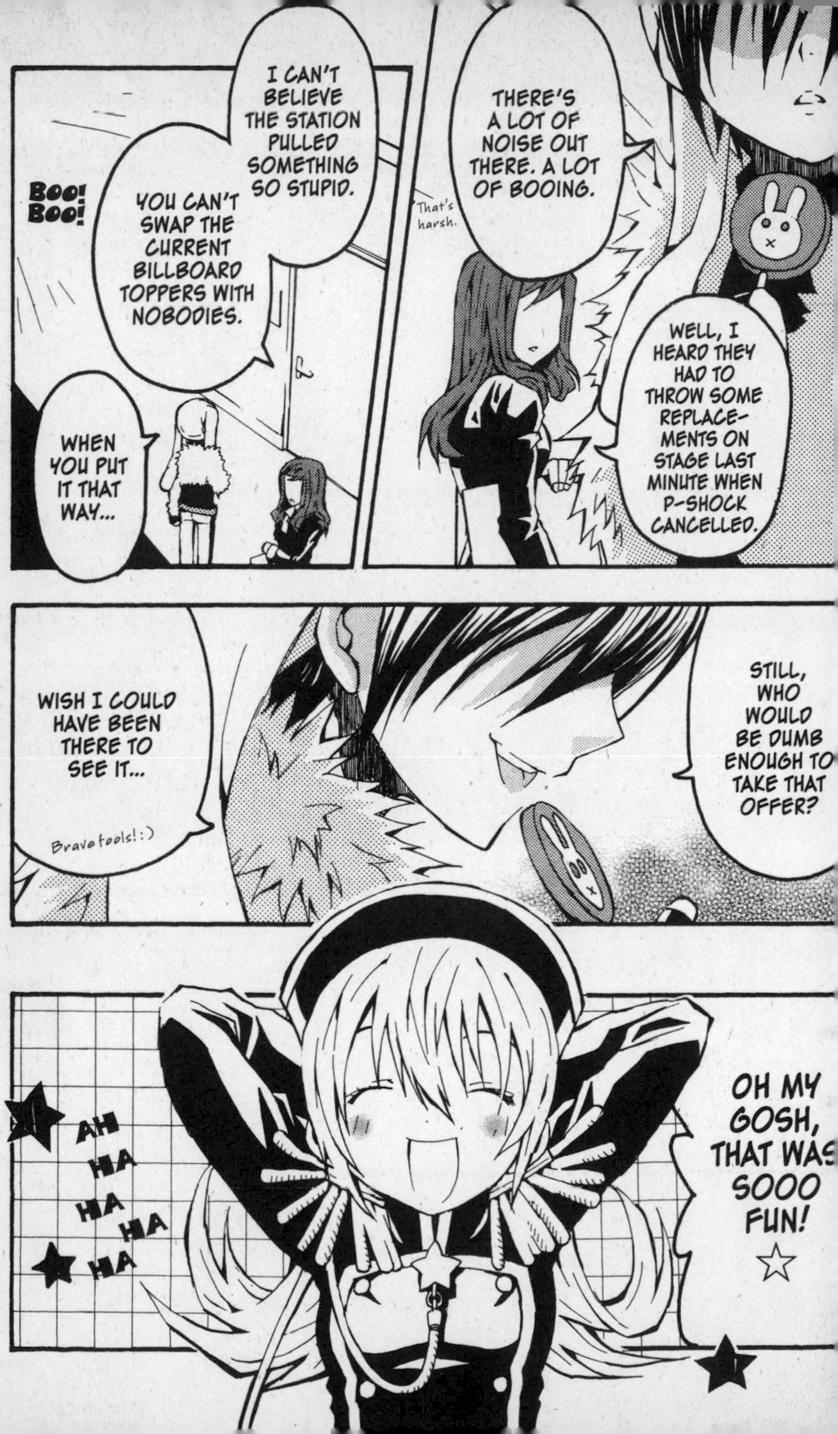
THERE'S A LOT OF NOISE OUT THERE. A LOT OF BOOING.
That's harsh.
WELL, I HEARD THEY HAD TO THROW SOME REPLACE-MENTS ON STAGE LAST MINUTE WHEN P-SHOCK CANCELLED.
I CAN'T BELIEVE THE STATION PULLED SOMETHING SO STUPID.
BOO! BOO!
YOU CAN'T SWAP THE CURRENT BILLBOARD TOPPERS WITH NOBODIES.
WHEN YOU PUT IT THAT WAY...
STILL, WHO WOULD BE DUMB ENOUGH TO TAKE THAT OFFER?
WISH I COULD HAVE BEEN THERE TO SEE IT...
Brave fools!:)
OH MY GOSH, THAT WAS SOOO FUN! ☆
AH HA HA HA HA

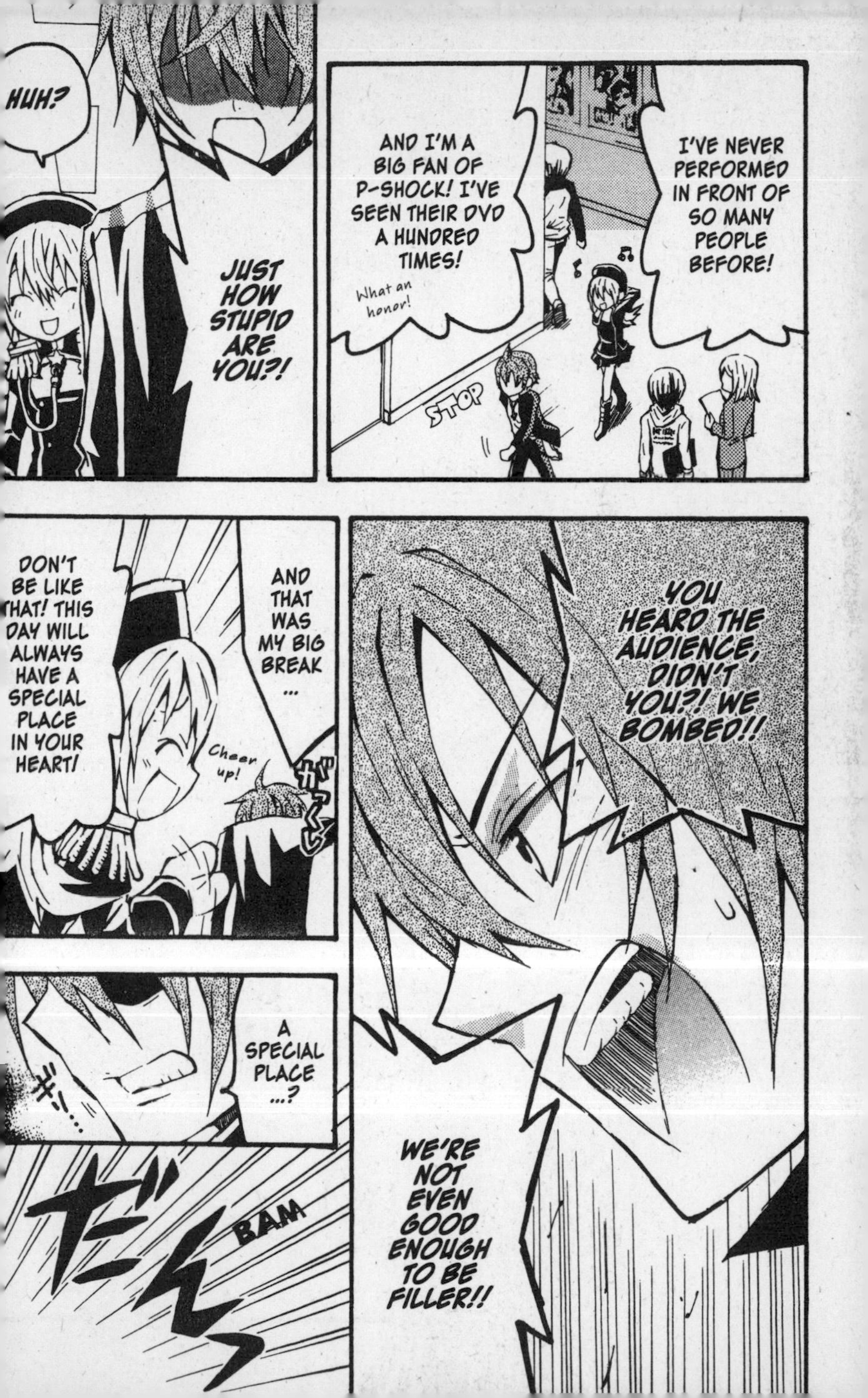
I'VE NEVER PERFORMED IN FRONT OF SO MANY PEOPLE BEFORE!
AND I'M A BIG FAN OF P-SHOCK! I'VE SEEN THEIR DVD A HUNDRED TIMES!
What an honor!
STOP
HUH?
JUST HOW STUPID ARE YOU?!
YOU HEARD THE AUDIENCE, DIDN'T YOU?! WE BOMBED!!
WE'RE NOT EVEN GOOD ENOUGH TO BE FILLER!!
AND THAT WAS MY BIG BREAK...
DON'T BE LIKE THAT! THIS DAY WILL ALWAYS HAVE A SPECIAL PLACE IN YOUR HEART!
Cheer up!
A SPECIAL PLACE...?
BAM

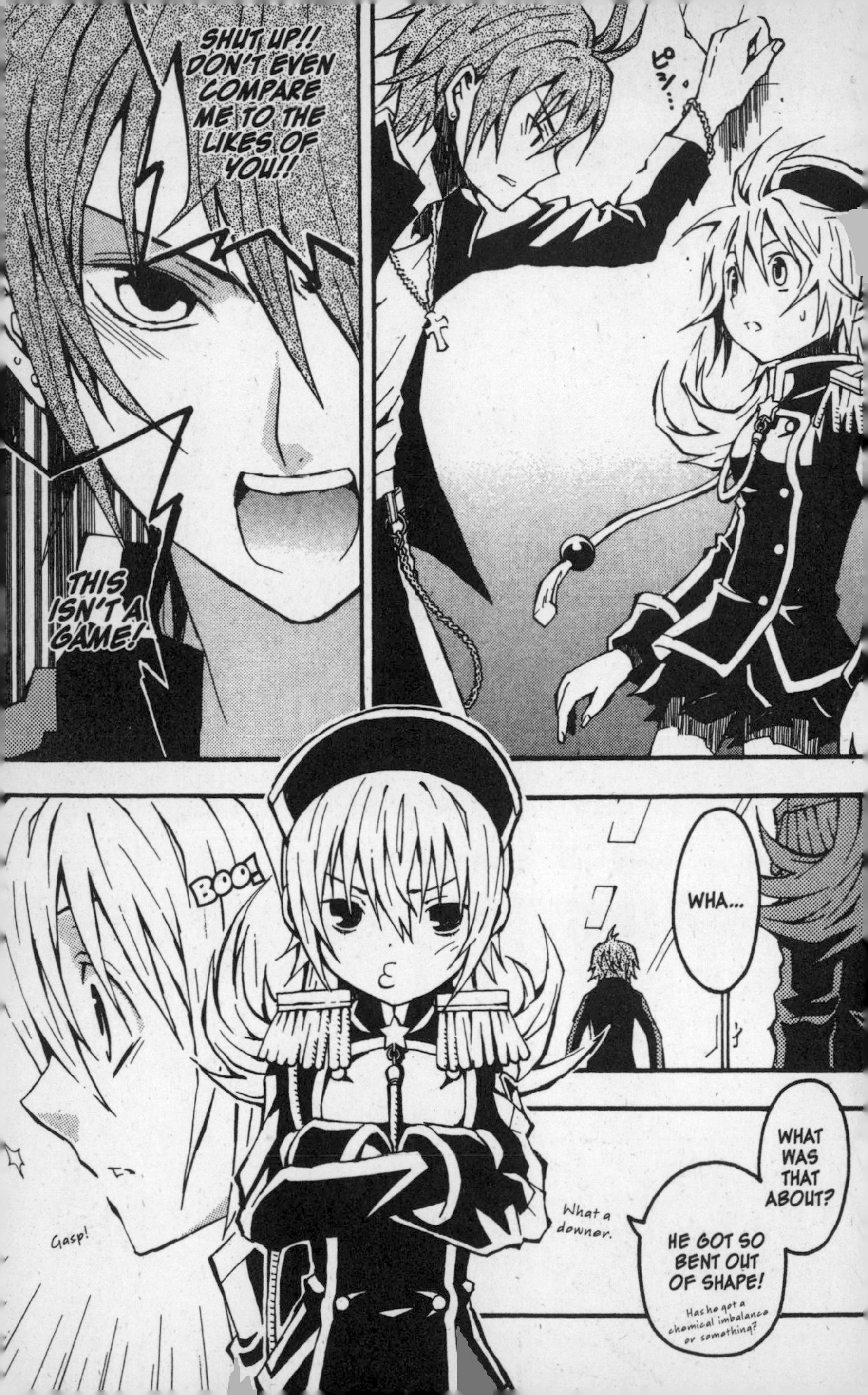
SHUT UP!! DON'T EVEN COMPARE ME TO THE LIKES OF YOU!!
THIS ISN'T A GAME!
WHA...
BOO!
WHAT WAS THAT ABOUT?
HE GOT SO BENT OUT OF SHAPE!
Has he got a chemical imbalance or something?
What a downer.
Gasp!

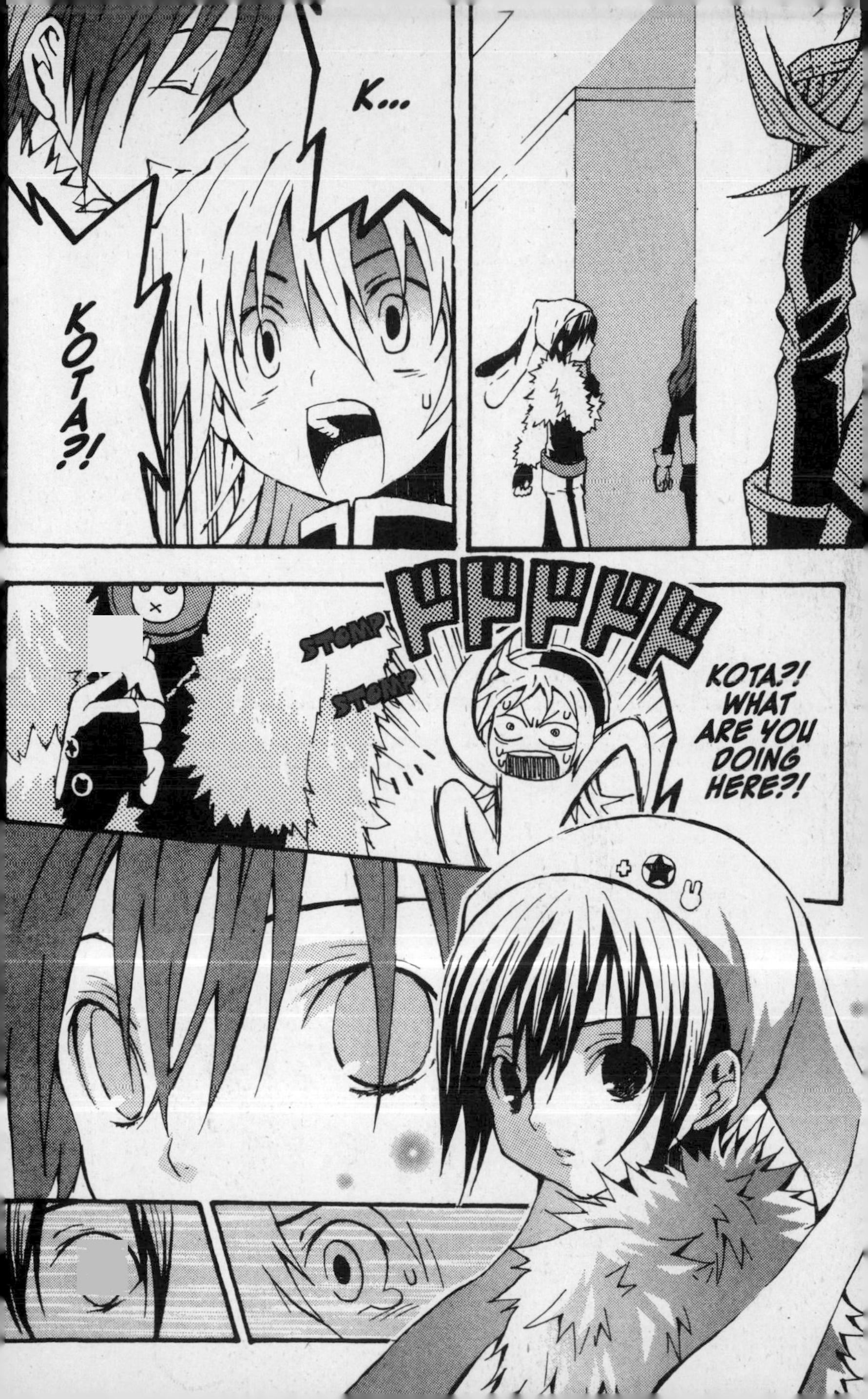
K...
KOTA?!
KOTA?! WHAT ARE YOU DOING HERE?!
STOMP
STOMP

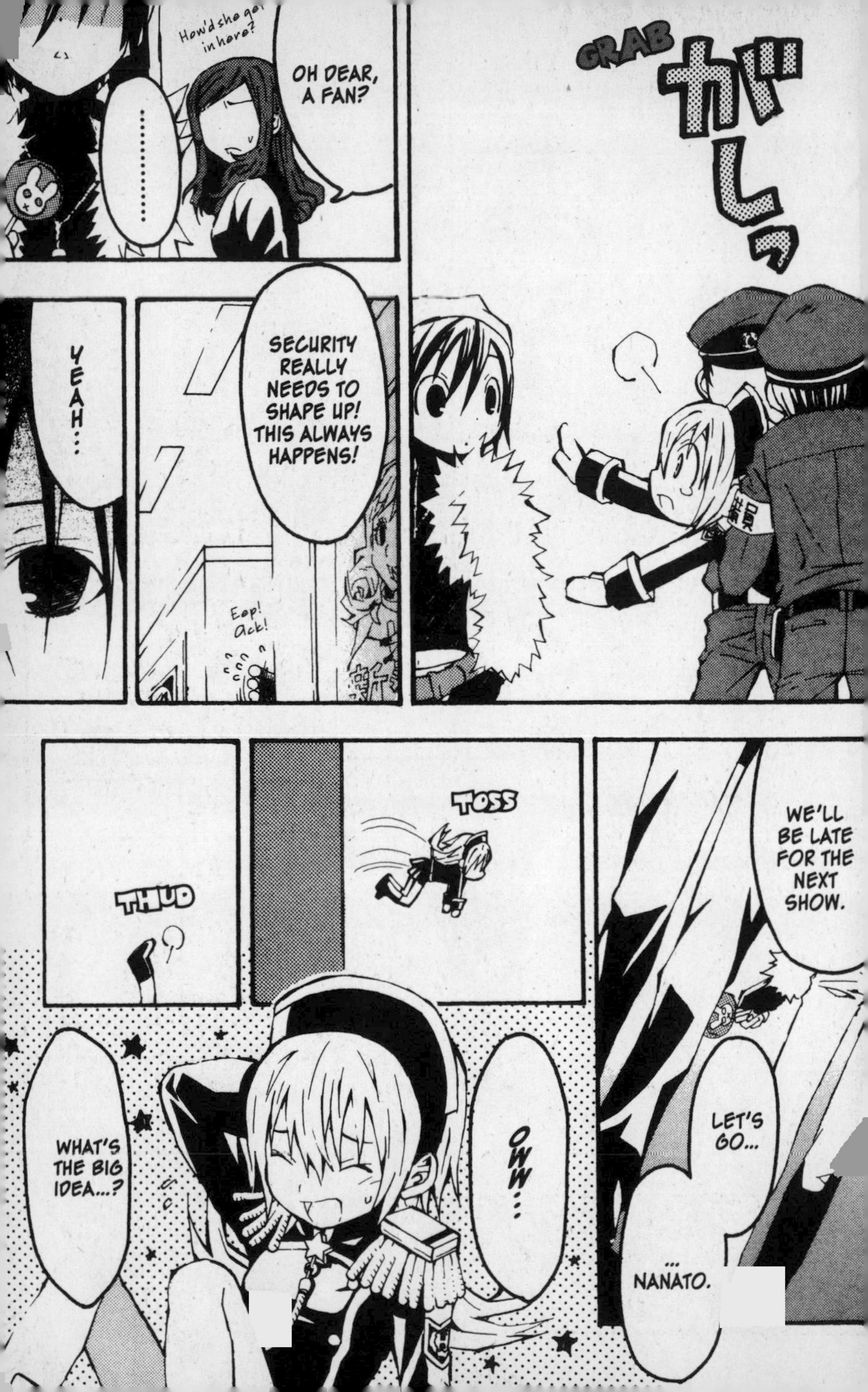
GRAB
がしっ
OH DEAR, A FAN?
How'd she get in here?
......
SECURITY REALLY NEEDS TO SHAPE UP! THIS ALWAYS HAPPENS!
Eep! Ack!
YEAH...
WE'LL BE LATE FOR THE NEXT SHOW.
LET'S GO...
...NANATO.
TOSS
THUD
OWW...
WHAT'S THE BIG IDEA...?

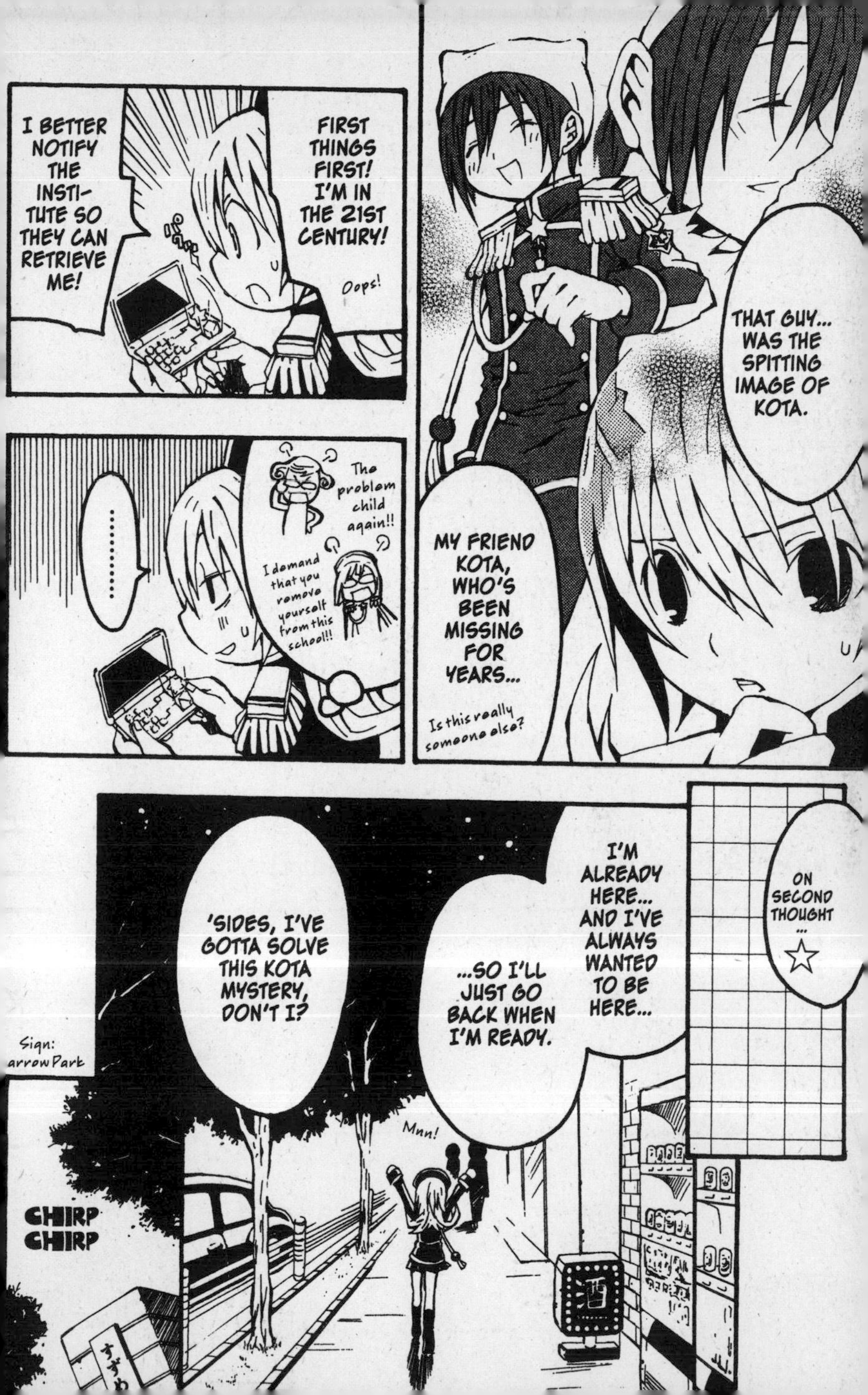
THAT GUY... WAS THE SPITTING IMAGE OF KOTA.
MY FRIEND KOTA, WHO'S BEEN MISSING FOR YEARS...
Is this really someone else?
FIRST THINGS FIRST! I'M IN THE 21ST CENTURY!
Oops!
I BETTER NOTIFY THE INSTI-TUTE SO THEY CAN RETRIEVE ME!
The problem child again!!
I demand that you remove yourself from this school!!
......
ON SECOND THOUGHT... ☆
I'M ALREADY HERE... AND I'VE ALWAYS WANTED TO BE HERE...
...SO I'LL JUST GO BACK WHEN I'M READY.
'SIDES, I'VE GOTTA SOLVE THIS KOTA MYSTERY, DON'T I?
Mnn!
Sign: arrowPark
CHIRP CHIRP
すずめ

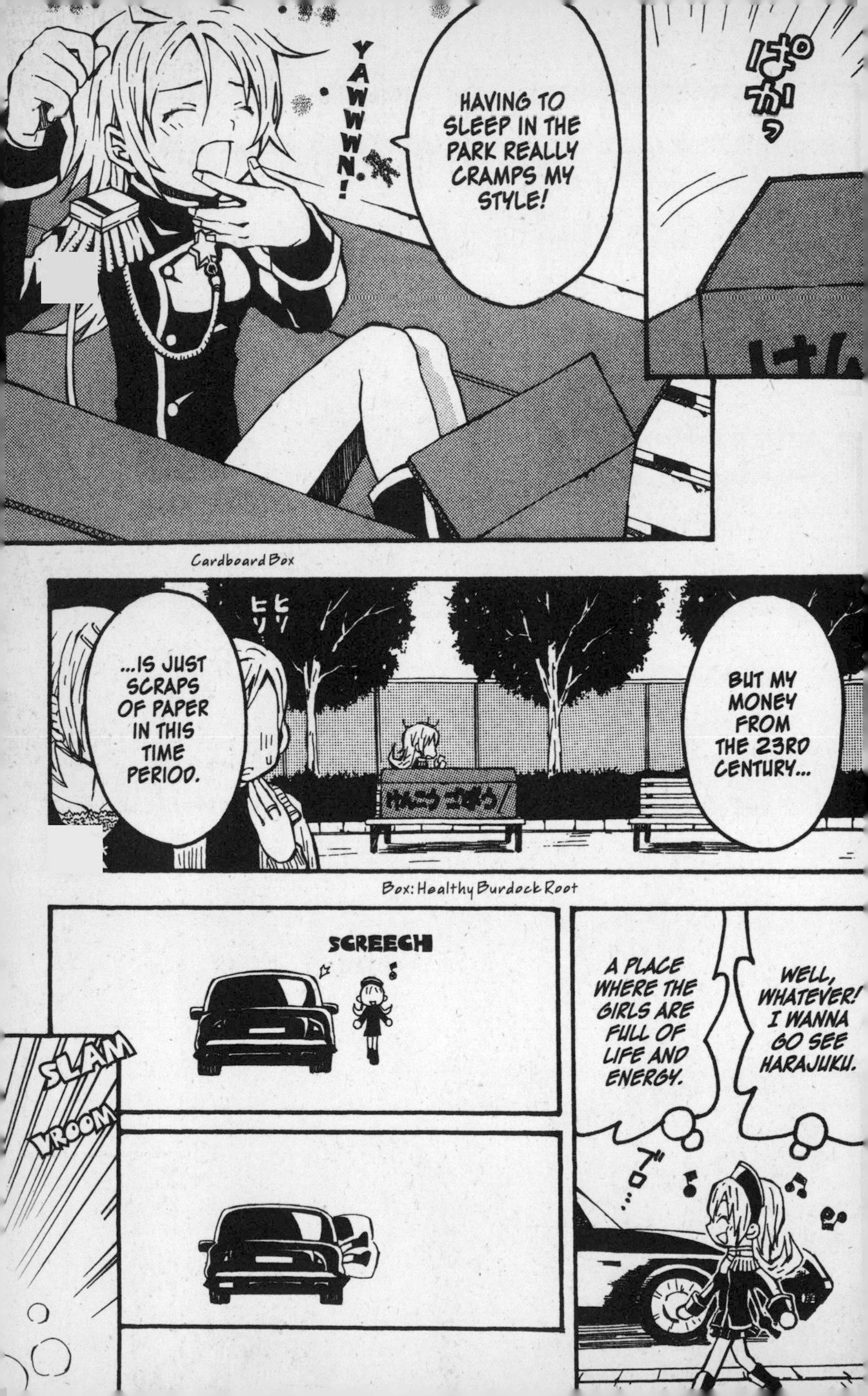
ぱかっ
YAWWWN!
HAVING TO SLEEP IN THE PARK REALLY CRAMPS MY STYLE!
Cardboard Box
BUT MY MONEY FROM THE 23RD CENTURY...
ヒソヒソ
...IS JUST SCRAPS OF PAPER IN THIS TIME PERIOD.
Box: Healthy Burdock Root
WELL, WHATEVER! I WANNA GO SEE HARAJUKU.
A PLACE WHERE THE GIRLS ARE FULL OF LIFE AND ENERGY.
ブロ...
SCREECH
SLAM
VROOM

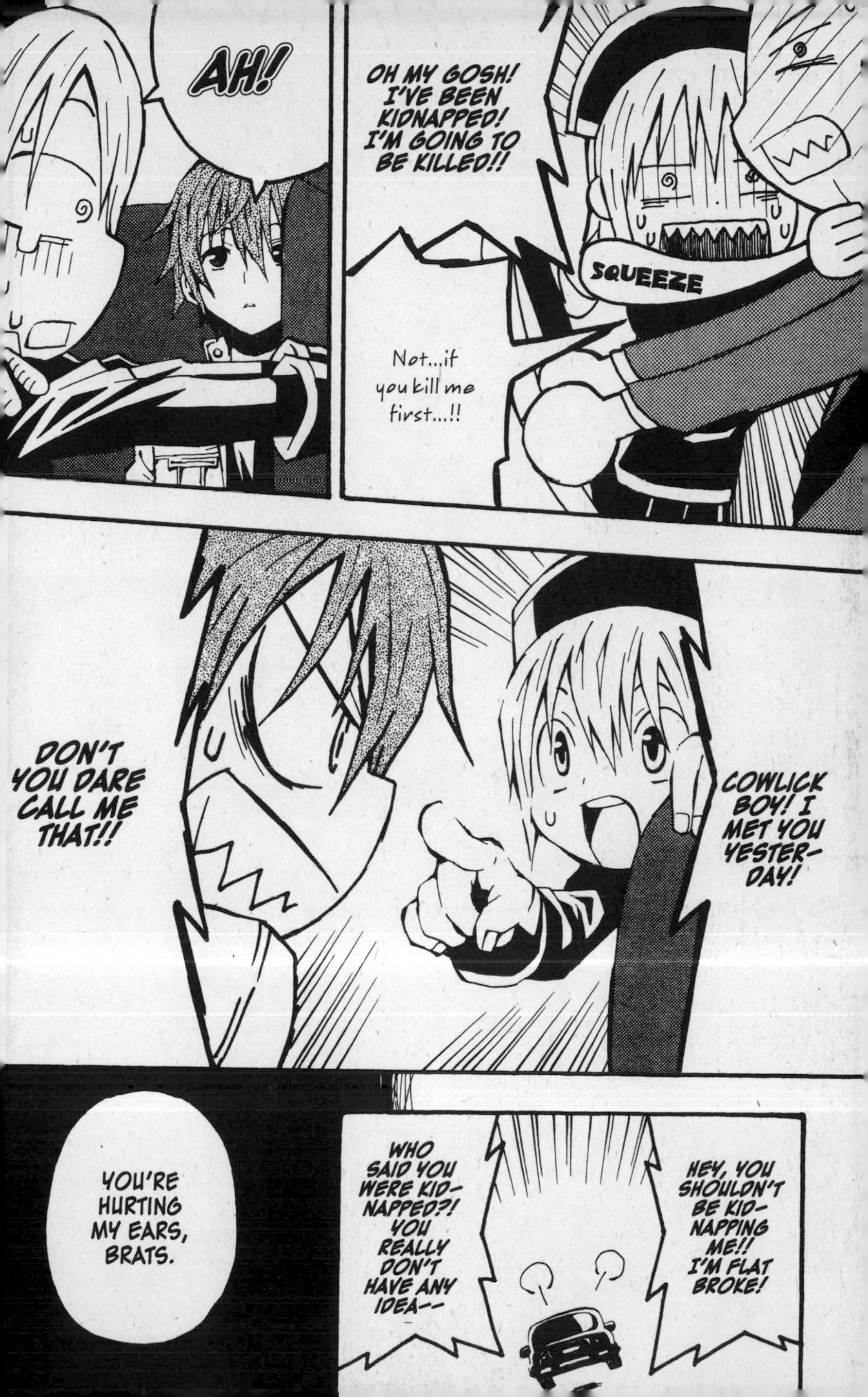
OH MY GOSH! I'VE BEEN KIDNAPPED! I'M GOING TO BE KILLED!!
SQUEEZE
Not...if you kill me first...!!
AH!
COWLICK BOY! I MET YOU YESTER-DAY!
DON'T YOU DARE CALL ME THAT!!
HEY, YOU SHOULDN'T BE KID-NAPPING ME!! I'M FLAT BROKE!
WHO SAID YOU WERE KID-NAPPED?! YOU REALLY DON'T HAVE ANY IDEA--
YOU'RE HURTING MY EARS, BRATS.

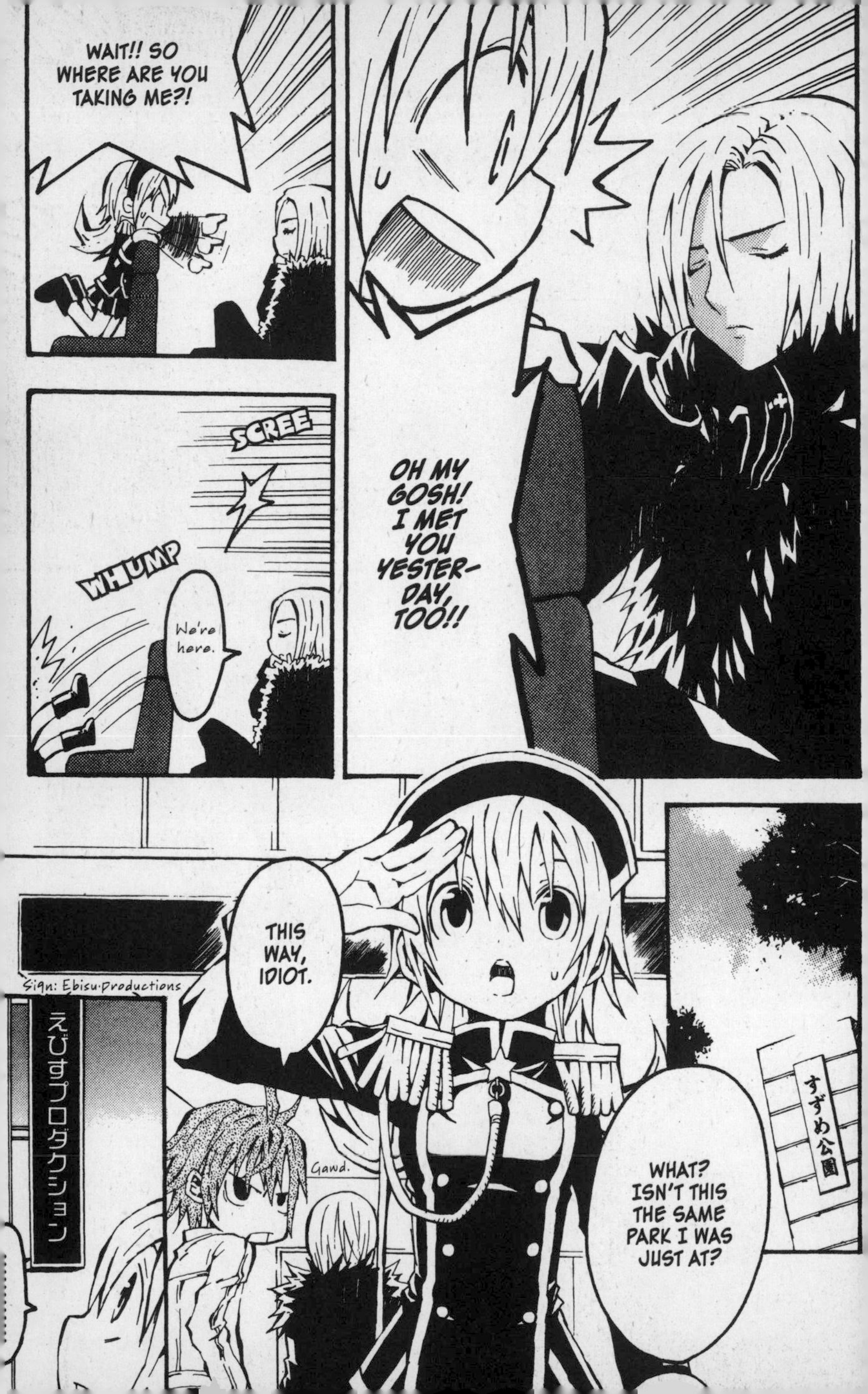
OH MY GOSH! I MET YOU YESTER-DAY, TOO!!
WAIT!! SO WHERE ARE YOU TAKING ME?!
SCREE
WHUMP
We're here.
WHAT? ISN'T THIS THE SAME PARK I WAS JUST AT?
すずめ公園
THIS WAY, IDIOT.
Sign: Ebisu·Productions
えびすプロダクション
Gawd.

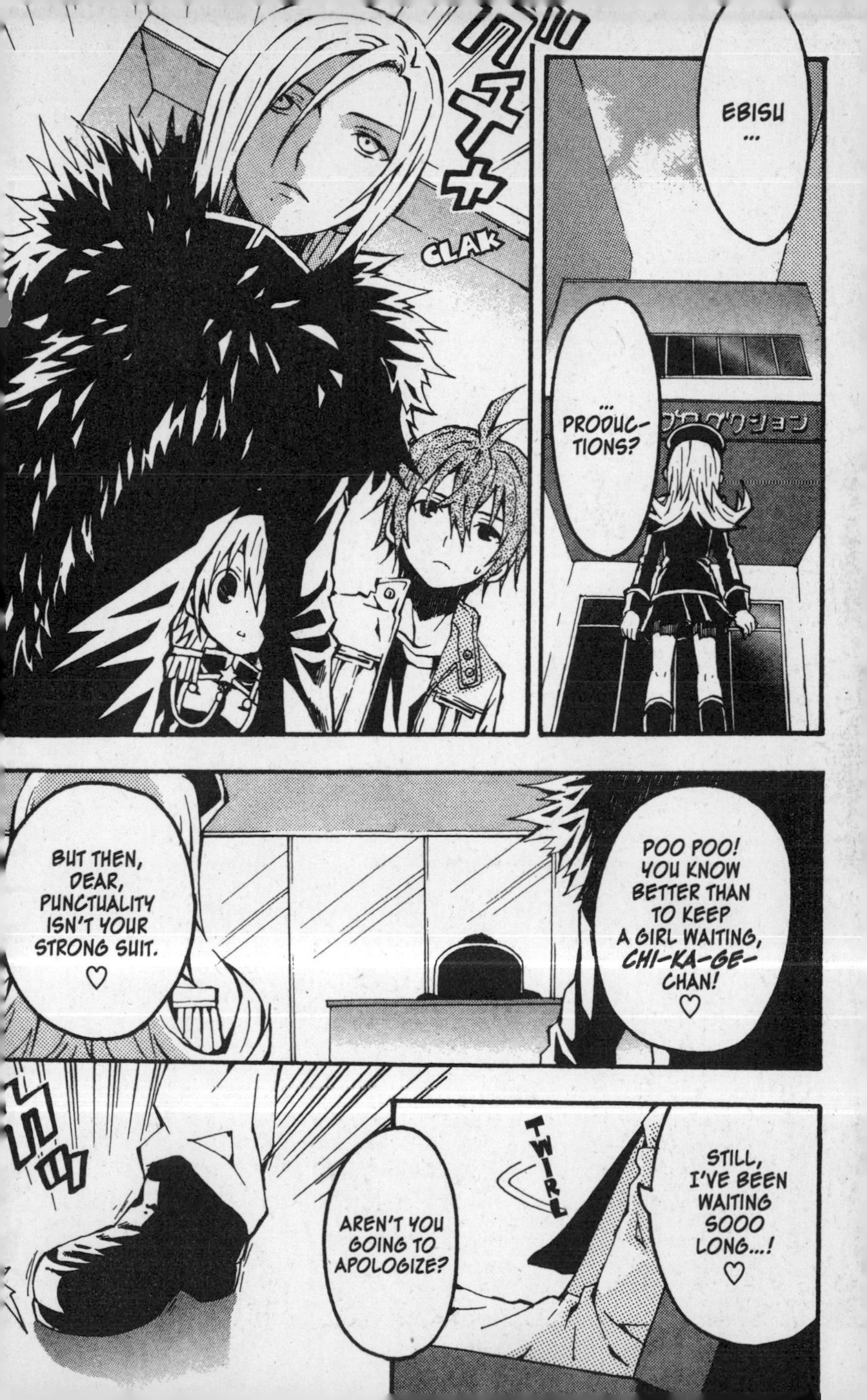
EBISU ...
... PRODUC-TIONS?
CLAK
POO POO! YOU KNOW BETTER THAN TO KEEP A GIRL WAITING, CHI-KA-GE-CHAN! ♡
BUT THEN, DEAR, PUNCTUALITY ISN'T YOUR STRONG SUIT. ♡
STILL, I'VE BEEN WAITING SOOO LONG...! ♡
TWIRL
AREN'T YOU GOING TO APOLOGIZE?

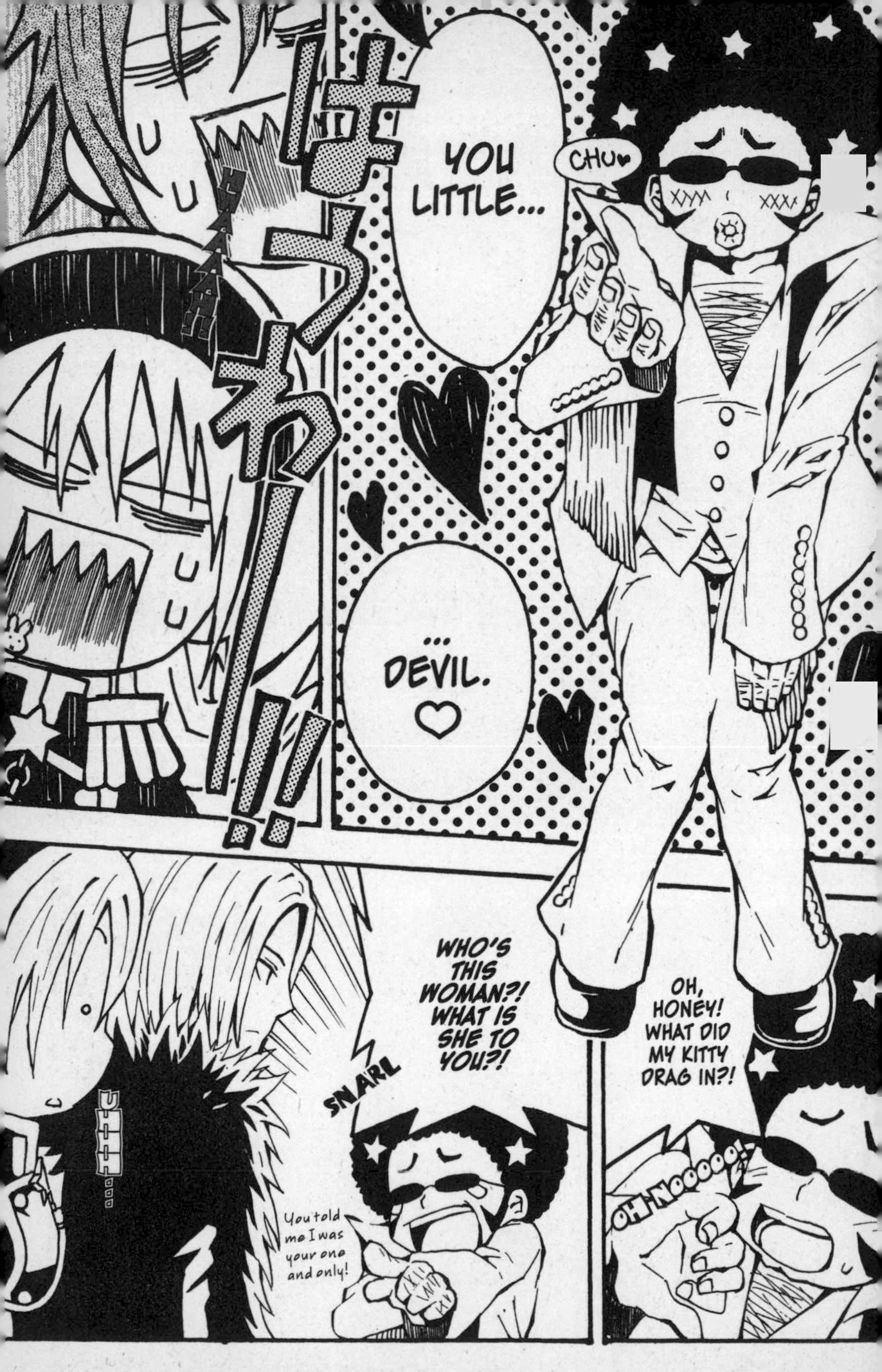
CHU♥
YOU LITTLE...
...DEVIL. ♡
WHAAAAT
OH, HONEY! WHAT DID MY KITTY DRAG IN?!
OH-NOOOOO!
WHO'S THIS WOMAN?! WHAT IS SHE TO YOU?!
SNARL
You told me I was your one and only!
UHHH...

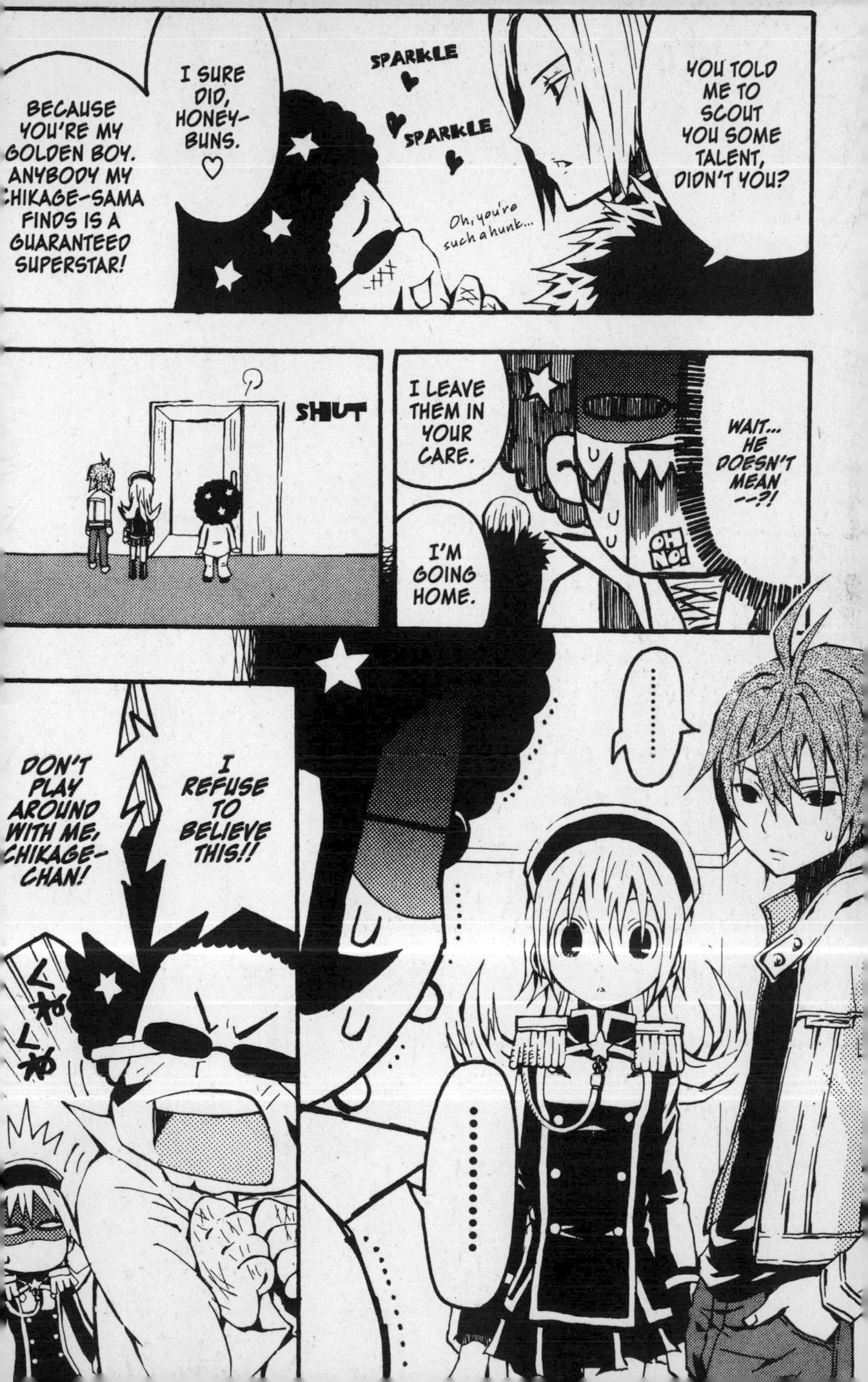
YOU TOLD ME TO SCOUT YOU SOME TALENT, DIDN'T YOU?
SPARKLE
SPARKLE
Oh, you're such a hunk...
I SURE DID, HONEY-BUNS. ♡
BECAUSE YOU'RE MY GOLDEN BOY. ANYBODY MY CHIKAGE-SAMA FINDS IS A GUARANTEED SUPERSTAR!
WAIT... HE DOESN'T MEAN --?!
I LEAVE THEM IN YOUR CARE.
OH NO!
I'M GOING HOME.
SHUT
......
......
I REFUSE TO BELIEVE THIS!!
DON'T PLAY AROUND WITH ME, CHIKAGE-CHAN!
くねくね

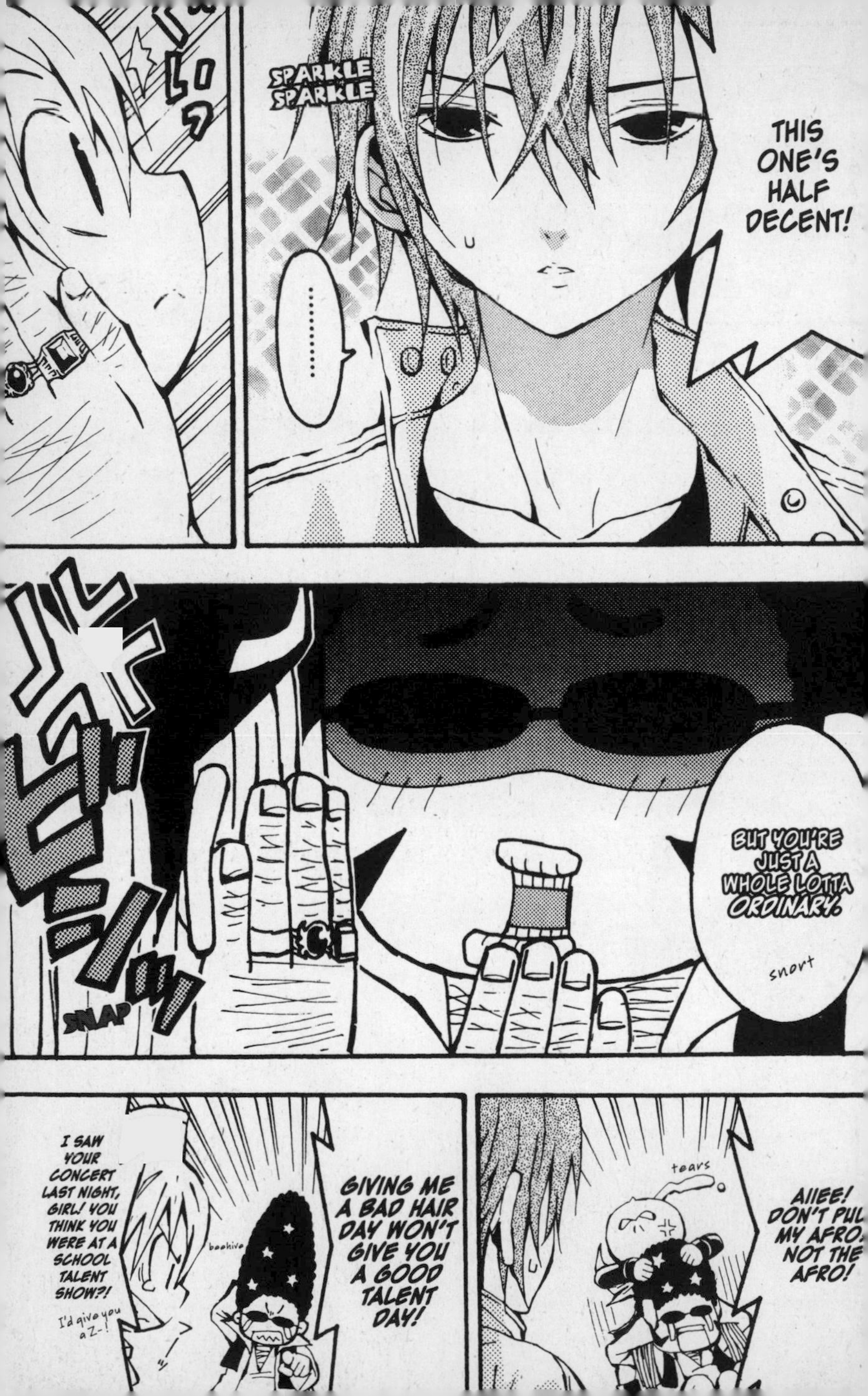
SPARKLE SPARKLE
THIS ONE'S HALF DECENT!
......
BUT YOU'RE JUST A WHOLE LOTTA ORDINARY.
snort
SNAP
tears
AIIEE! DON'T PUL MY AFRO, NOT THE AFRO!
I SAW YOUR CONCERT LAST NIGHT, GIRL! YOU THINK YOU WERE AT A SCHOOL TALENT SHOW?!
beehive
I'd give you a Z-!
GIVING ME A BAD HAIR DAY WON'T GIVE YOU A GOOD TALENT DAY!

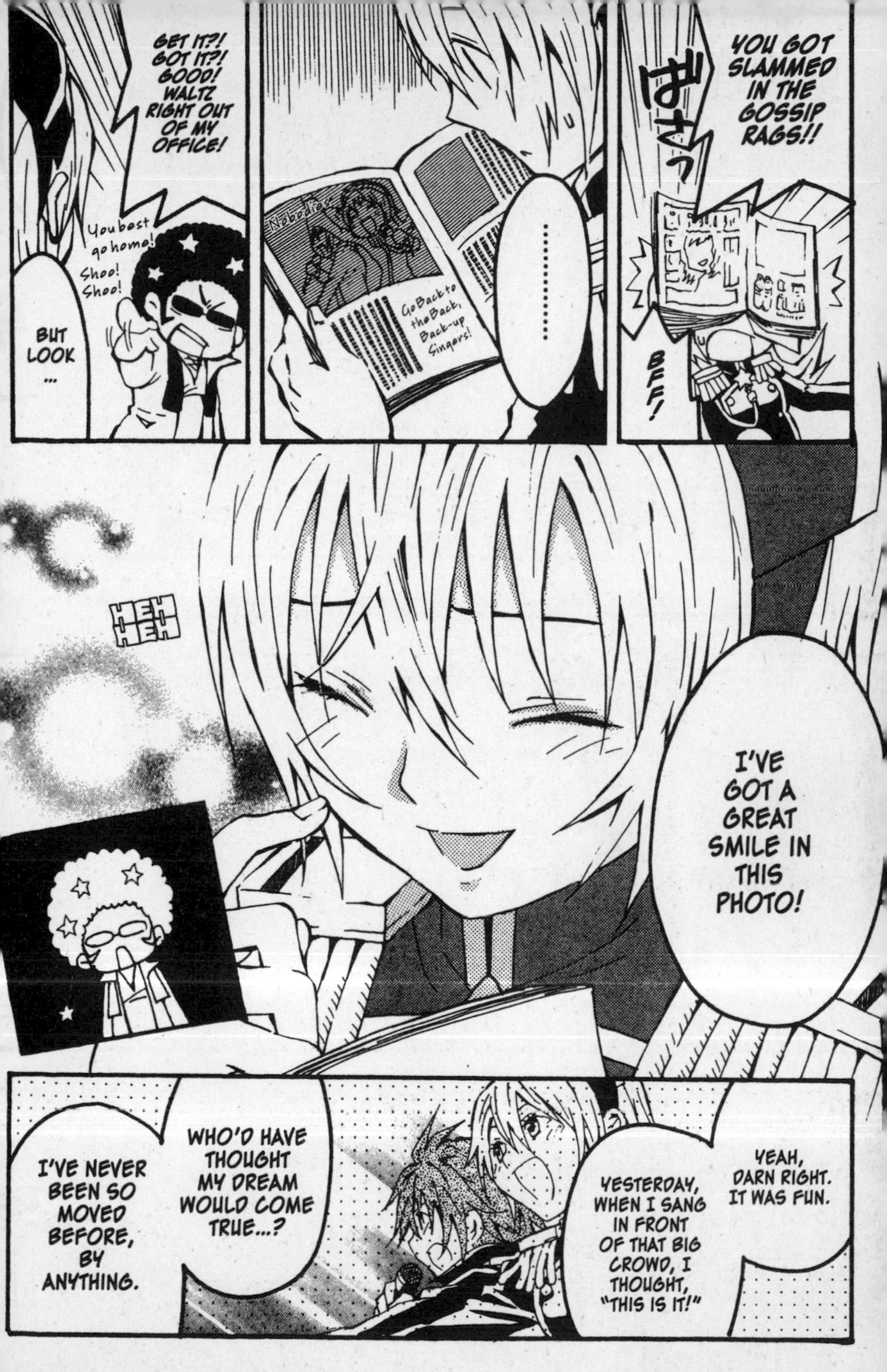
YOU GOT SLAMMED IN THE GOSSIP RAGS!!
BFF!
......
Nobodies
Go Back to the Back, Back-up Singers!
GET IT?! GOT IT?! GOOD! WALTZ RIGHT OUT OF MY OFFICE!
You best go home!
Shoo! Shoo!
BUT LOOK ...
I'VE GOT A GREAT SMILE IN THIS PHOTO!
HEH HEH
YEAH, DARN RIGHT. IT WAS FUN.
YESTERDAY, WHEN I SANG IN FRONT OF THAT BIG CROWD, I THOUGHT, "THIS IS IT!"
WHO'D HAVE THOUGHT MY DREAM WOULD COME TRUE...?
I'VE NEVER BEEN SO MOVED BEFORE, BY ANYTHING.

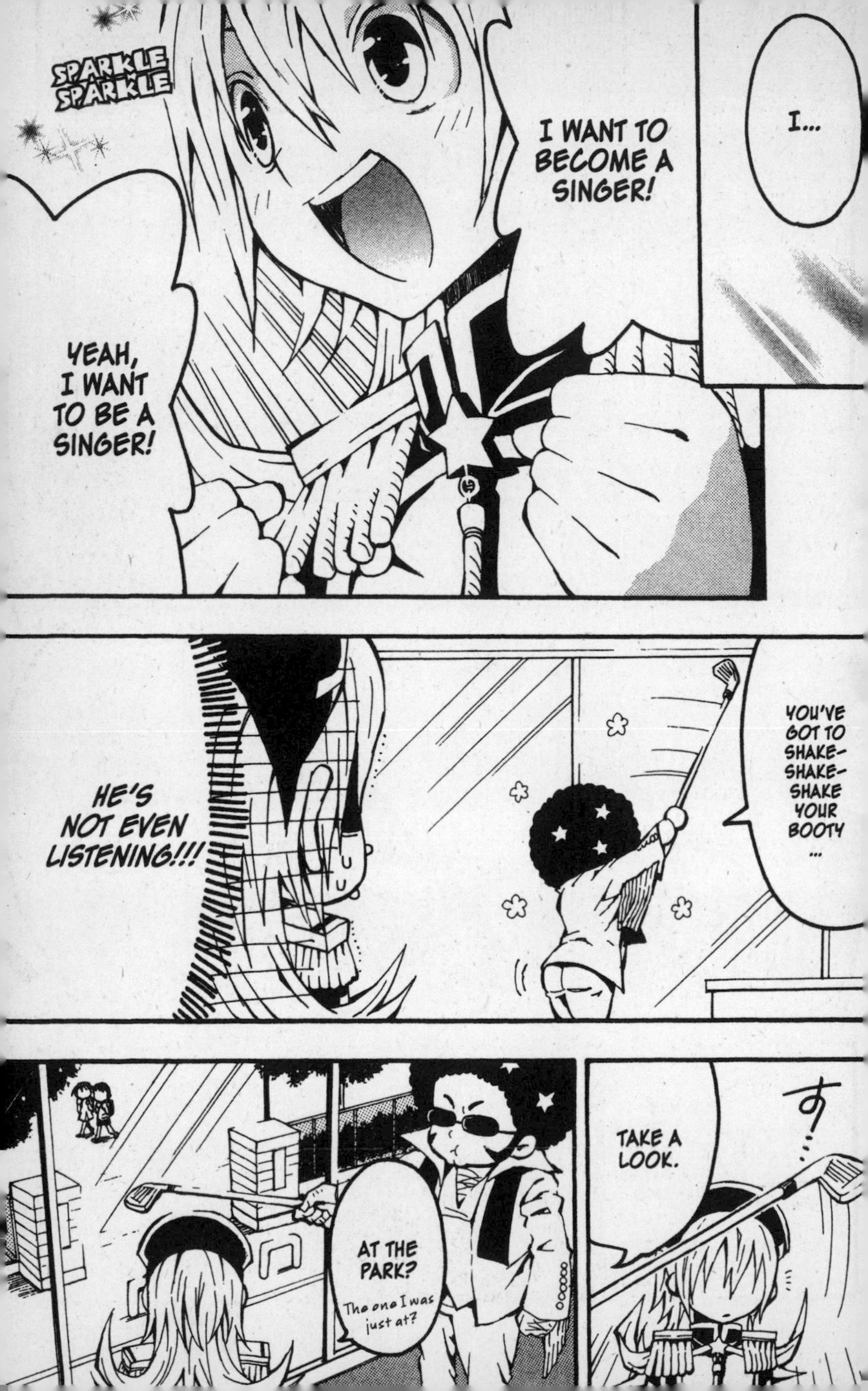
I...
I WANT TO BECOME A SINGER!
SPARKLE SPARKLE
YEAH, I WANT TO BE A SINGER!
YOU'VE GOT TO SHAKE-SHAKE-SHAKE YOUR BOOTY ...
HE'S NOT EVEN LISTENING!!!
す…
TAKE A LOOK.
AT THE PARK?
The one I was just at?

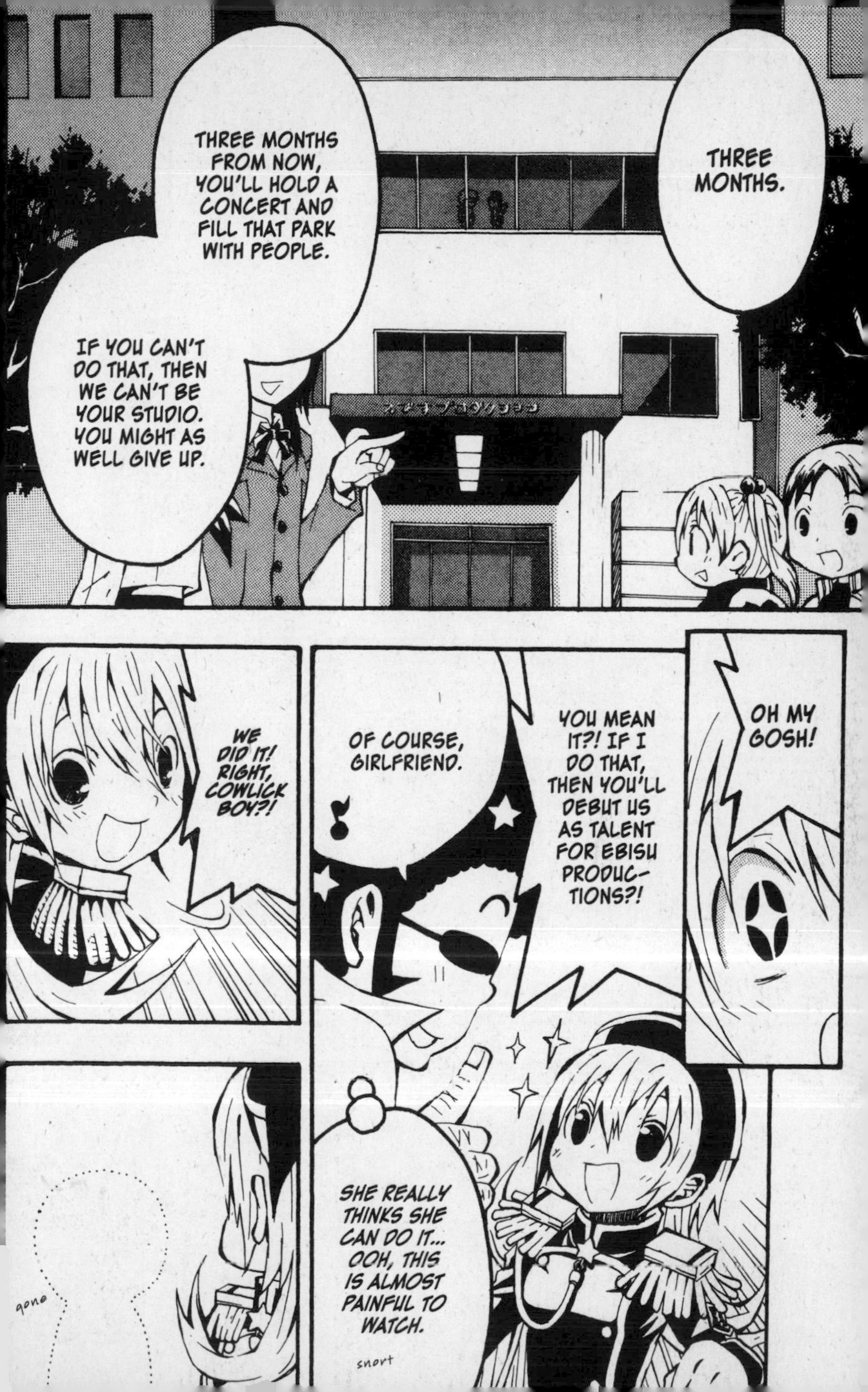
THREE MONTHS.
THREE MONTHS FROM NOW, YOU'LL HOLD A CONCERT AND FILL THAT PARK WITH PEOPLE.
IF YOU CAN'T DO THAT, THEN WE CAN'T BE YOUR STUDIO. YOU MIGHT AS WELL GIVE UP.
OH MY GOSH!
YOU MEAN IT?! IF I DO THAT, THEN YOU'LL DEBUT US AS TALENT FOR EBISU PRODUCTIONS?!
OF COURSE, GIRLFRIEND.
WE DID IT! RIGHT, COWLICK BOY?!
SHE REALLY THINKS SHE CAN DO IT... OOH, THIS IS ALMOST PAINFUL TO WATCH.
snort
gone

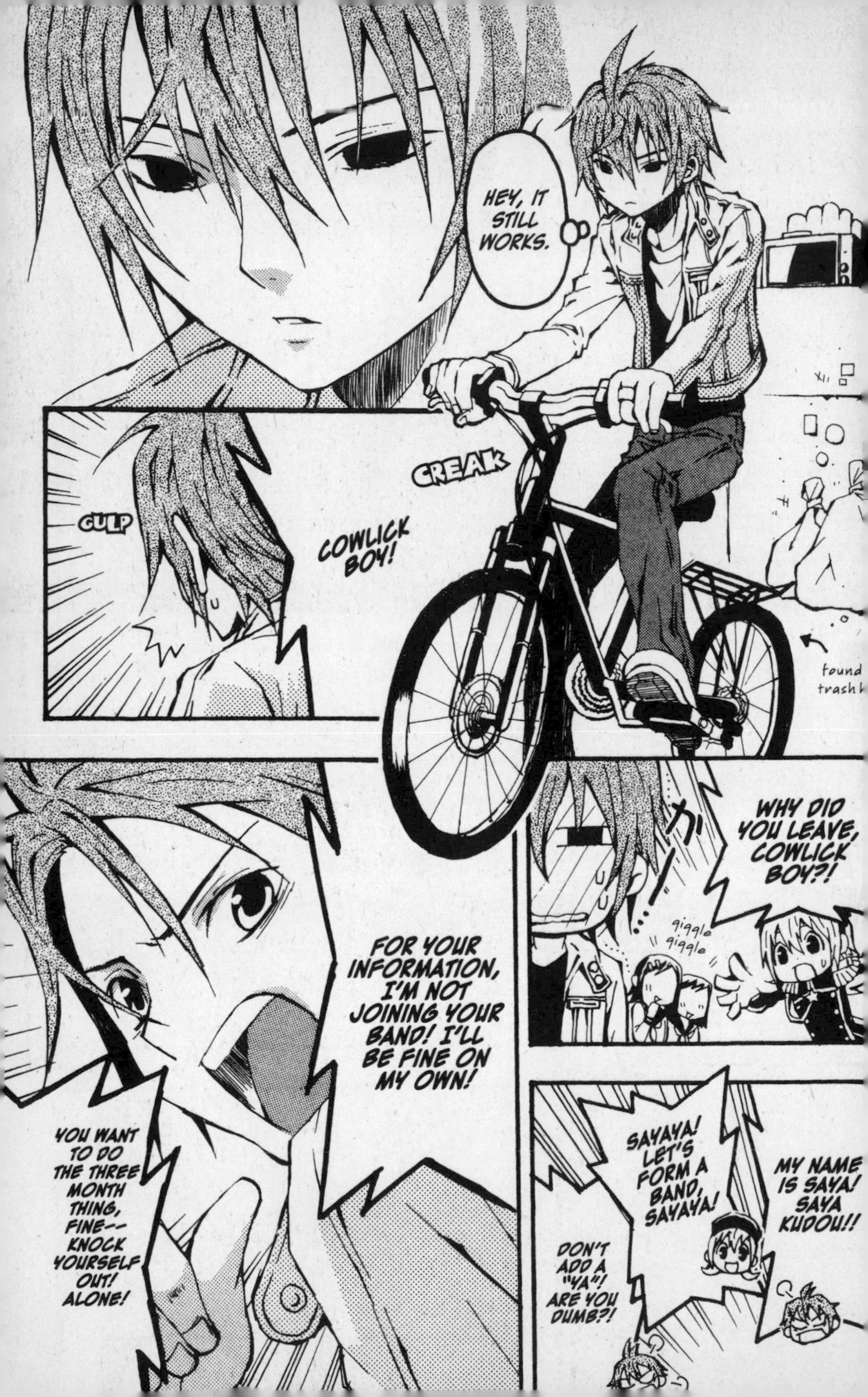
HEY, IT STILL WORKS.
CREAK
found trash
COWLICK BOY!
GULP
WHY DID YOU LEAVE, COWLICK BOY?!
giggle giggle
SAYAYA! LET'S FORM A BAND, SAYAYA!
MY NAME IS SAYA! SAYA KUDOU!!
DON'T ADD A "YA"! ARE YOU DUMB?!
FOR YOUR INFORMATION, I'M NOT JOINING YOUR BAND! I'LL BE FINE ON MY OWN!
YOU WANT TO DO THE THREE MONTH THING, FINE--KNOCK YOURSELF OUT! ALONE!

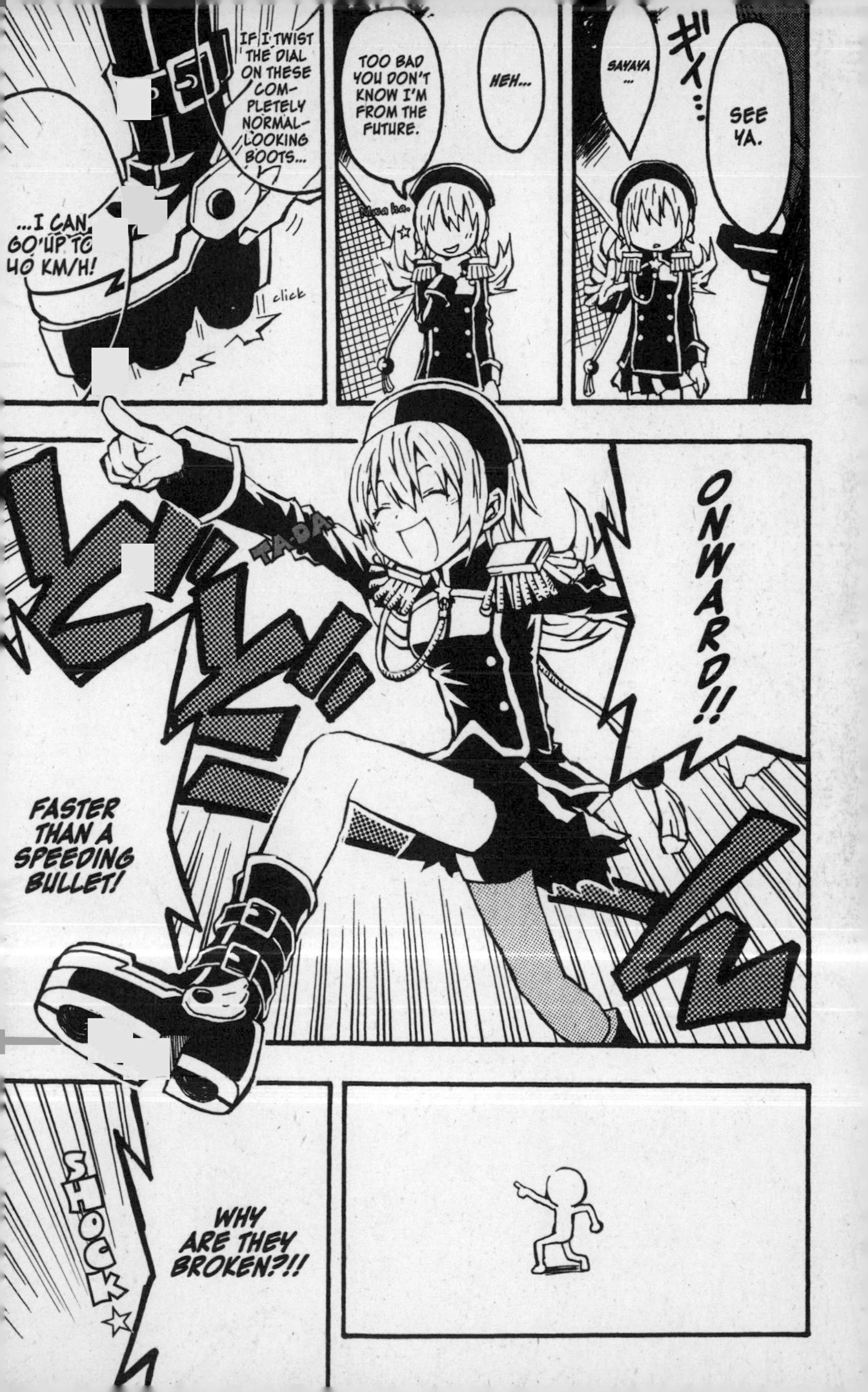
ギイ…
SEE YA.
SAYAYA...
HEH...
TOO BAD YOU DON'T KNOW I'M FROM THE FUTURE.
Nwa ha.
IF I TWIST THE DIAL ON THESE COMPLETELY NORMAL-LOOKING BOOTS...
...I CAN GO UP TO 40 KM/H!
click
ONWARD!!
TA-DA
FASTER THAN A SPEEDING BULLET!
SHOCK☆
WHY ARE THEY BROKEN?!!

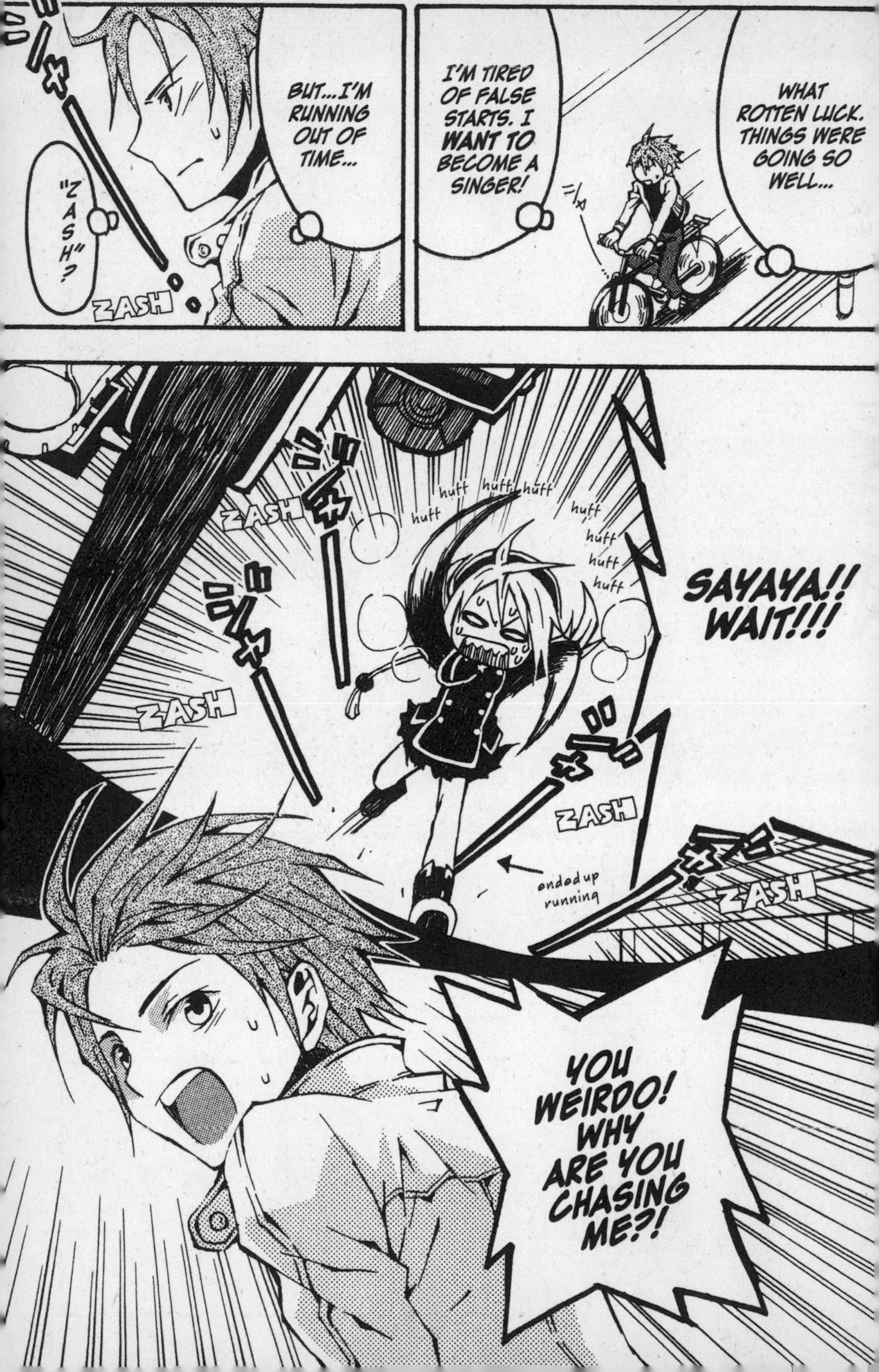
WHAT ROTTEN LUCK. THINGS WERE GOING SO WELL...
I'M TIRED OF FALSE STARTS. I WANT TO BECOME A SINGER!
BUT...I'M RUNNING OUT OF TIME...
"ZASH"?
ZASH
SAYAYA!! WAIT!!!
huff huff huff huff huff huff huff huff
ZASH
ZASH
ZASH
ZASH
ended up running
YOU WEIRDO! WHY ARE YOU CHASING ME?!

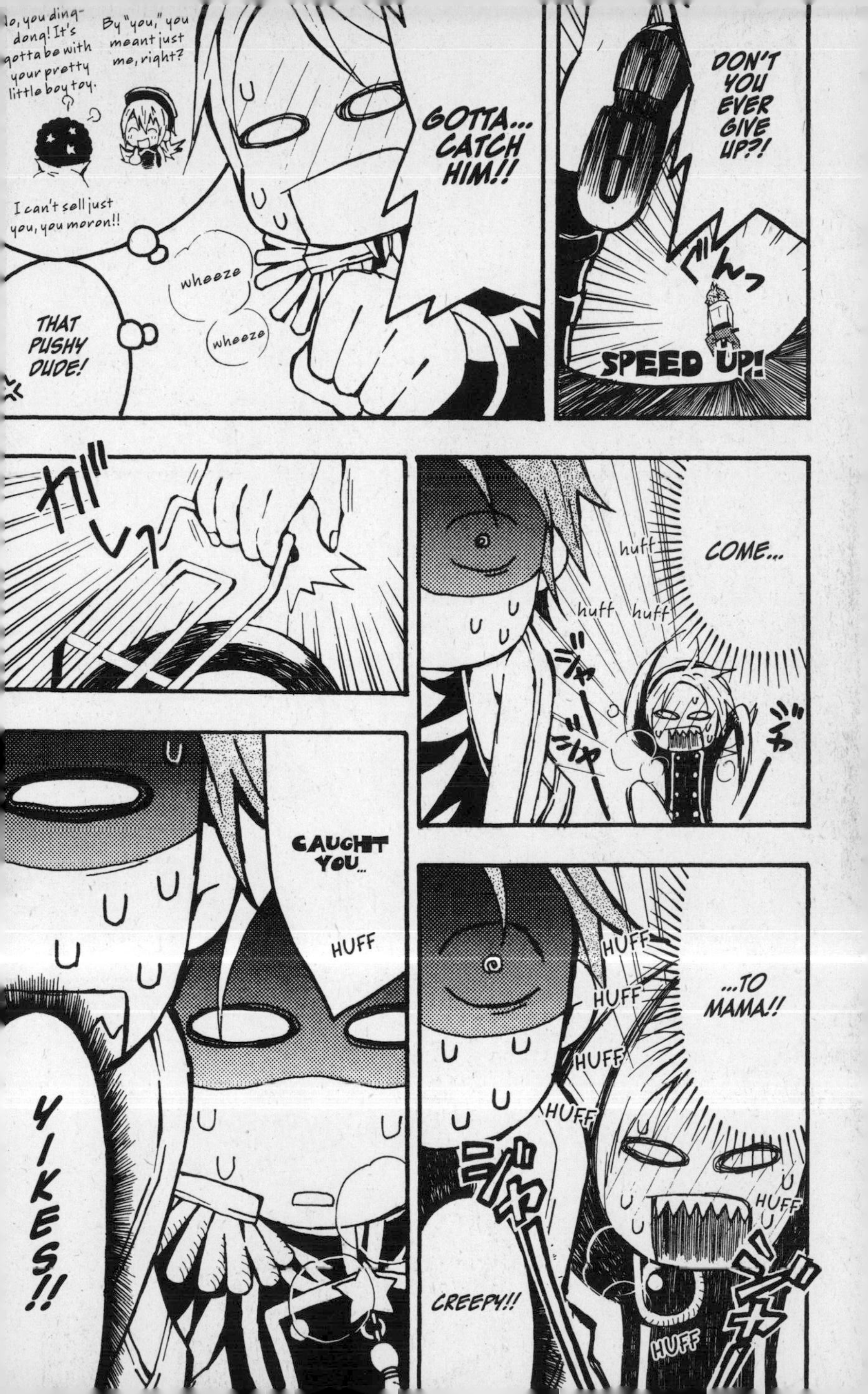
DON'T YOU EVER GIVE UP?!
SPEED UP!
GOTTA... CATCH HIM!!
By "you," you meant just me, right?
No, you ding-dong! It's gotta be with your pretty little boy toy.
I can't sell just you, you moron!!
wheeze
wheeze
THAT PUSHY DUDE!
COME...
huff
huff huff
...TO MAMA!!
HUFF
HUFF
HUFF
HUFF
HUFF
HUFF
CREEPY!!
CAUGHT YOU...
HUFF
YIKES!!

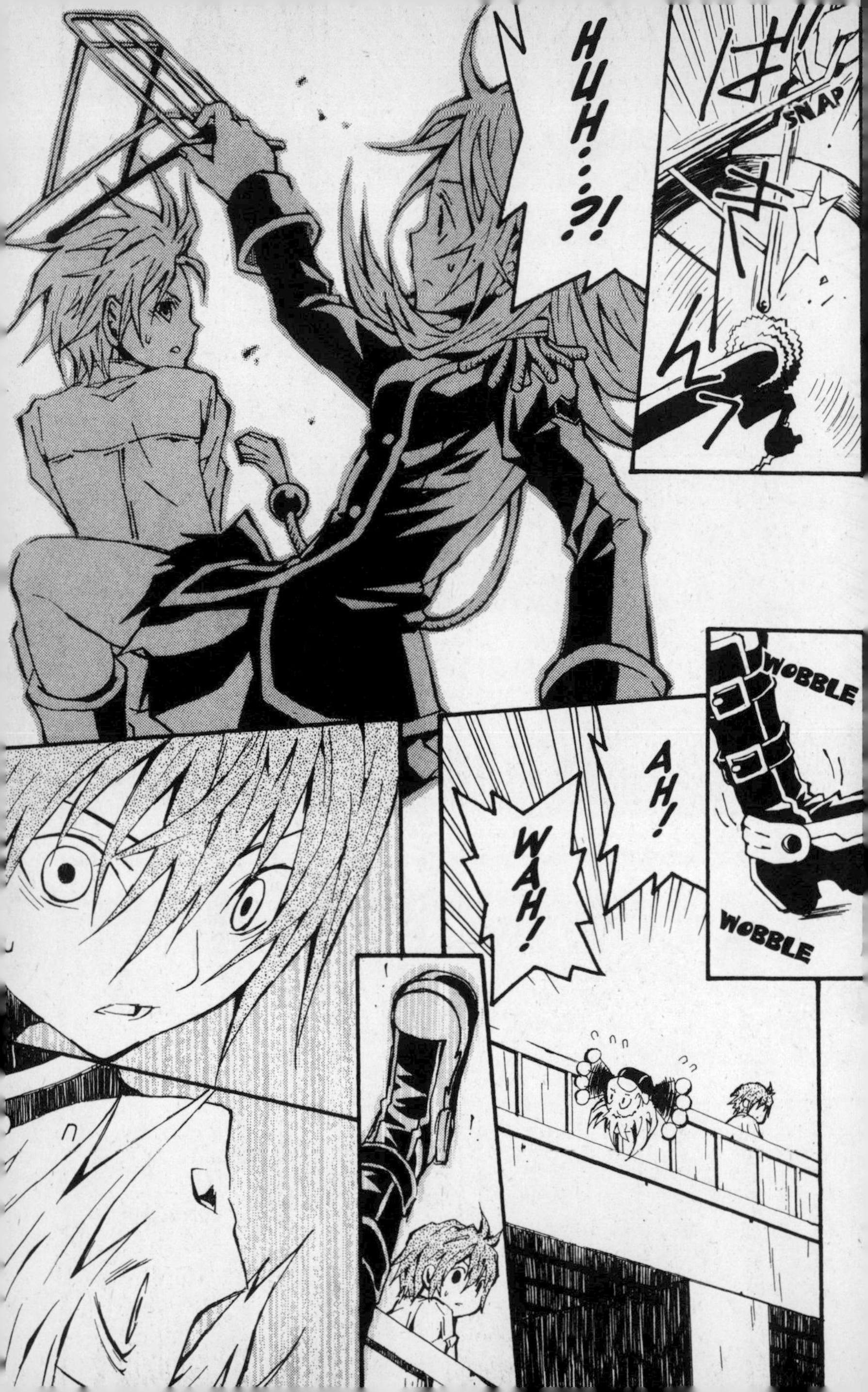
SNAP
HUH...?!
WOBBLE
WOBBLE
AH!
WAH!

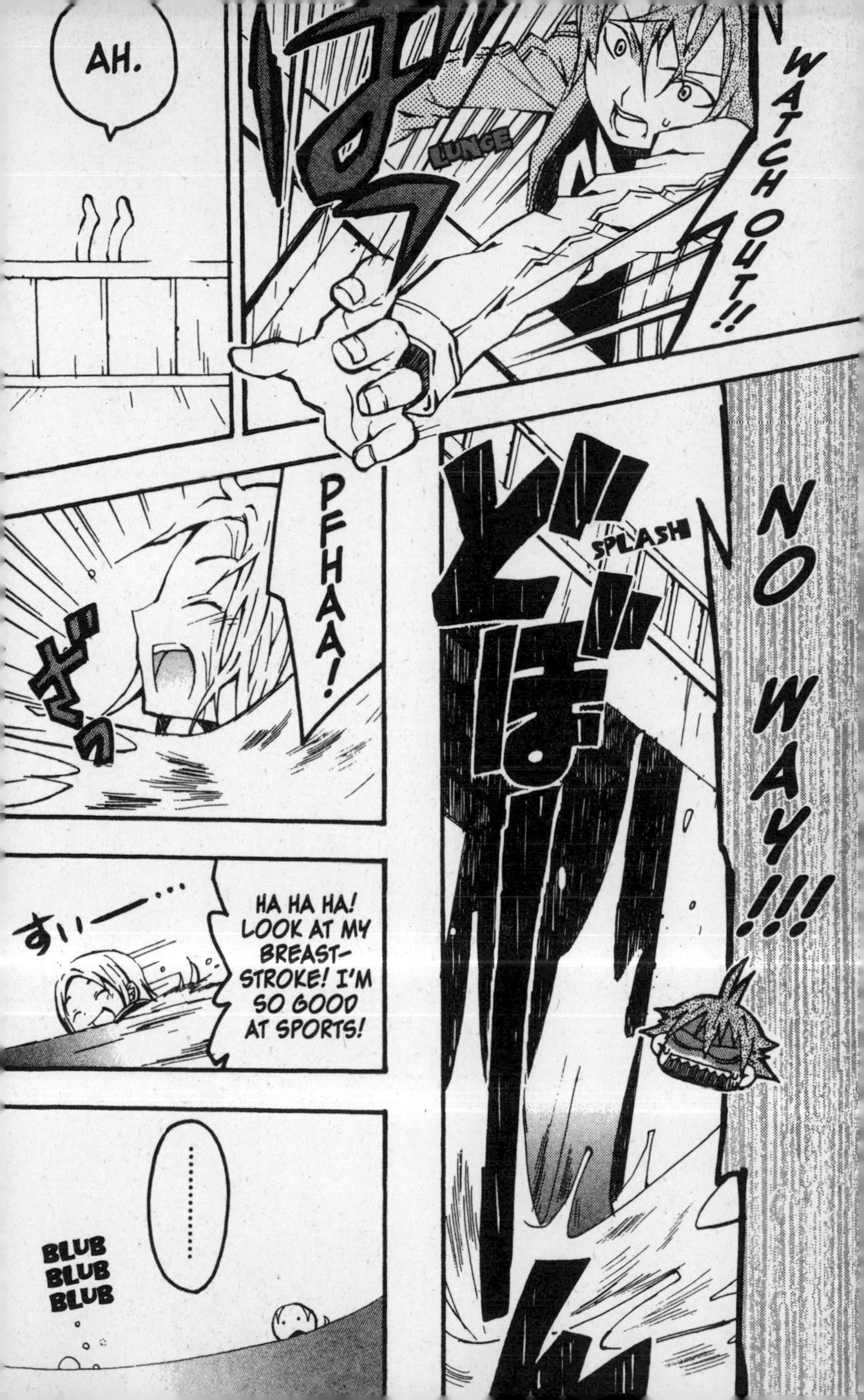

WATCH OUT!!
LUNGE
AH.
NO WAY!!!
SPLASH
PFHAA!
HA HA HA! LOOK AT MY BREAST-STROKE! I'M SO GOOD AT SPORTS!
......
BLUB BLUB BLUB

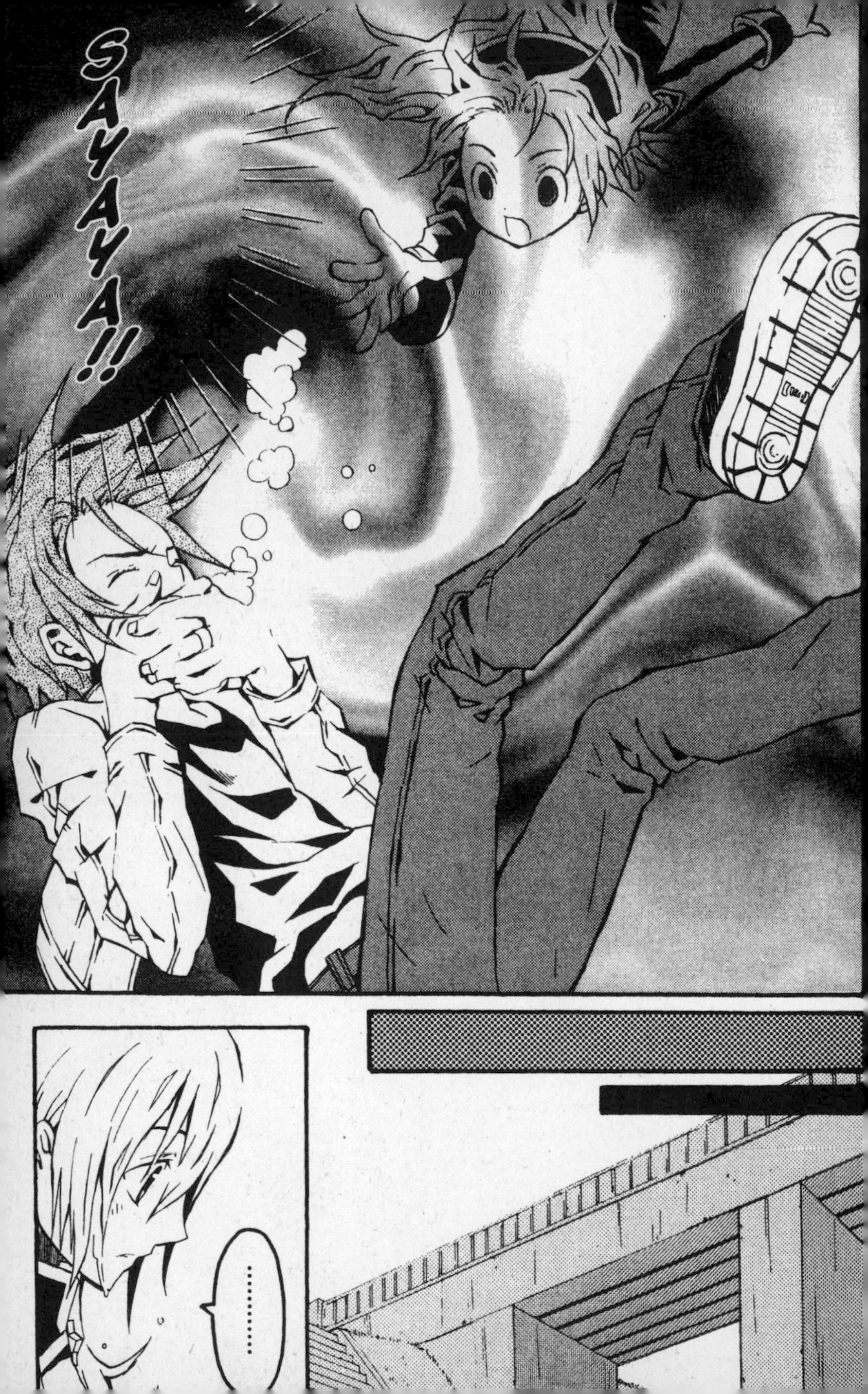
SAYAYAYA!!
......

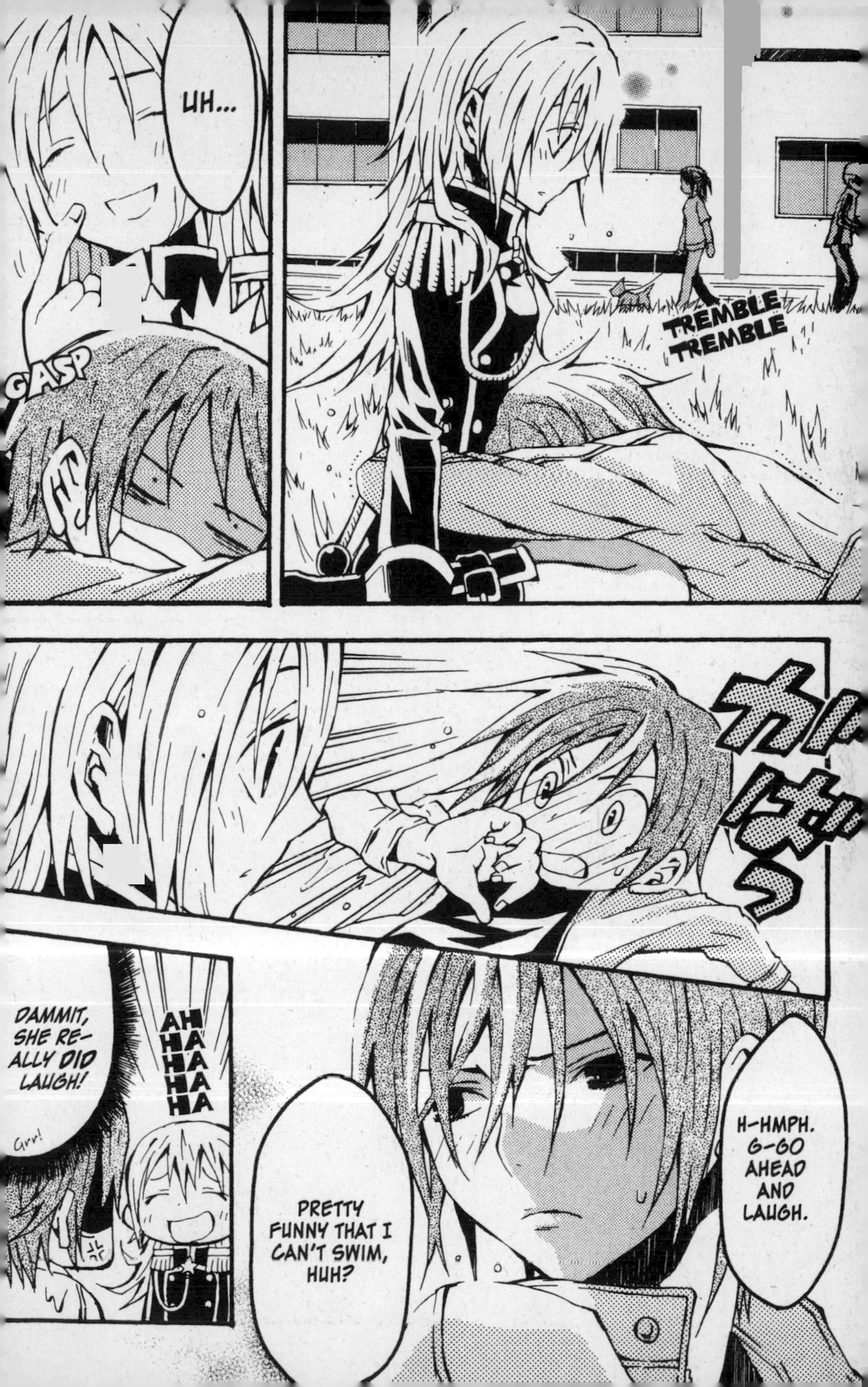
TREMBLE TREMBLE
UH...
GASP
H-HMPH. G-GO AHEAD AND LAUGH.
PRETTY FUNNY THAT I CAN'T SWIM, HUH?
AHAHAHAHAHA
DAMMIT, SHE RE-ALLY DID LAUGH!
Grr!

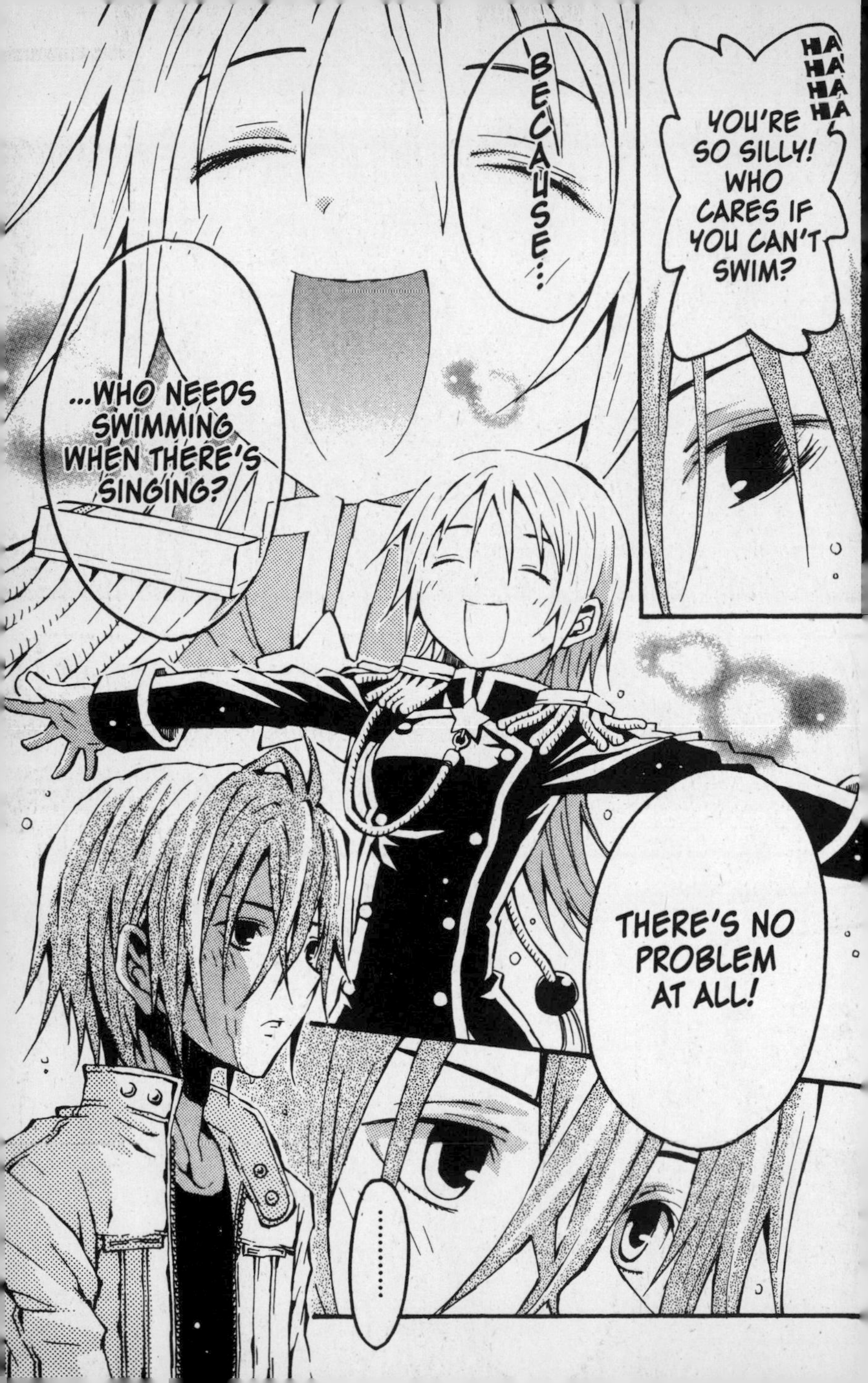
HA HA HA HA
YOU'RE SO SILLY! WHO CARES IF YOU CAN'T SWIM?
BECAUSE...
...WHO NEEDS SWIMMING WHEN THERE'S SINGING?
THERE'S NO PROBLEM AT ALL!
......

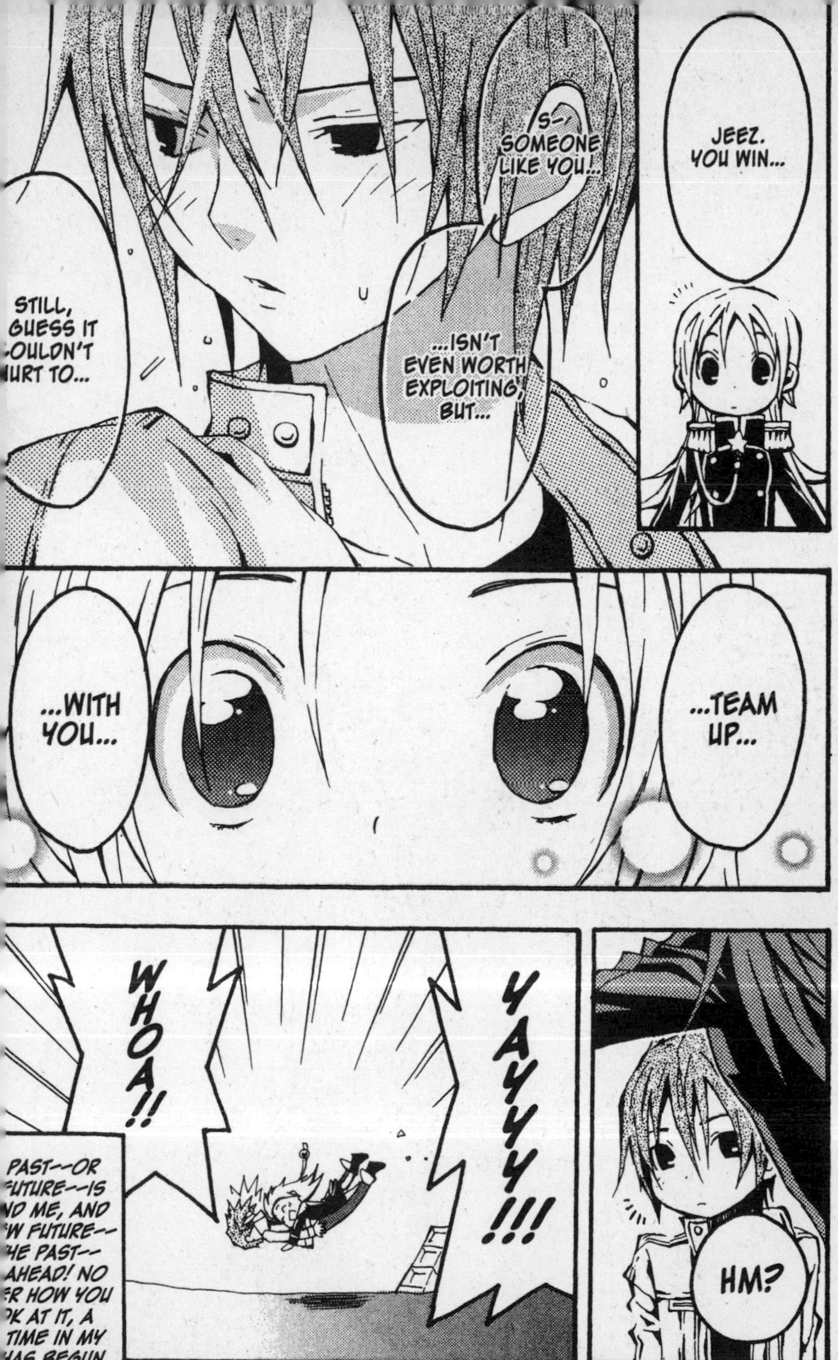
JEEZ. YOU WIN...
S-- SOMEONE LIKE YOU...
...ISN'T EVEN WORTH EXPLOITING, BUT...
STILL, GUESS IT OULDN'T URT TO...
...TEAM UP...
...WITH YOU...
HM?
YAYYY!!!
WHOA!!
PAST--OR UTURE--IS ND ME, AND W FUTURE-- HE PAST-- AHEAD! NO ER HOW YOU OK AT IT, A TIME IN MY HAS BEGUN.

Stage 1 "Future superstars★" / End

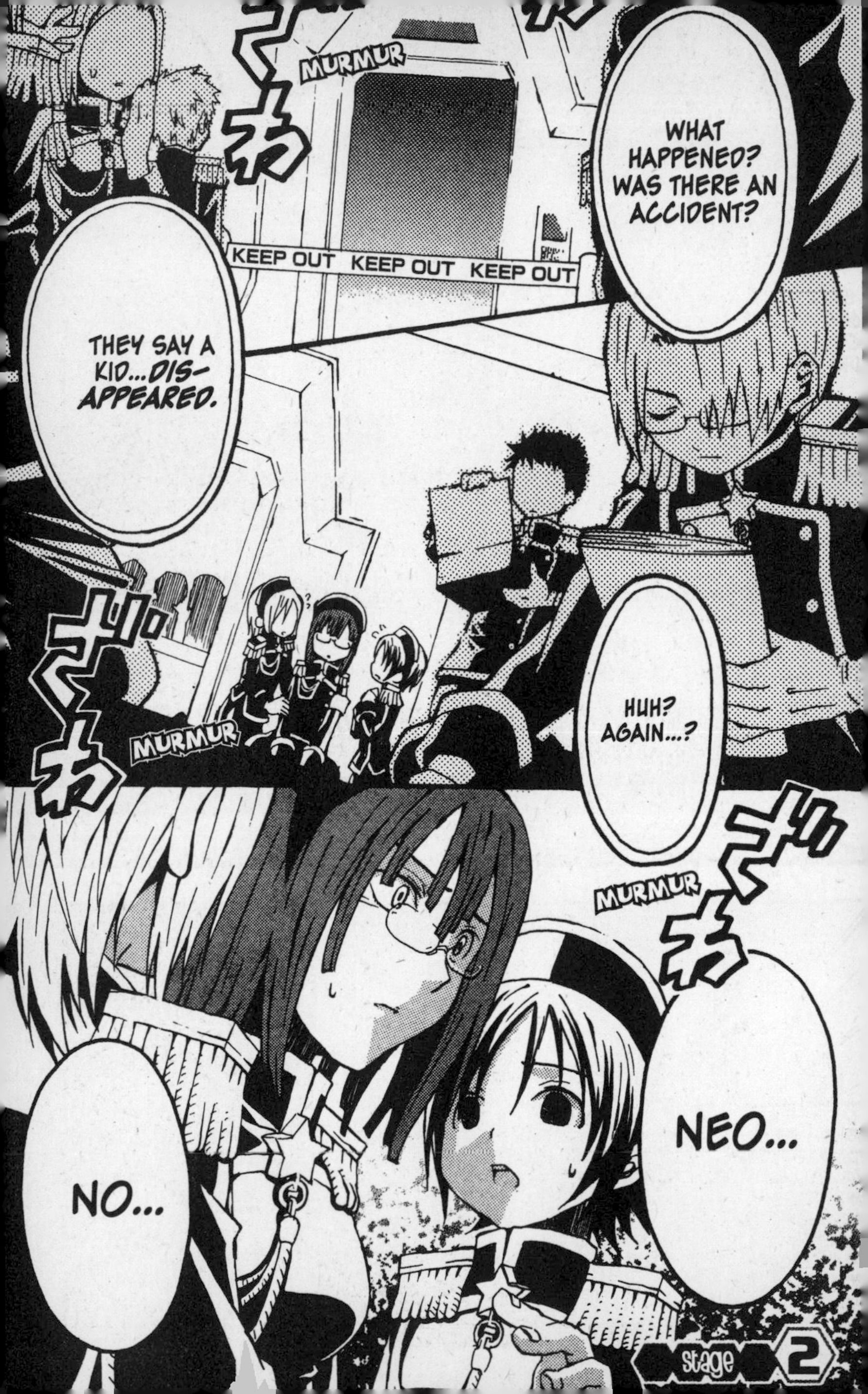
MURMUR
WHAT HAPPENED? WAS THERE AN ACCIDENT?
KEEP OUT KEEP OUT KEEP OUT
THEY SAY A KID...DIS-APPEARED.
HUH? AGAIN...?
MURMUR
MURMUR
NEO...
NO...
stage 2

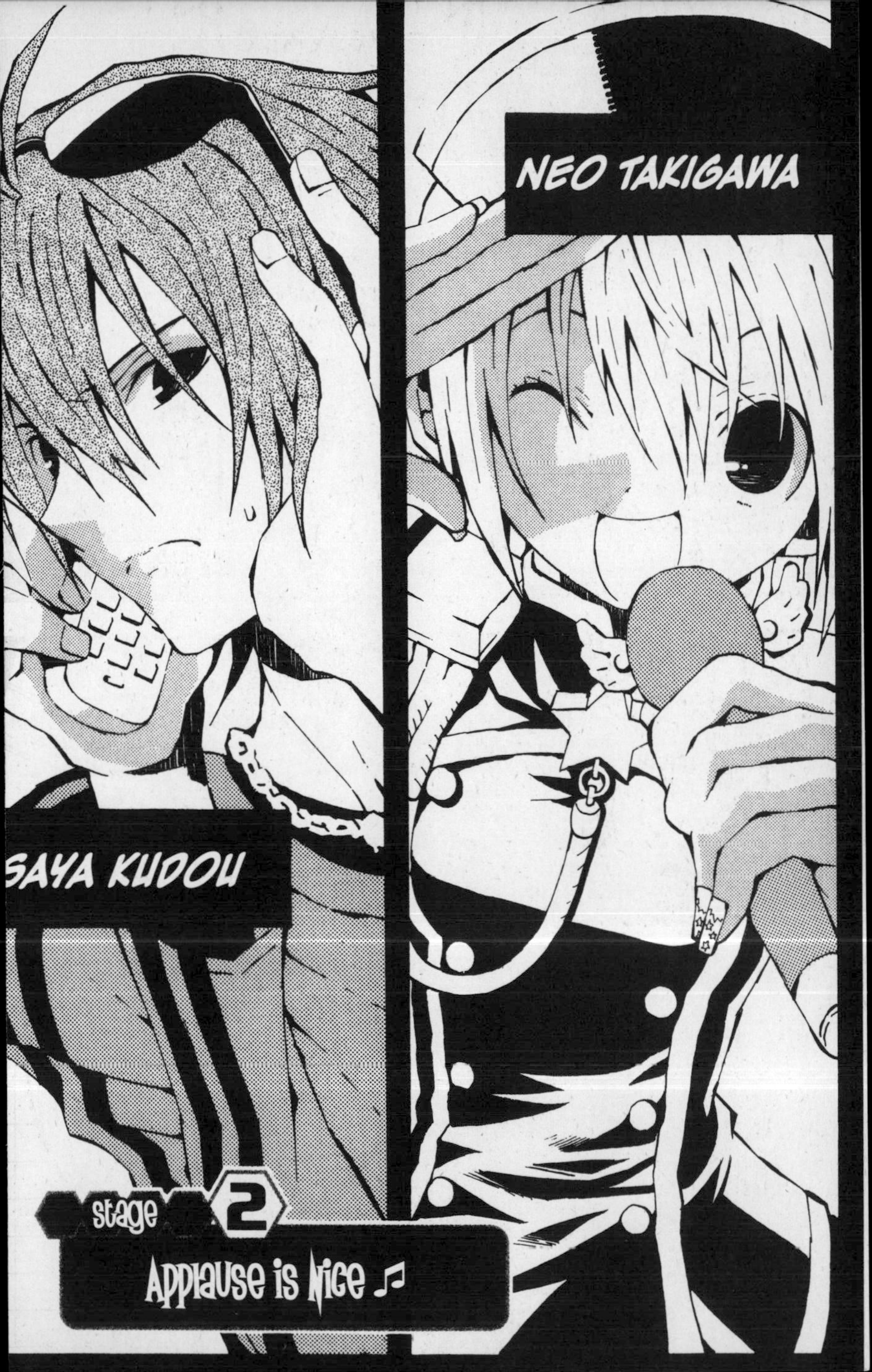
NEO TAKIGAWA
SAYA KUDOU
stage 2
Applause is Nice ♫

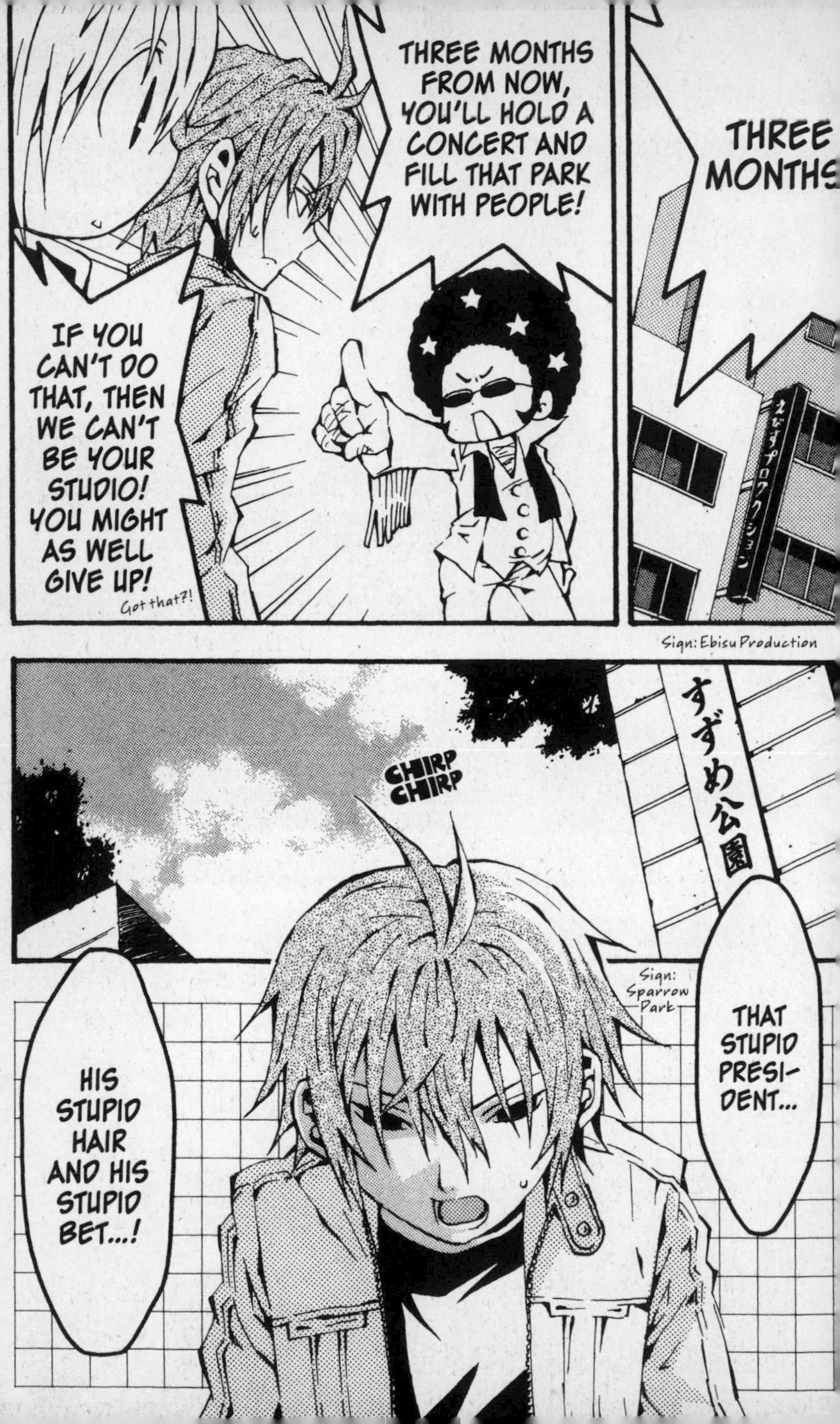
THREE MONTHS
えびすプロダクション
Sign: Ebisu Production
THREE MONTHS FROM NOW, YOU'LL HOLD A CONCERT AND FILL THAT PARK WITH PEOPLE!
IF YOU CAN'T DO THAT, THEN WE CAN'T BE YOUR STUDIO! YOU MIGHT AS WELL GIVE UP!
Got that?!
すずめ公園
Sign: Sparrow Park
CHIRP CHIRP
THAT STUPID PRESIDENT...
HIS STUPID HAIR AND HIS STUPID BET...!

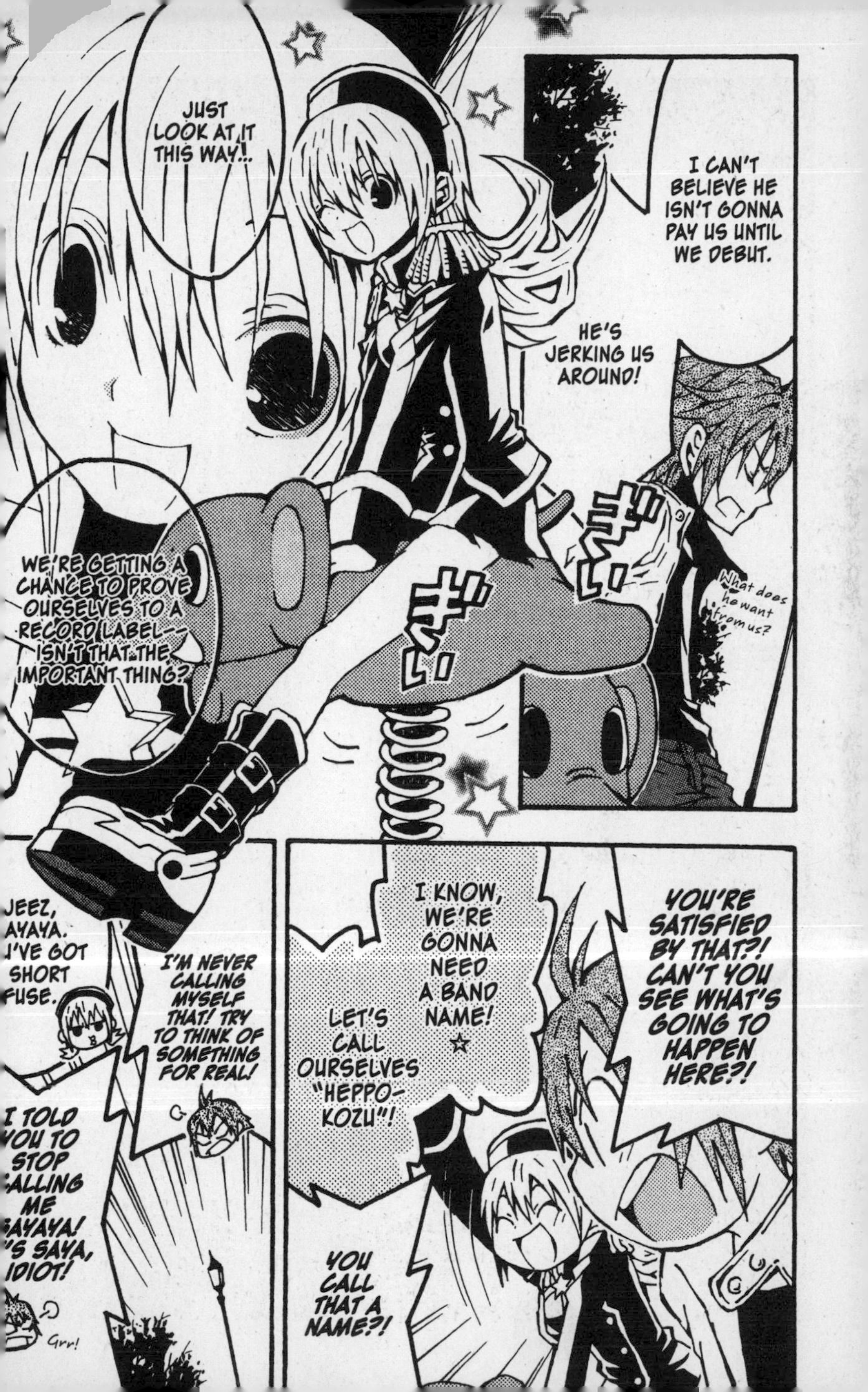
I CAN'T BELIEVE HE ISN'T GONNA PAY US UNTIL WE DEBUT.
HE'S JERKING US AROUND!
What does he want from us?
JUST LOOK AT IT THIS WAY!..
WE'RE GETTING A CHANCE TO PROVE OURSELVES TO A RECORD LABEL--ISN'T THAT THE IMPORTANT THING?
ぎしっ
ぎしっ
YOU'RE SATISFIED BY THAT?! CAN'T YOU SEE WHAT'S GOING TO HAPPEN HERE?!
I KNOW, WE'RE GONNA NEED A BAND NAME!
LET'S CALL OURSELVES "HEPPO-KOZU"!
YOU CALL THAT A NAME?!
I'M NEVER CALLING MYSELF THAT! TRY TO THINK OF SOMETHING FOR REAL!
JEEZ, AYAYA. U'VE GOT SHORT FUSE.
I TOLD YOU TO STOP ALLING ME SAYAYA! 'S SAYA, IDIOT!
Grr!

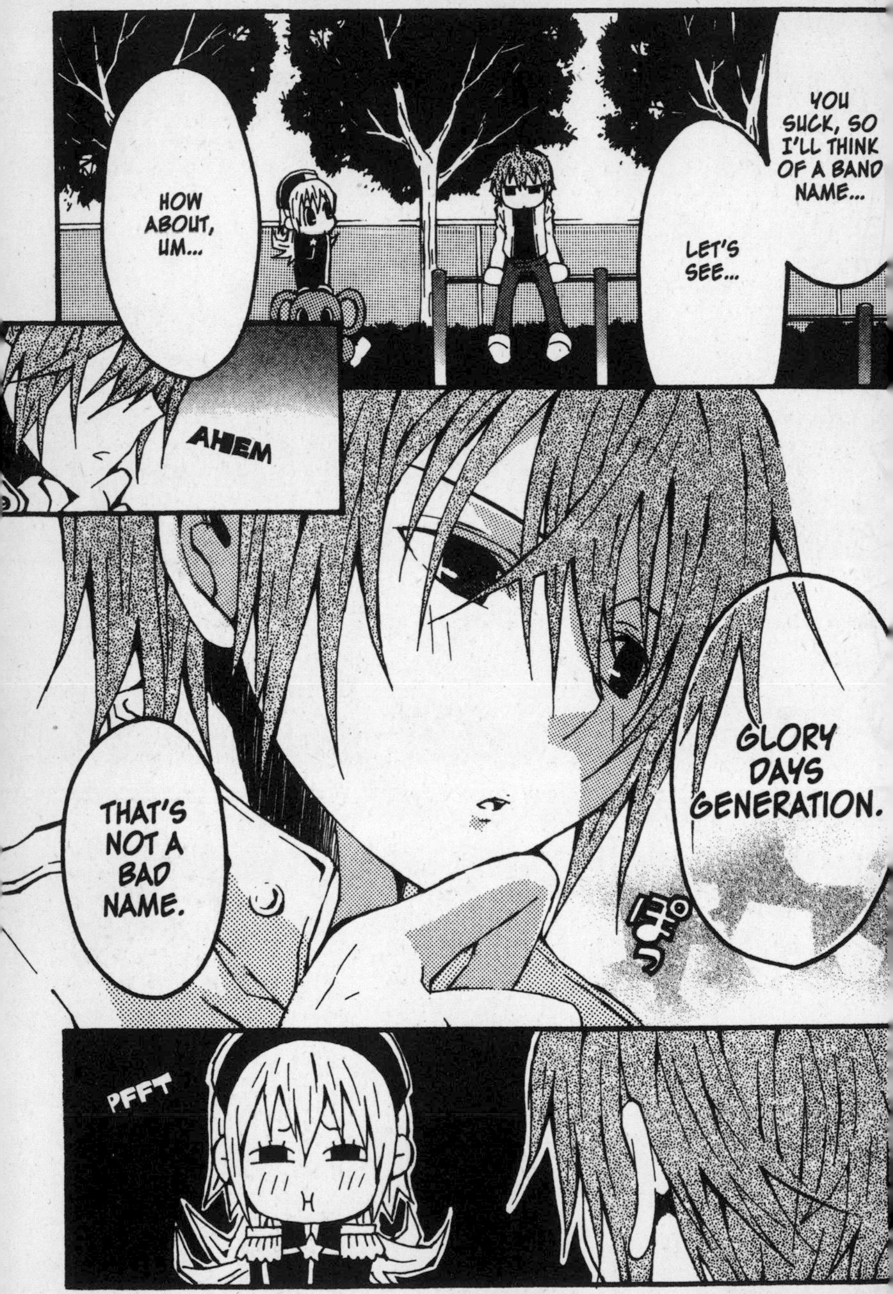
YOU SUCK, SO I'LL THINK OF A BAND NAME...
LET'S SEE...
HOW ABOUT, UM...
AHEM
GLORY DAYS GENERATION.
ぽっ
THAT'S NOT A BAD NAME.
PFFT

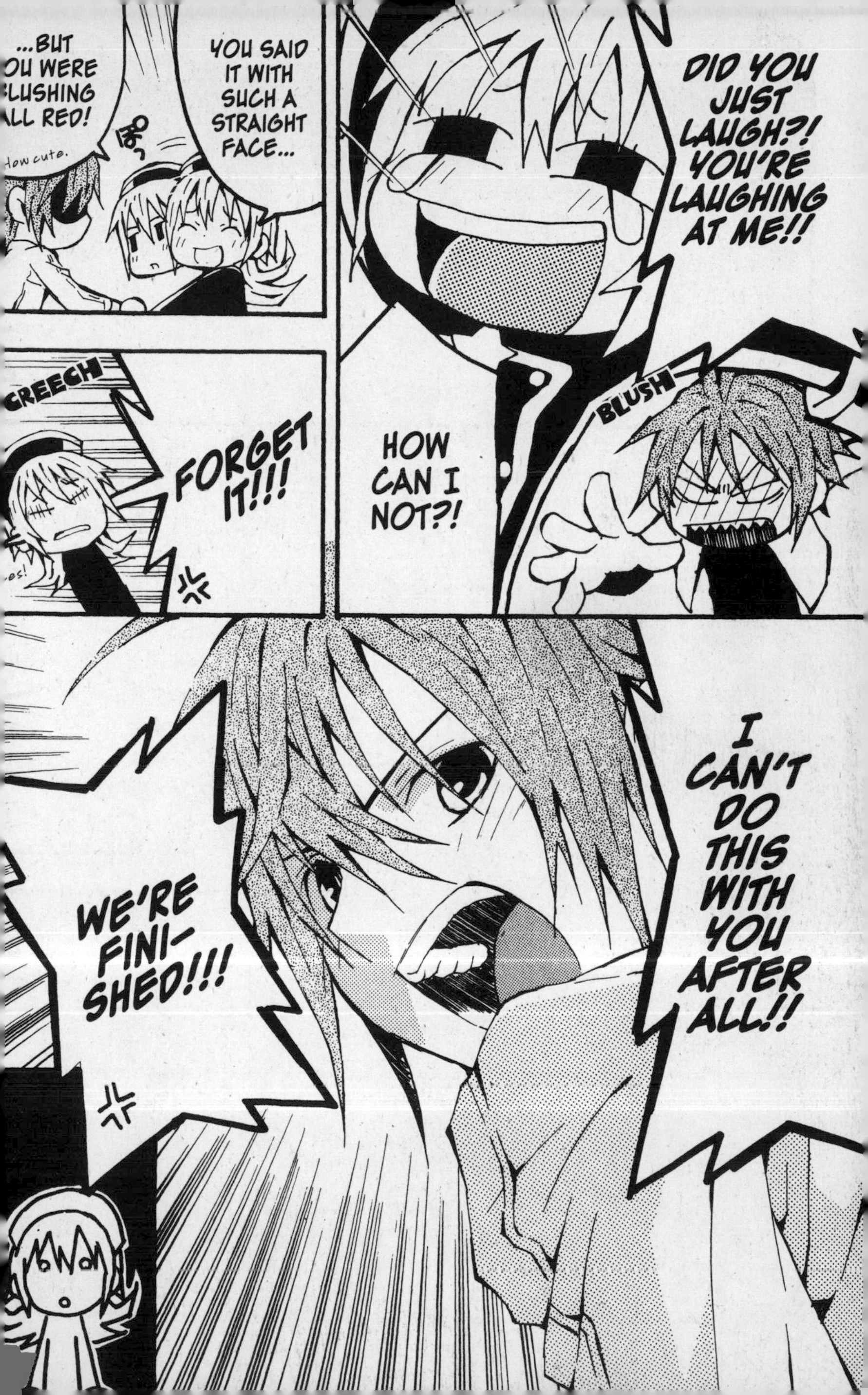
DID YOU JUST LAUGH?! YOU'RE LAUGHING AT ME!!
BLUSH
HOW CAN I NOT?!
YOU SAID IT WITH SUCH A STRAIGHT FACE...
...BUT OU WERE LUSHING LL RED!
ぽっ
How cute.
CREECH
FORGET IT!!!
I CAN'T DO THIS WITH YOU AFTER ALL!!
WE'RE FINI-SHED!!!

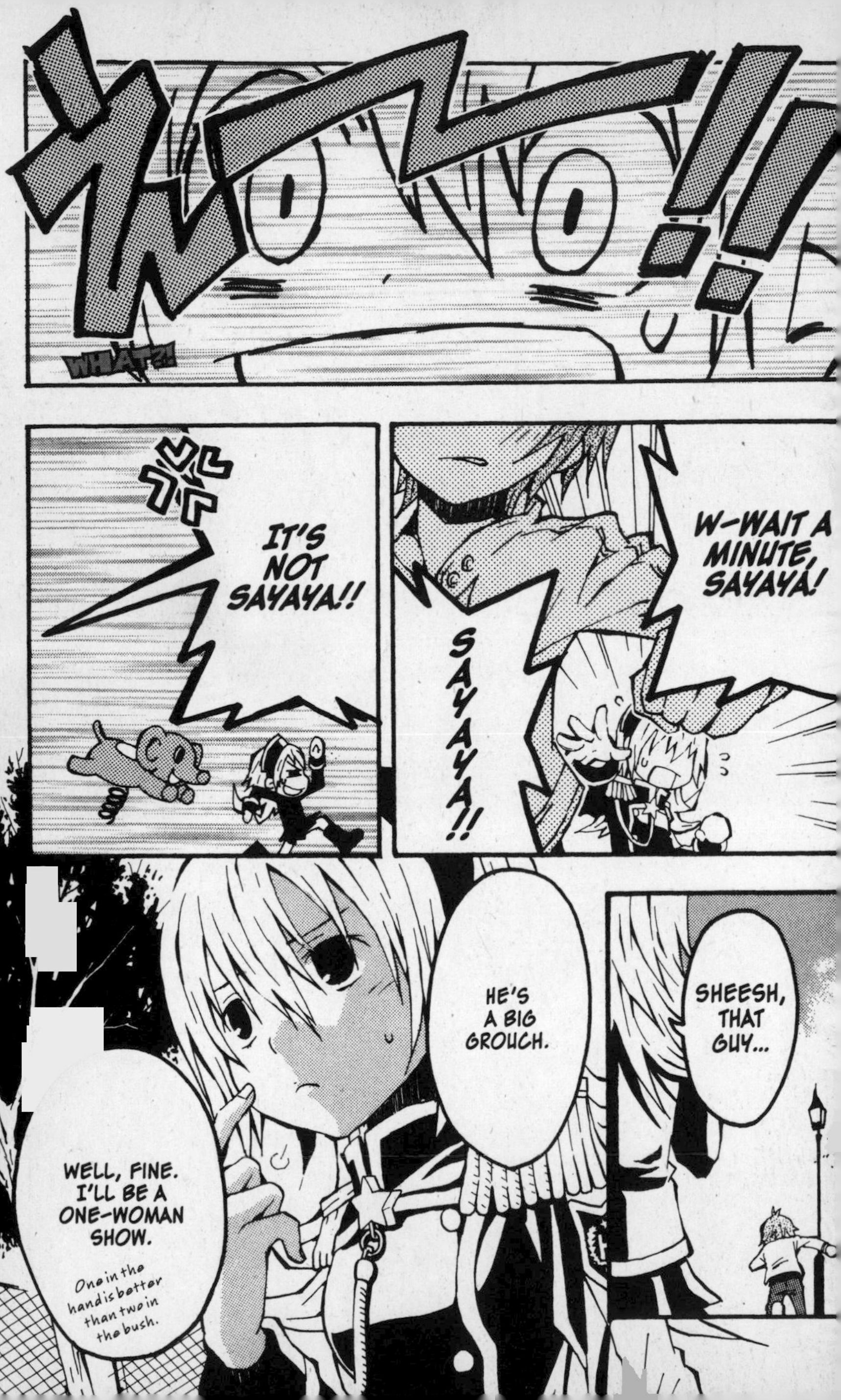
WHAT?!
W-WAIT A MINUTE, SAYAYA!
SAYAYA!!
IT'S NOT SAYAYA!!
SHEESH, THAT GUY...
HE'S A BIG GROUCH.
WELL, FINE. I'LL BE A ONE-WOMAN SHOW.
One in the hand is better than two in the bush.

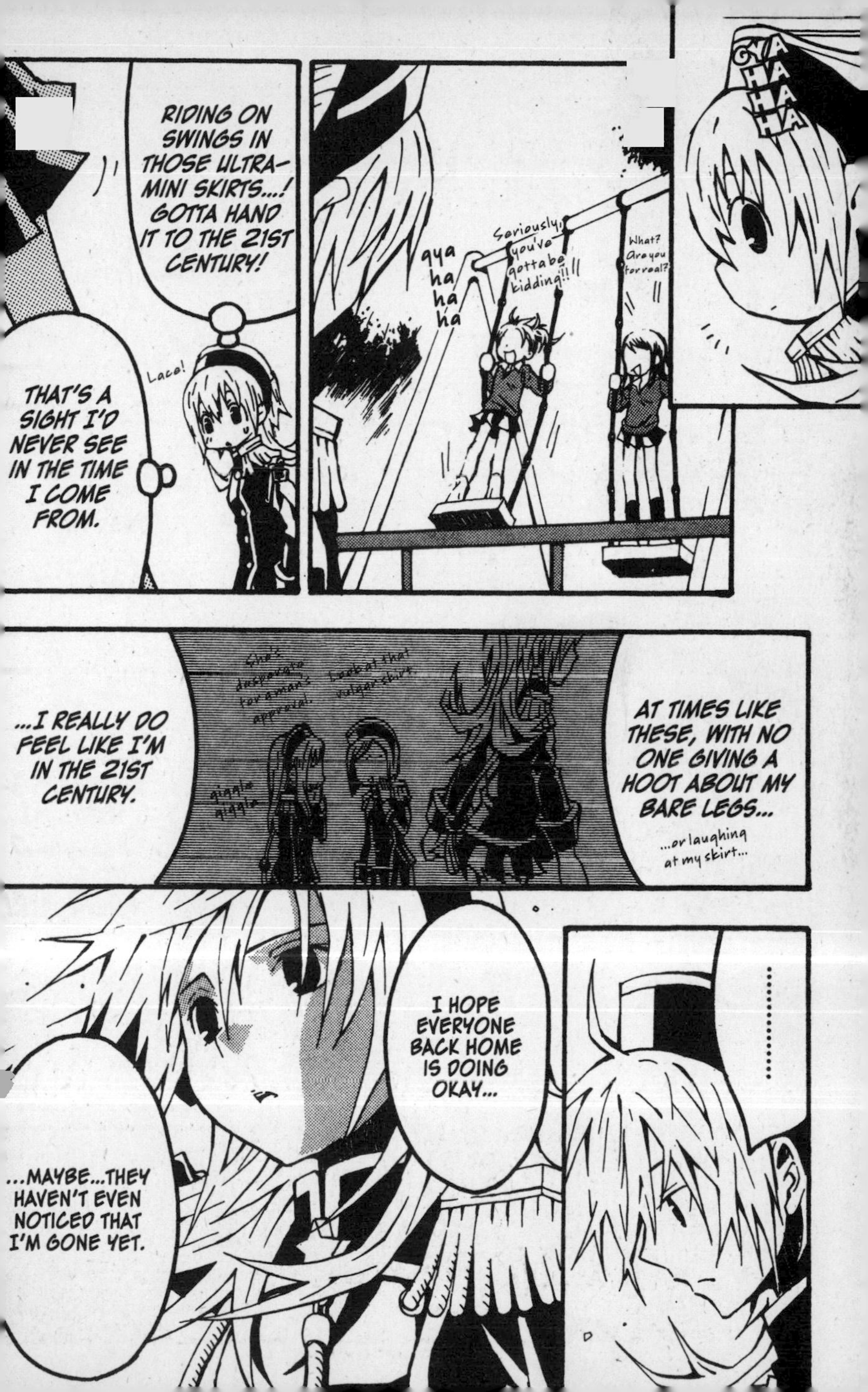
GYAHAHAHAHA
What? Are you for real?
Seriously, you've gotta be kidding!!
gya ha ha ha
RIDING ON SWINGS IN THOSE ULTRA-MINI SKIRTS...! GOTTA HAND IT TO THE 21ST CENTURY!
Laco!
THAT'S A SIGHT I'D NEVER SEE IN THE TIME I COME FROM.
AT TIMES LIKE THESE, WITH NO ONE GIVING A HOOT ABOUT MY BARE LEGS...
...or laughing at my skirt...
Look at that vulgar skirt.
She's desperate for a man's approval.
giggle giggle
...I REALLY DO FEEL LIKE I'M IN THE 21ST CENTURY.
I HOPE EVERYONE BACK HOME IS DOING OKAY...
...MAYBE...THEY HAVEN'T EVEN NOTICED THAT I'M GONE YET.

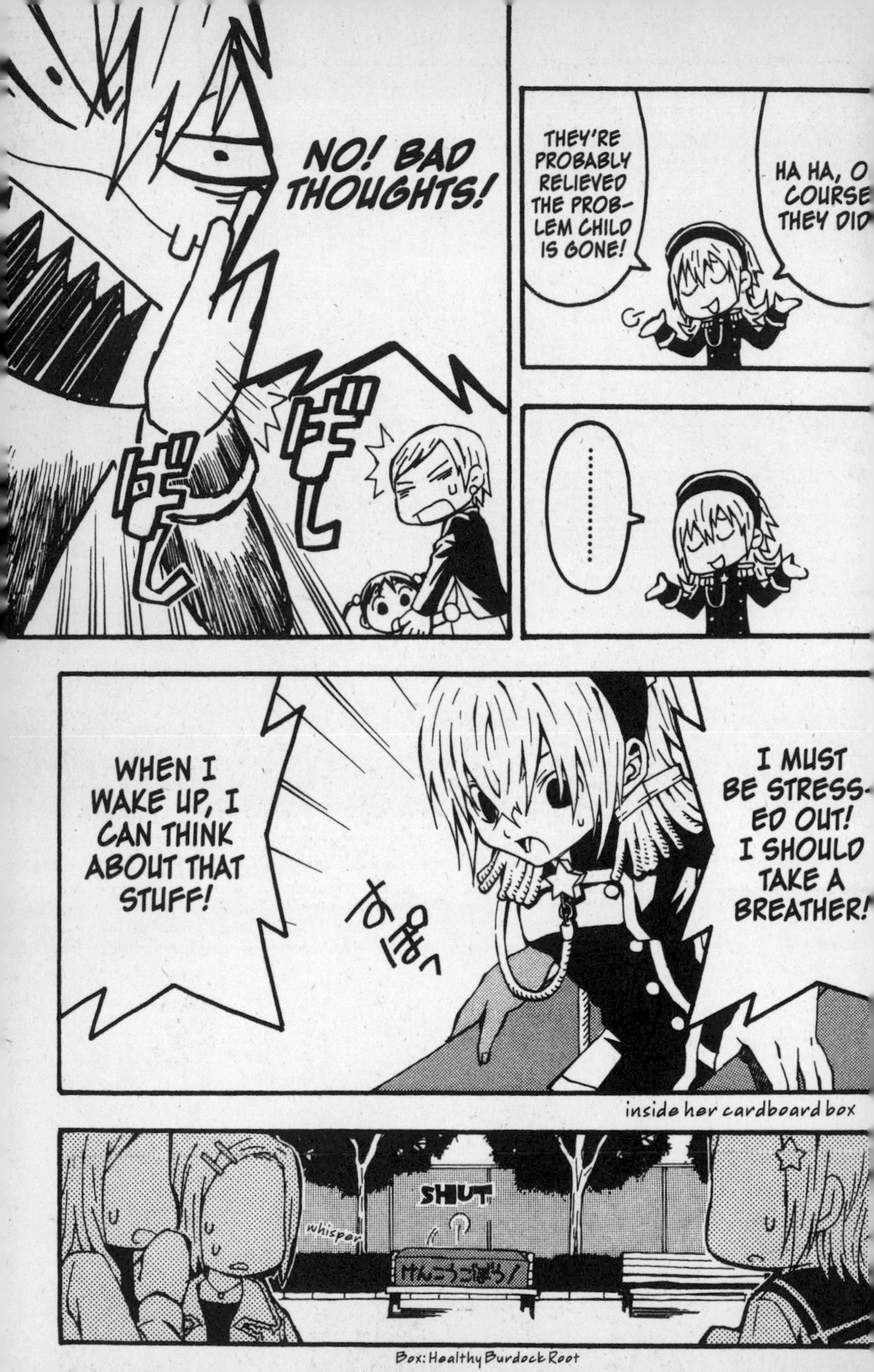
HA HA, O COURSE THEY DID
THEY'RE PROBABLY RELIEVED THE PROB-LEM CHILD IS GONE!
......
NO! BAD THOUGHTS!
ばし
ばし
I MUST BE STRESS-ED OUT! I SHOULD TAKE A BREATHER!
WHEN I WAKE UP, I CAN THINK ABOUT THAT STUFF!
inside her cardboard box
SHUT
whisper
けんこうごぼう!
Box: Healthy Burdock Root

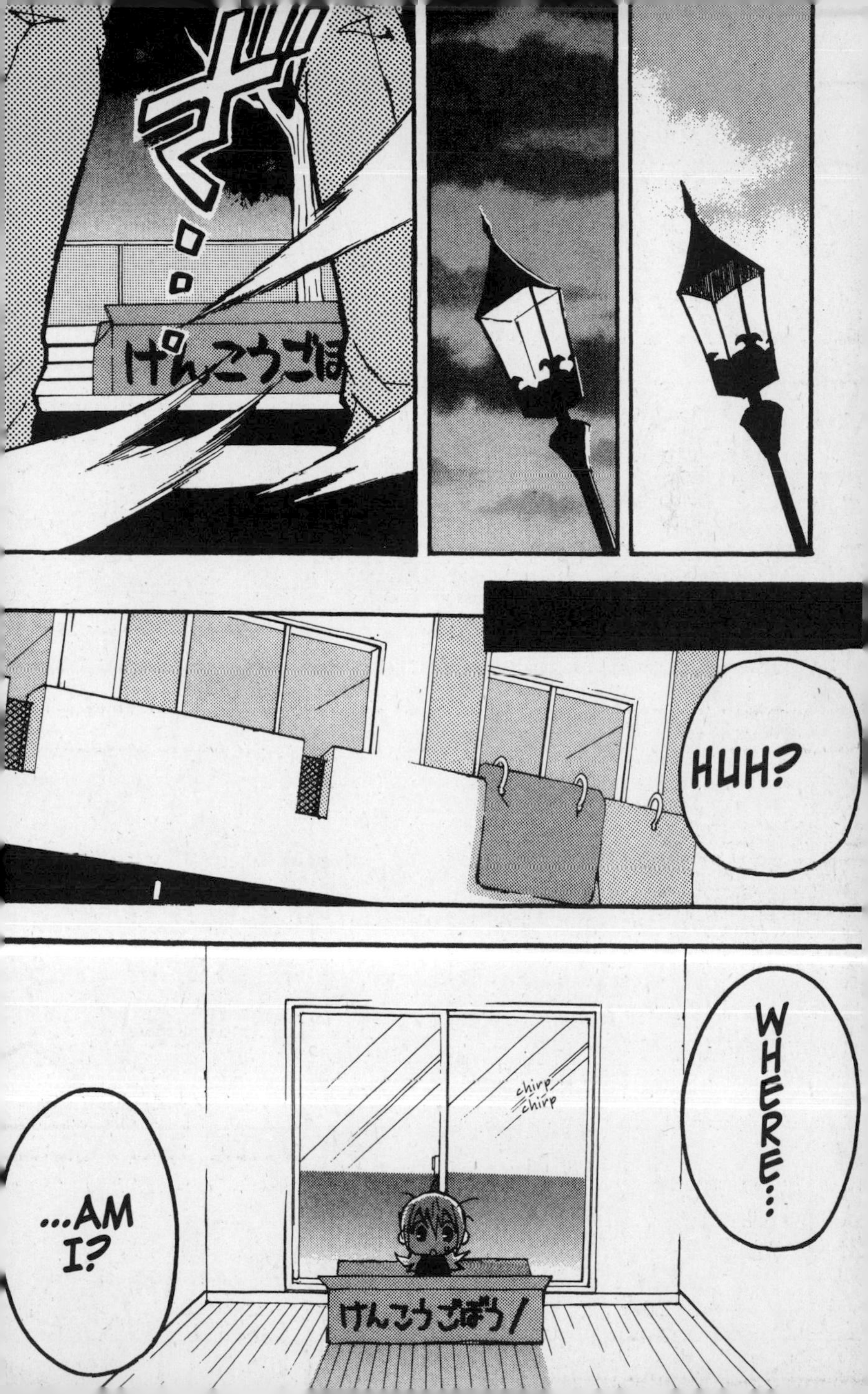
けんこうごぼ
HUH?
WHERE...
chirp chirp
...AM I?
けんこうごぼう!

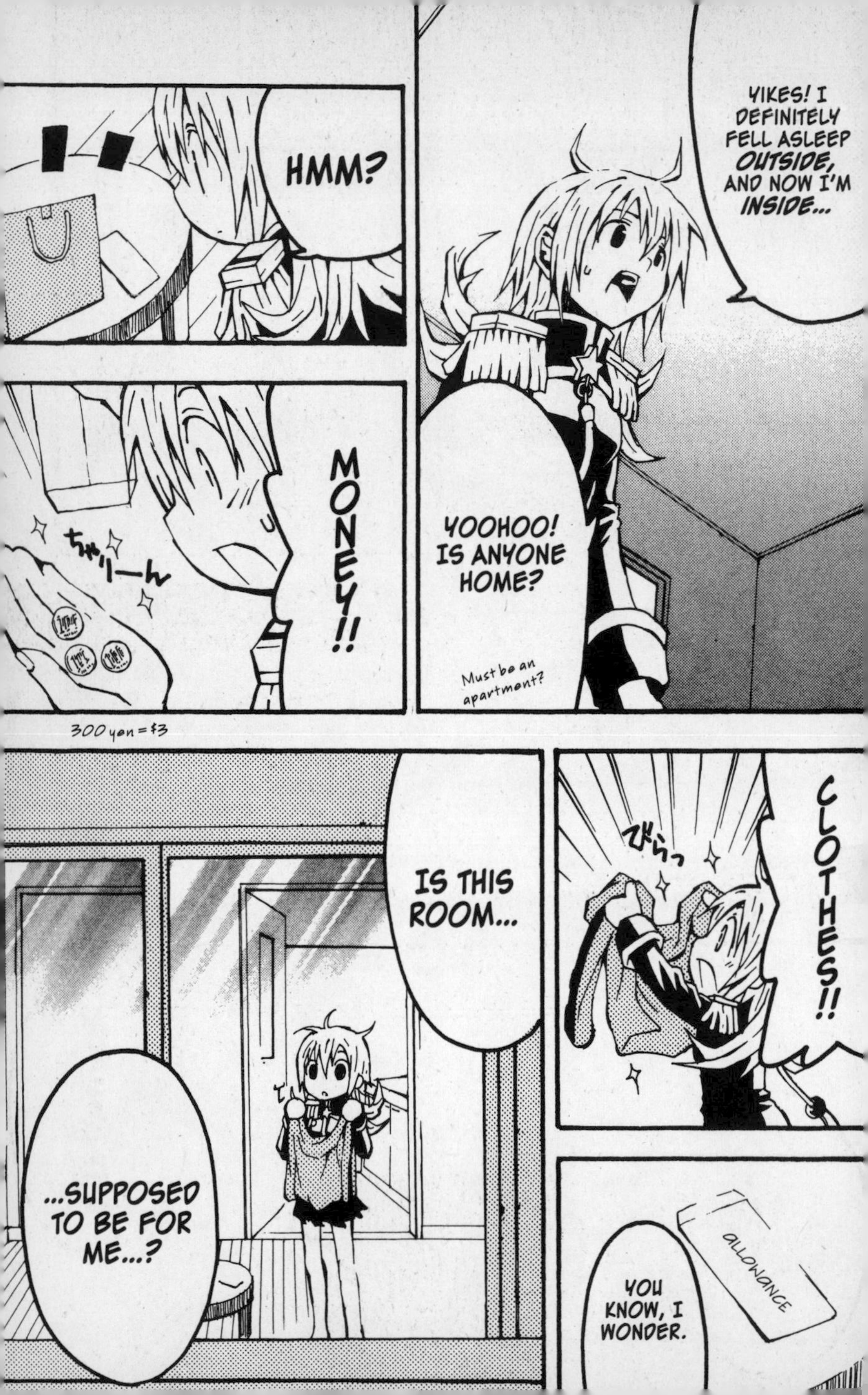
YIKES! I DEFINITELY FELL ASLEEP *OUTSIDE*, AND NOW I'M *INSIDE*...
YOOHOO! IS ANYONE HOME?
Must be an apartment?
HMM?
MONEY!!
ちゃりーん
300 yen = $3
CLOTHES!!
びらっ
ALLOWANCE
YOU KNOW, I WONDER.
IS THIS ROOM...
...SUPPOSED TO BE FOR ME...?

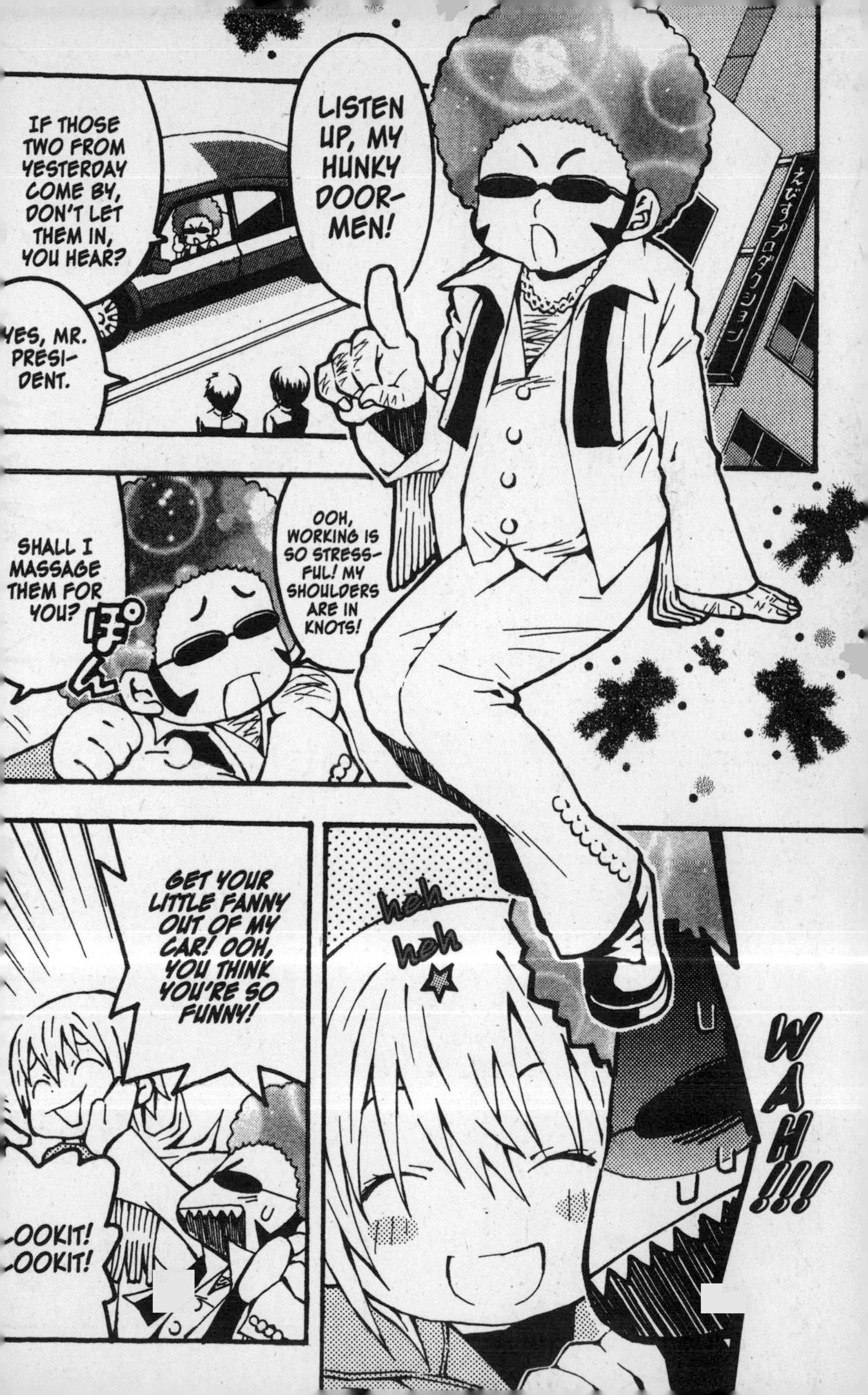

LISTEN UP, MY HUNKY DOOR-MEN!
えびすプロダクション
IF THOSE TWO FROM YESTERDAY COME BY, DON'T LET THEM IN, YOU HEAR?
YES, MR. PRESI-DENT.
OOH, WORKING IS SO STRESS-FUL! MY SHOULDERS ARE IN KNOTS!
SHALL I MASSAGE THEM FOR YOU?
ぽん
heh heh
WAH!!!
GET YOUR LITTLE FANNY OUT OF MY CAR! OOH, YOU THINK YOU'RE SO FUNNY!
-OOKIT!
-OOKIT!

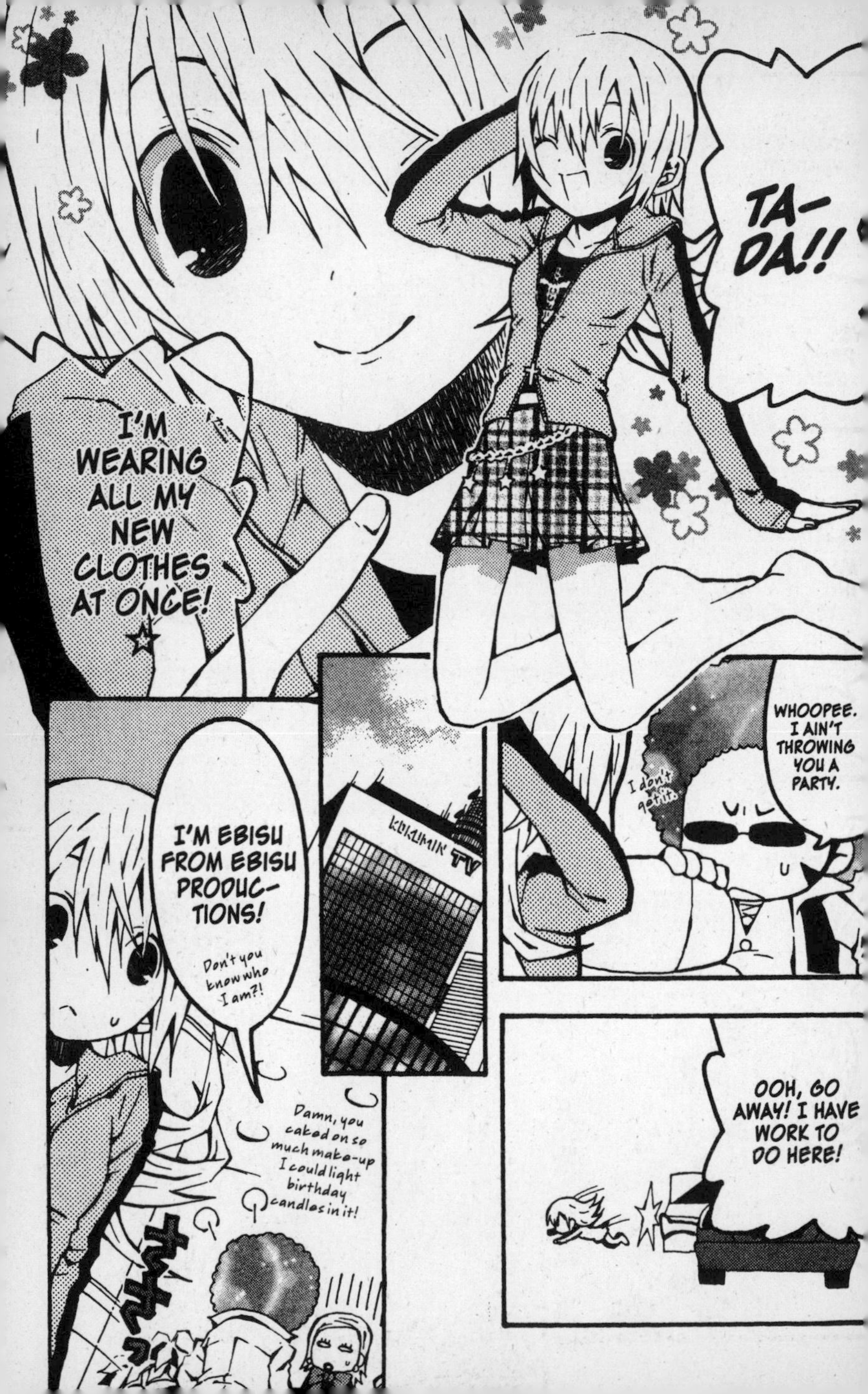
TA-DA!!
I'M WEARING ALL MY NEW CLOTHES AT ONCE!
WHOOPEE. I AIN'T THROWING YOU A PARTY.
I don't get it.
OOH, GO AWAY! I HAVE WORK TO DO HERE!
KOKUMIN TV
I'M EBISU FROM EBISU PRODUC-TIONS!
Don't you know who I am?!
Damn, you caked on so much make-up I could light birthday candles in it!

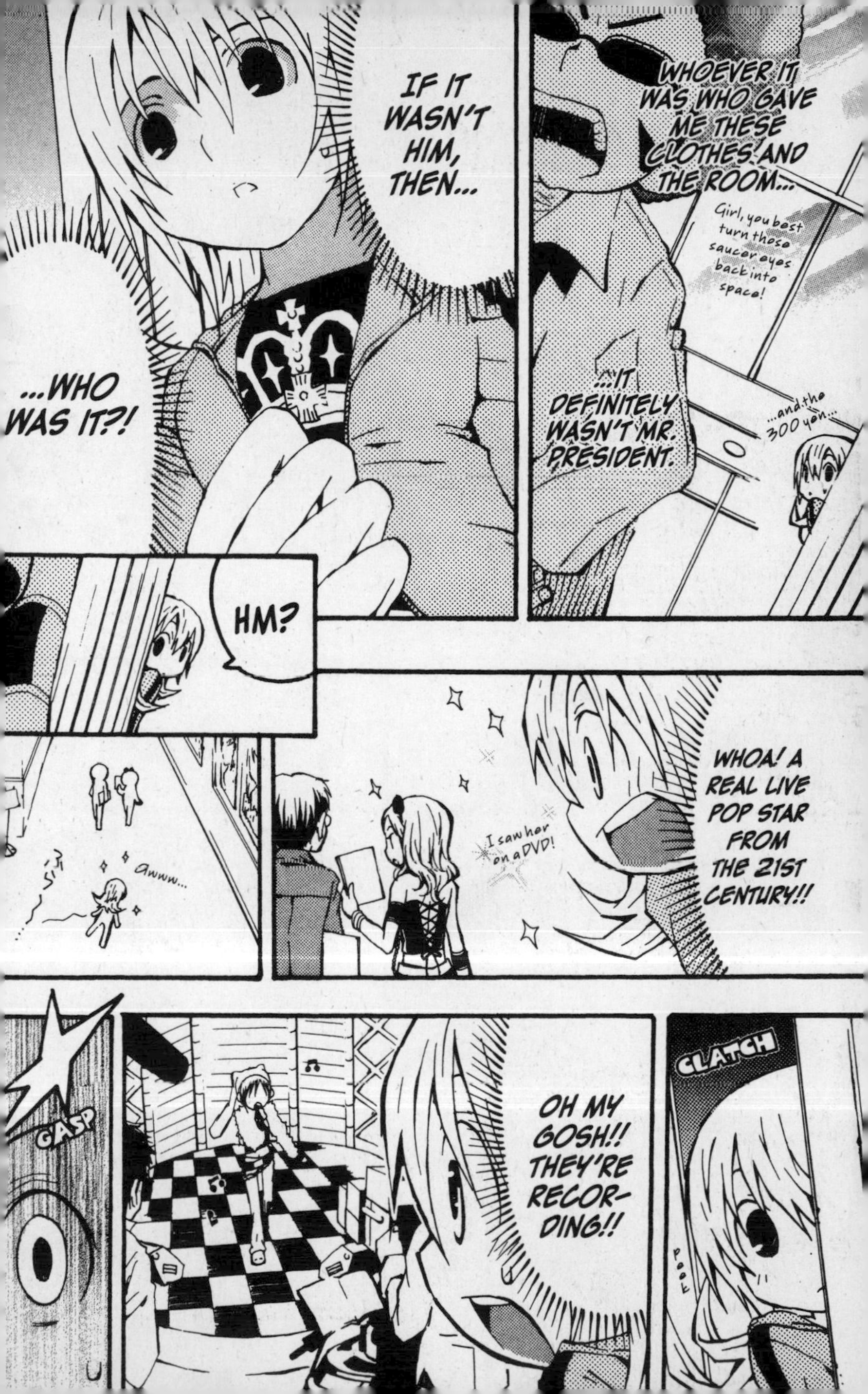
WHOEVER IT WAS WHO GAVE ME THESE CLOTHES AND THE ROOM...
Girl, you best turn those saucer eyes back into space!
...IT DEFINITELY WASN'T MR. PRESIDENT.
...and the 300 yen...
IF IT WASN'T HIM, THEN...
...WHO WAS IT?!
HM?
WHOA! A REAL LIVE POP STAR FROM THE 21ST CENTURY!!
I saw her on a DVD!
awww...
CLATCH
OH MY GOSH!! THEY'RE RECOR-DING!!
GASP

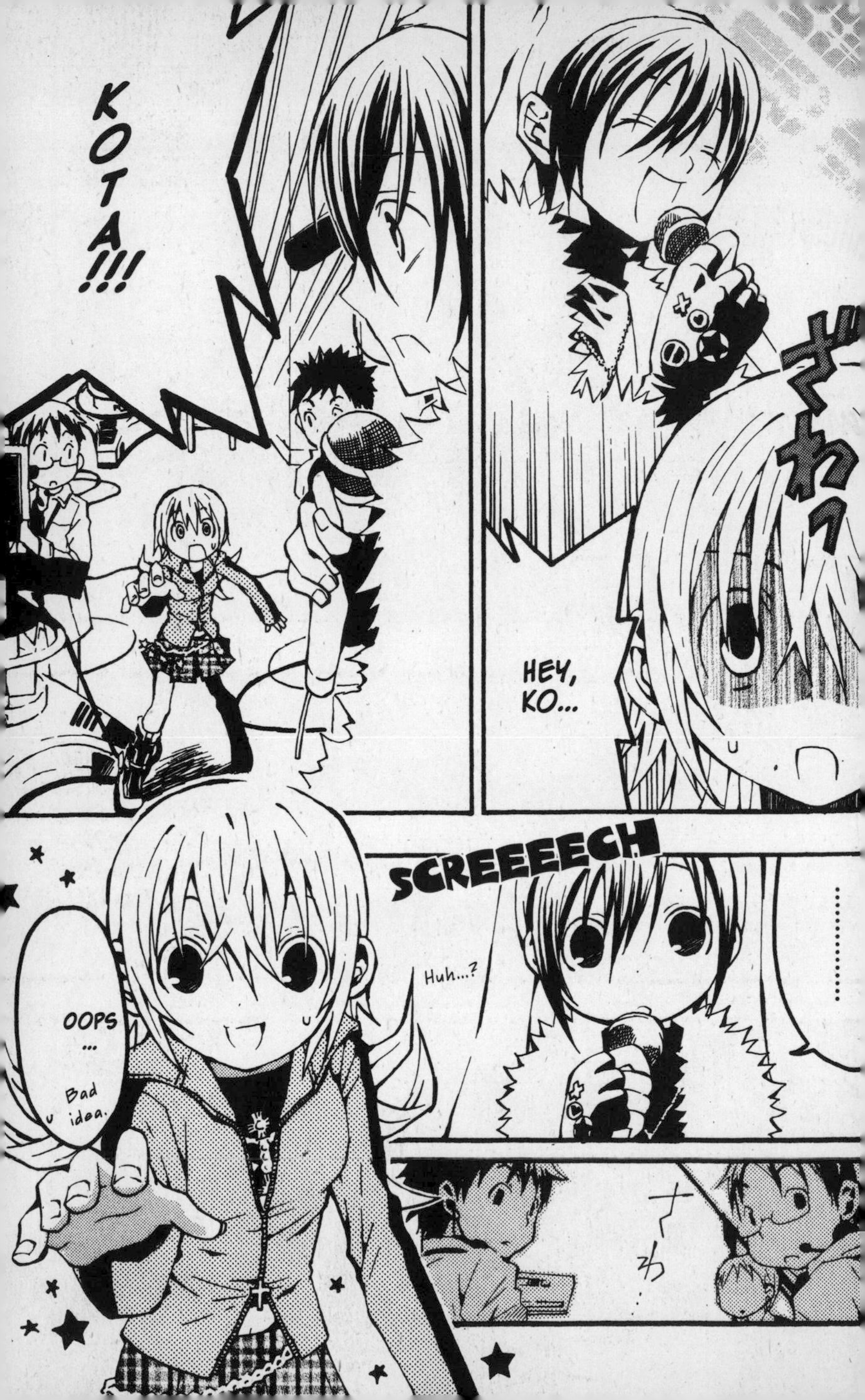

ざわっ
HEY, KO...
KOTA!!!
SCREEEECH
......
Huh...?
ざわ…
OOPS ...
Bad idea.

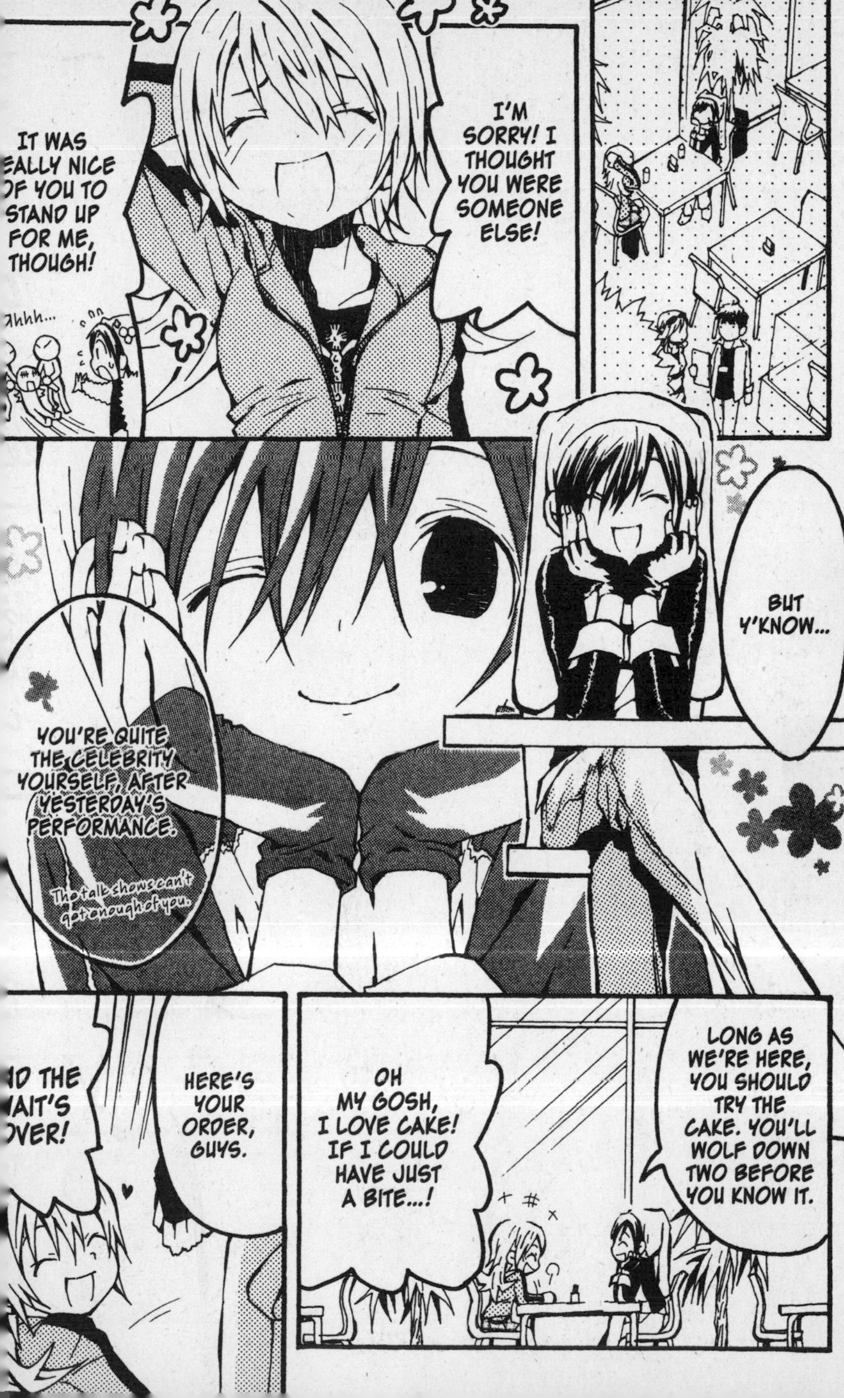
I'M SORRY! I THOUGHT YOU WERE SOMEONE ELSE!
IT WAS EALLY NICE OF YOU TO STAND UP FOR ME, THOUGH!
Ahhh...
BUT Y'KNOW...
YOU'RE QUITE THE CELEBRITY YOURSELF, AFTER YESTERDAY'S PERFORMANCE.
The talk shows can't get enough of you.
LONG AS WE'RE HERE, YOU SHOULD TRY THE CAKE. YOU'LL WOLF DOWN TWO BEFORE YOU KNOW IT.
OH MY GOSH, I LOVE CAKE! IF I COULD HAVE JUST A BITE...!
HERE'S YOUR ORDER, GUYS.
ND THE AIT'S OVER!

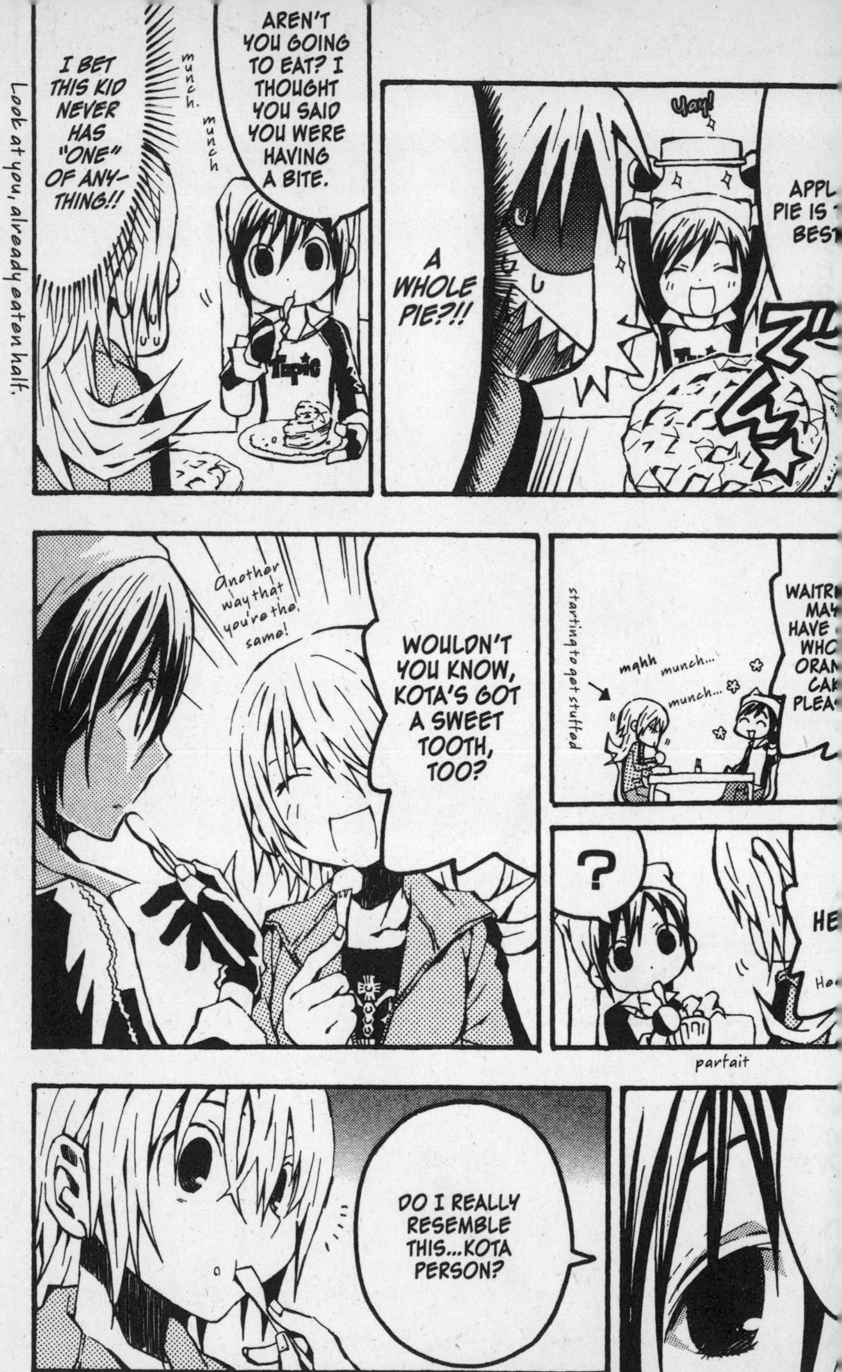
Yay!
APPL PIE IS BEST
A WHOLE PIE?!!
AREN'T YOU GOING TO EAT? I THOUGHT YOU SAID YOU WERE HAVING A BITE.
munch. munch
I BET THIS KID NEVER HAS "ONE" OF ANY-THING!!
Look at you, already eaten half.
WAITR MAY HAVE WHO ORAN CAK PLEA
starting to get stuffed
mghh munch... munch...
?
HE
He
parfait
Another way that you're the same!
WOULDN'T YOU KNOW, KOTA'S GOT A SWEET TOOTH, TOO?
DO I REALLY RESEMBLE THIS...KOTA PERSON?

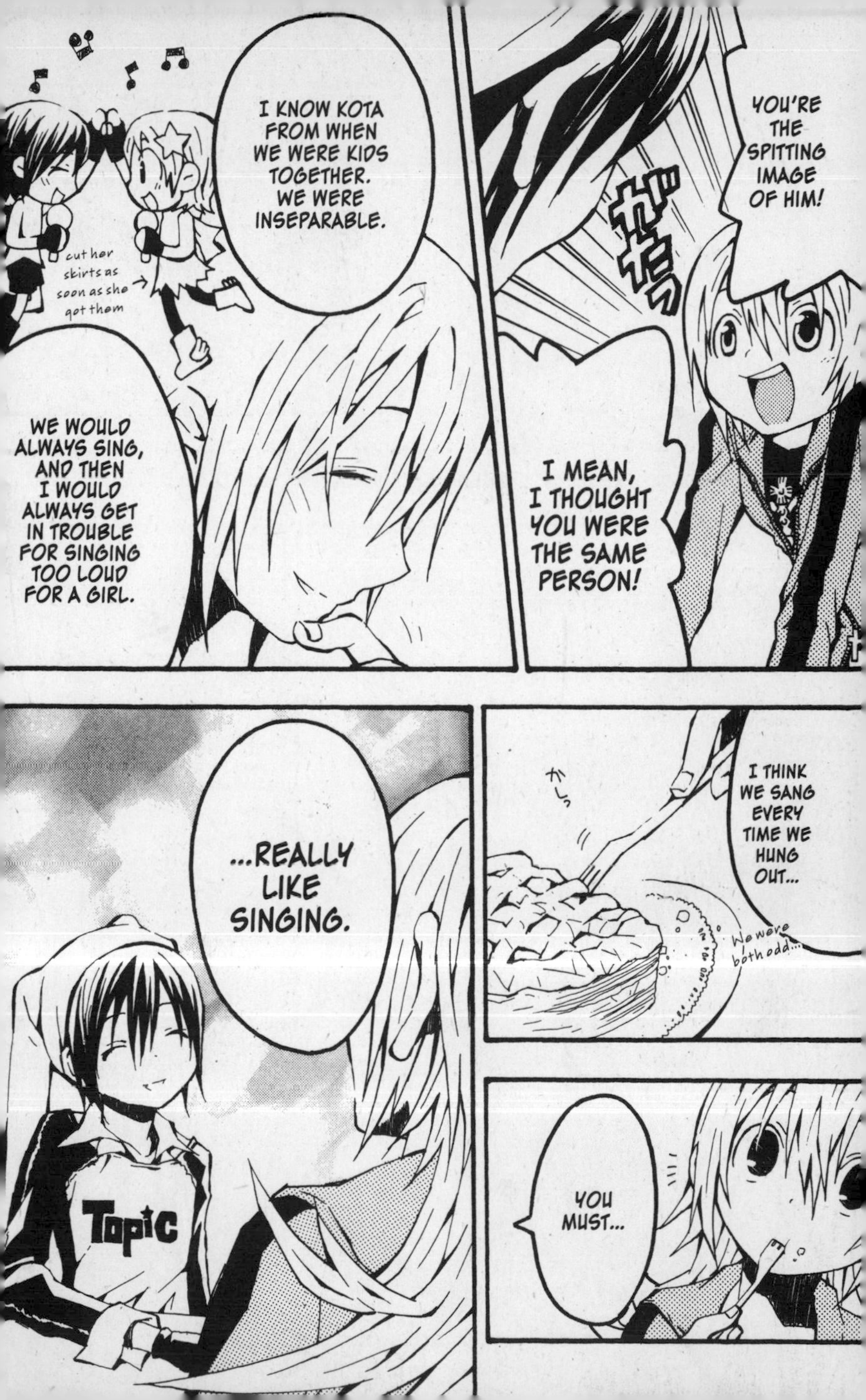
がたっ
YOU'RE THE SPITTING IMAGE OF HIM!
I MEAN, I THOUGHT YOU WERE THE SAME PERSON!
I KNOW KOTA FROM WHEN WE WERE KIDS TOGETHER. WE WERE INSEPARABLE.
cut her skirts as soon as she got them
WE WOULD ALWAYS SING, AND THEN I WOULD ALWAYS GET IN TROUBLE FOR SINGING TOO LOUD FOR A GIRL.
I THINK WE SANG EVERY TIME WE HUNG OUT...
We were both odd...
かしっ
YOU MUST...
...REALLY LIKE SINGING.
Topic

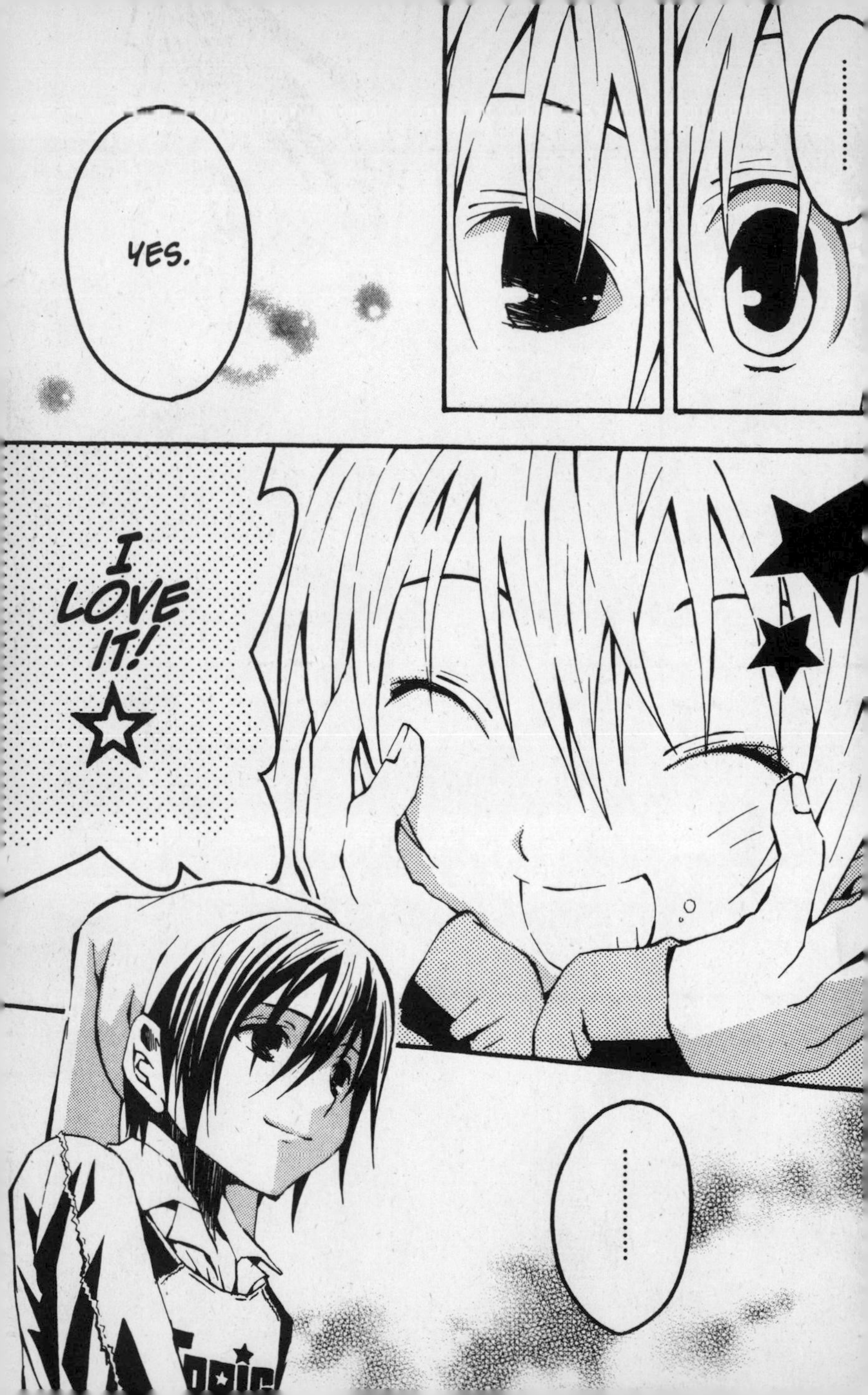
......
YES.
I LOVE IT! ☆
......

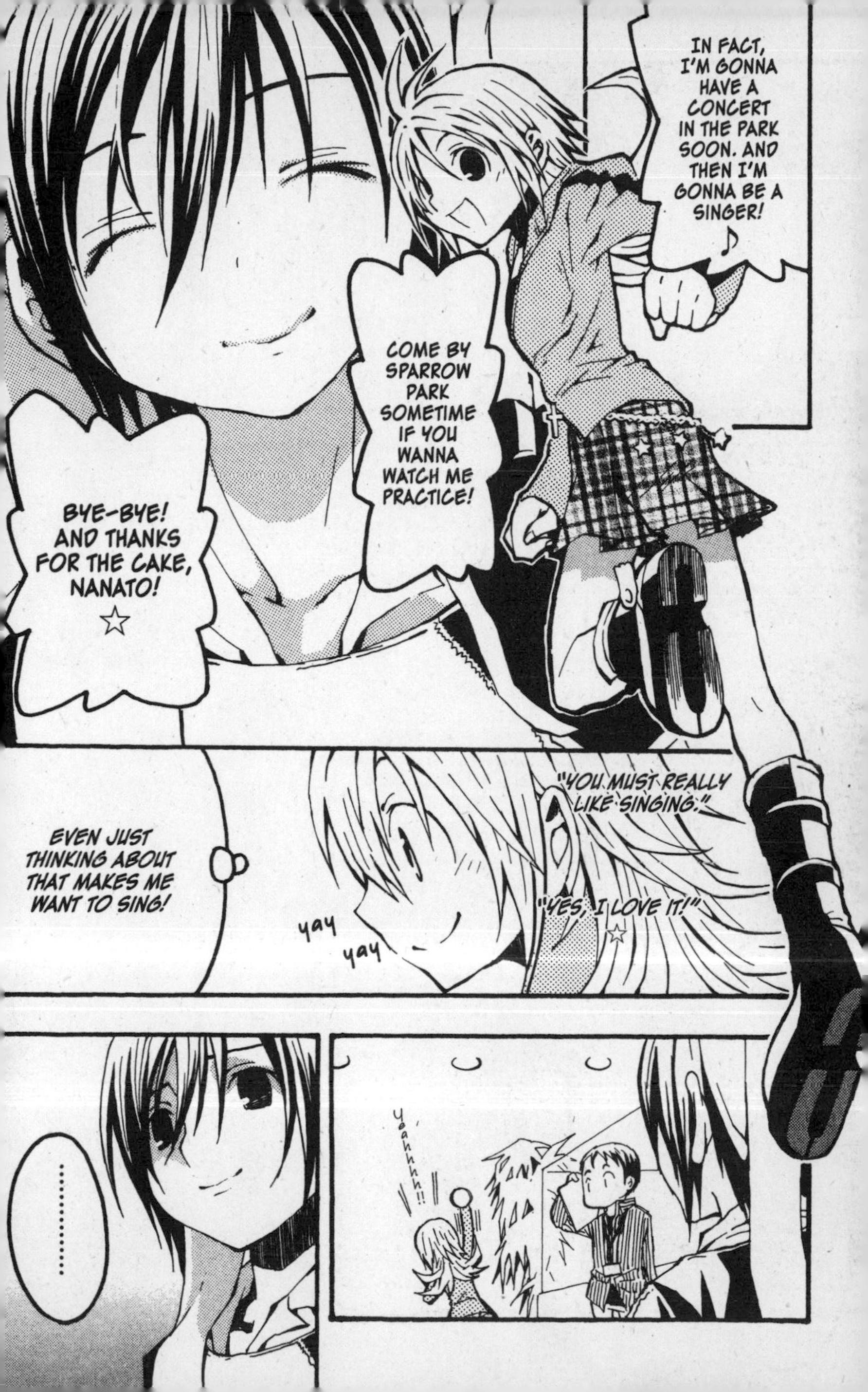
IN FACT, I'M GONNA HAVE A CONCERT IN THE PARK SOON. AND THEN I'M GONNA BE A SINGER! ♪
COME BY SPARROW PARK SOMETIME IF YOU WANNA WATCH ME PRACTICE!
BYE-BYE! AND THANKS FOR THE CAKE, NANATO! ☆
"YOU MUST REALLY LIKE SINGING."
"YES, I LOVE IT!" ☆
yay yay
EVEN JUST THINKING ABOUT THAT MAKES ME WANT TO SING!
Yeahhhh!!
......

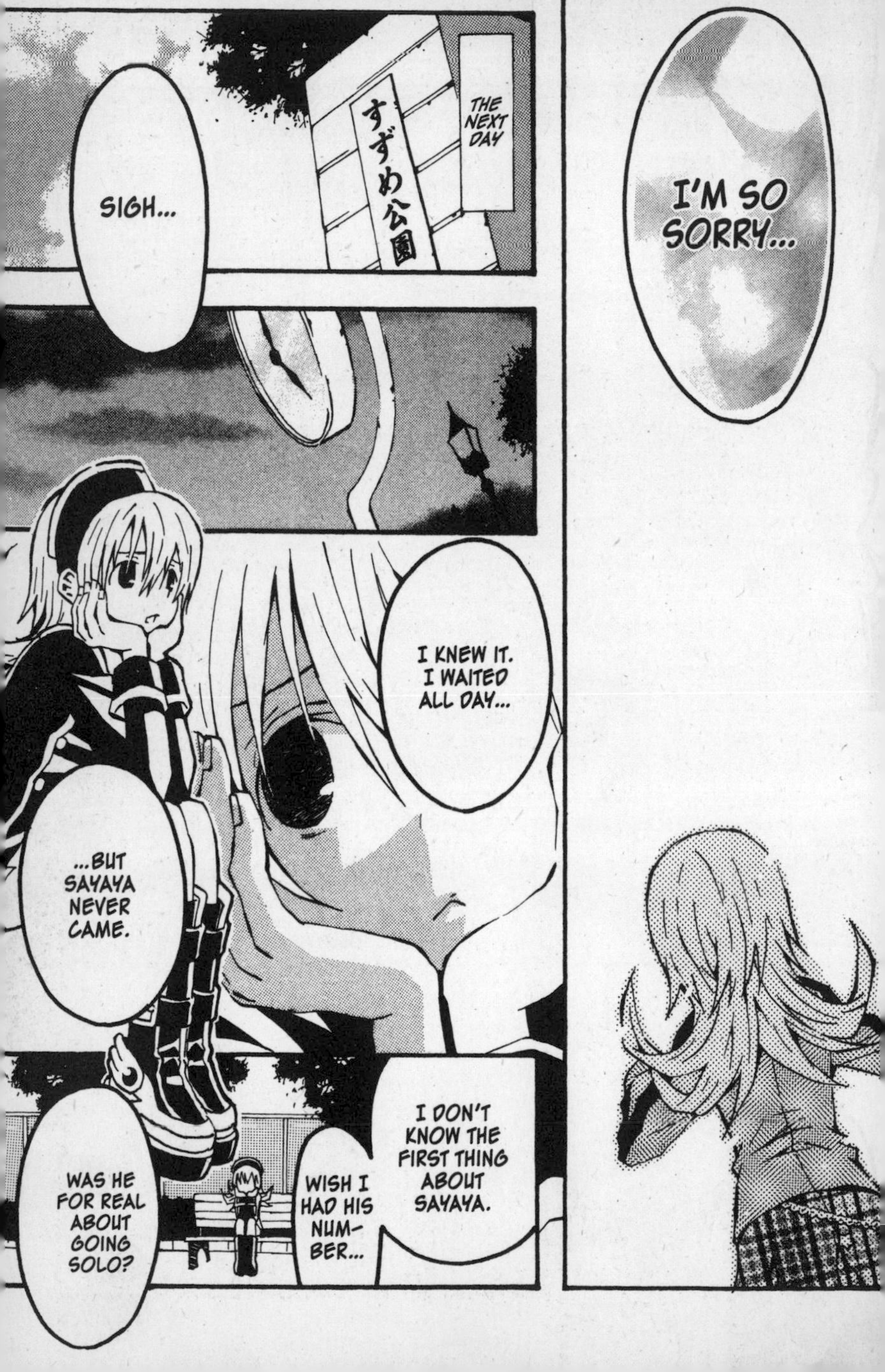
I'M SO SORRY...
THE NEXT DAY
すずめ公園
SIGH...
I KNEW IT. I WAITED ALL DAY...
...BUT SAYAYA NEVER CAME.
I DON'T KNOW THE FIRST THING ABOUT SAYAYA.
WISH I HAD HIS NUM-BER...
WAS HE FOR REAL ABOUT GOING SOLO?

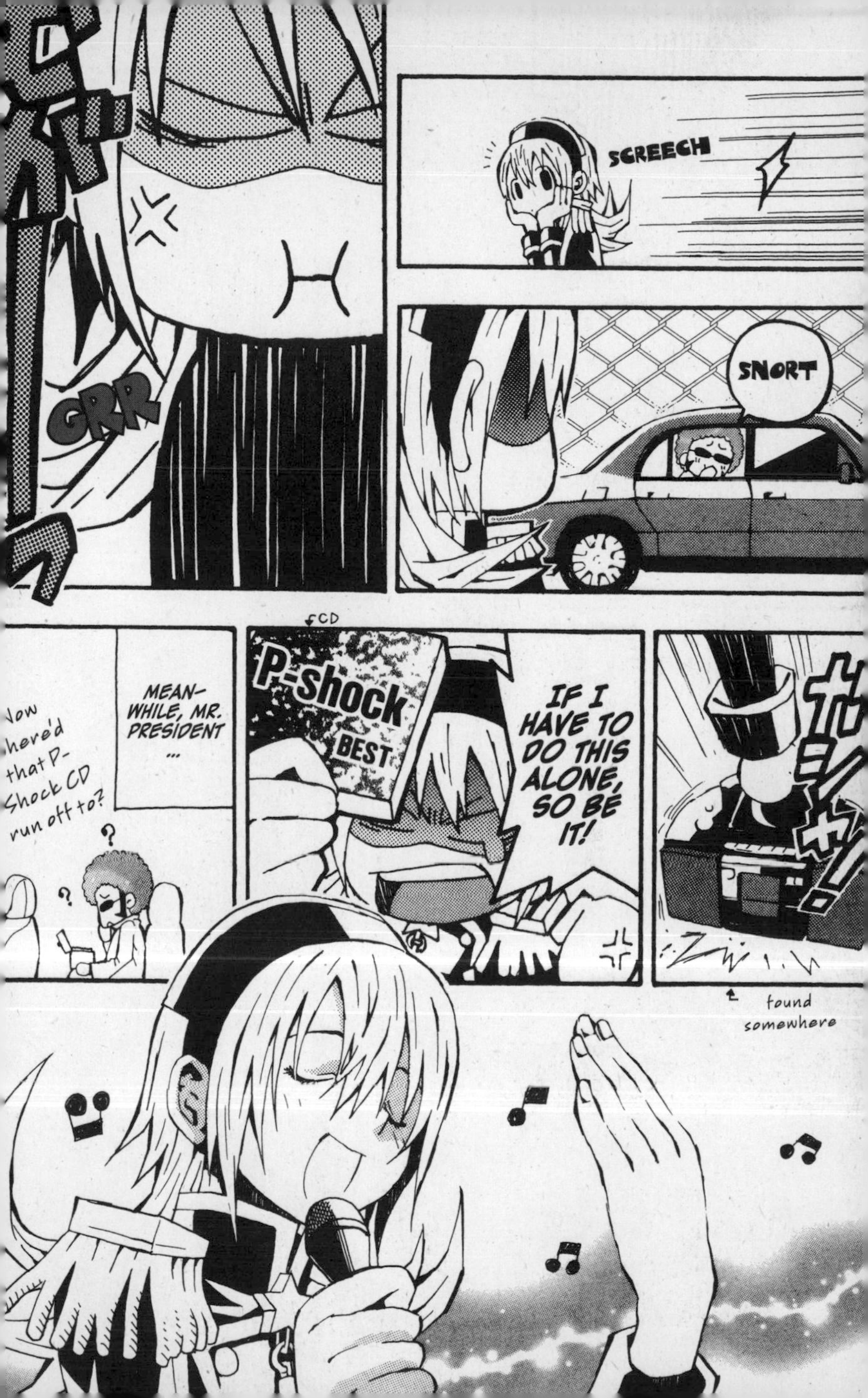
SCREECH
SNORT
GRR
found somewhere
CD
P-shock BEST
IF I HAVE TO DO THIS ALONE, SO BE IT!
MEAN-WHILE, MR. PRESIDENT ...
Now where'd that P-Shock CD run off to?
?
?

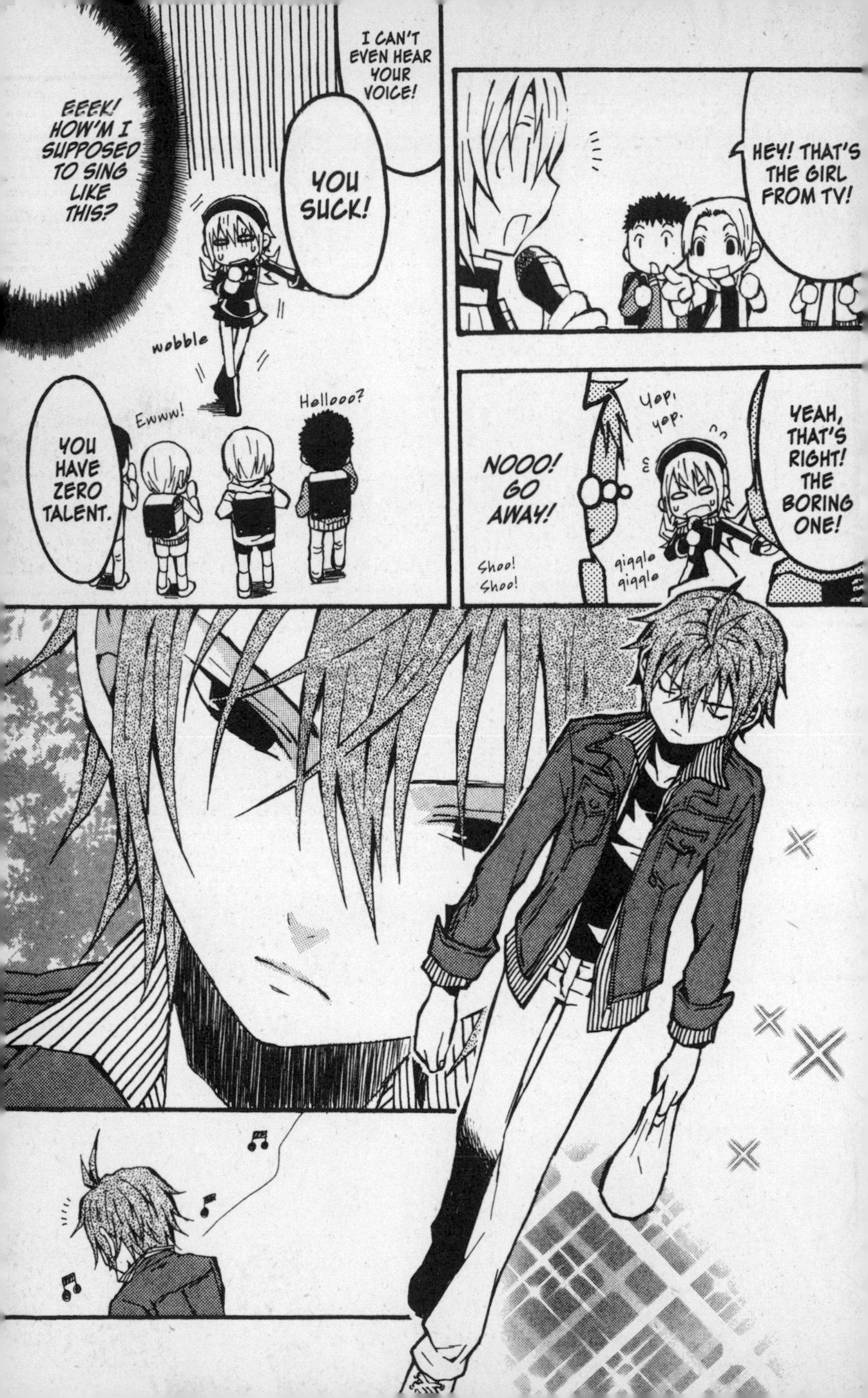
HEY! THAT'S THE GIRL FROM TV!
YEAH, THAT'S RIGHT! THE BORING ONE!
Yep, yep.
NOOO! GO AWAY!
giggle giggle
Shoo! Shoo!
I CAN'T EVEN HEAR YOUR VOICE!
YOU SUCK!
EEEK! HOW'M I SUPPOSED TO SING LIKE THIS?
wobble
Hellooo?
Ewww!
YOU HAVE ZERO TALENT.

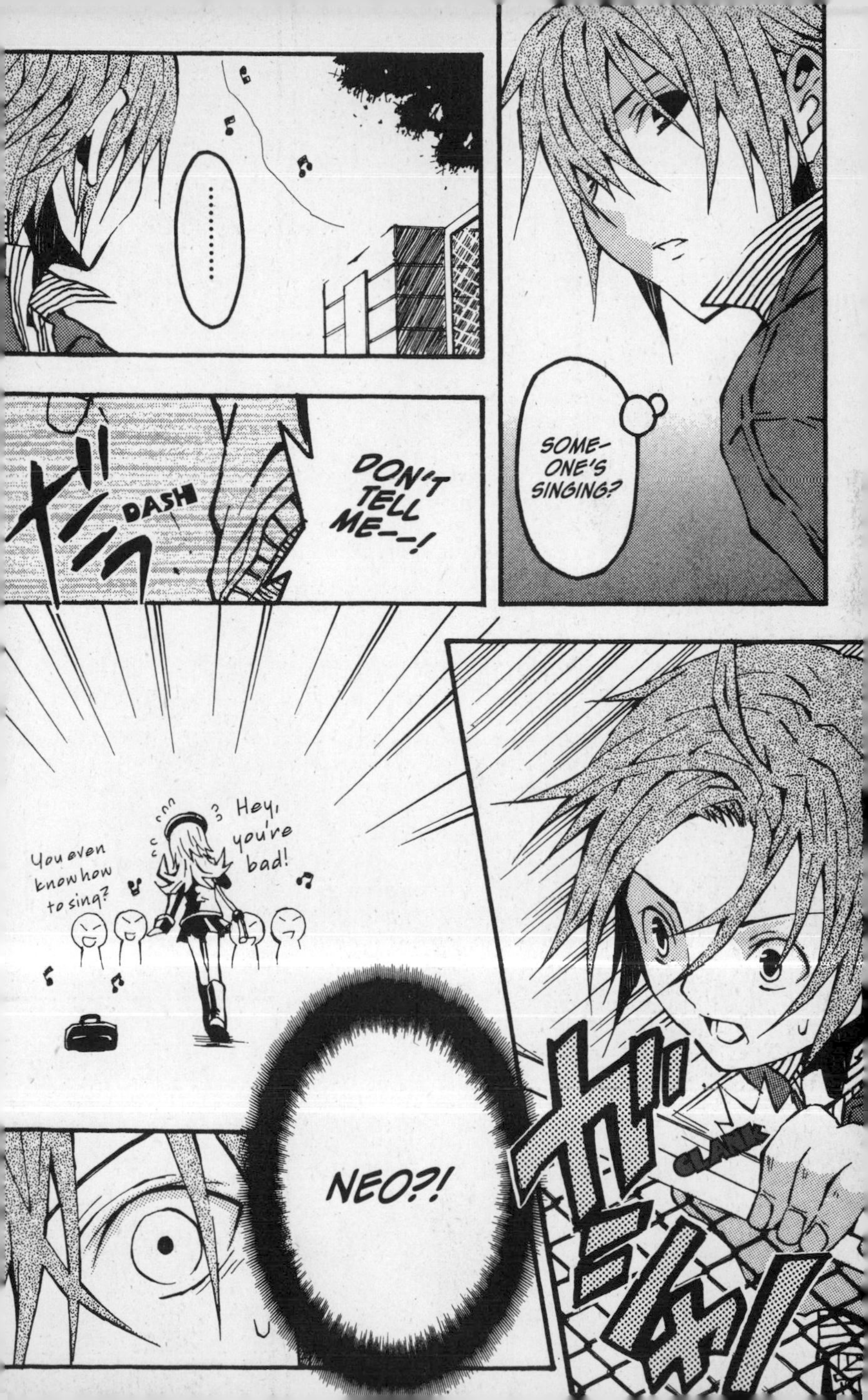
SOME-ONE'S SINGING?
......
DON'T TELL ME--!
DASH
CLANK
Hey, you're bad!
You even know how to sing?
NEO?!

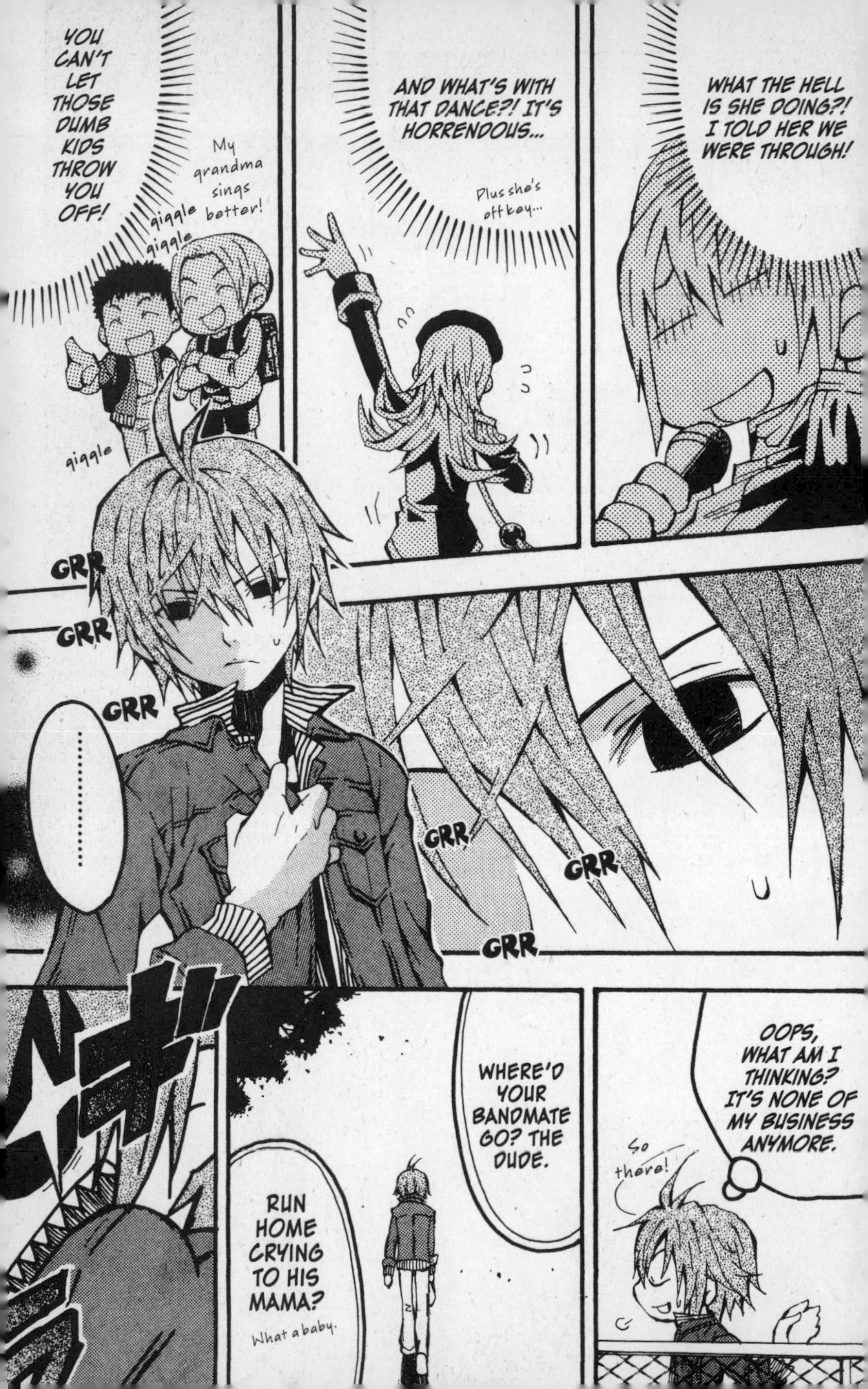
WHAT THE HELL IS SHE DOING?! I TOLD HER WE WERE THROUGH!
AND WHAT'S WITH THAT DANCE?! IT'S HORRENDOUS...
Plus she's off key...
YOU CAN'T LET THOSE DUMB KIDS THROW YOU OFF!
My grandma sings better!
giggle giggle
giggle
GRR
GRR
GRR
GRR
GRR
GRR
......
OOPS, WHAT AM I THINKING? IT'S NONE OF MY BUSINESS ANYMORE.
So there!
WHERE'D YOUR BANDMATE GO? THE DUDE.
RUN HOME CRYING TO HIS MAMA?
What a baby.

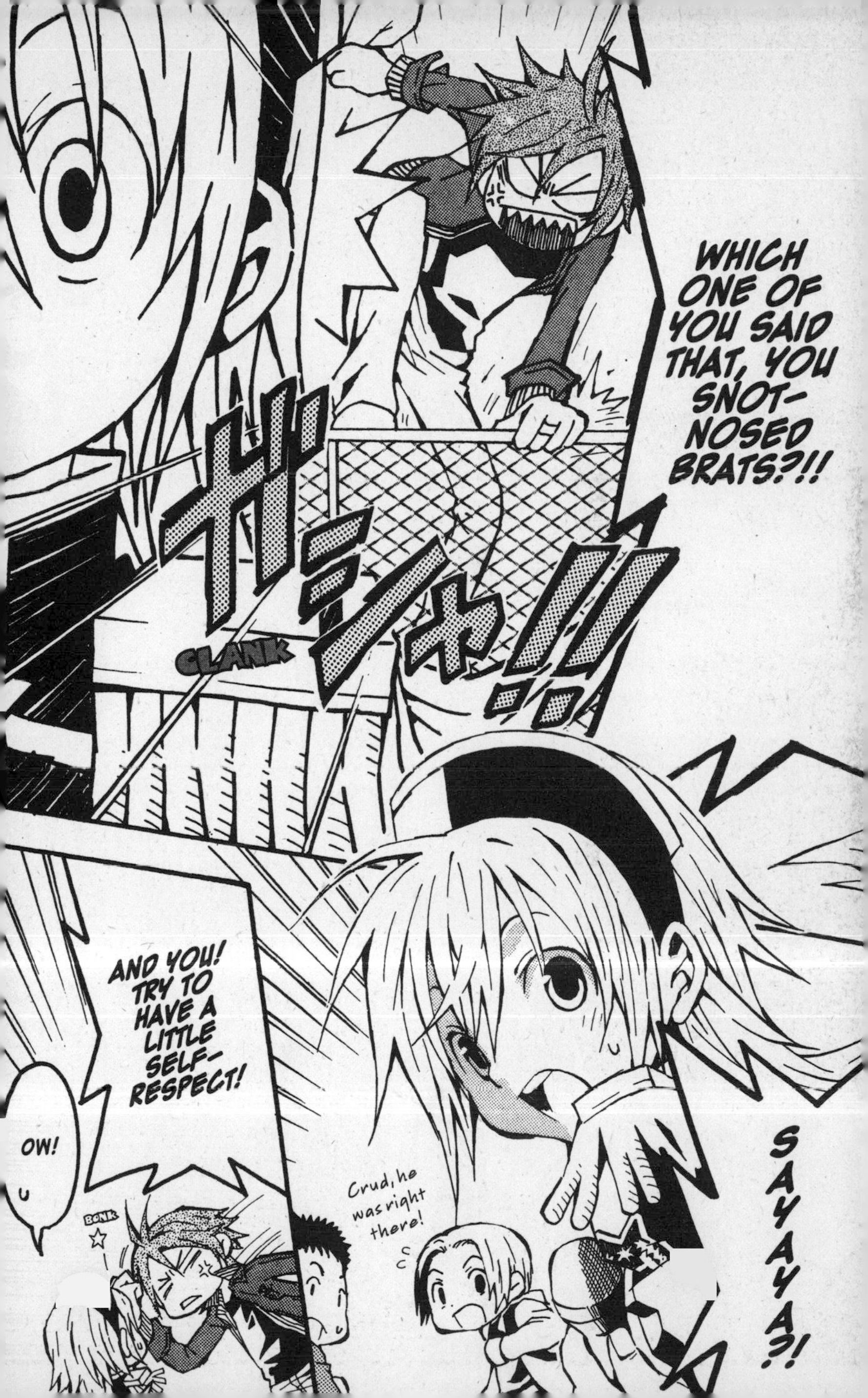
WHICH ONE OF YOU SAID THAT, YOU SNOT-NOSED BRATS?!!
ガシャン!!
CLANK
SAYAYA?!
Crud, he was right there!
AND YOU! TRY TO HAVE A LITTLE SELF-RESPECT!
BONK
OW!

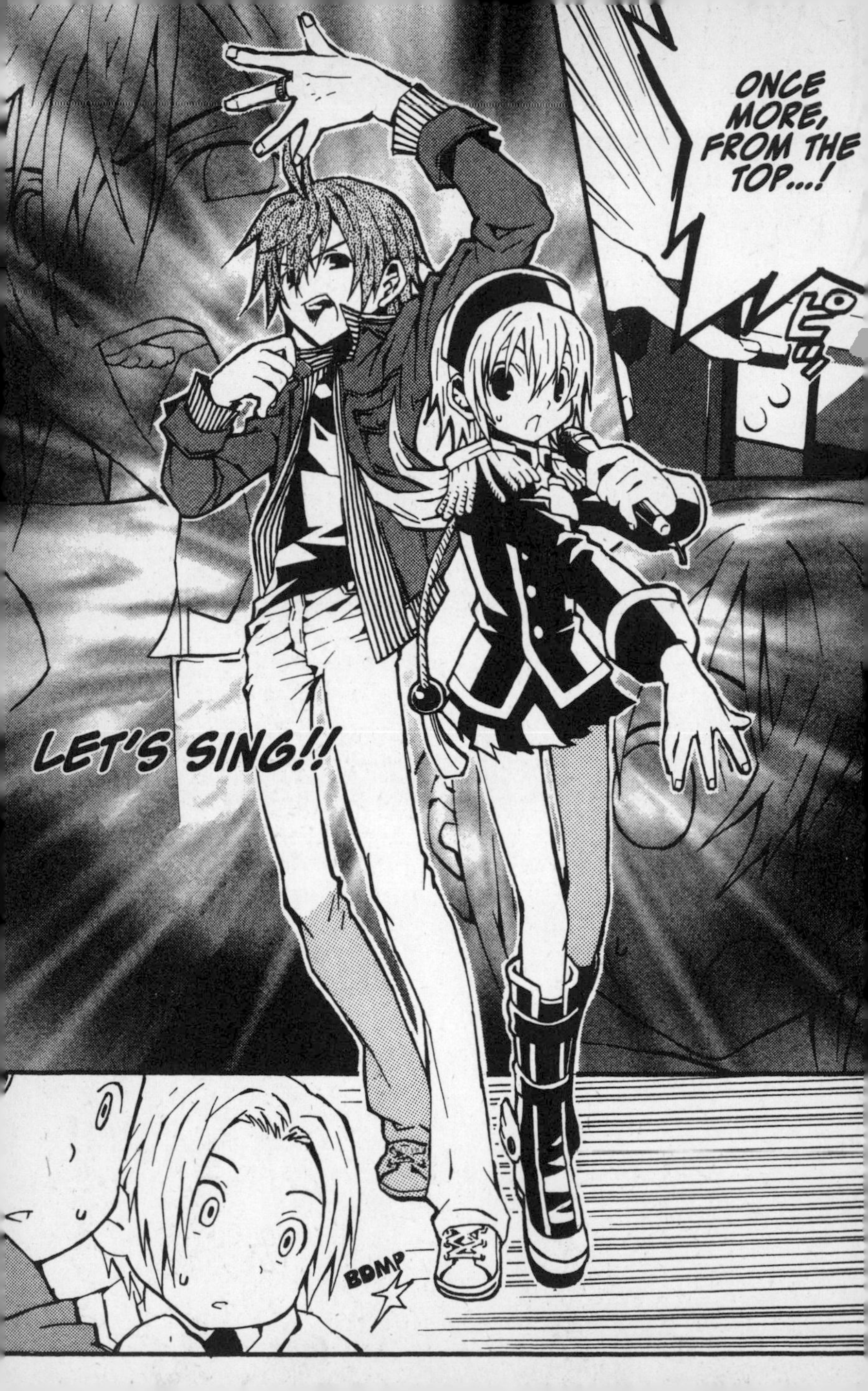
ONCE MORE, FROM THE TOP...!
LET'S SING!!
BDMP

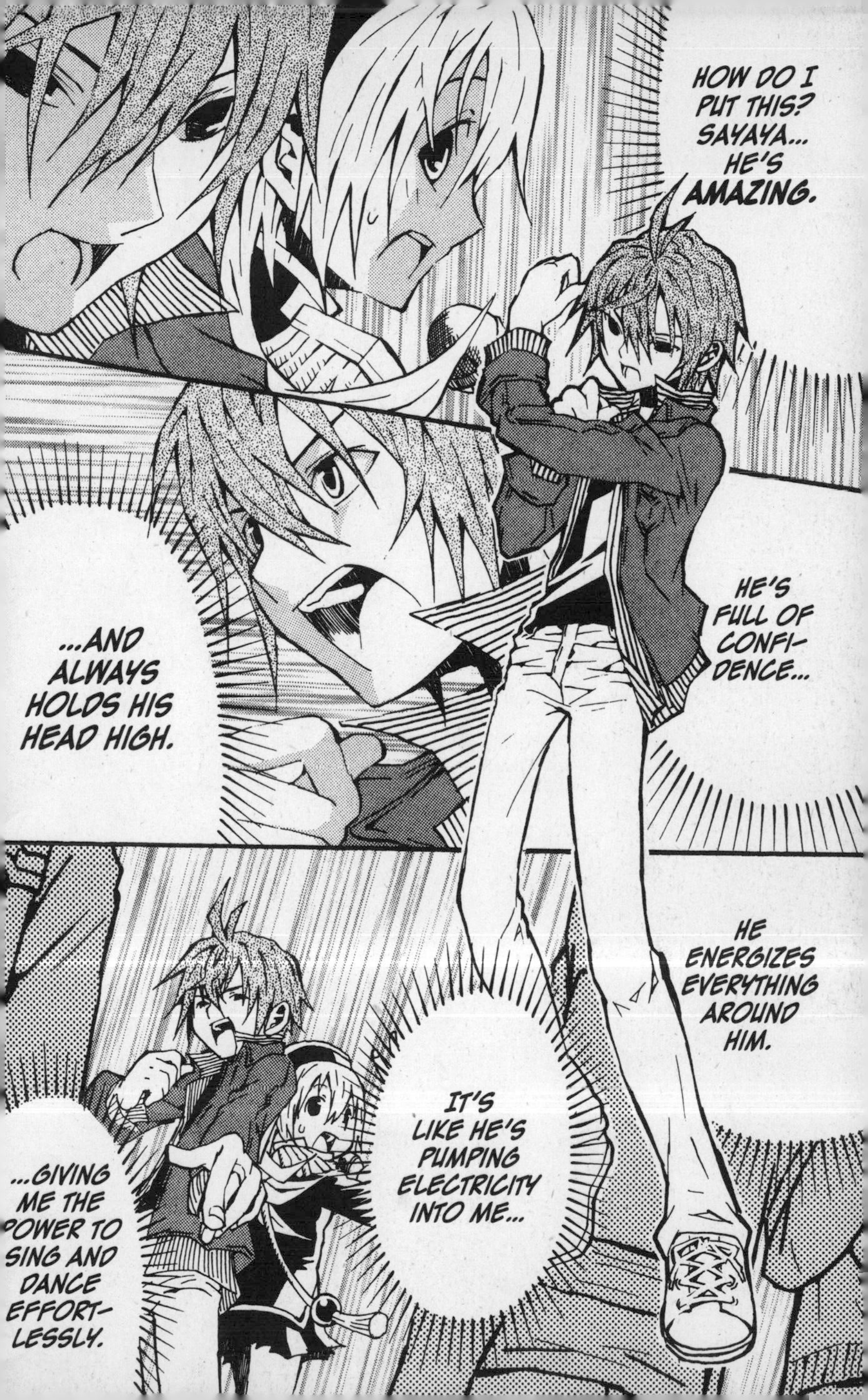
HOW DO I PUT THIS? SAYAYA... HE'S **AMAZING.**
HE'S FULL OF CONFI-DENCE...
...AND ALWAYS HOLDS HIS HEAD HIGH.
HE ENERGIZES EVERYTHING AROUND HIM.
IT'S LIKE HE'S PUMPING ELECTRICITY INTO ME...
...GIVING ME THE POWER TO SING AND DANCE EFFORT-LESSLY.

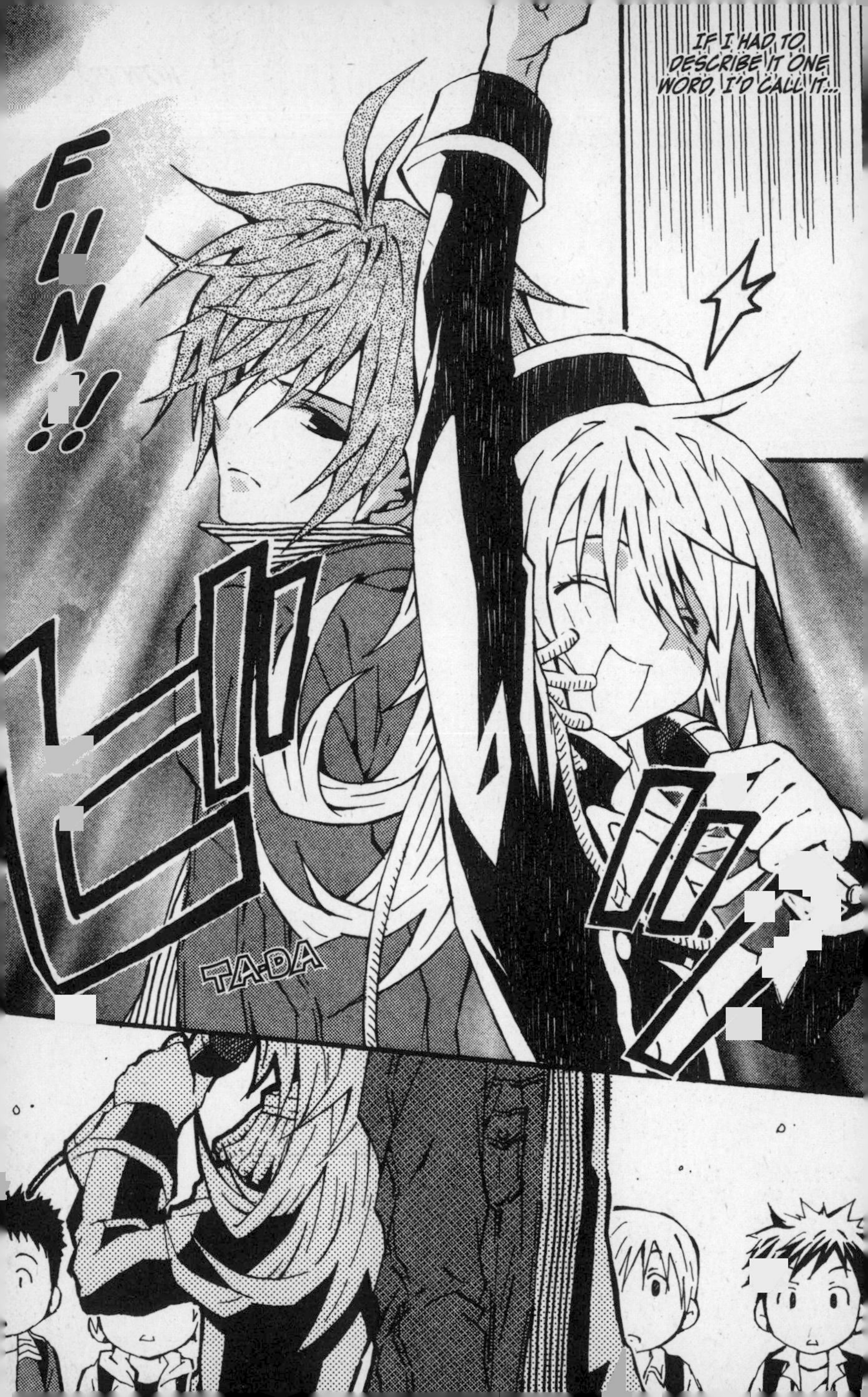
IF I HAD TO DESCRIBE IT ONE WORD, I'D CALL IT...
FUN!!
TA-DA

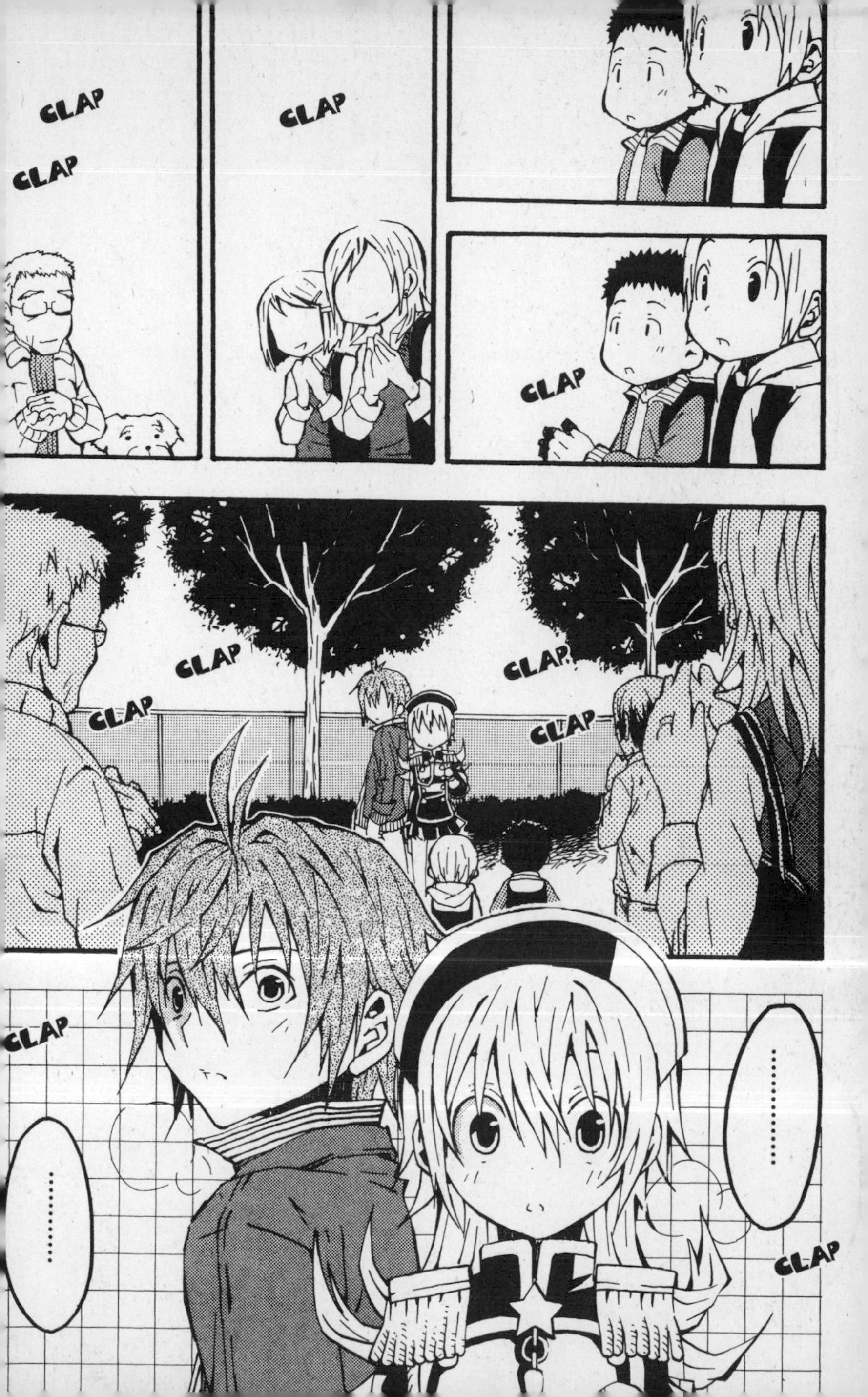
CLAP
CLAP
CLAP
CLAP
CLAP
CLAP
CLAP
CLAP
....
CLAP
....
CLAP

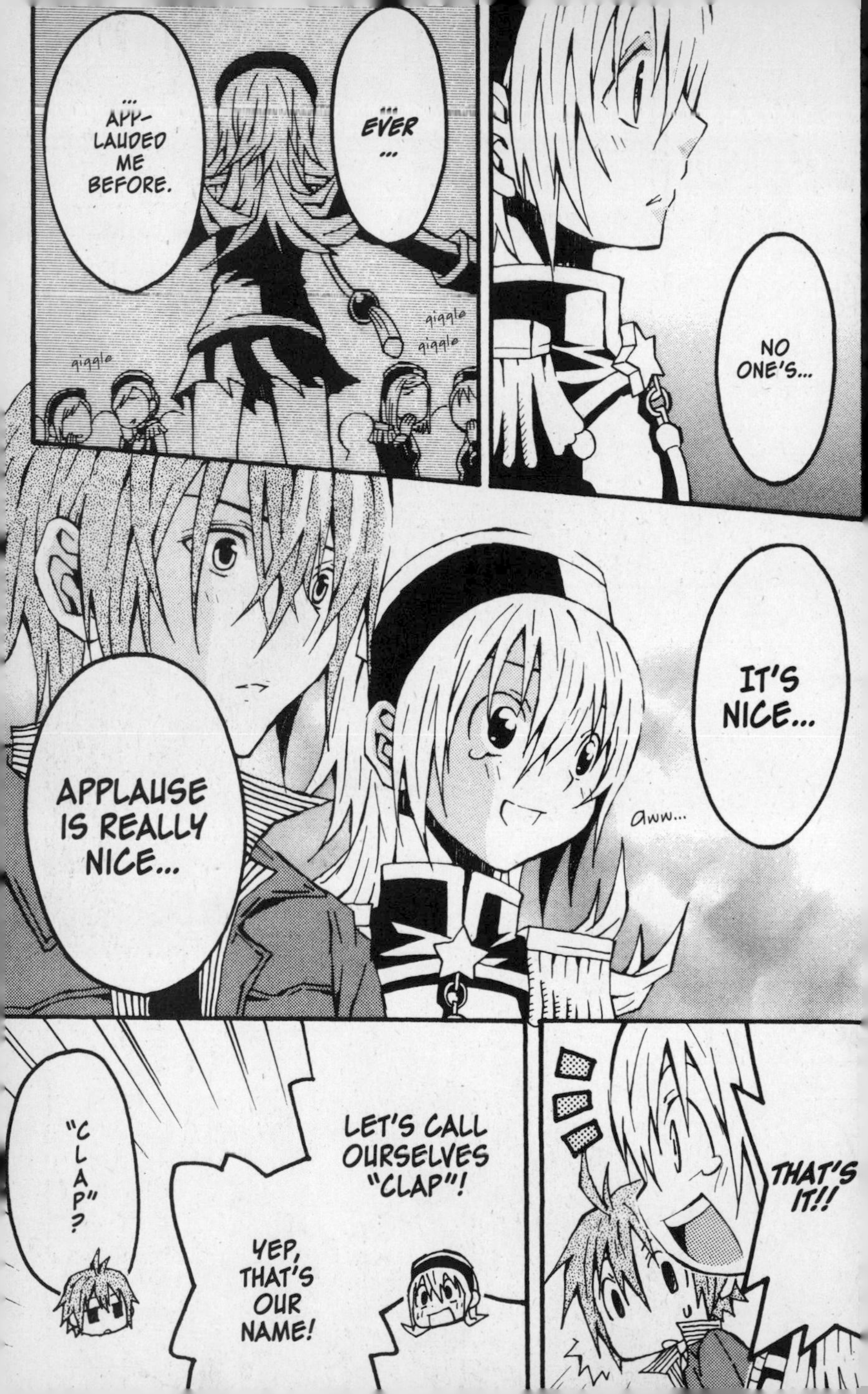
NO ONE'S...
...EVER...
...APP-LAUDED ME BEFORE.
giggle
giggle
giggle
IT'S NICE...
aww...
APPLAUSE IS REALLY NICE...
THAT'S IT!!
LET'S CALL OURSELVES "CLAP"!
YEP, THAT'S OUR NAME!
"CLAP"?

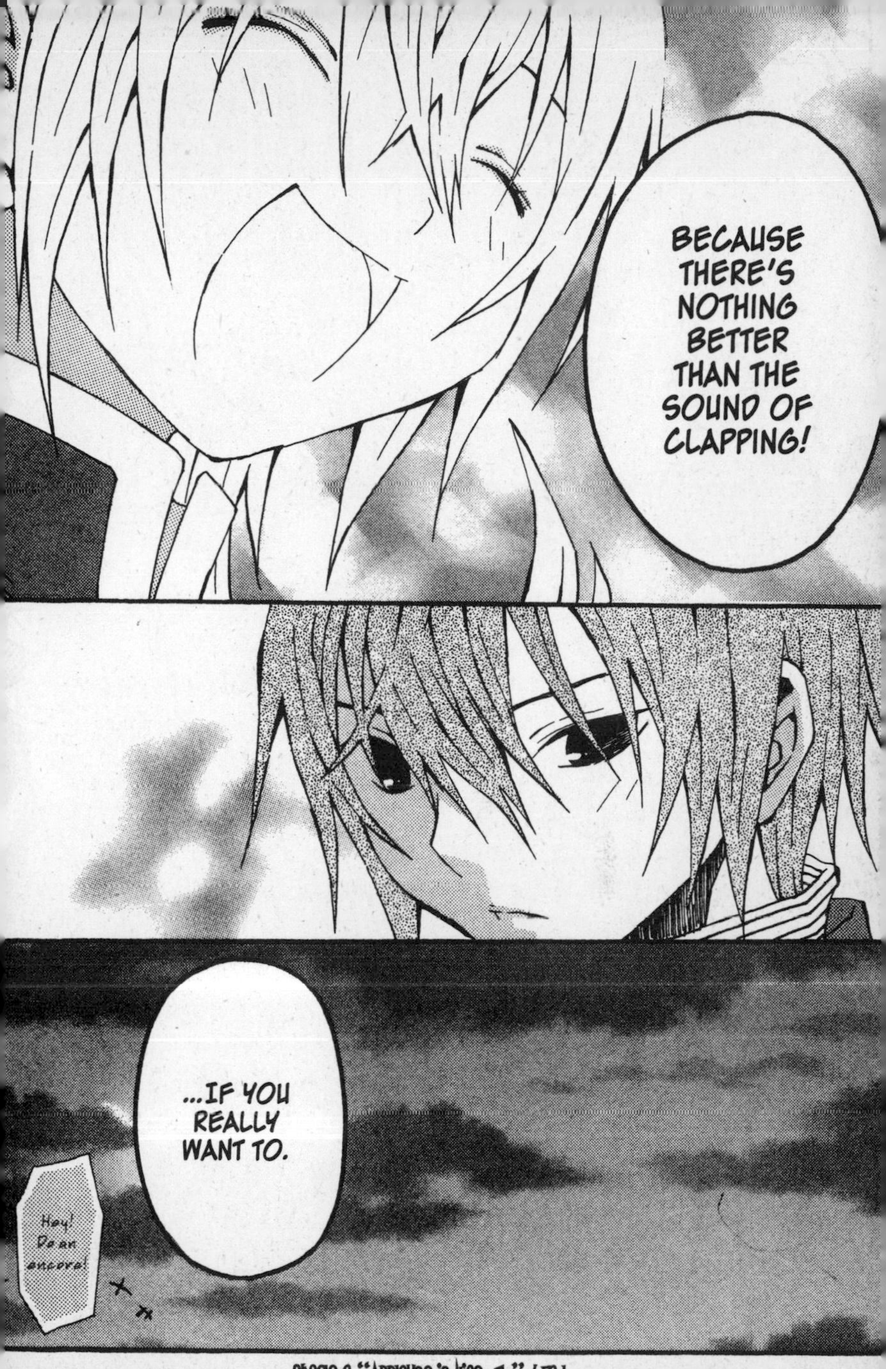
BECAUSE THERE'S NOTHING BETTER THAN THE SOUND OF CLAPPING!
...IF YOU REALLY WANT TO.
Hey! Do an encore!

stage 2 "Applause is Nice ♫" / End

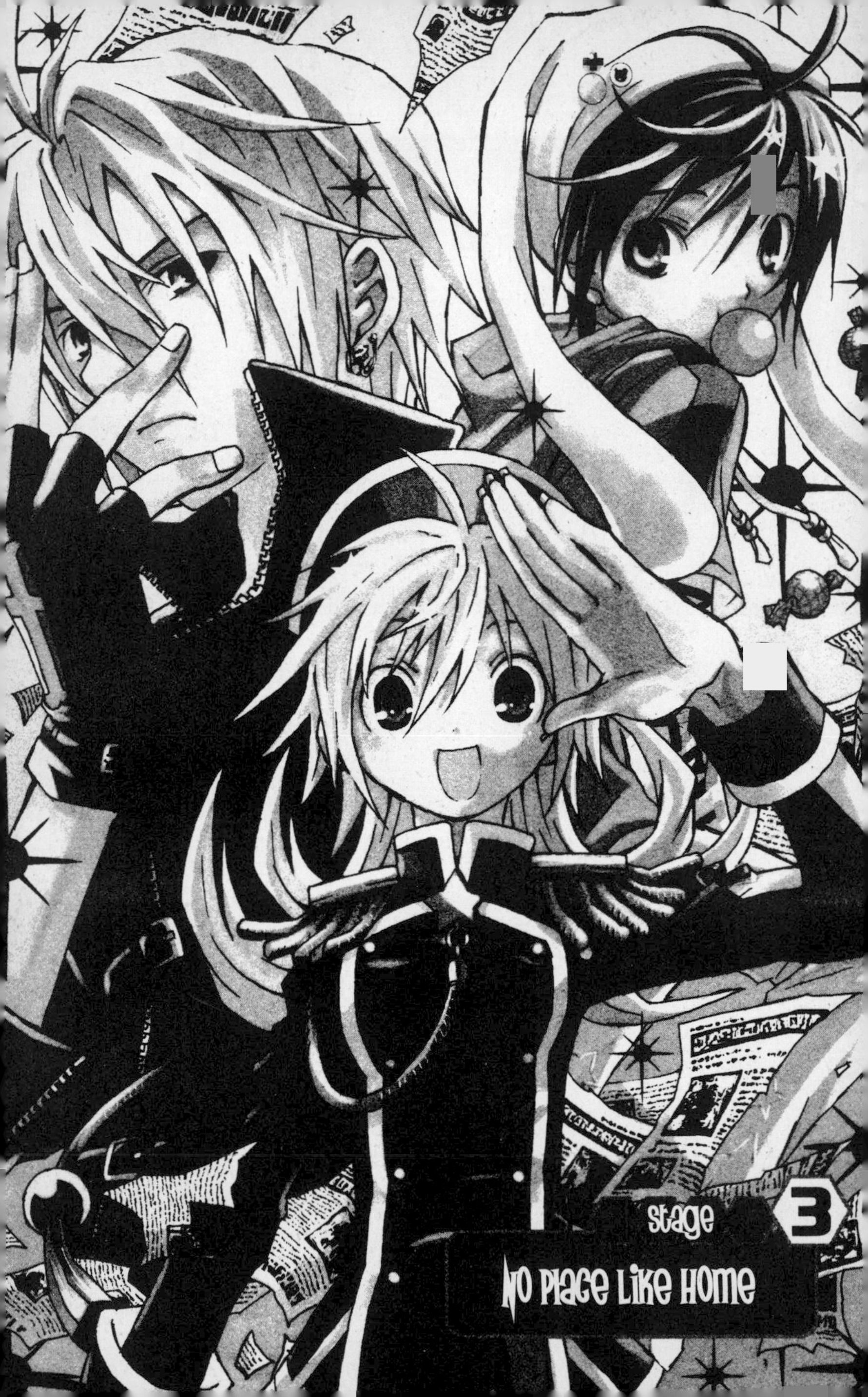
Stage 3
No Place Like Home

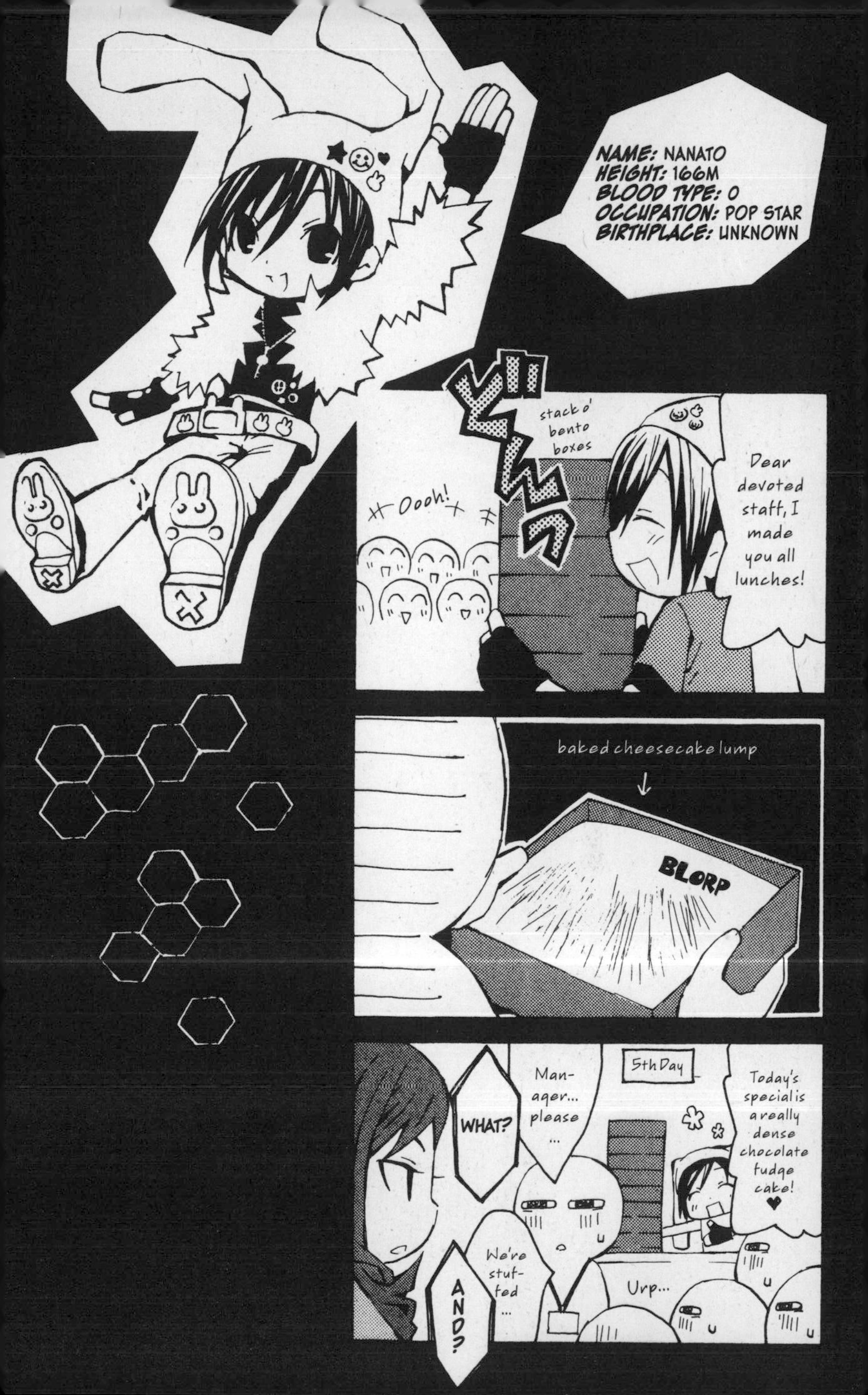

NAME: NANATO
HEIGHT: 166M
BLOOD TYPE: O
OCCUPATION: POP STAR
BIRTHPLACE: UNKNOWN
Dear devoted staff, I made you all lunches!
stack o' bento boxes
Oooh!
baked cheesecake lump
BLORP
Today's special is a really dense chocolate fudge cake!
5th Day
Man-ager... please...
WHAT?
Urp...
We're stuf-fed...
AND?

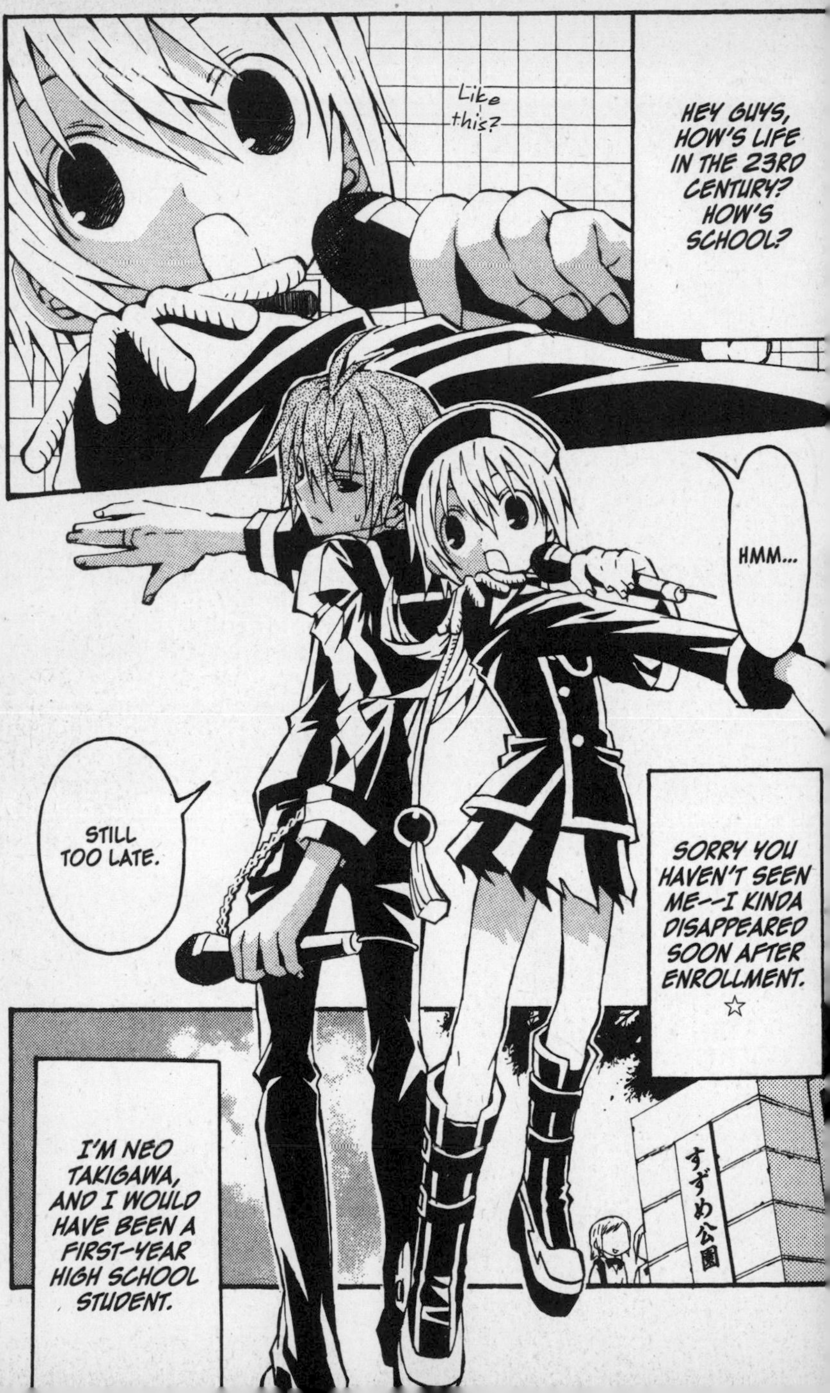
HEY GUYS, HOW'S LIFE IN THE 23RD CENTURY? HOW'S SCHOOL?
Like this?
HMM...
SORRY YOU HAVEN'T SEEN ME--I KINDA DISAPPEARED SOON AFTER ENROLLMENT. ☆
STILL TOO LATE.
すずめ公園
I'M NEO TAKIGAWA, AND I WOULD HAVE BEEN A FIRST-YEAR HIGH SCHOOL STUDENT.

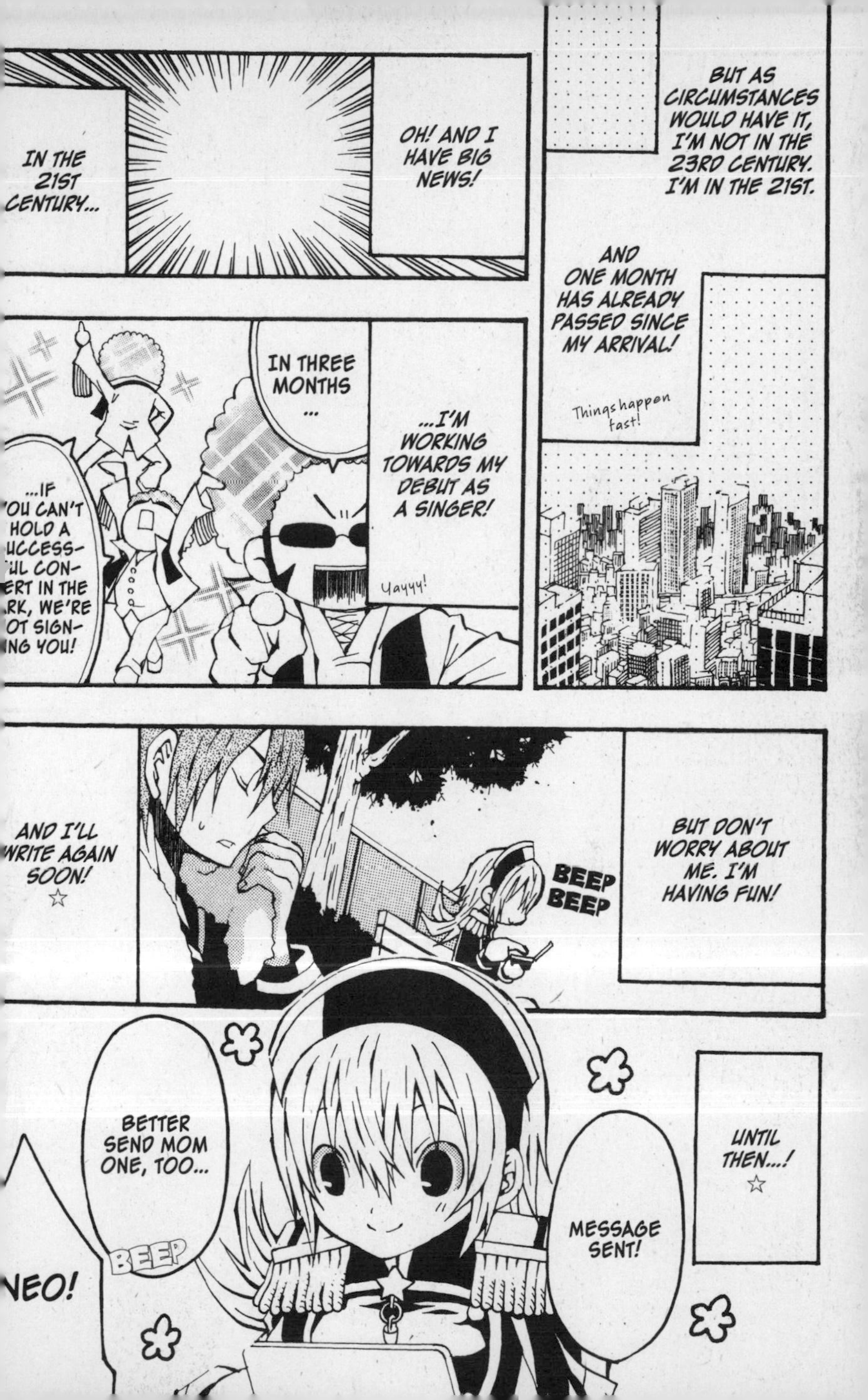
BUT AS CIRCUMSTANCES WOULD HAVE IT, I'M NOT IN THE 23RD CENTURY. I'M IN THE 21ST.
AND ONE MONTH HAS ALREADY PASSED SINCE MY ARRIVAL!
Things happen fast!
OH! AND I HAVE BIG NEWS!
IN THE 21ST CENTURY...
IN THREE MONTHS...
...I'M WORKING TOWARDS MY DEBUT AS A SINGER!
Yayyy!
...IF OU CAN'T HOLD A UCCESS-UL CON-ERT IN THE ARK, WE'RE OT SIGN-NG YOU!
BUT DON'T WORRY ABOUT ME. I'M HAVING FUN!
BEEP BEEP
AND I'LL WRITE AGAIN SOON! ☆
UNTIL THEN...! ☆
MESSAGE SENT!
BETTER SEND MOM ONE, TOO...
BEEP
NEO!

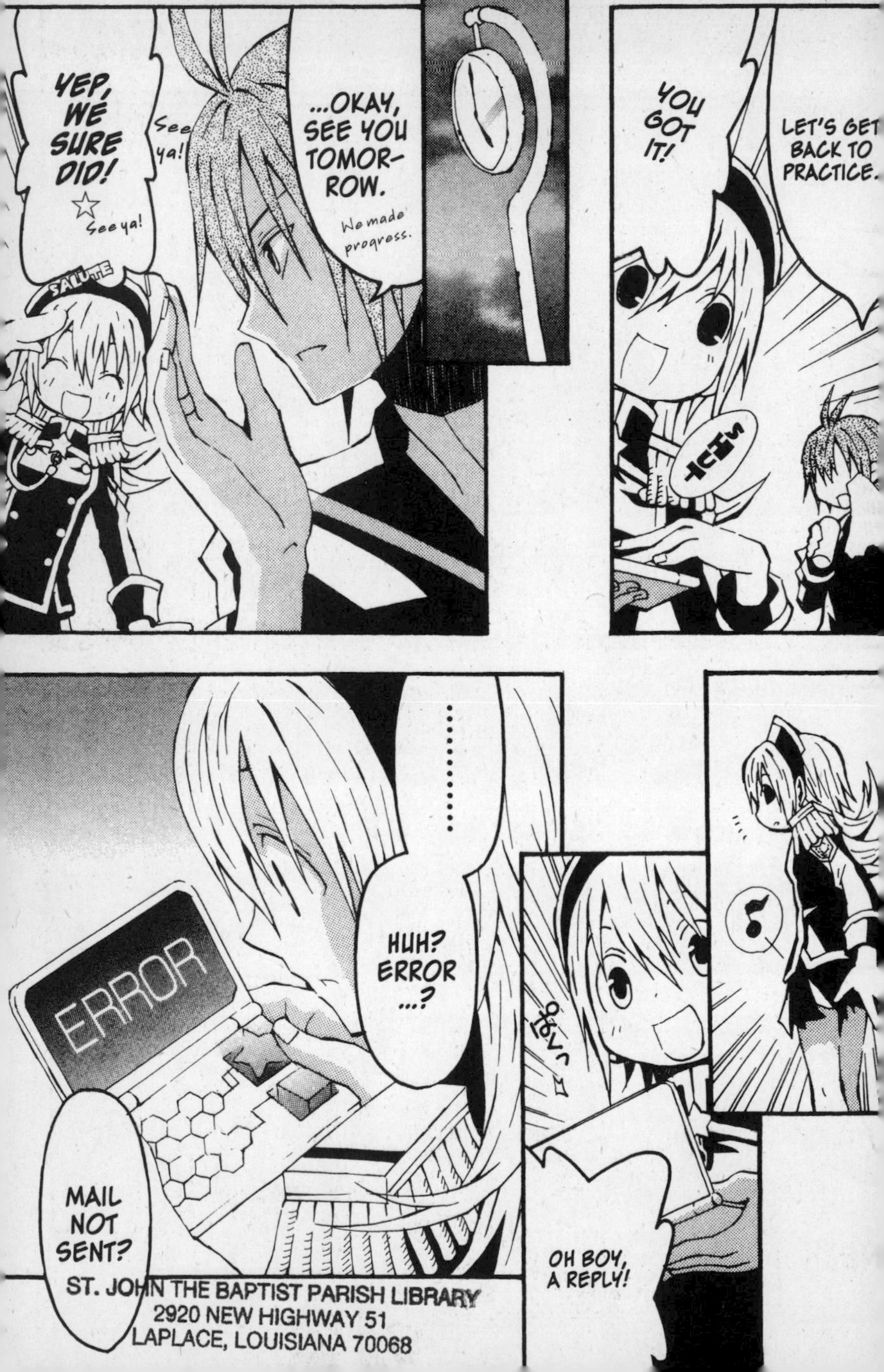

LET'S GET BACK TO PRACTICE.
YOU GOT IT!
...OKAY, SEE YOU TOMORROW.
We made progress.
YEP, WE SURE DID! ☆
See ya!
See ya!
SALUTE
...
OH BOY, A REPLY!
......
HUH? ERROR ...?
ERROR
MAIL NOT SENT?

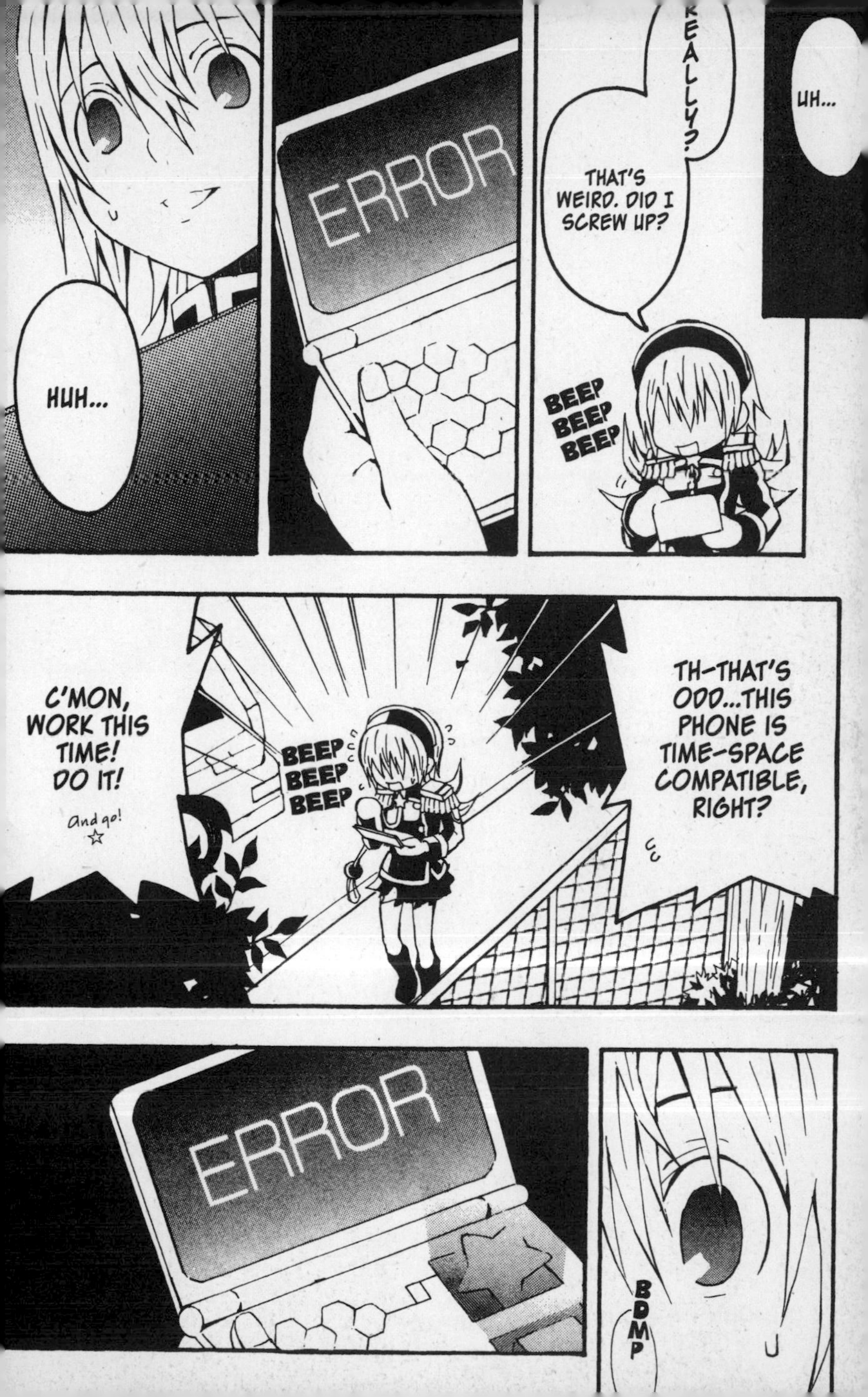
UH...
REALLY?
THAT'S WEIRD. DID I SCREW UP?
BEEP BEEP BEEP
ERROR
HUH...
TH-THAT'S ODD...THIS PHONE IS TIME-SPACE COMPATIBLE, RIGHT?
BEEP BEEP BEEP
C'MON, WORK THIS TIME! DO IT!
and go! ☆
BDMP
ERROR

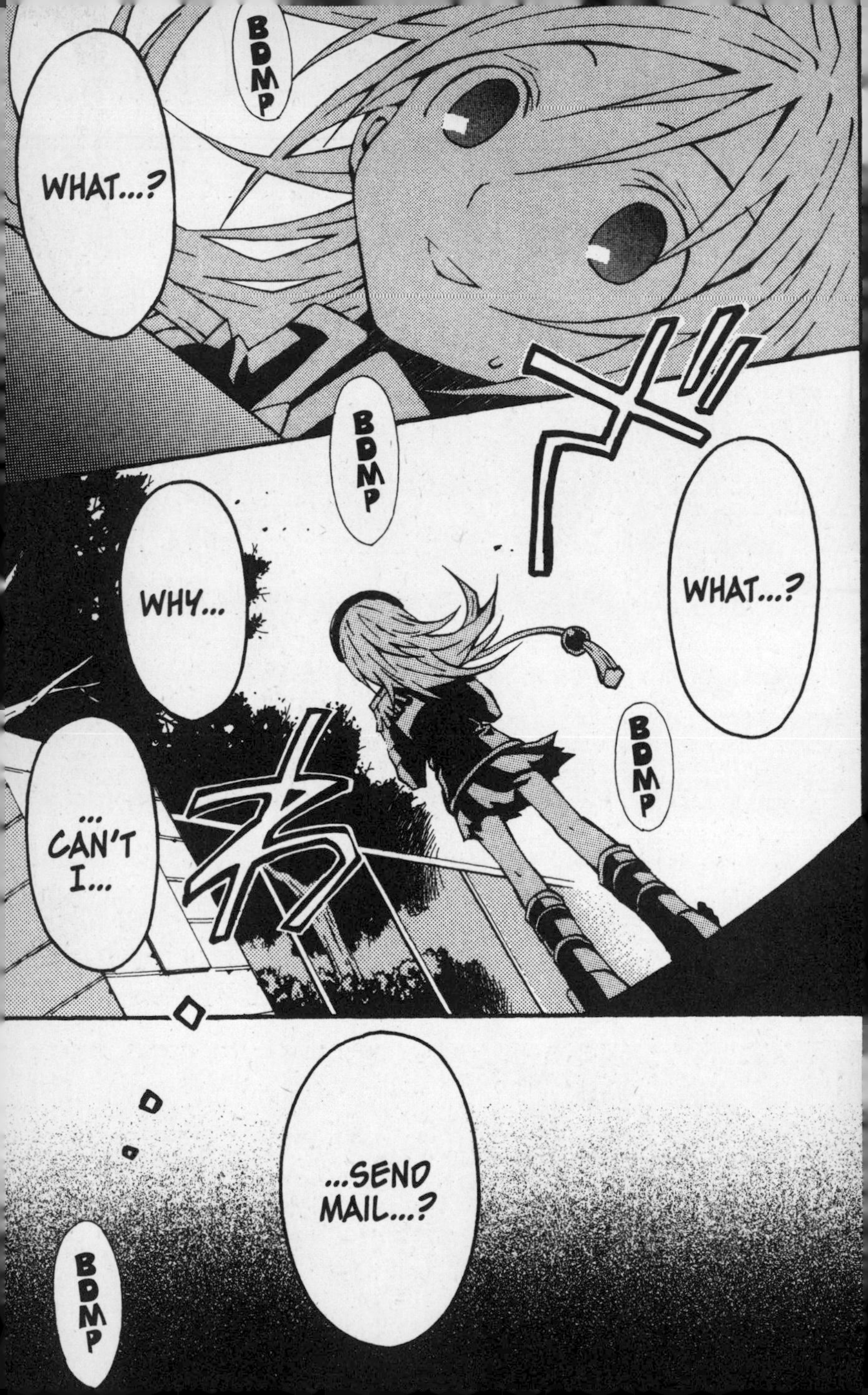
BDMP
WHAT...?
BDMP
WHAT...?
BDMP
WHY...
... CAN'T I...
...SEND MAIL...?
BDMP

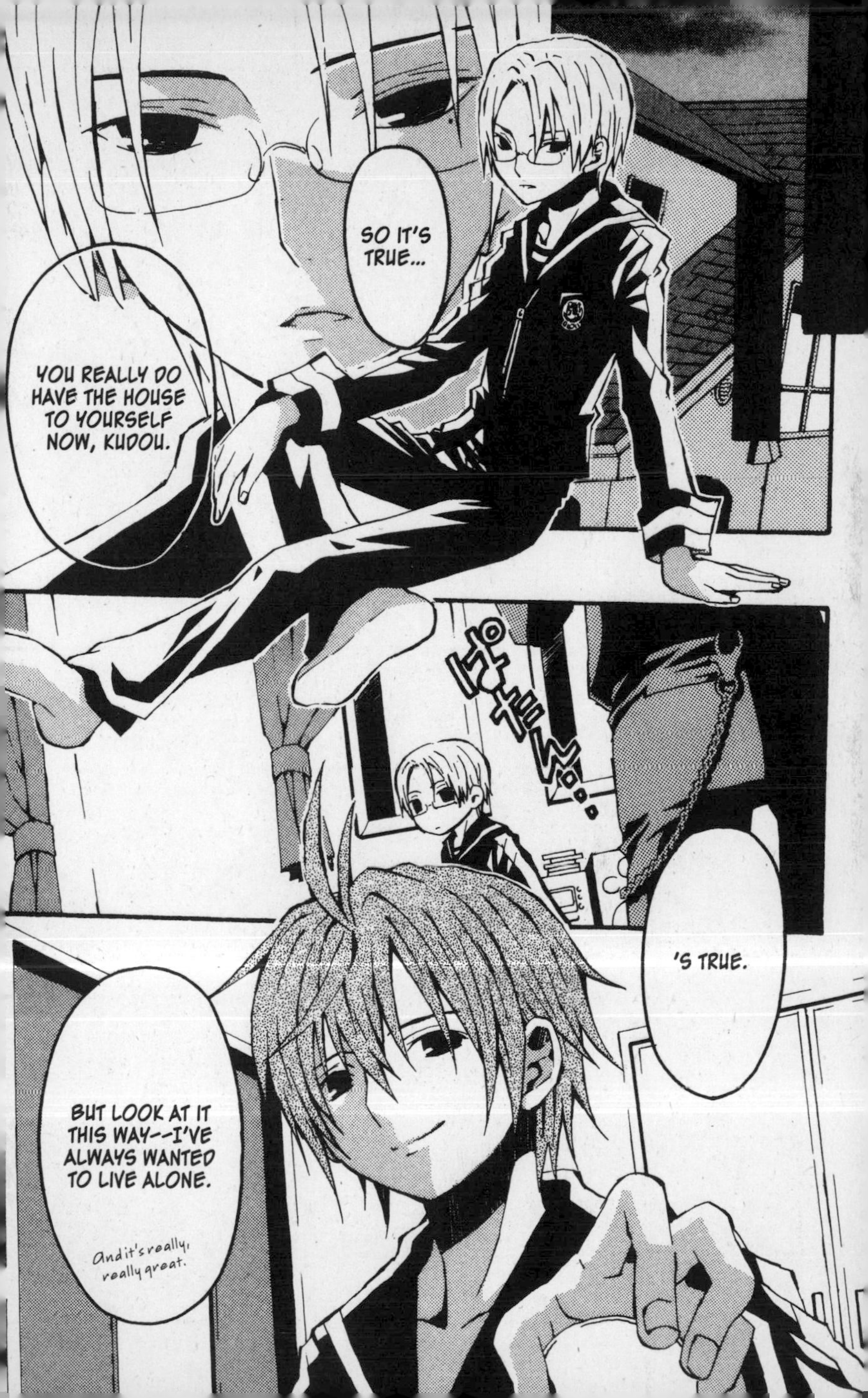
SO IT'S TRUE...
YOU REALLY DO HAVE THE HOUSE TO YOURSELF NOW, KUDOU.
'S TRUE.
BUT LOOK AT IT THIS WAY--I'VE ALWAYS WANTED TO LIVE ALONE.
And it's really, really great.

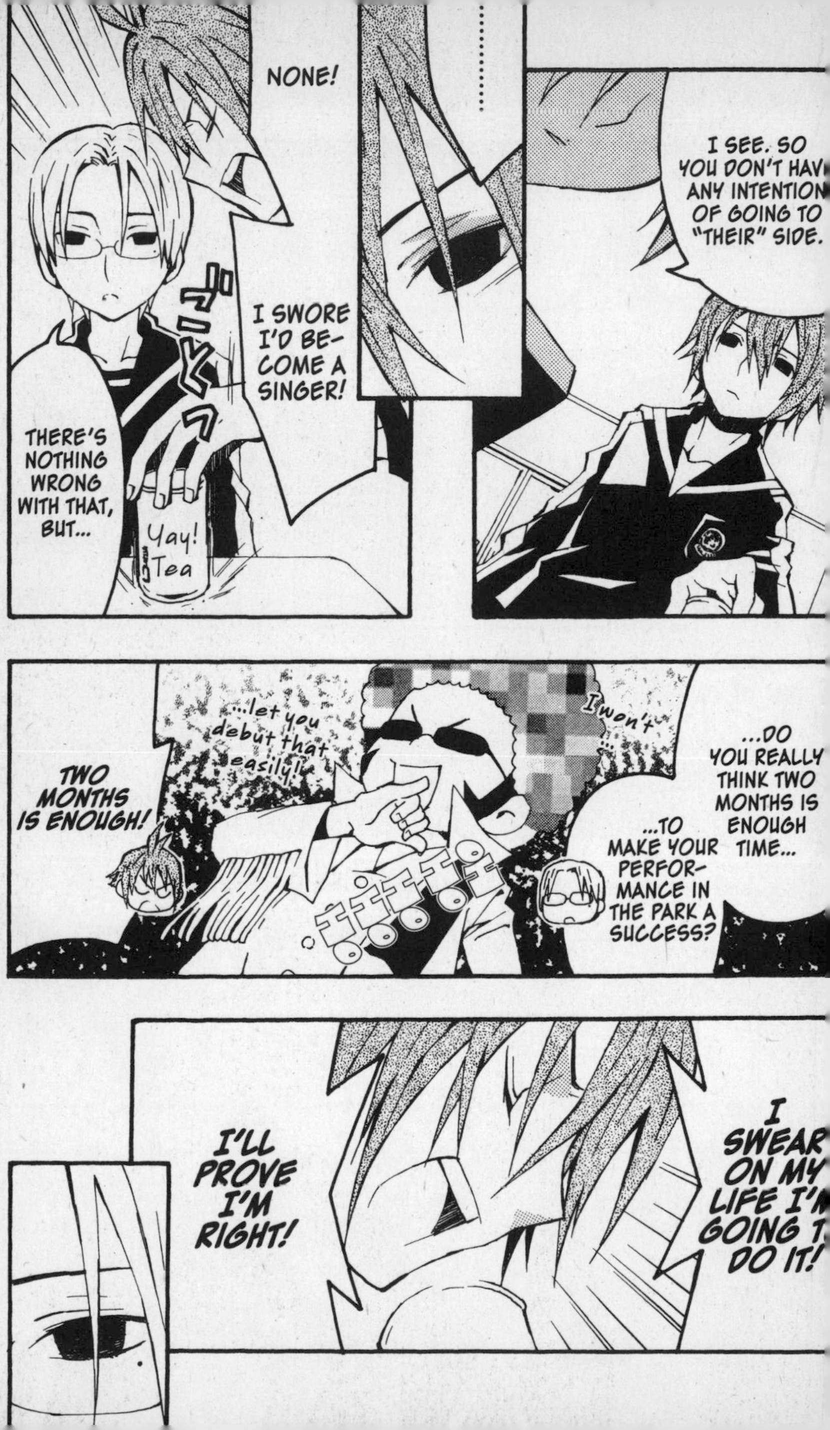
I SEE. SO YOU DON'T HAV ANY INTENTION OF GOING TO "THEIR" SIDE.
NONE!
I SWORE I'D BE-COME A SINGER!
THERE'S NOTHING WRONG WITH THAT, BUT...
Yay! Tea
...DO YOU REALLY THINK TWO MONTHS IS ENOUGH TIME...
...TO MAKE YOUR PERFOR-MANCE IN THE PARK A SUCCESS?
I won't...
...let you debut that easily!
TWO MONTHS IS ENOUGH!
I SWEAR ON MY LIFE I' GOING T DO IT!
I'LL PROVE I'M RIGHT!

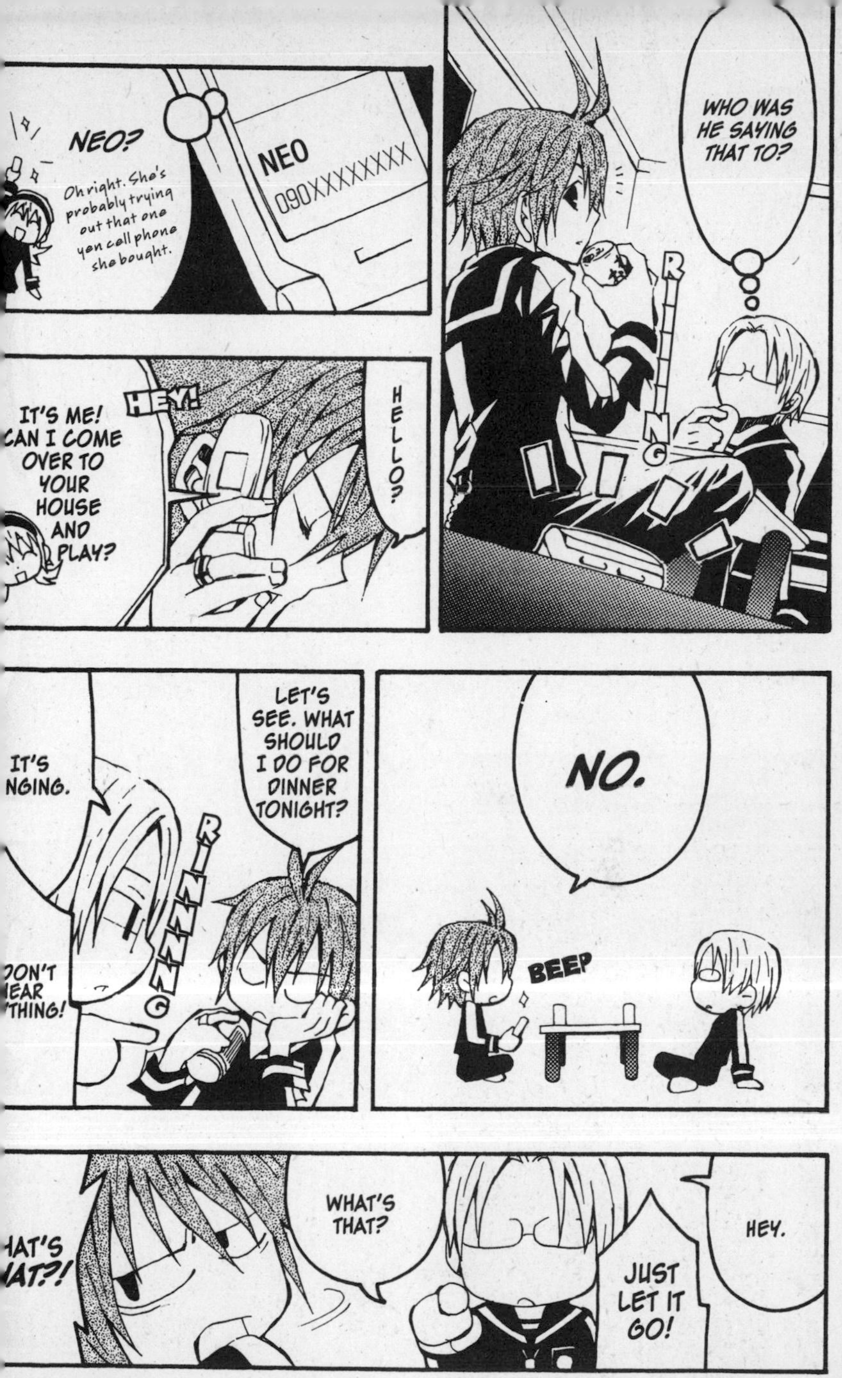
WHO WAS HE SAYING THAT TO?
RING
NEO?
NEO
090XXXXXXXX
Oh right. She's probably trying out that one yen cell phone she bought.
HELLO?
HEY!
IT'S ME! CAN I COME OVER TO YOUR HOUSE AND PLAY?
NO.
BEEP
LET'S SEE. WHAT SHOULD I DO FOR DINNER TONIGHT?
RINNNNG
IT'S NGING.
DON'T HEAR THING!
HEY.
JUST LET IT GO!
WHAT'S THAT?
HAT'S HAT?!

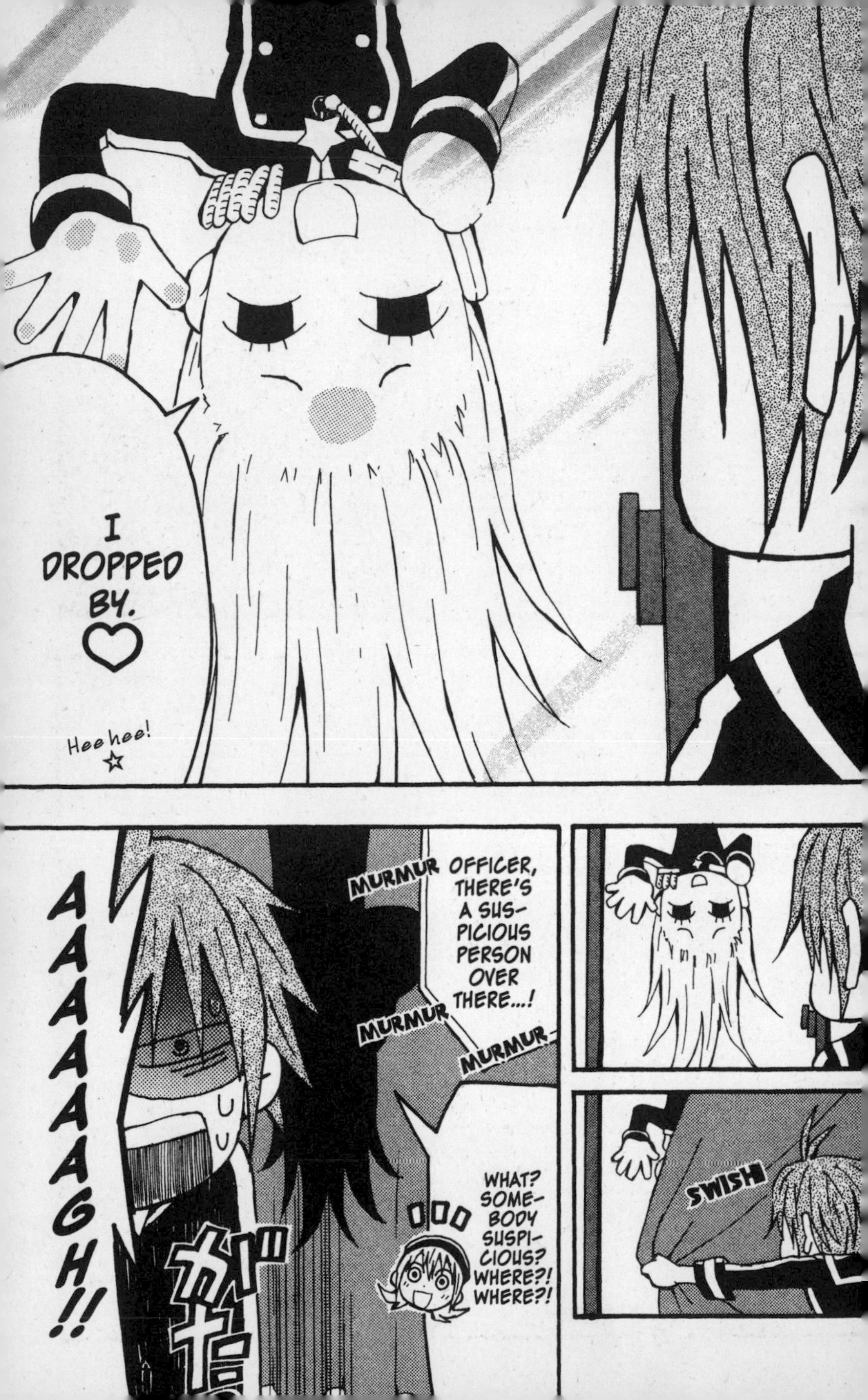
I DROPPED BY. ♡
Hee hee! ☆
SWISH
MURMUR
OFFICER, THERE'S A SUS-PICIOUS PERSON OVER THERE...!
MURMUR
MURMUR
WHAT? SOME-BODY SUSPI-CIOUS? WHERE?! WHERE?!
AAAAAAAGH!!

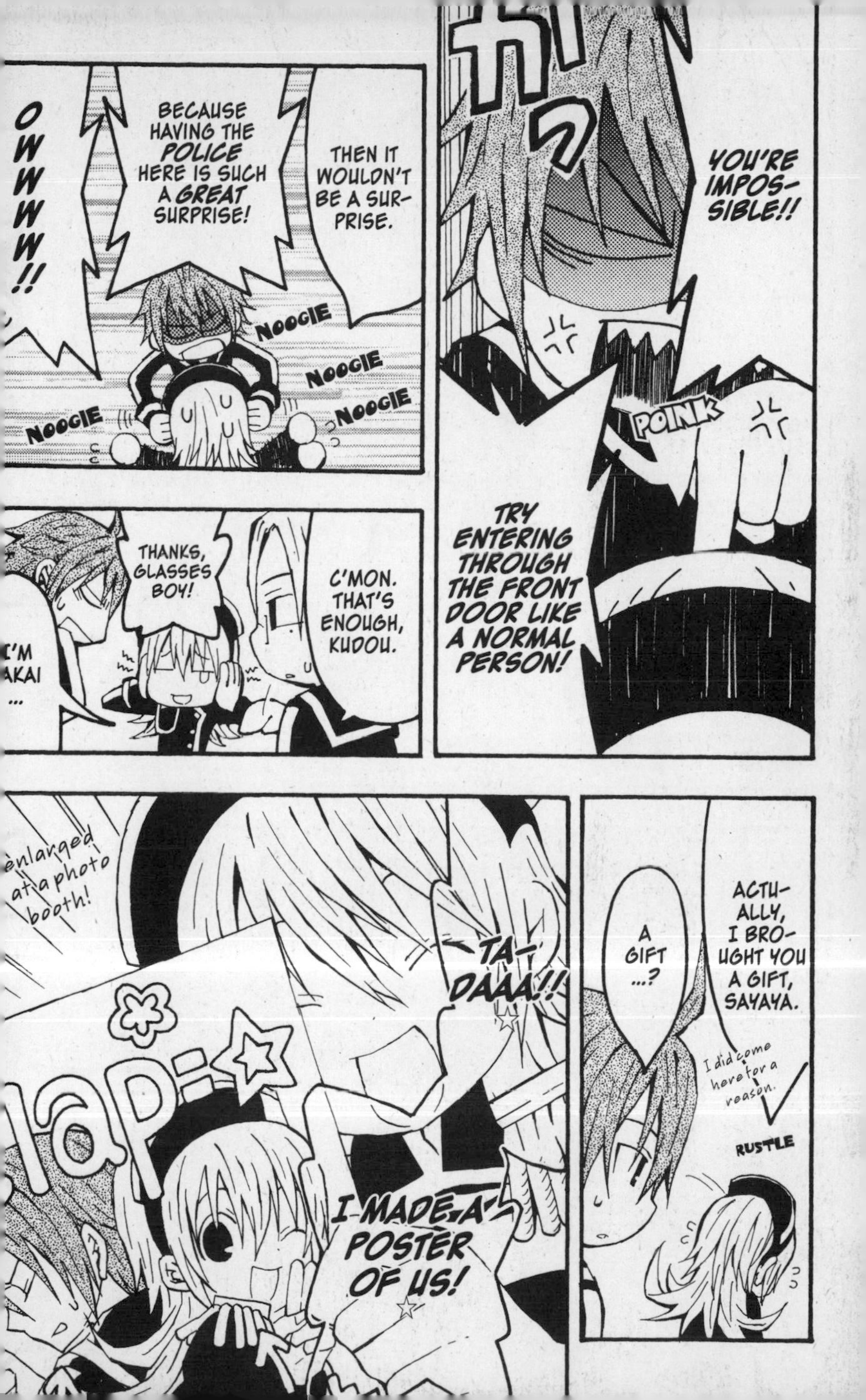
YOU'RE IMPOS-SIBLE!!
POINK
TRY ENTERING THROUGH THE FRONT DOOR LIKE A NORMAL PERSON!
THEN IT WOULDN'T BE A SUR-PRISE.
BECAUSE HAVING THE POLICE HERE IS SUCH A GREAT SURPRISE!
OWWWWW!!
NOOGIE
NOOGIE
NOOGIE
NOOGIE
C'MON. THAT'S ENOUGH, KUDOU.
THANKS, GLASSES BOY!
'M AKAI ...
ACTU-ALLY, I BRO-UGHT YOU A GIFT, SAYAYA.
I did come here for a reason.
A GIFT ...?
RUSTLE
TA-DAAA!!
enlarged at a photo booth!
I MADE A POSTER OF US!

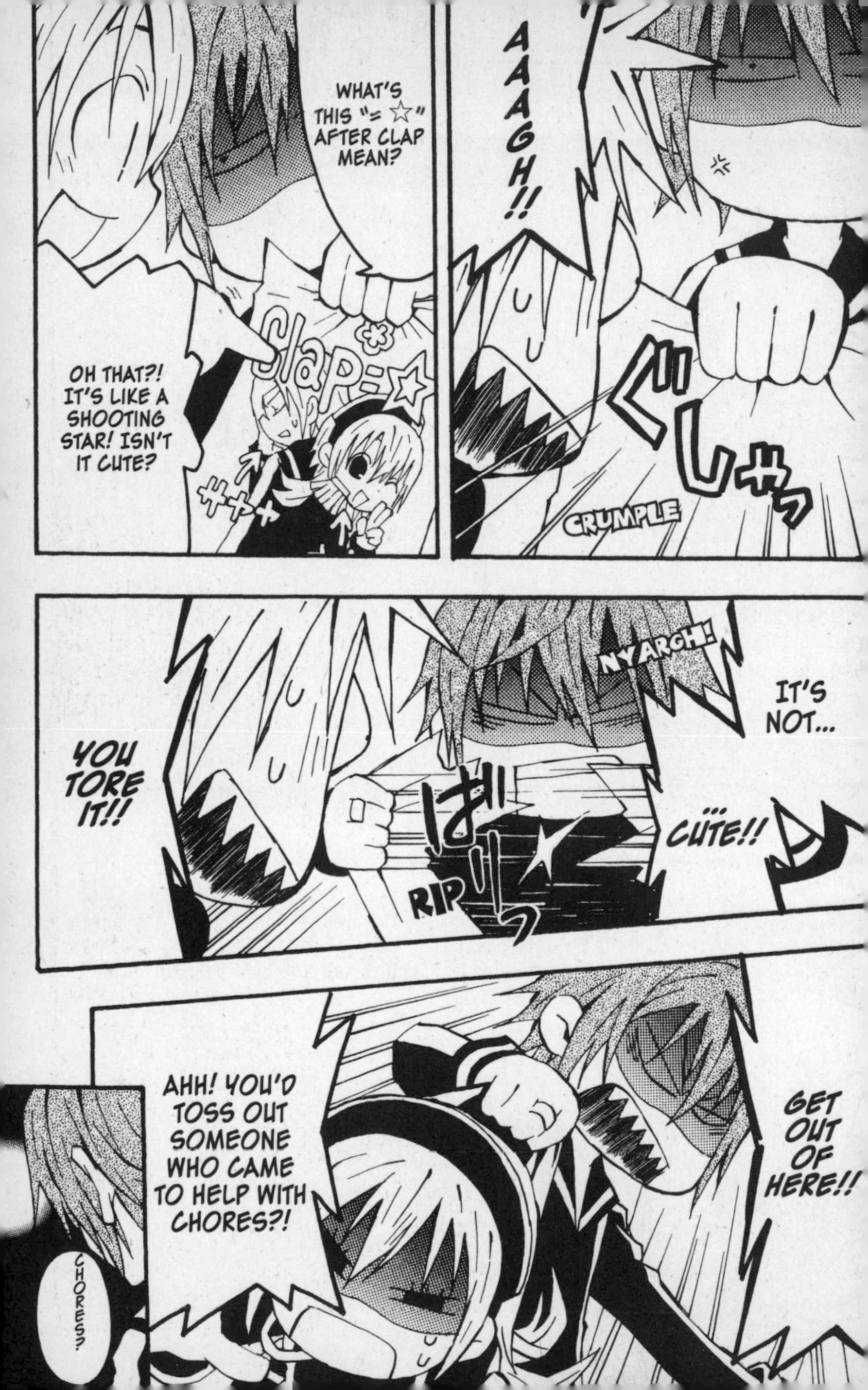
AAAGH!!
ぐしゃっ
CRUMPLE
WHAT'S THIS "=☆" AFTER CLAP MEAN?
clap=☆
OH THAT?! IT'S LIKE A SHOOTING STAR! ISN'T IT CUTE?
IT'S NOT...
...CUTE!!
NYARGH!
ばりっ
RIP
YOU TORE IT!!
GET OUT OF HERE!!
AHH! YOU'D TOSS OUT SOMEONE WHO CAME TO HELP WITH CHORES?!
CHORES?

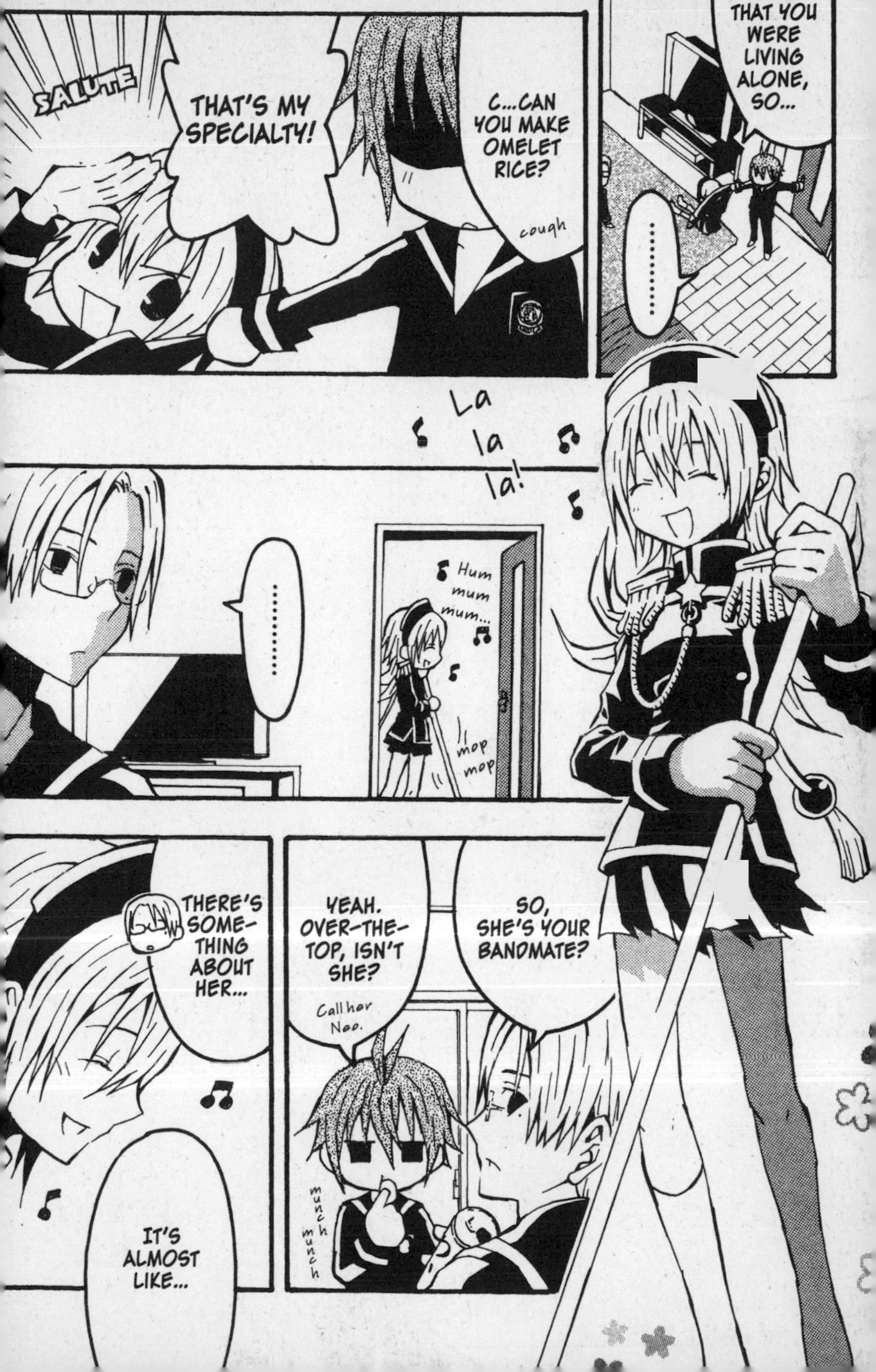
I HEARD THAT YOU WERE LIVING ALONE, SO...
......
C...CAN YOU MAKE OMELET RICE?
cough
THAT'S MY SPECIALTY!
SALUTE
La la la!
......
Hum mum mum...
mop mop
SO, SHE'S YOUR BANDMATE?
YEAH. OVER-THE-TOP, ISN'T SHE?
Call her Neo.
munch munch
THERE'S SOME-THING ABOUT HER...
IT'S ALMOST LIKE...

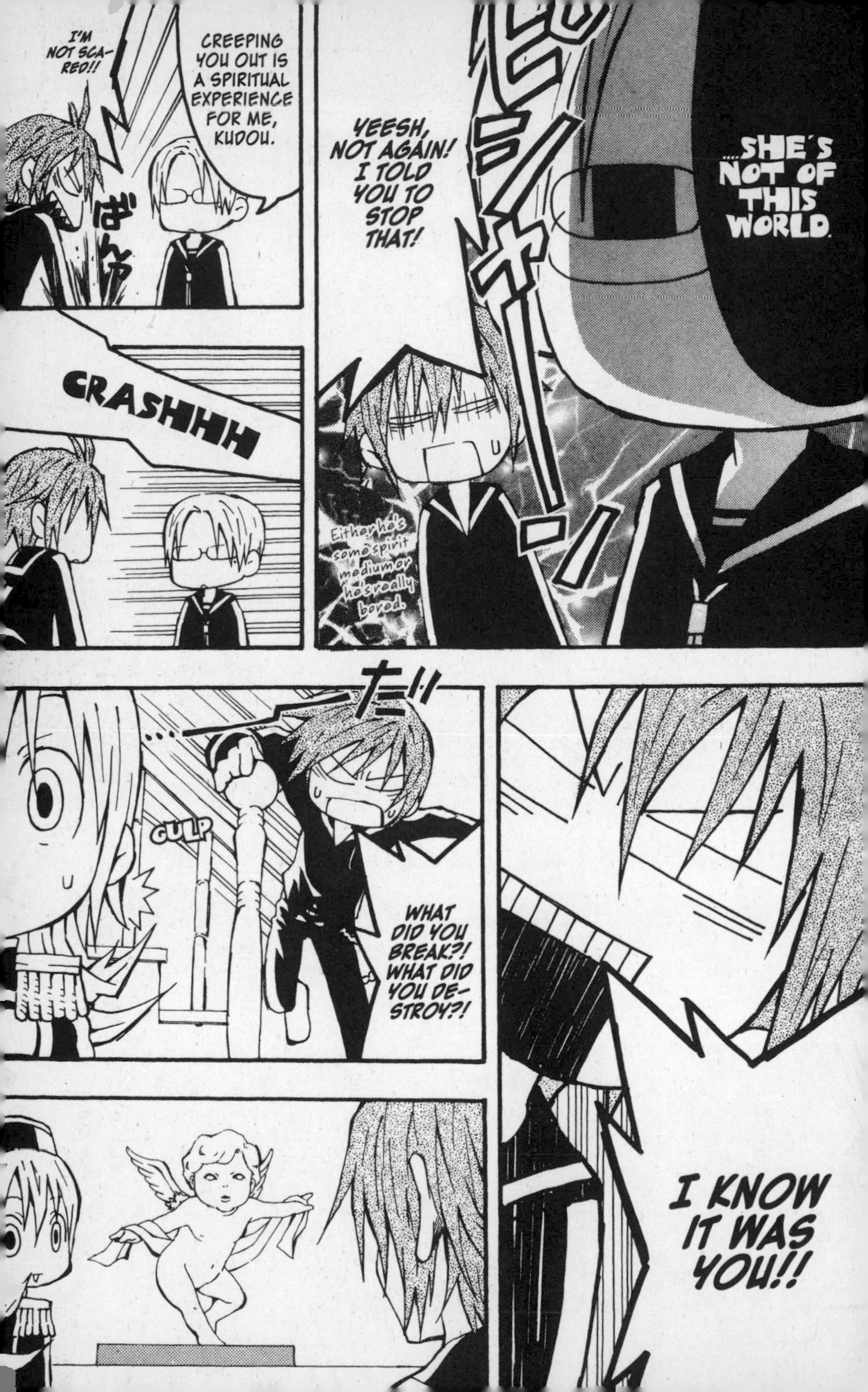
...SHE'S NOT OF THIS WORLD.
YEESH, NOT AGAIN! I TOLD YOU TO STOP THAT!
Either he's some spirit medium or he's really bored.
CREEPING YOU OUT IS A SPIRITUAL EXPERIENCE FOR ME, KUDOU.
I'M NOT SCA-RED!!
ばん
CRASHHHH
I KNOW IT WAS YOU!!
たッ
...
GULP
WHAT DID YOU BREAK?! WHAT DID YOU DESTROY?!

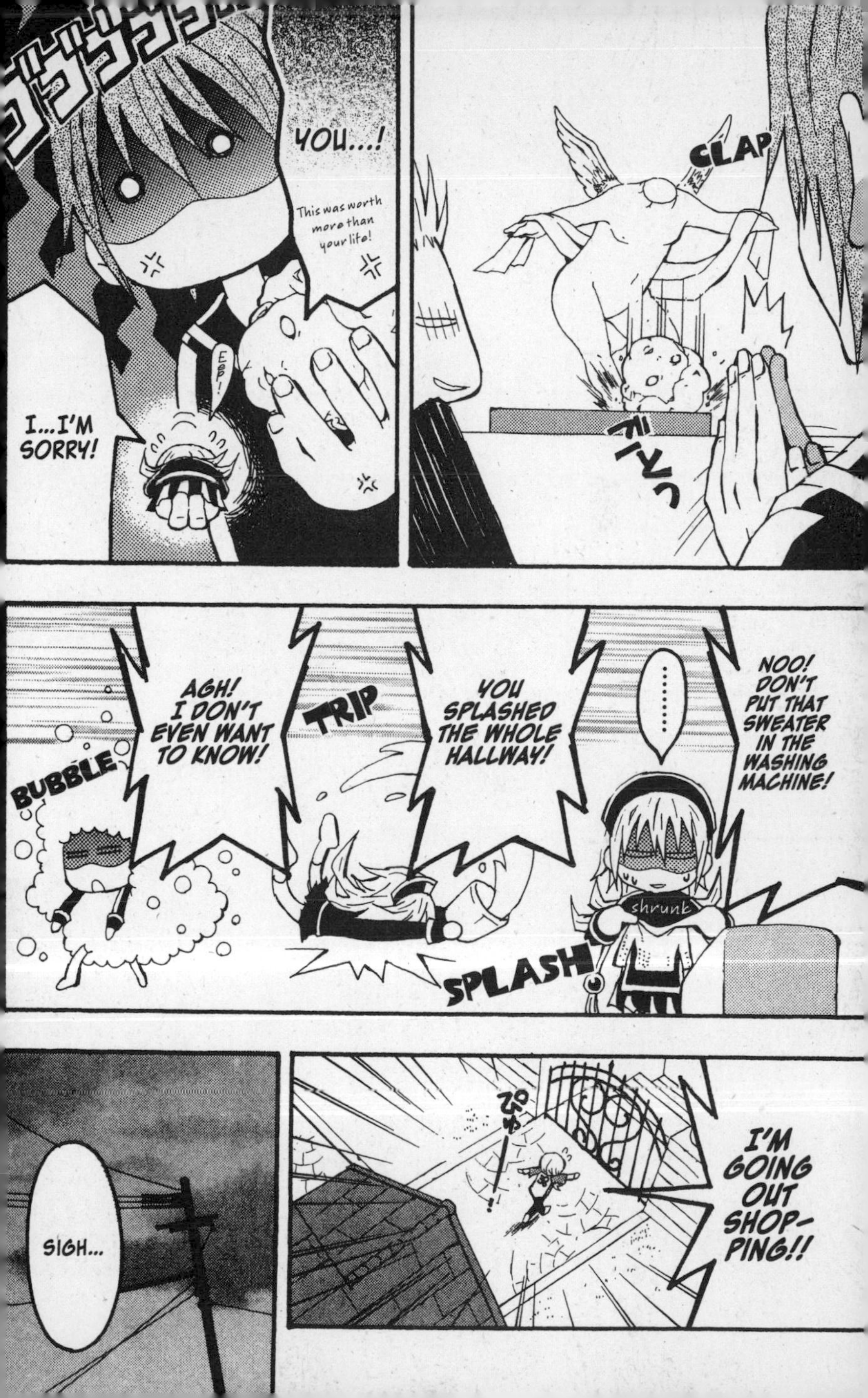
CLAP
YOU...!
This was worth more than your life!
EEP!
I...I'M SORRY!
NOO! DON'T PUT THAT SWEATER IN THE WASHING MACHINE!
......
shrunk
SPLASH
YOU SPLASHED THE WHOLE HALLWAY!
TRIP
AGH! I DON'T EVEN WANT TO KNOW!
BUBBLE
I'M GOING OUT SHOP-PING!!
SIGH...

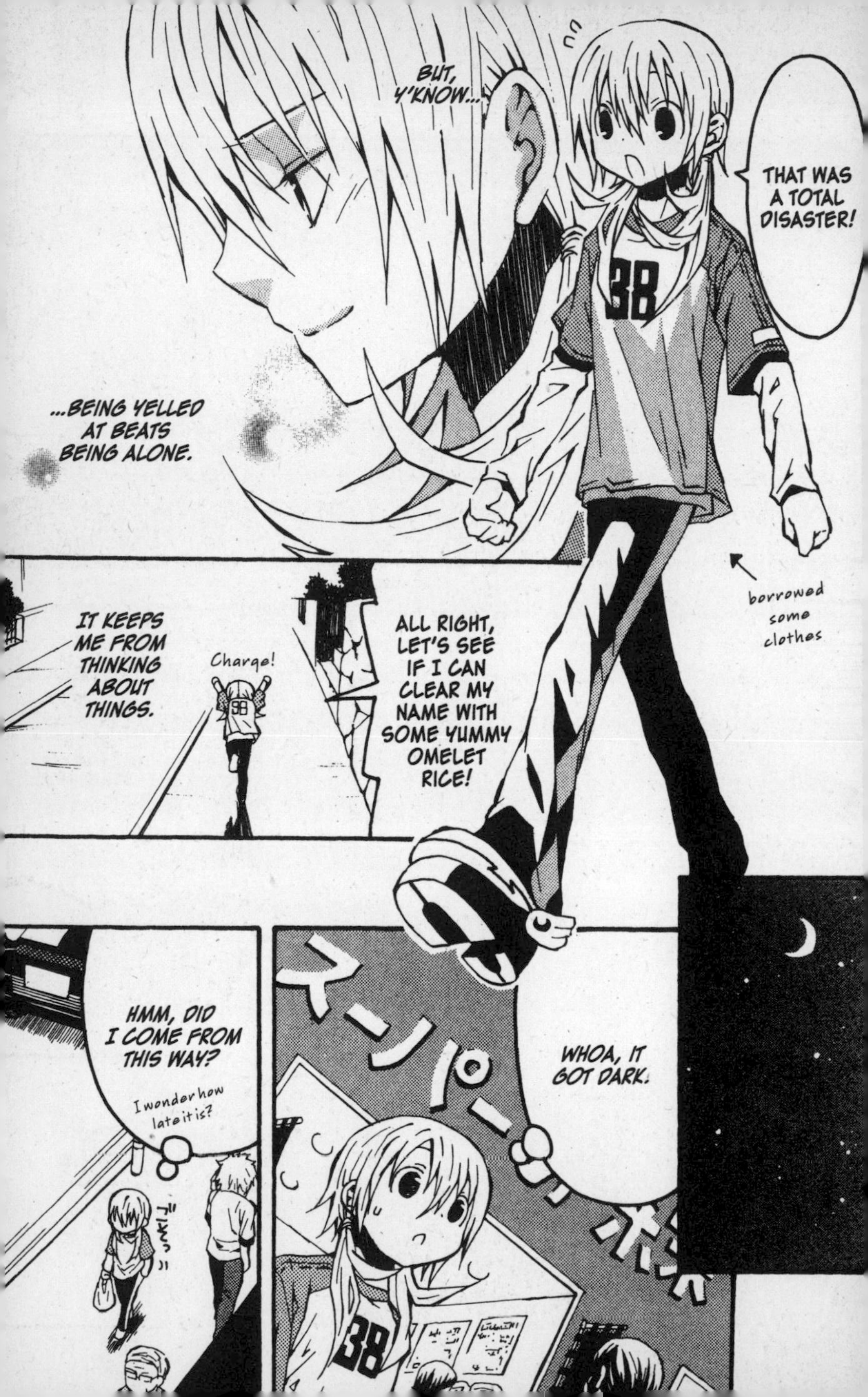
THAT WAS A TOTAL DISASTER!
BUT, Y'KNOW...
...BEING YELLED AT BEATS BEING ALONE.
borrowed some clothes
ALL RIGHT, LET'S SEE IF I CAN CLEAR MY NAME WITH SOME YUMMY OMELET RICE!
Charge!
IT KEEPS ME FROM THINKING ABOUT THINGS.
WHOA, IT GOT DARK.
HMM, DID I COME FROM THIS WAY?
I wonder how late it is?

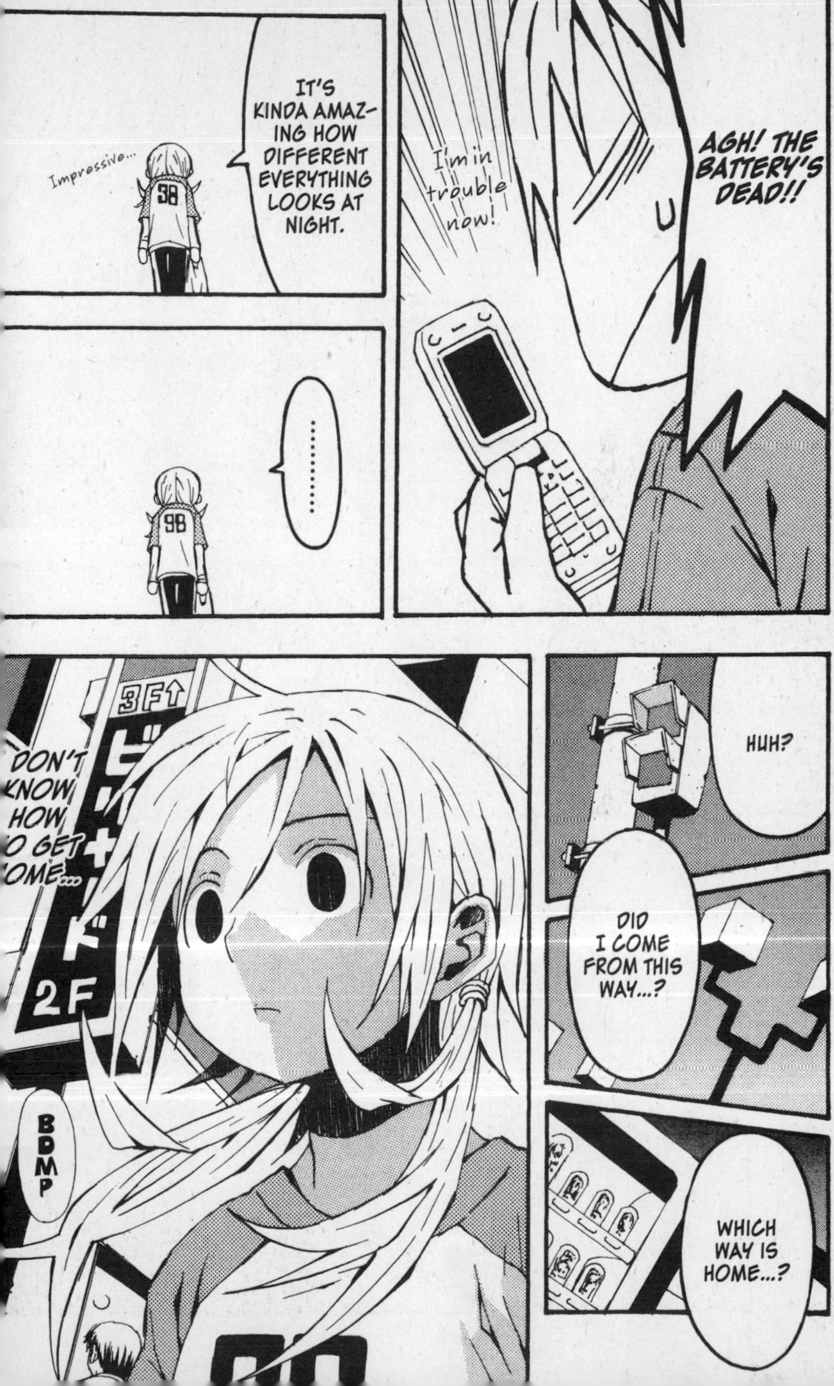
AGH! THE BATTERY'S DEAD!!
I'm in trouble now!
IT'S KINDA AMAZING HOW DIFFERENT EVERYTHING LOOKS AT NIGHT.
Impressive...
......
HUH?
DID I COME FROM THIS WAY...?
WHICH WAY IS HOME...?
3F↑
DON'T KNOW HOW O GET OME...
2F
BDMP

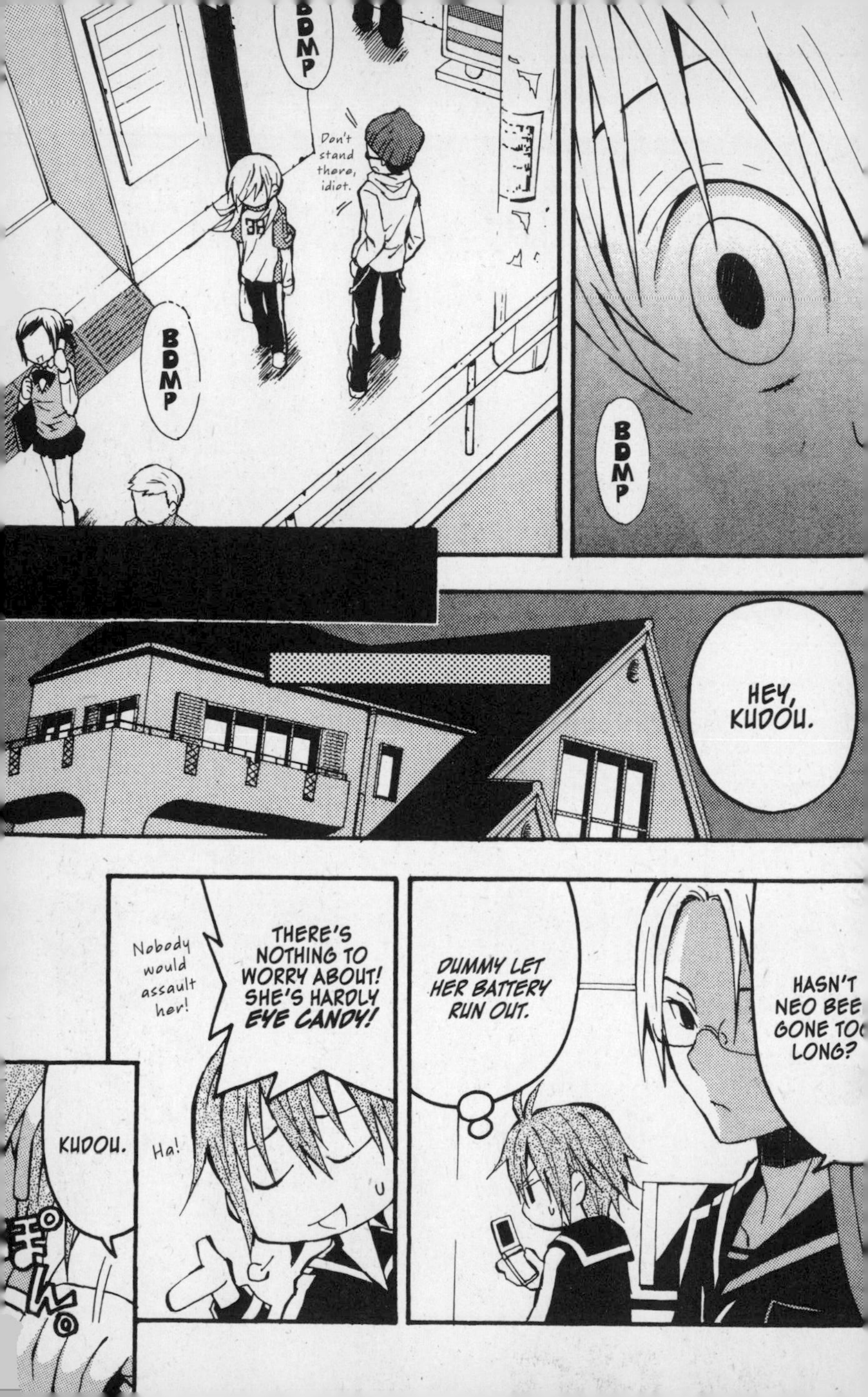

BDMP
BDMP
Don't stand there, idiot.
BDMP
HEY, KUDOU.
HASN'T NEO BEE GONE TO LONG?
DUMMY LET HER BATTERY RUN OUT.
THERE'S NOTHING TO WORRY ABOUT! SHE'S HARDLY EYE CANDY!
Nobody would assault her!
Ha!
KUDOU.
ぽん。

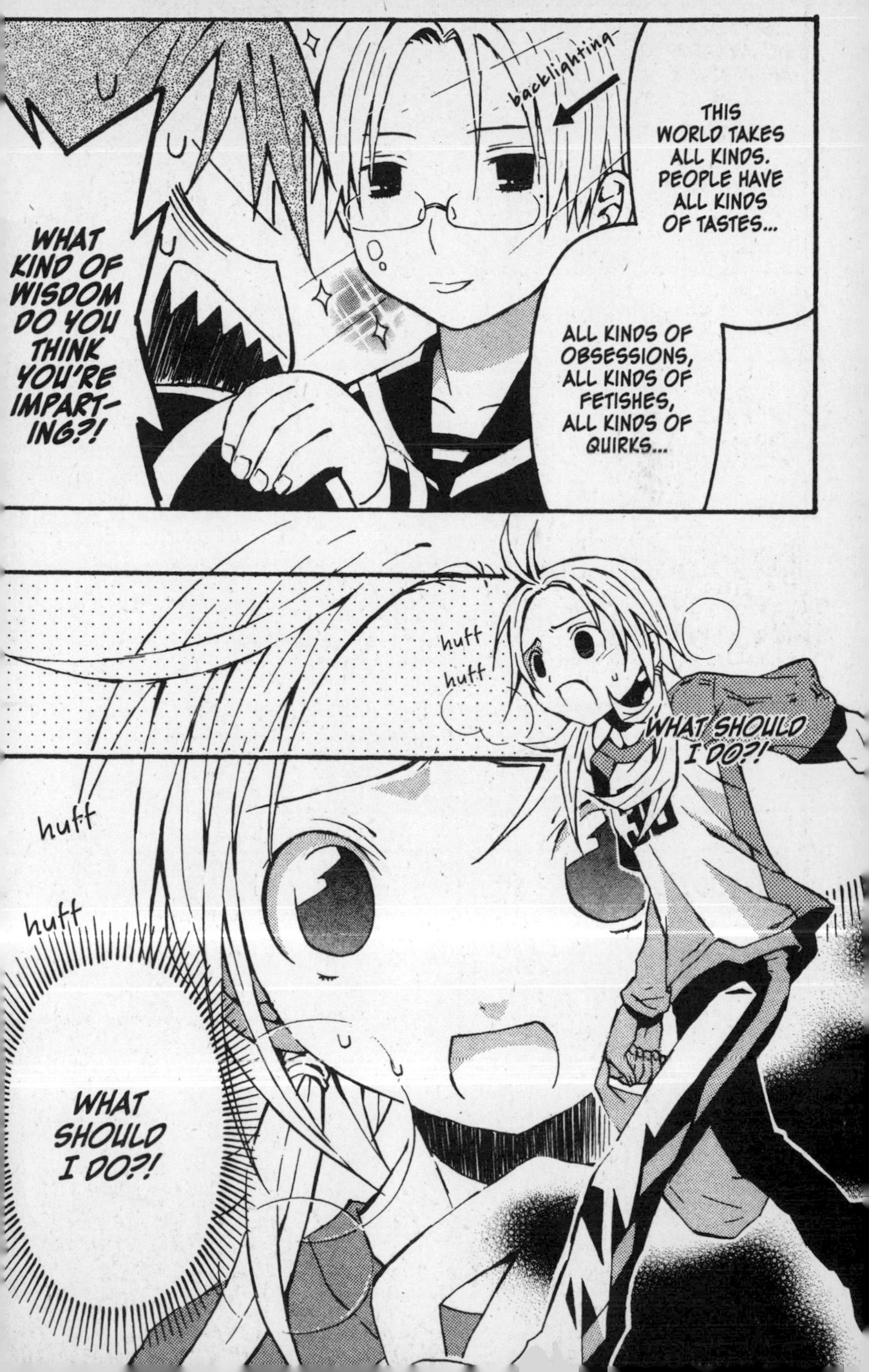
backlighting
THIS WORLD TAKES ALL KINDS. PEOPLE HAVE ALL KINDS OF TASTES...
ALL KINDS OF OBSESSIONS, ALL KINDS OF FETISHES, ALL KINDS OF QUIRKS...
WHAT KIND OF WISDOM DO YOU THINK YOU'RE IMPARTING?!
huff
huff
WHAT SHOULD I DO?!
huff
huff
WHAT SHOULD I DO?!

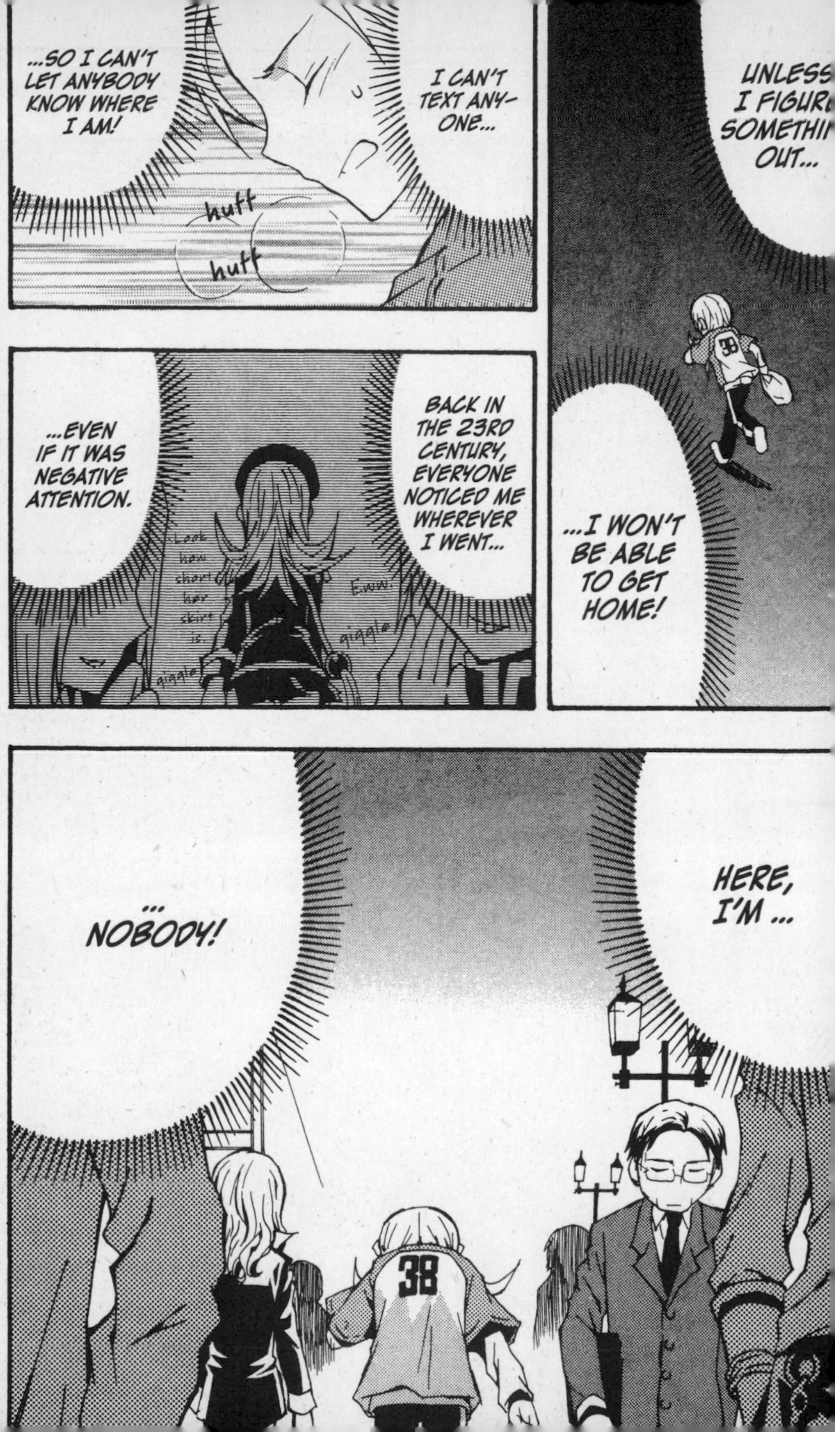
UNLESS I FIGUR SOMETHI OUT...
...I WON'T BE ABLE TO GET HOME!
I CAN'T TEXT ANY-ONE...
...SO I CAN'T LET ANYBODY KNOW WHERE I AM!
huff
huff
BACK IN THE 23RD CENTURY, EVERYONE NOTICED ME WHEREVER I WENT...
...EVEN IF IT WAS NEGATIVE ATTENTION.
Eww.
giggle
Look how short her skirt is.
giggle
HERE, I'M ...
... NOBODY!

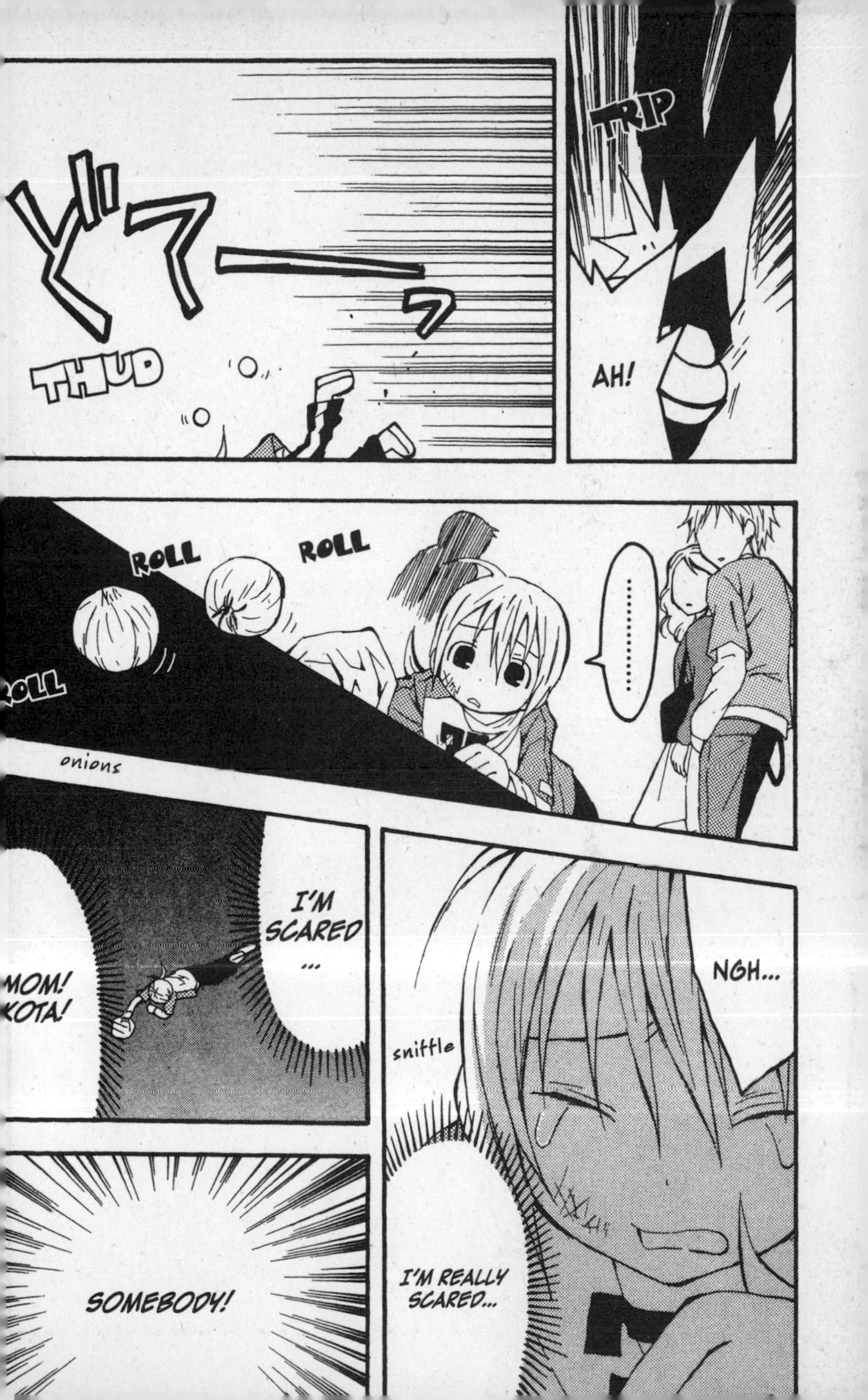
TRIP
AH!
ドバァーーッ
THUD
......
ROLL
ROLL
ROLL
onions
NGH...
snifflle
I'M REALLY SCARED...
I'M SCARED ...
MOM! KOTA!
SOMEBODY!

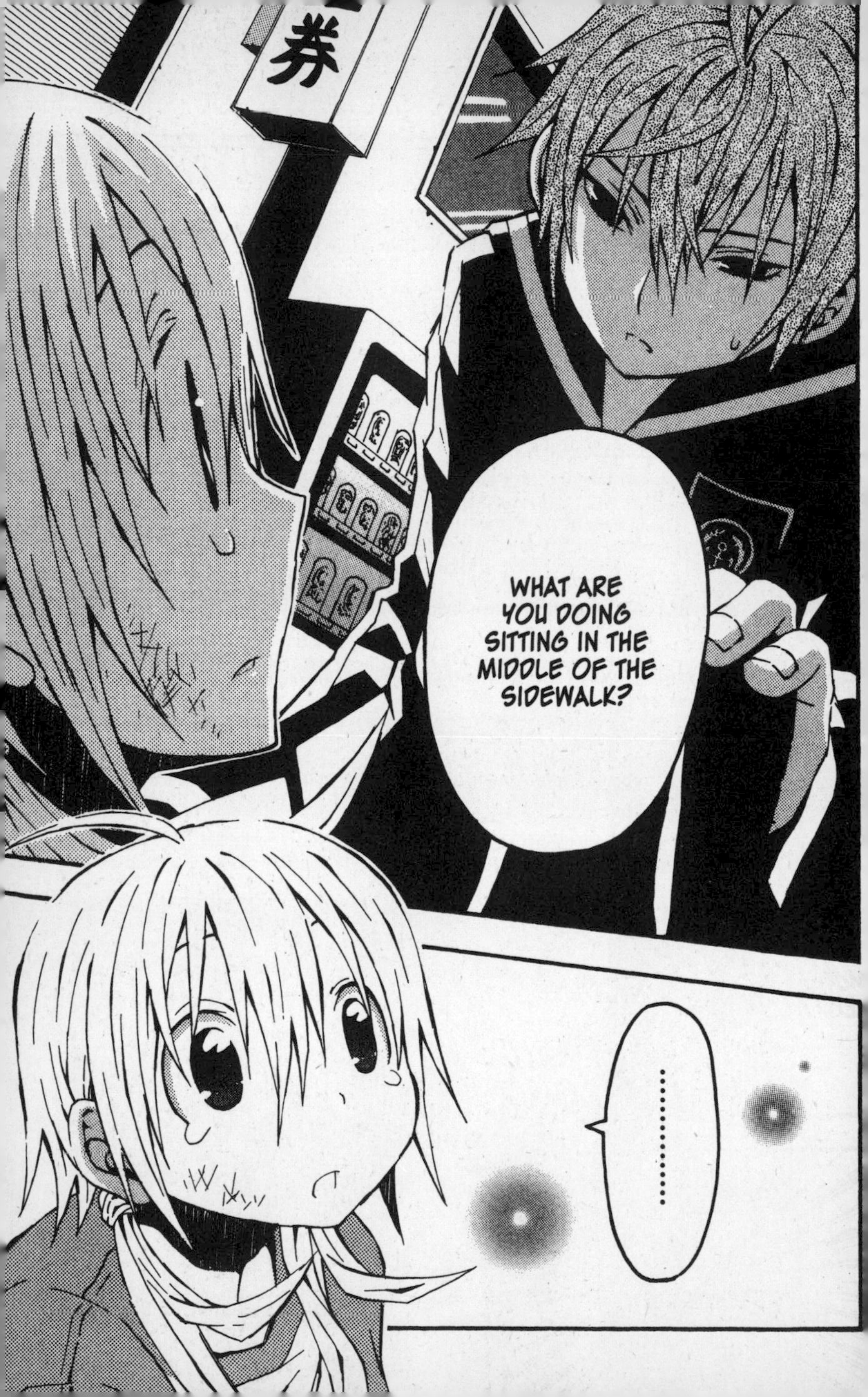

券
WHAT ARE YOU DOING SITTING IN THE MIDDLE OF THE SIDEWALK?
......

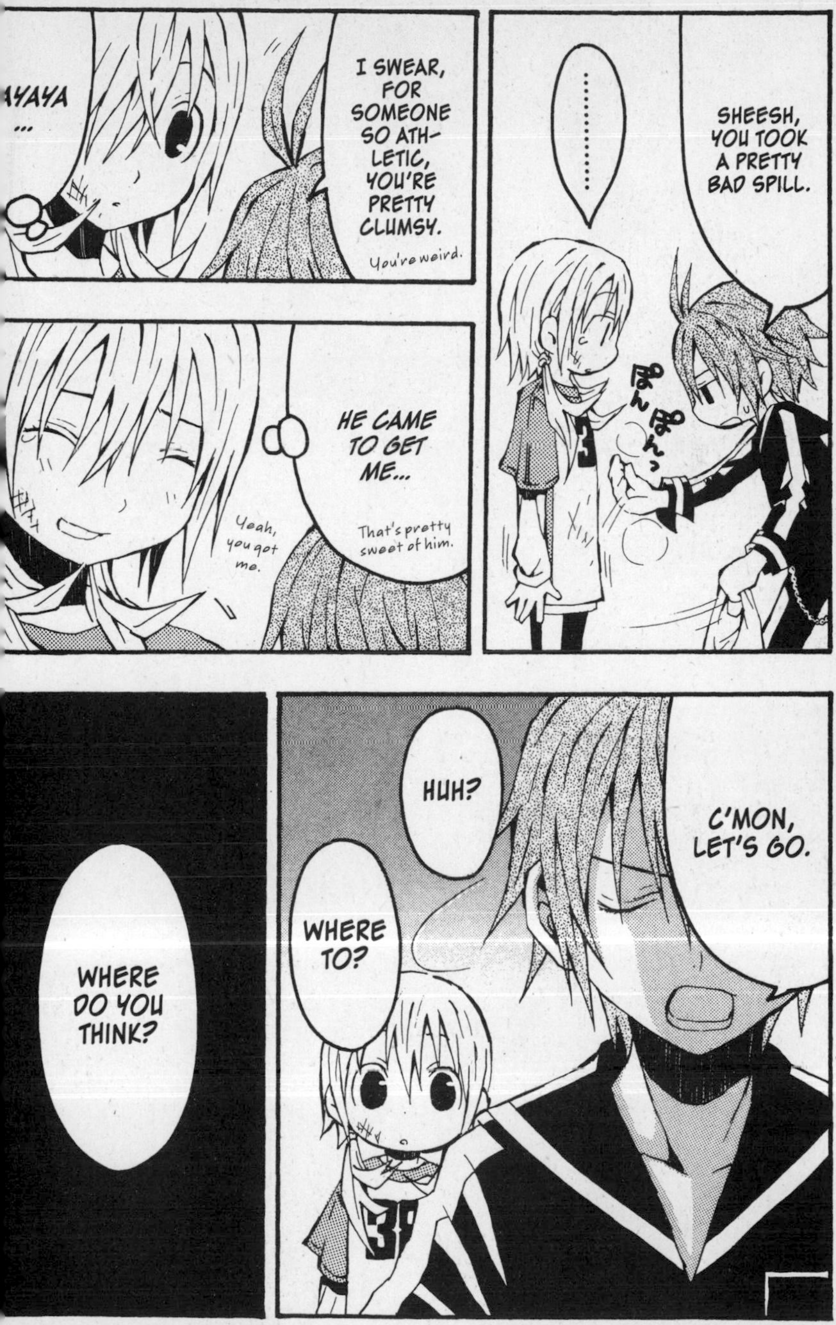
SHEESH, YOU TOOK A PRETTY BAD SPILL.
......
ぽん ぽんっ
I SWEAR, FOR SOMEONE SO ATH-LETIC, YOU'RE PRETTY CLUMSY.
AYAYA ...
You're weird.
HE CAME TO GET ME...
That's pretty sweet of him.
Yeah, you got me.
C'MON, LET'S GO.
HUH?
WHERE TO?
WHERE DO YOU THINK?

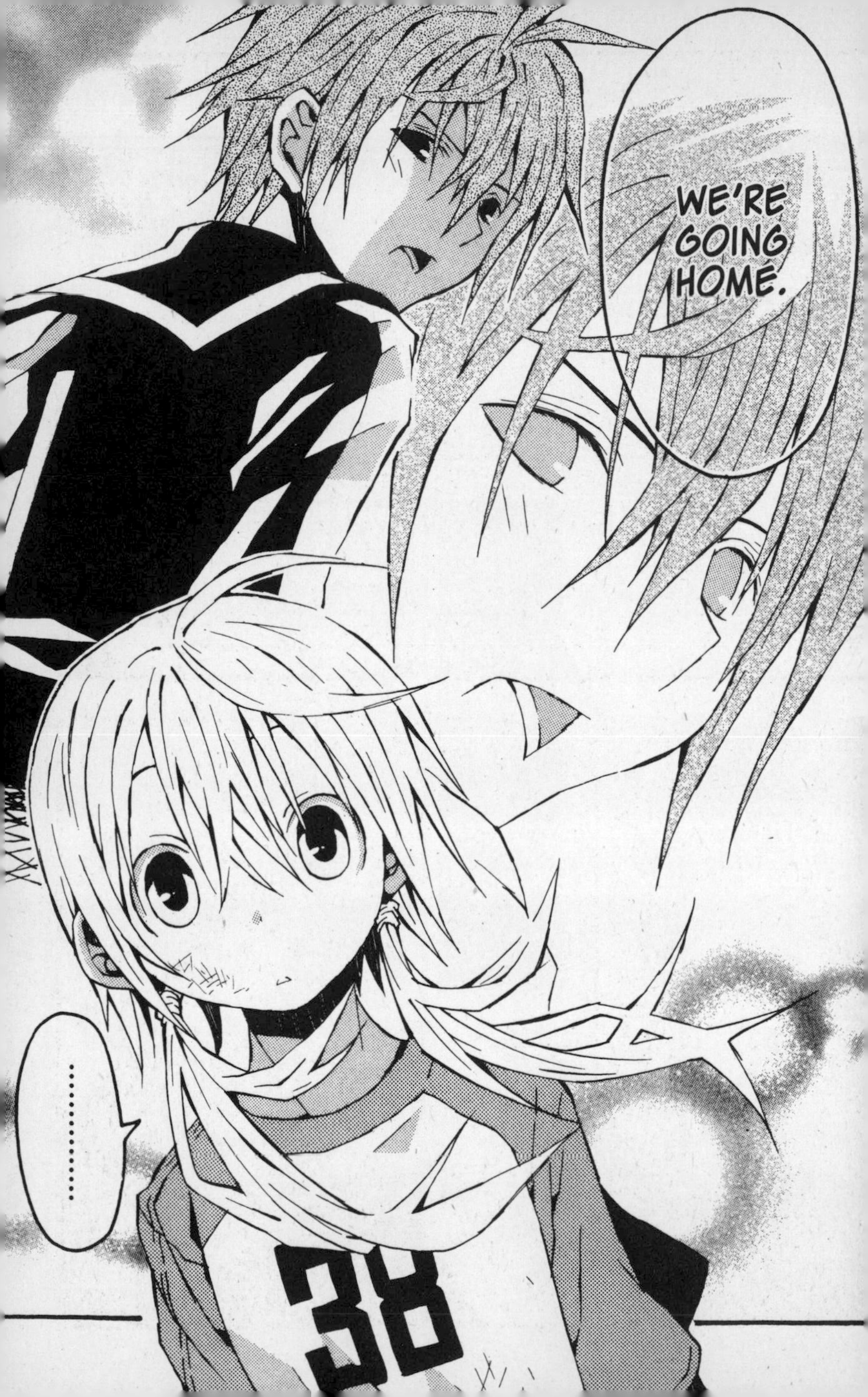
WE'RE GOING HOME.
......

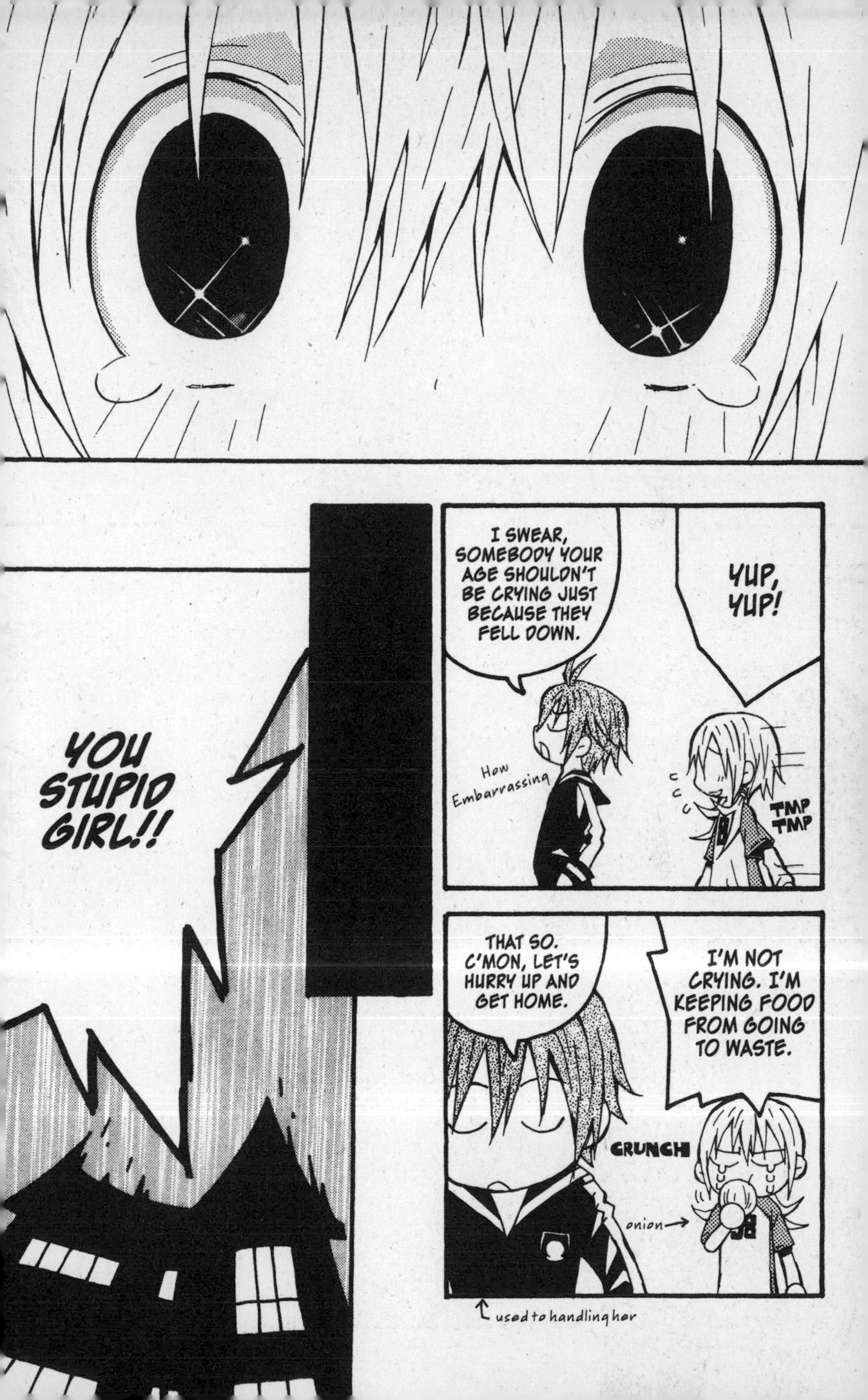
I SWEAR, SOMEBODY YOUR AGE SHOULDN'T BE CRYING JUST BECAUSE THEY FELL DOWN.
YUP, YUP!
TMP TMP
How Embarrassing
I'M NOT CRYING. I'M KEEPING FOOD FROM GOING TO WASTE.
THAT SO. C'MON, LET'S HURRY UP AND GET HOME.
CRUNCH
onion
used to handling her
YOU STUPID GIRL!!

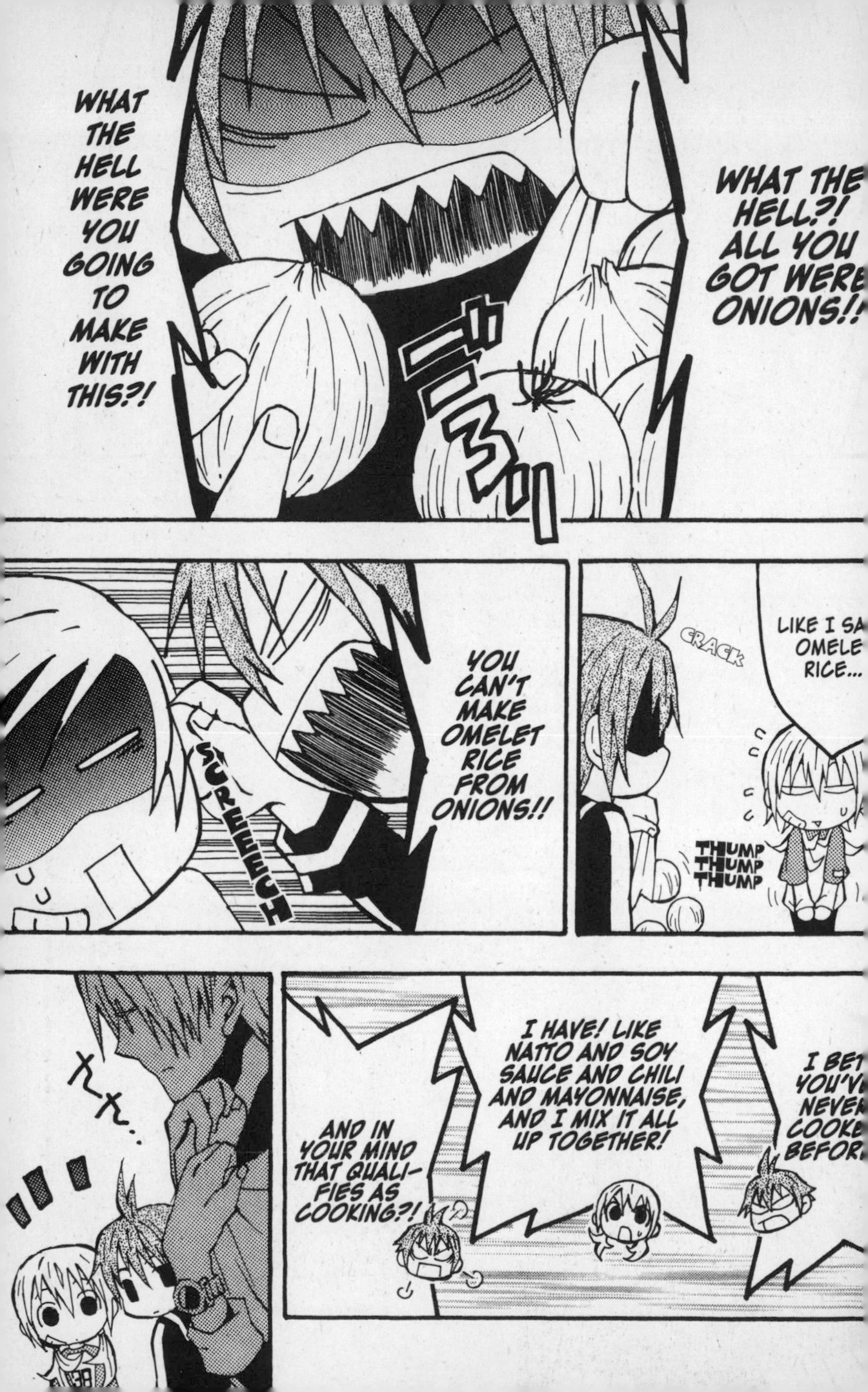
WHAT THE HELL?! ALL YOU GOT WERE ONIONS!!
WHAT THE HELL WERE YOU GOING TO MAKE WITH THIS?!
LIKE I SA OMELE RICE...
CRACK
THUMP THUMP THUMP
YOU CAN'T MAKE OMELET RICE FROM ONIONS!!
SCREEEECH
I BET YOU'V NEVER COOKE BEFOR
I HAVE! LIKE NATTO AND SOY SAUCE AND CHILI AND MAYONNAISE, AND I MIX IT ALL UP TOGETHER!
AND IN YOUR MIND THAT QUALI-FIES AS COOKING?!

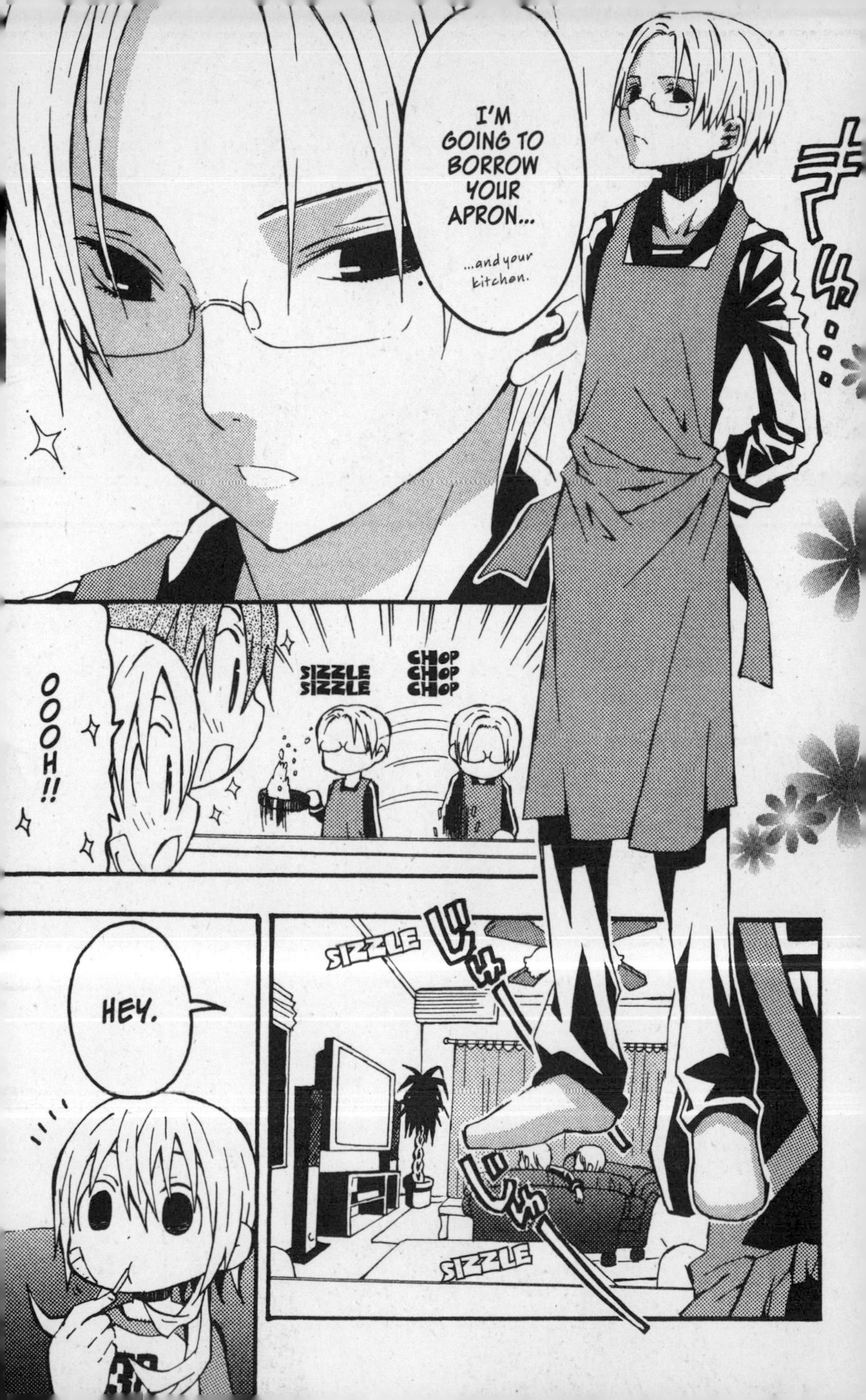
I'M GOING TO BORROW YOUR APRON...
...and your kitchen.
SIZZLE SIZZLE
CHOP CHOP CHOP
OOOOH!!
SIZZLE
SIZZLE
HEY.

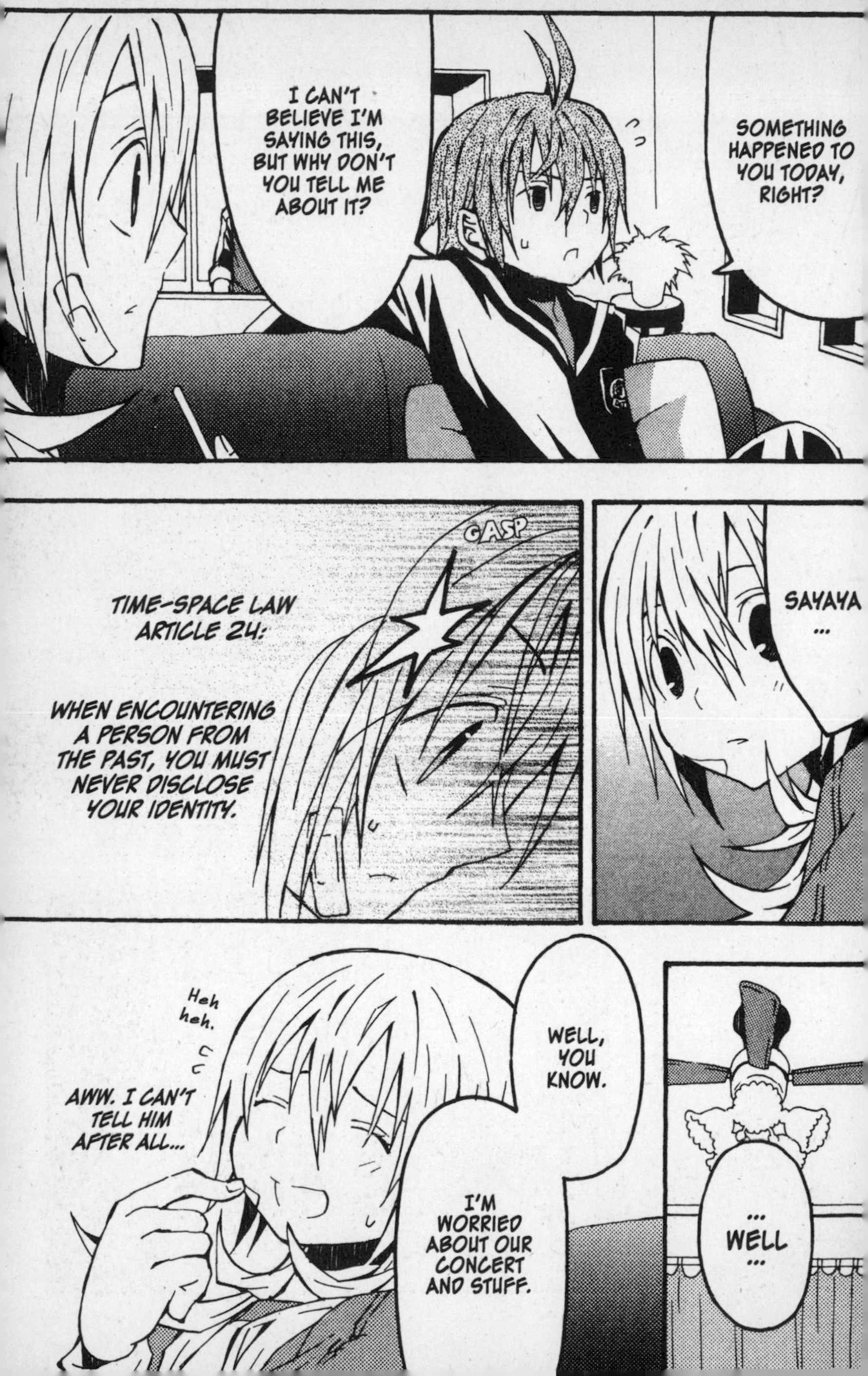
SOMETHING HAPPENED TO YOU TODAY, RIGHT?
I CAN'T BELIEVE I'M SAYING THIS, BUT WHY DON'T YOU TELL ME ABOUT IT?
SAYAYA ...
GASP
TIME-SPACE LAW ARTICLE 24:
WHEN ENCOUNTERING A PERSON FROM THE PAST, YOU MUST NEVER DISCLOSE YOUR IDENTITY.
... WELL ...
WELL, YOU KNOW.
I'M WORRIED ABOUT OUR CONCERT AND STUFF.
Heh heh.
AWW. I CAN'T TELL HIM AFTER ALL...

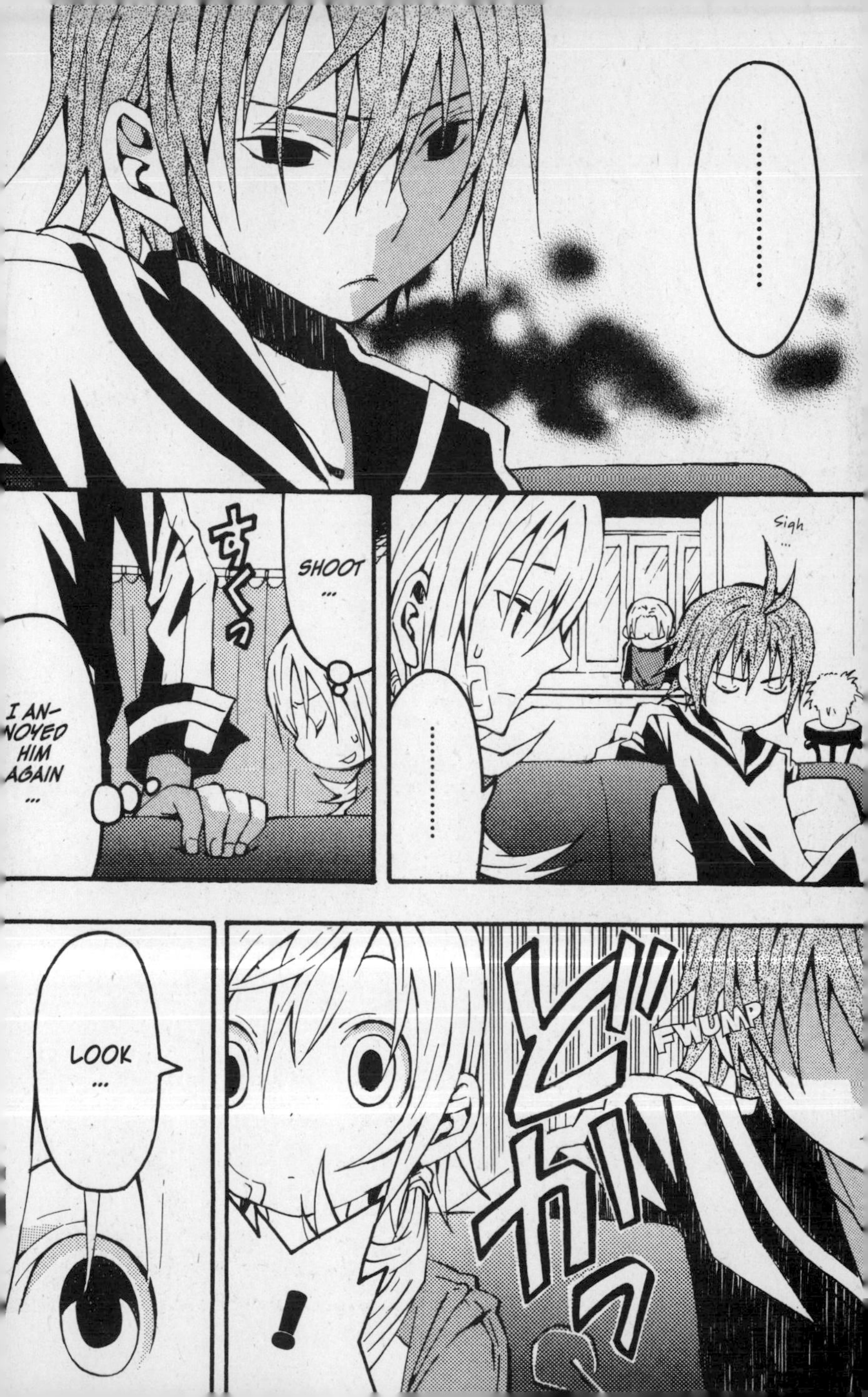
......
Sigh ...
......
すくっ
SHOOT ...
I AN-NOYED HIM AGAIN ...
どがっ
FWUMP
!
LOOK ...

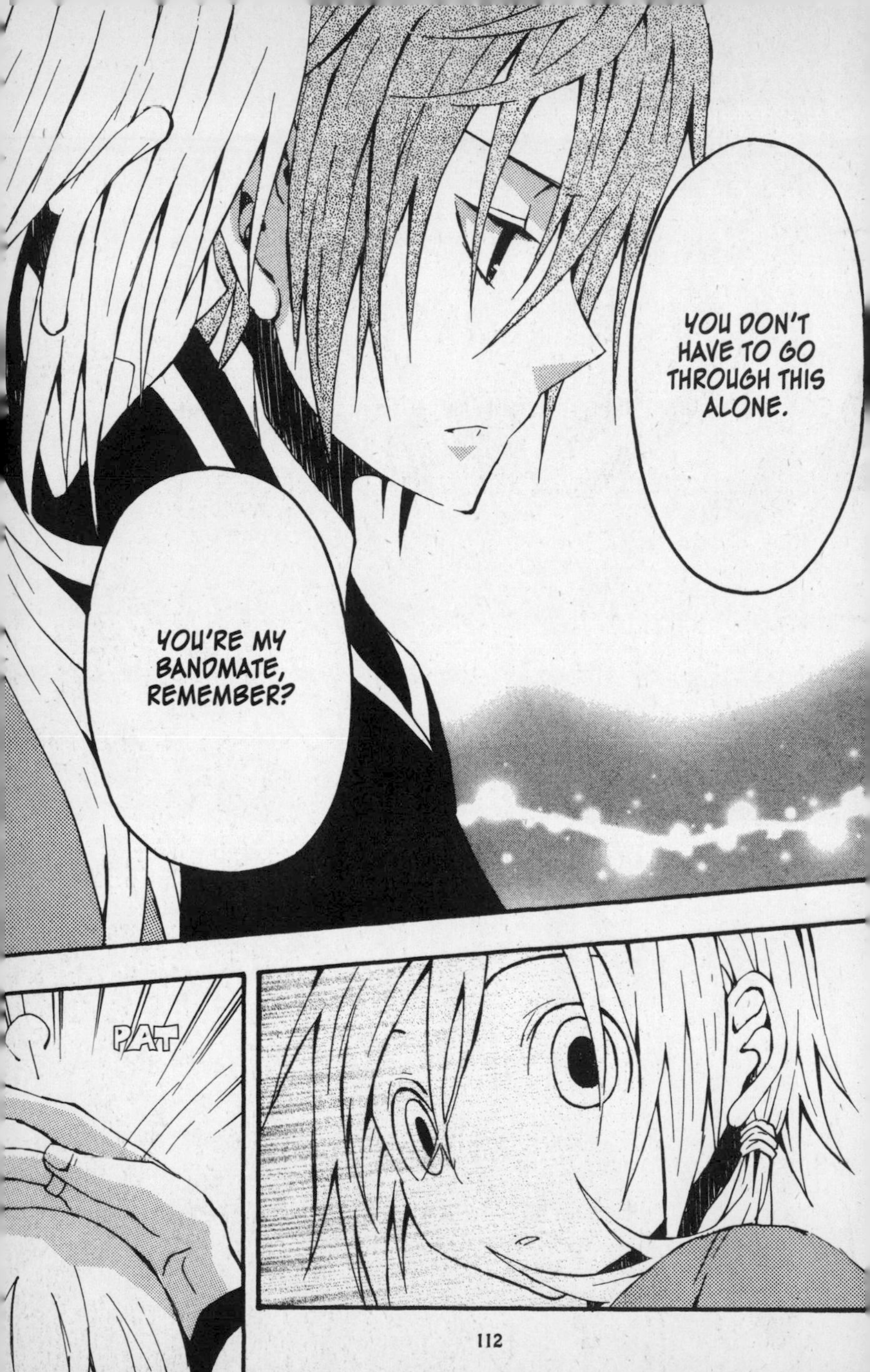
YOU DON'T HAVE TO GO THROUGH THIS ALONE.
YOU'RE MY BANDMATE, REMEMBER?
PAT

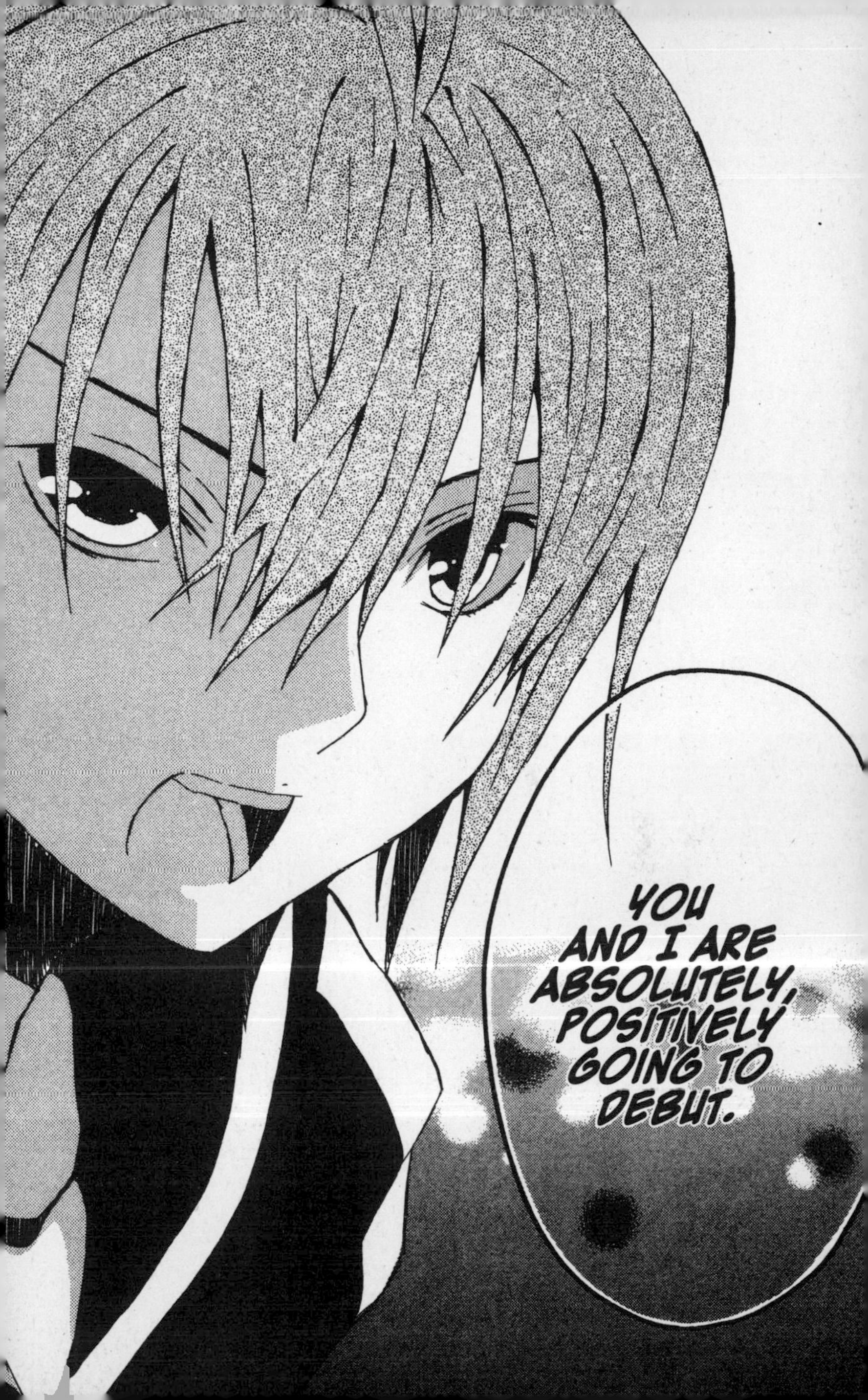
YOU AND I ARE ABSOLUTELY, POSITIVELY GOING TO DEBUT.

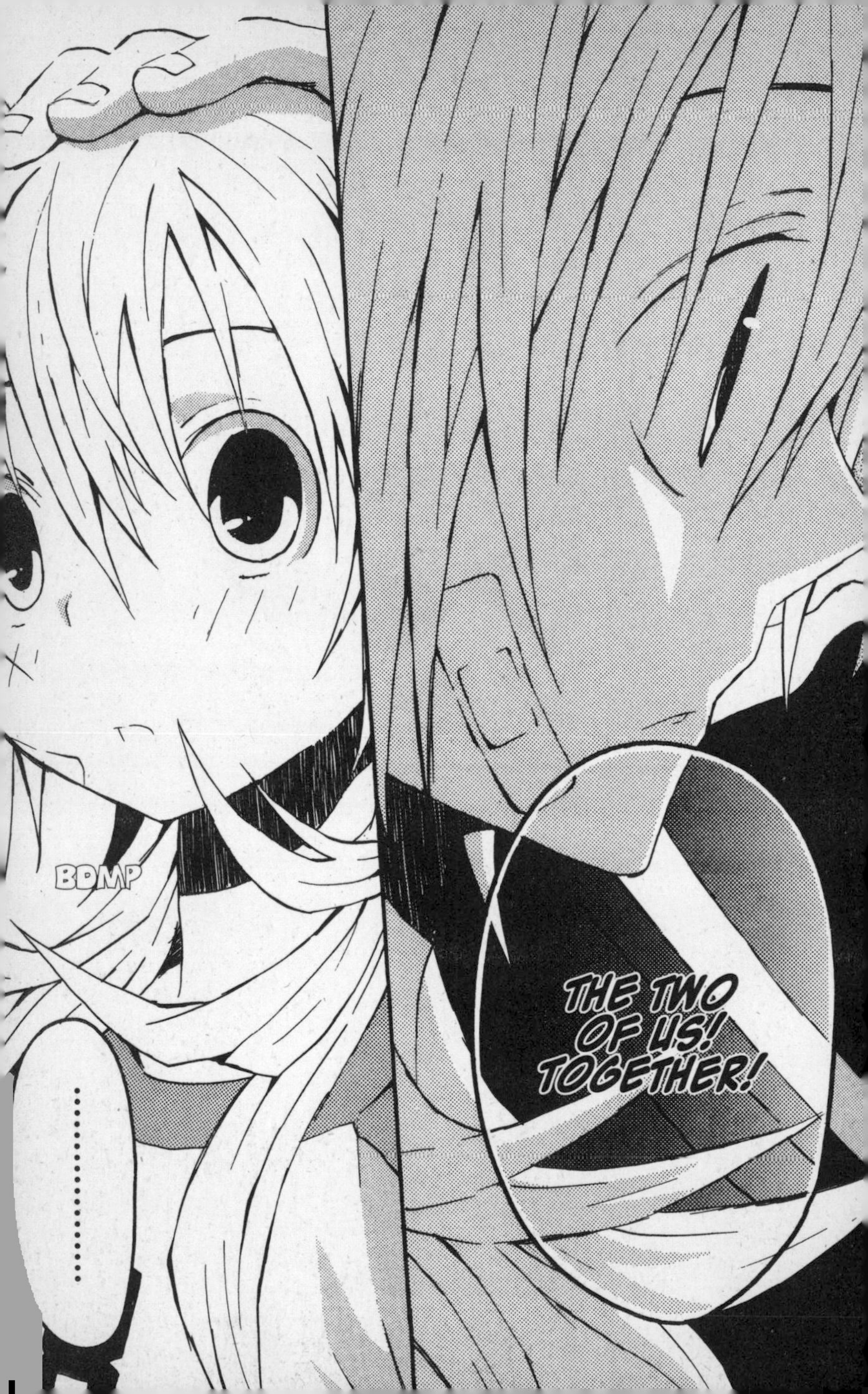
THE TWO OF US! TOGETHER!
BDMP
....

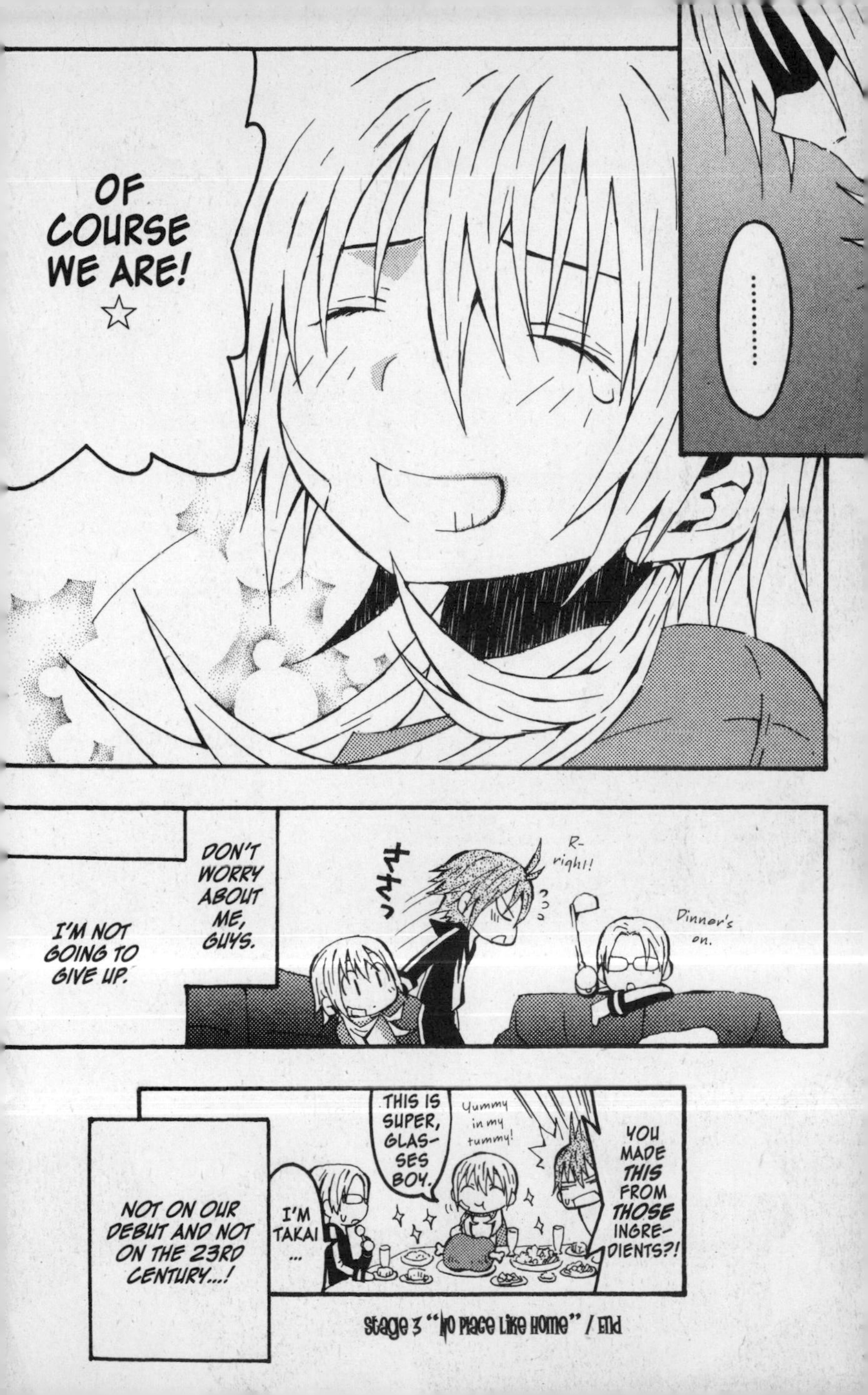
……
OF COURSE WE ARE! ☆
Dinner's on.
R-right!
DON'T WORRY ABOUT ME, GUYS.
I'M NOT GOING TO GIVE UP.
YOU MADE THIS FROM THOSE INGREDIENTS?!
Yummy in my tummy!
THIS IS SUPER, GLASSES BOY.
I'M TAKAI ...
NOT ON OUR DEBUT AND NOT ON THE 23RD CENTURY...!

Stage 3 "No Place Like Home" / End

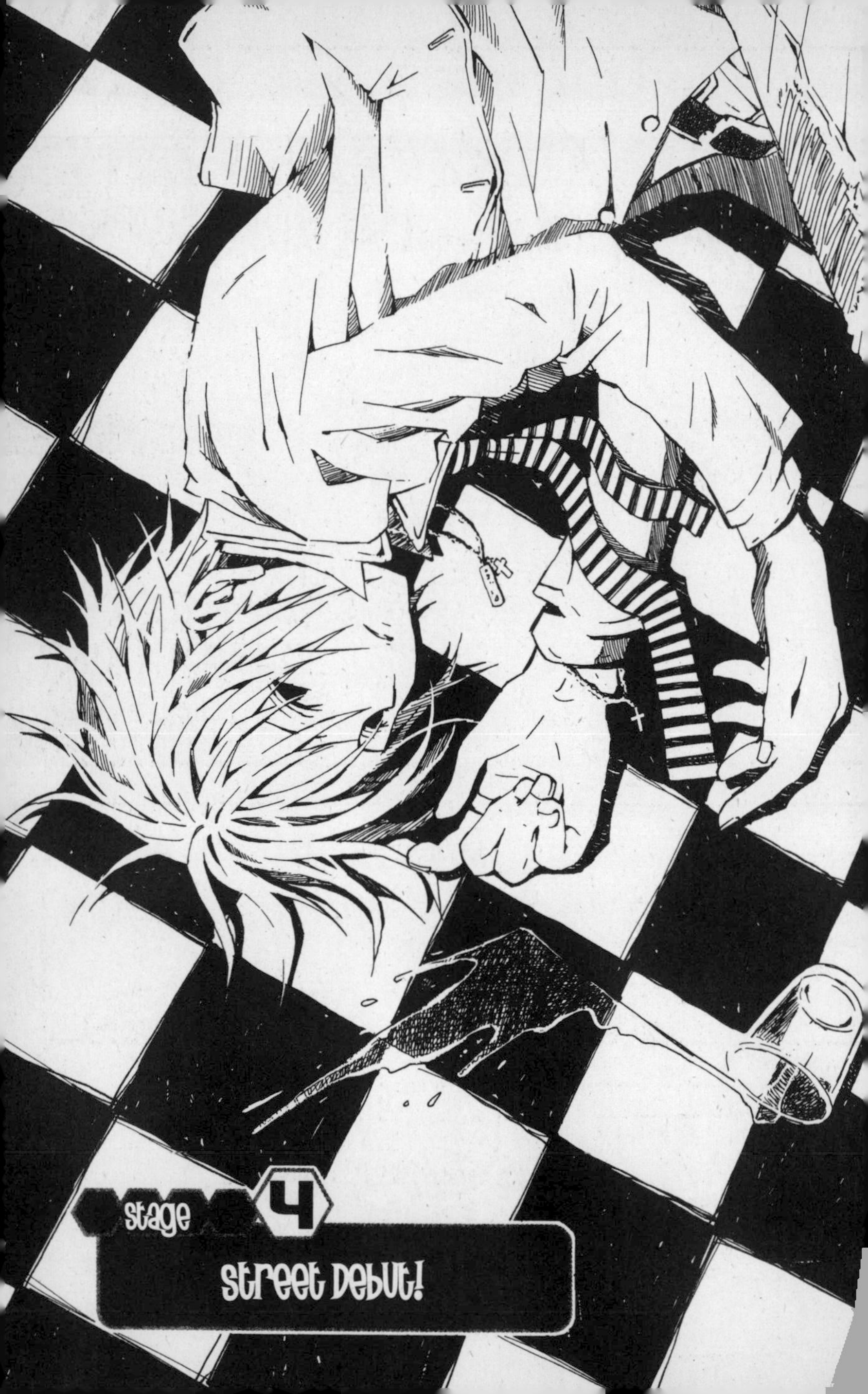
Stage 4
Street Debut!

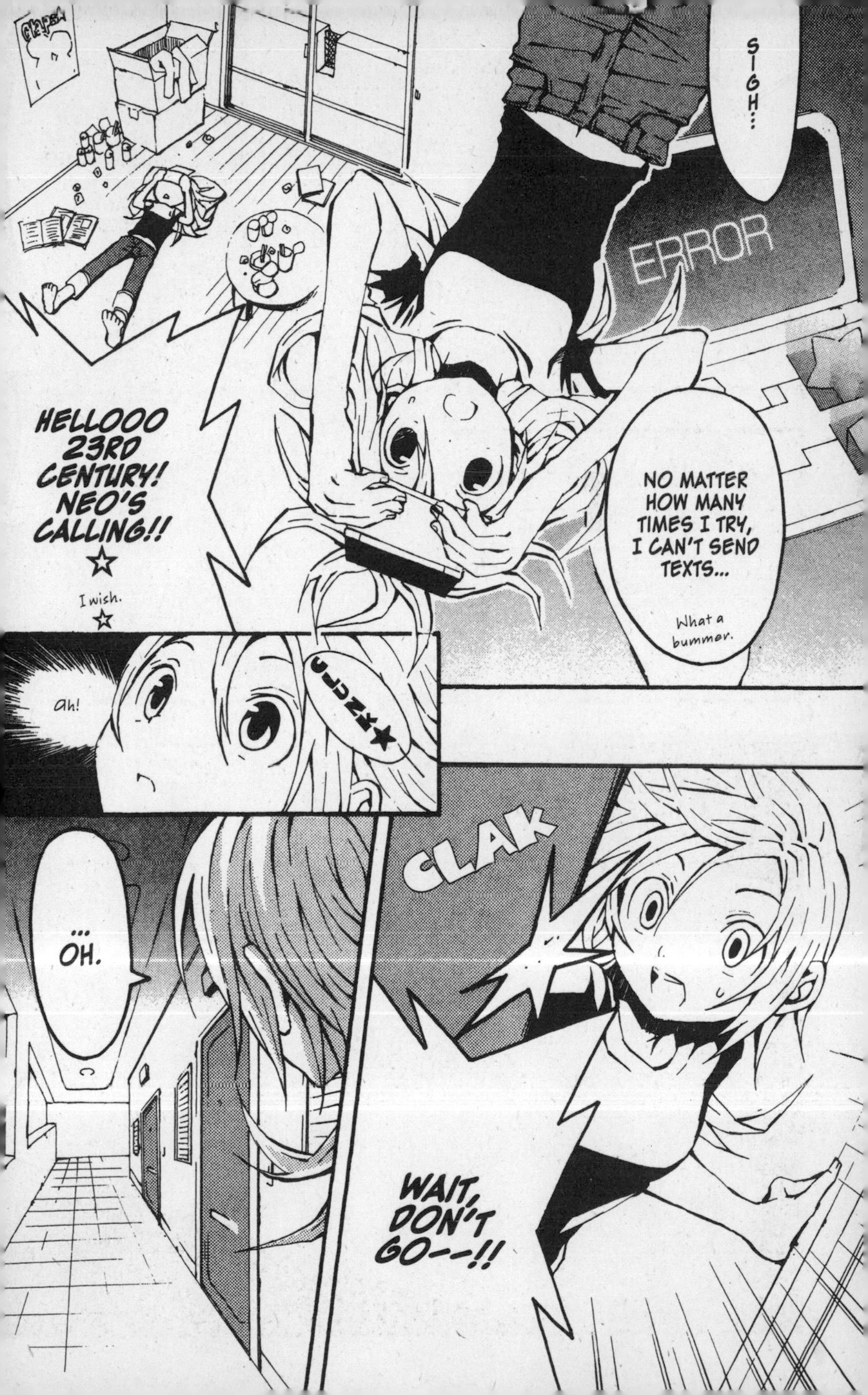
SIGH...
ERROR
NO MATTER HOW MANY TIMES I TRY, I CAN'T SEND TEXTS...
What a bummer.
HELLOOO 23RD CENTURY! NEO'S CALLING!! ☆
I wish. ☆
ah!
CLAK
...OH.
WAIT, DON'T GO--!!

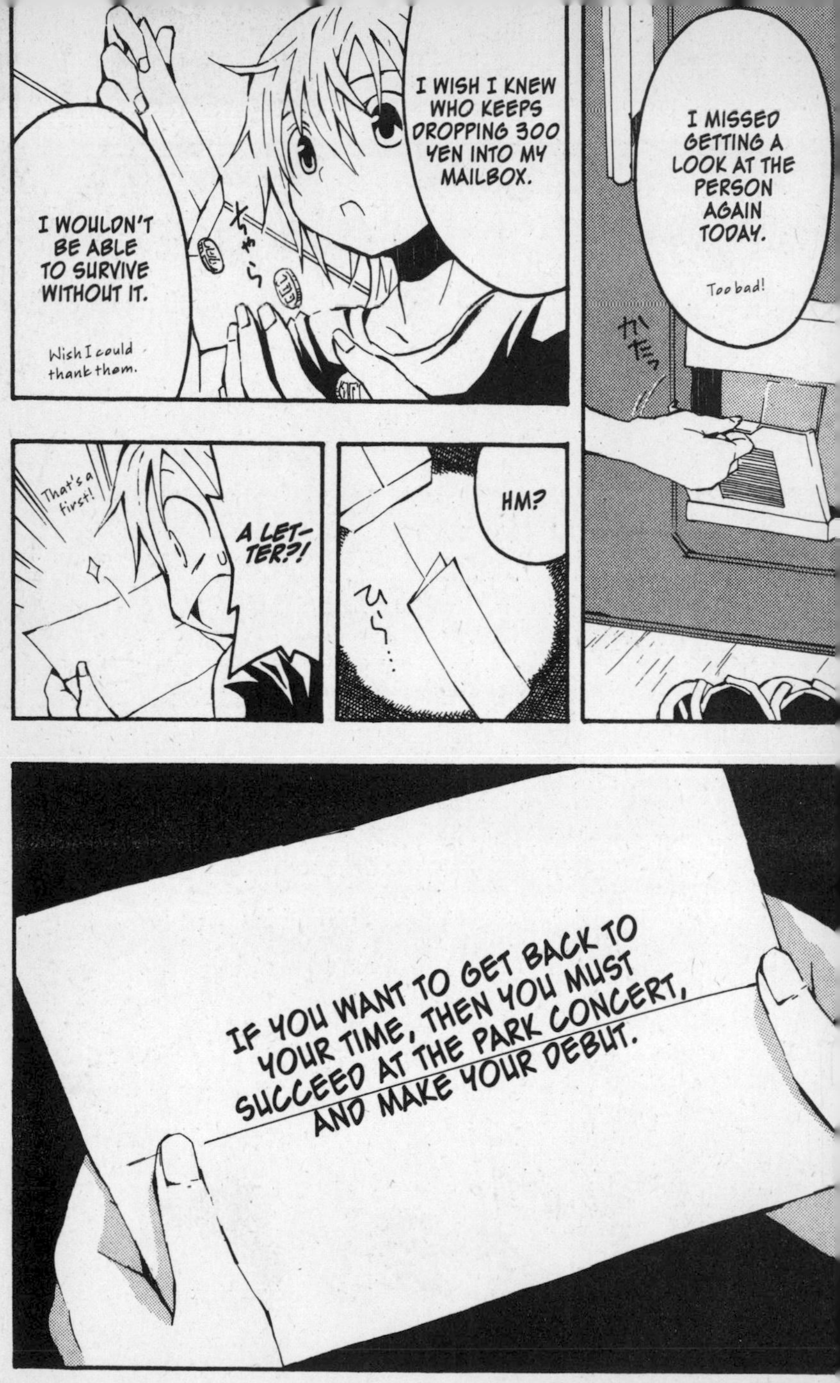
I MISSED GETTING A LOOK AT THE PERSON AGAIN TODAY.
Too bad!
I WISH I KNEW WHO KEEPS DROPPING 300 YEN INTO MY MAILBOX.
I WOULDN'T BE ABLE TO SURVIVE WITHOUT IT.
Wish I could thank them.
HM?
A LET-TER?!
That's a first!
IF YOU WANT TO GET BACK TO YOUR TIME, THEN YOU MUST SUCCEED AT THE PARK CONCERT, AND MAKE YOUR DEBUT.

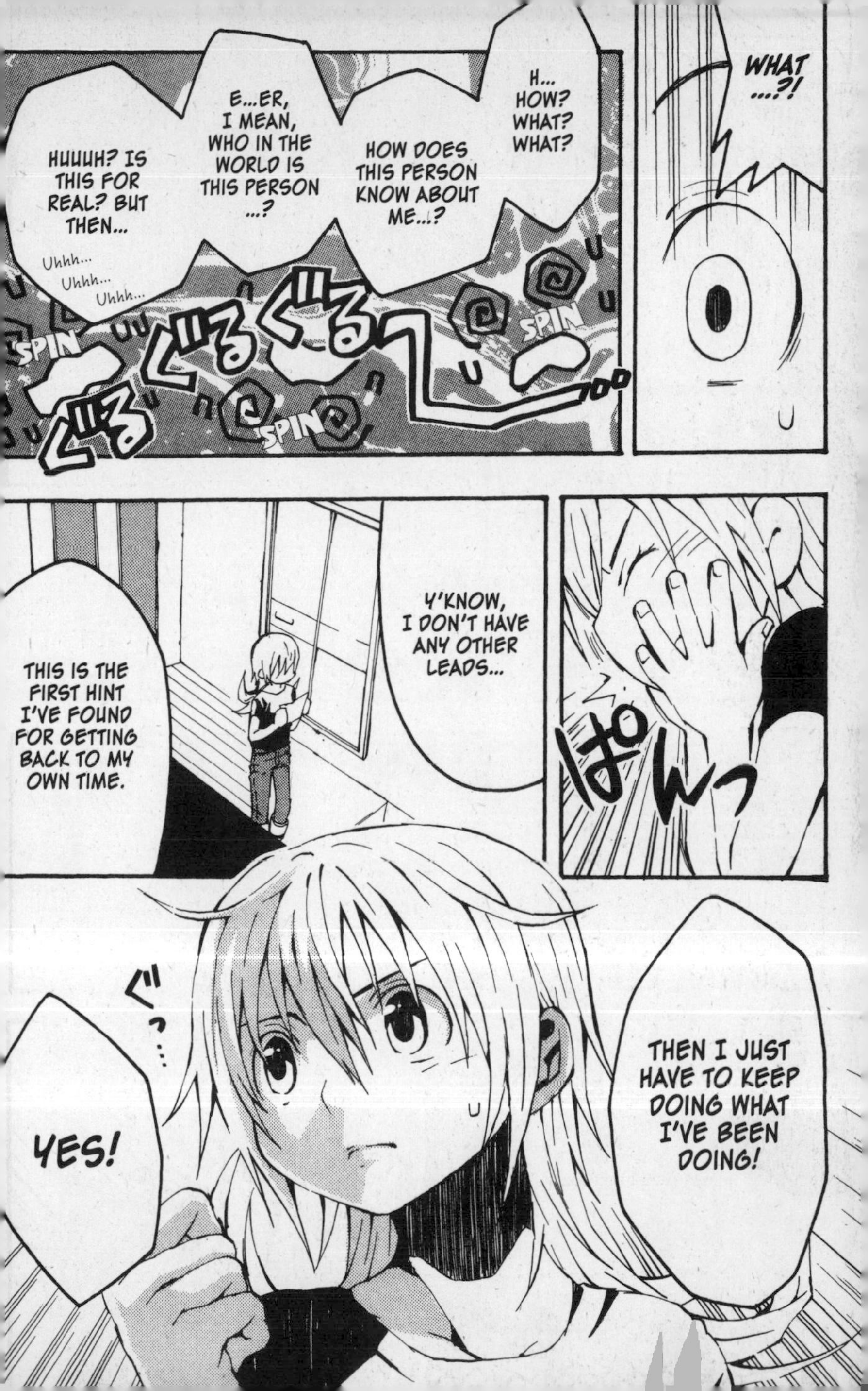
WHAT ....?!
H... HOW? WHAT? WHAT?
HOW DOES THIS PERSON KNOW ABOUT ME...?
E...ER, I MEAN, WHO IN THE WORLD IS THIS PERSON ...?
HUUUH? IS THIS FOR REAL? BUT THEN...
Uhhh... Uhhh... Uhhh...
SPIN
SPIN
SPIN
ぱんっ
Y'KNOW, I DON'T HAVE ANY OTHER LEADS...
THIS IS THE FIRST HINT I'VE FOUND FOR GETTING BACK TO MY OWN TIME.
THEN I JUST HAVE TO KEEP DOING WHAT I'VE BEEN DOING!
ぐっ…
YES!

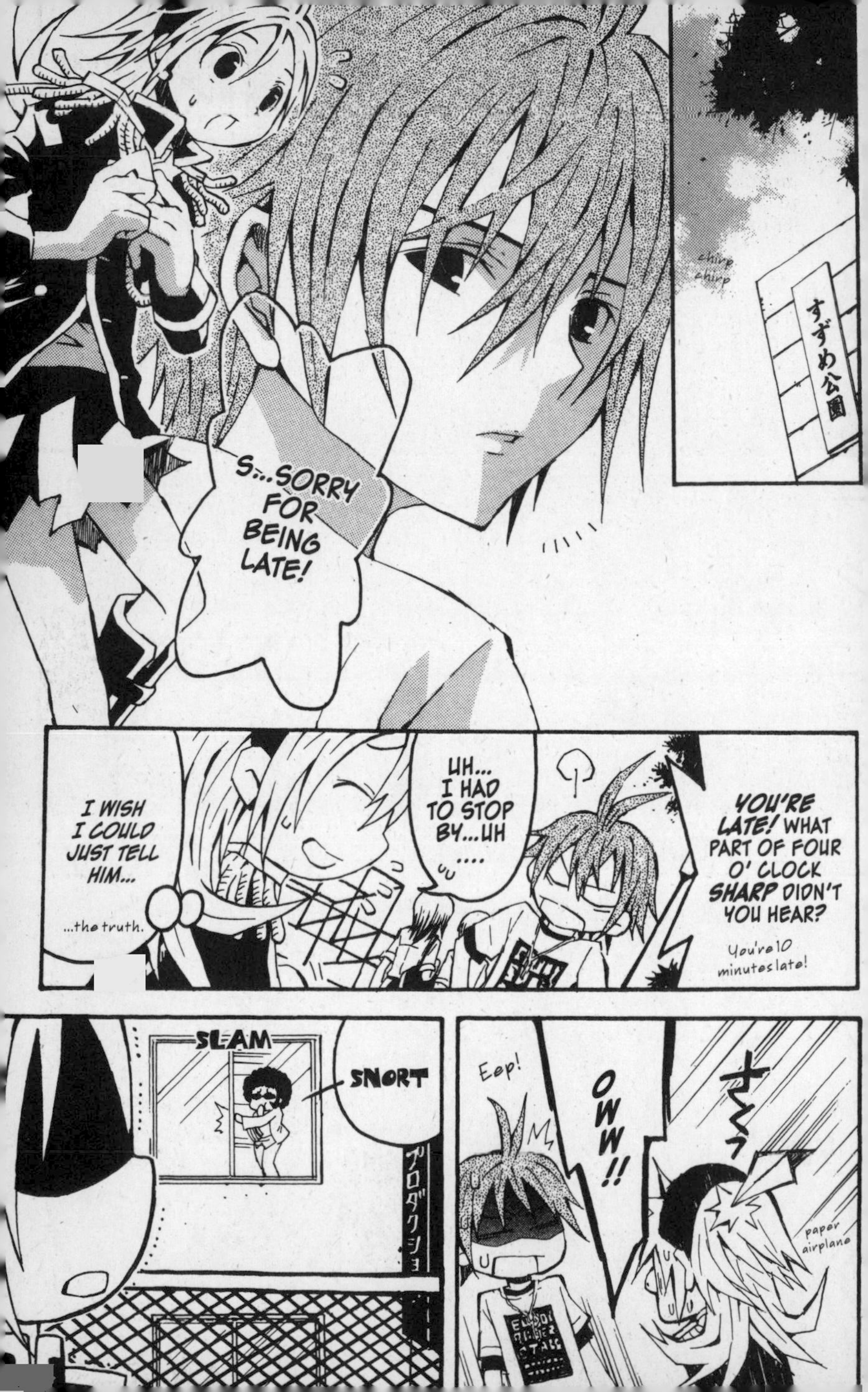

すずめ公園
chirp chirp
S...SORRY FOR BEING LATE!
YOU'RE LATE! WHAT PART OF FOUR O' CLOCK SHARP DIDN'T YOU HEAR?
You're 10 minutes late!
UH... I HAD TO STOP BY...UH ....
I WISH I COULD JUST TELL HIM...
...the truth.
paper airplane
OWW!!
Eep!
SNORT
SLAM
プロダクショ

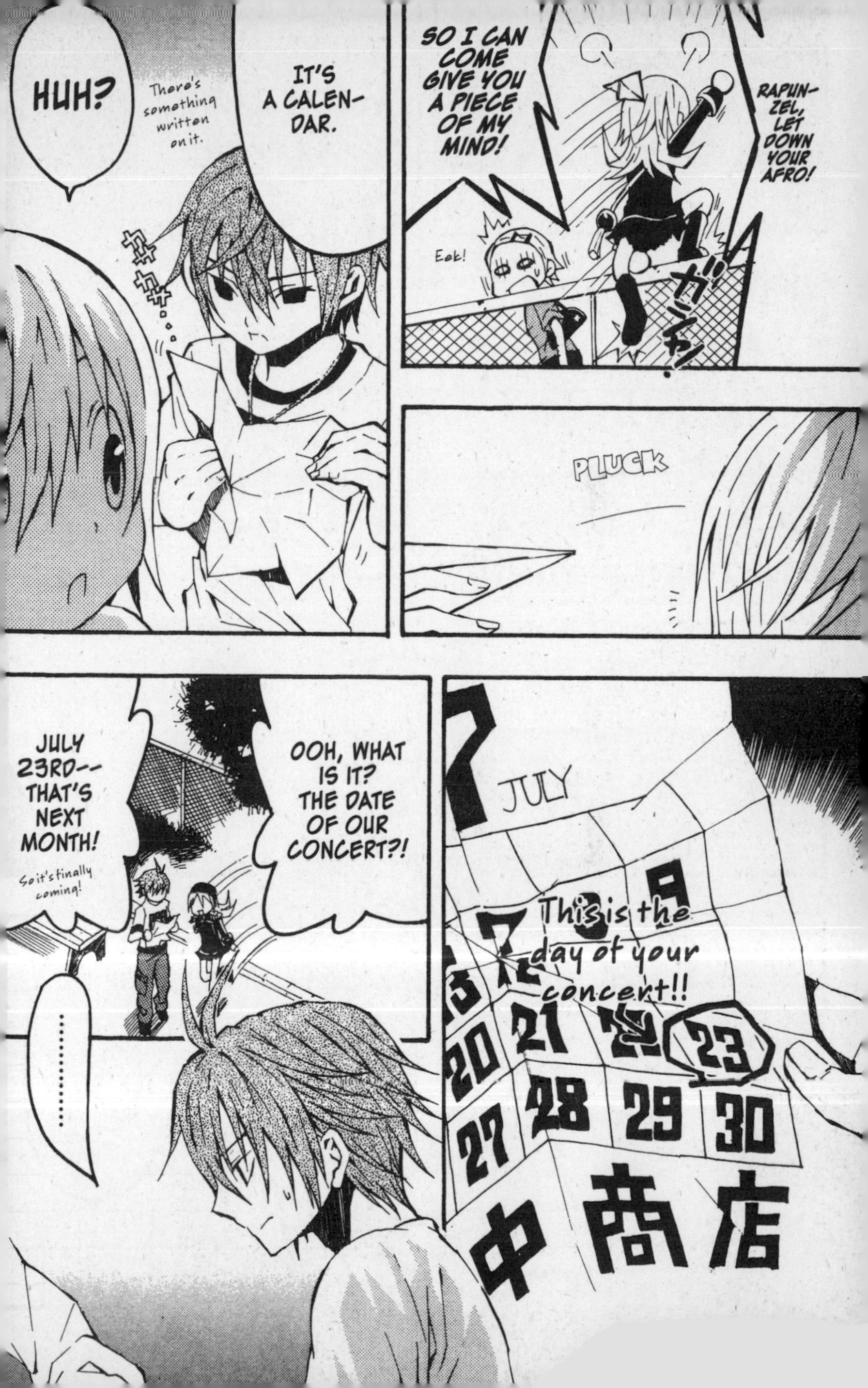
RAPUNZEL, LET DOWN YOUR AFRO!
SO I CAN COME GIVE YOU A PIECE OF MY MIND!
Eek!
PLUCK
IT'S A CALEN-DAR.
There's something written on it.
HUH?
JULY
This is the day of your concert!!
20 21 22 23
27 28 29 30
中商店
OOH, WHAT IS IT? THE DATE OF OUR CONCERT?!
JULY 23RD--THAT'S NEXT MONTH!
So it's finally coming!
......

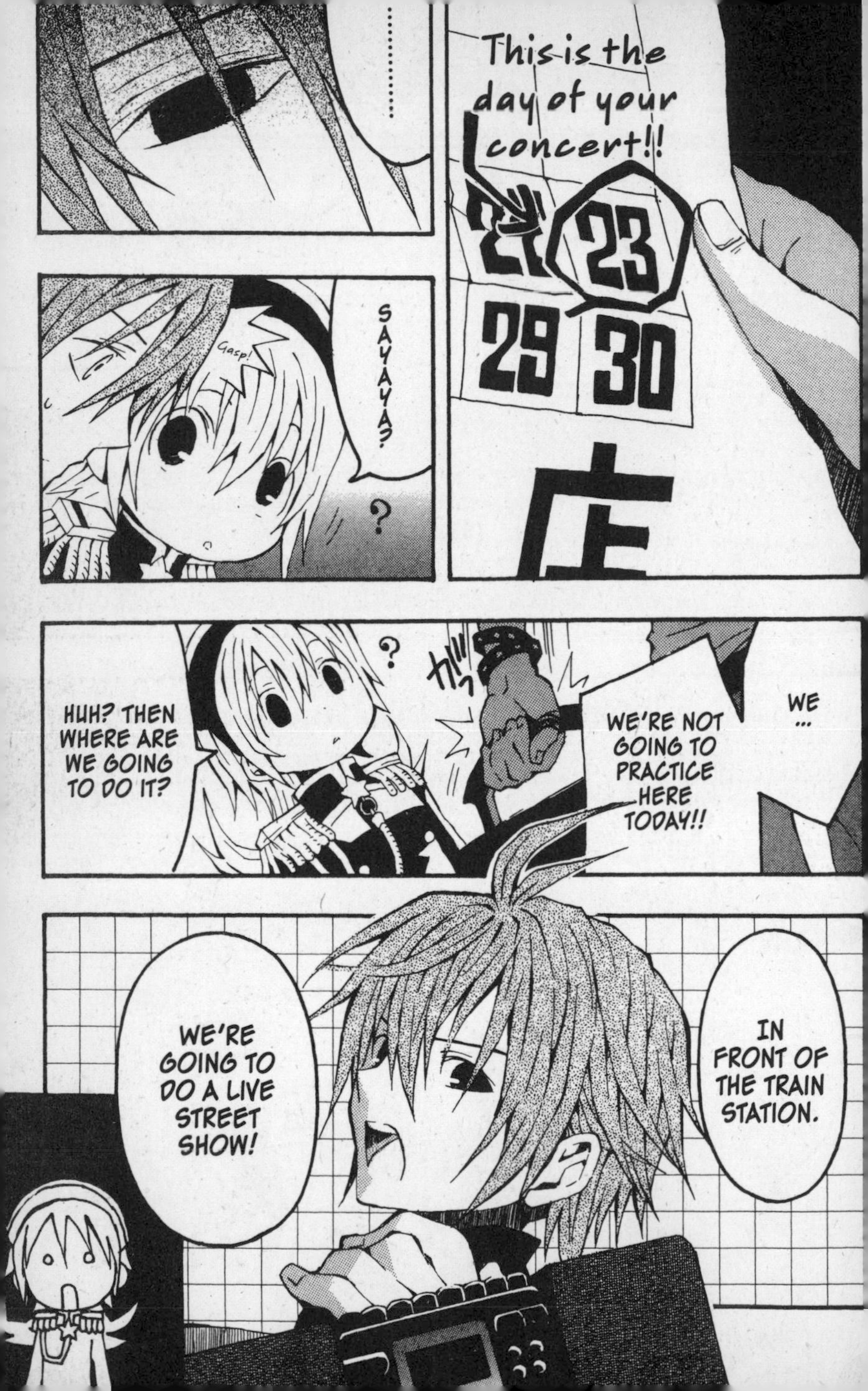
This is the day of your concert!!
23
29
30
......
SAYAYA?
Gasp!
?
WE ...
WE'RE NOT GOING TO PRACTICE HERE TODAY!!
HUH? THEN WHERE ARE WE GOING TO DO IT?
?
IN FRONT OF THE TRAIN STATION.
WE'RE GOING TO DO A LIVE STREET SHOW!

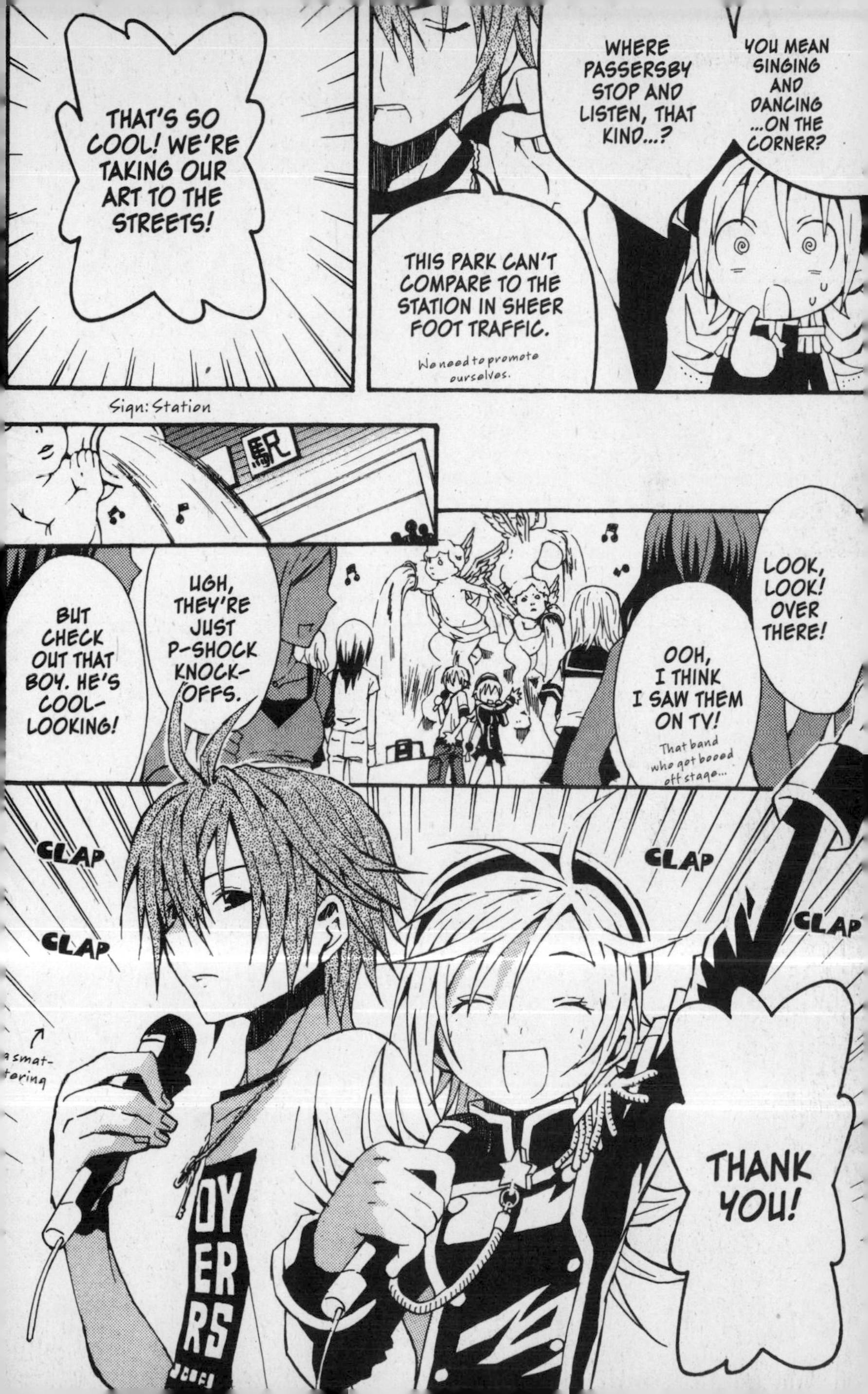
YOU MEAN SINGING AND DANCING ...ON THE CORNER?
WHERE PASSERSBY STOP AND LISTEN, THAT KIND...?
THIS PARK CAN'T COMPARE TO THE STATION IN SHEER FOOT TRAFFIC.
We need to promote ourselves.
THAT'S SO COOL! WE'RE TAKING OUR ART TO THE STREETS!
Sign: Station
駅
LOOK, LOOK! OVER THERE!
OOH, I THINK I SAW THEM ON TV!
That band who got booed off stage...
UGH, THEY'RE JUST P-SHOCK KNOCK-OFFS.
BUT CHECK OUT THAT BOY. HE'S COOL-LOOKING!
THANK YOU!
CLAP
CLAP
CLAP
CLAP
a smattering

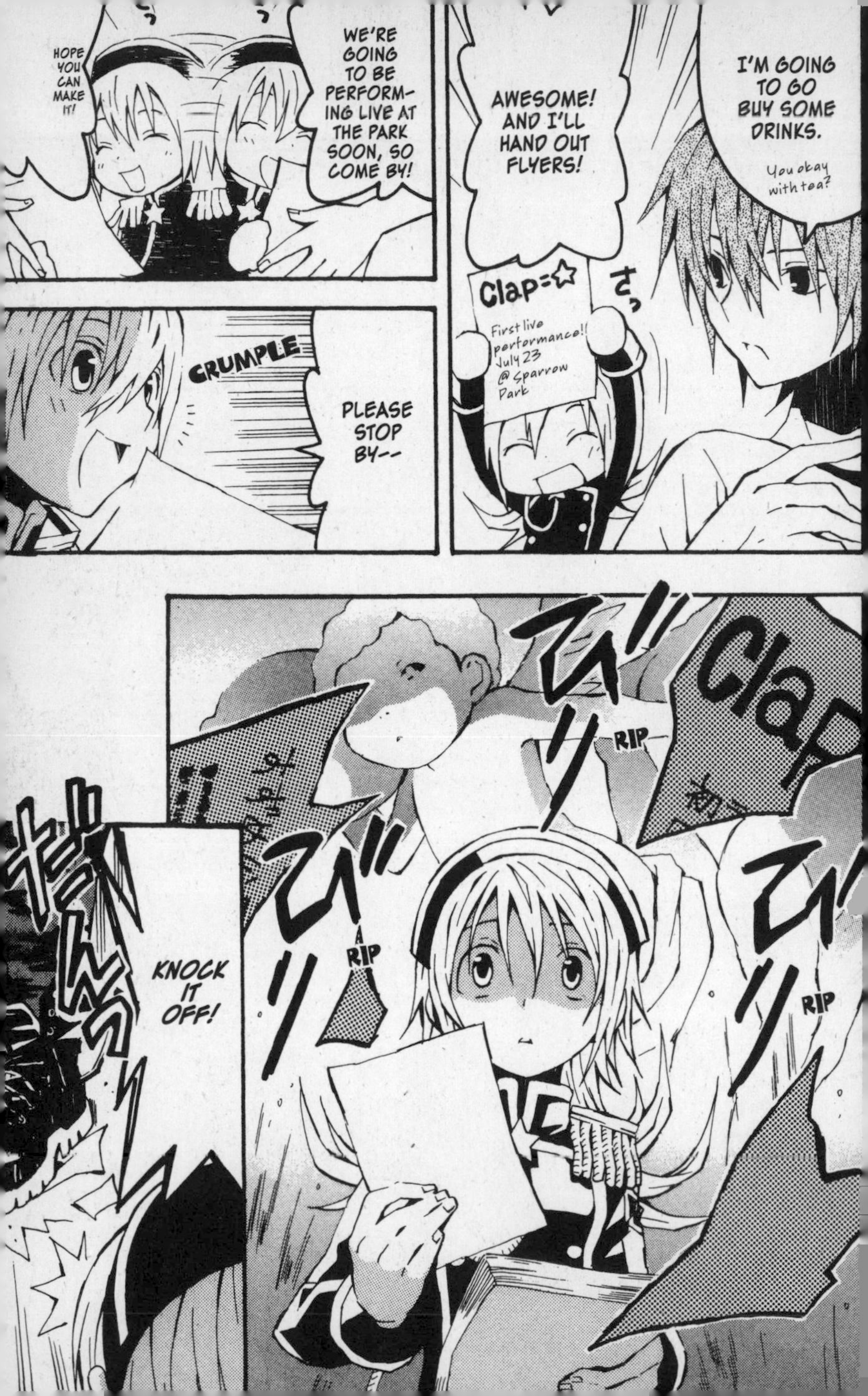

I'M GOING TO GO BUY SOME DRINKS.
You okay with tea?
AWESOME! AND I'LL HAND OUT FLYERS!
Clap=☆
First live performance!! July 23 @ Sparrow Park
WE'RE GOING TO BE PERFORMING LIVE AT THE PARK SOON, SO COME BY!
HOPE YOU CAN MAKE IT!
CRUMPLE
PLEASE STOP BY--
Clap
RIP
RIP
RIP
KNOCK IT OFF!

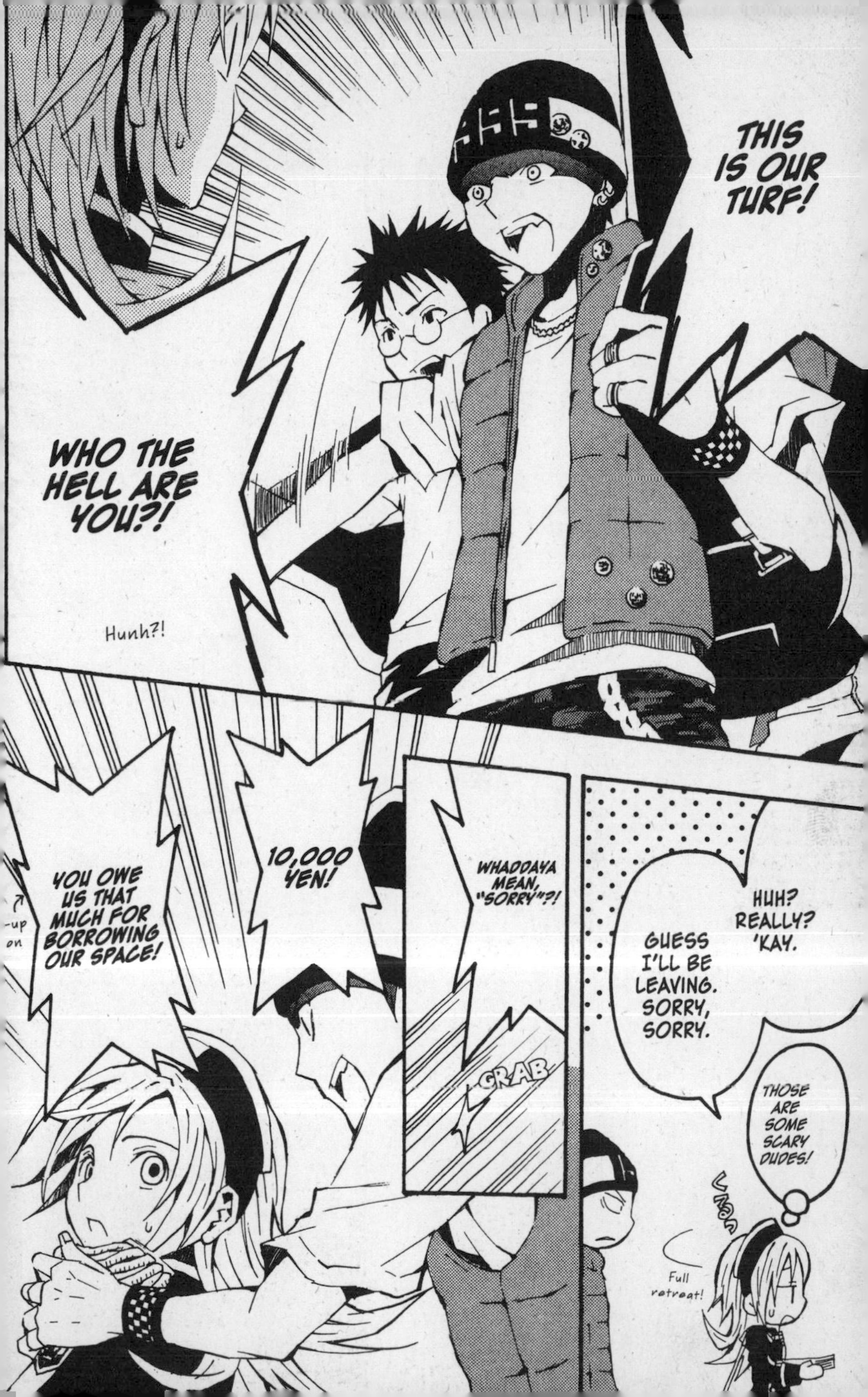
THIS IS OUR TURF!
WHO THE HELL ARE YOU?!
Hunh?!
HUH? REALLY? 'KAY.
GUESS I'LL BE LEAVING. SORRY, SORRY.
THOSE ARE SOME SCARY DUDES!
Full retreat!
WHADDAYA MEAN, "SORRY"?!
GRAB
10,000 YEN!
YOU OWE US THAT MUCH FOR BORROWING OUR SPACE!

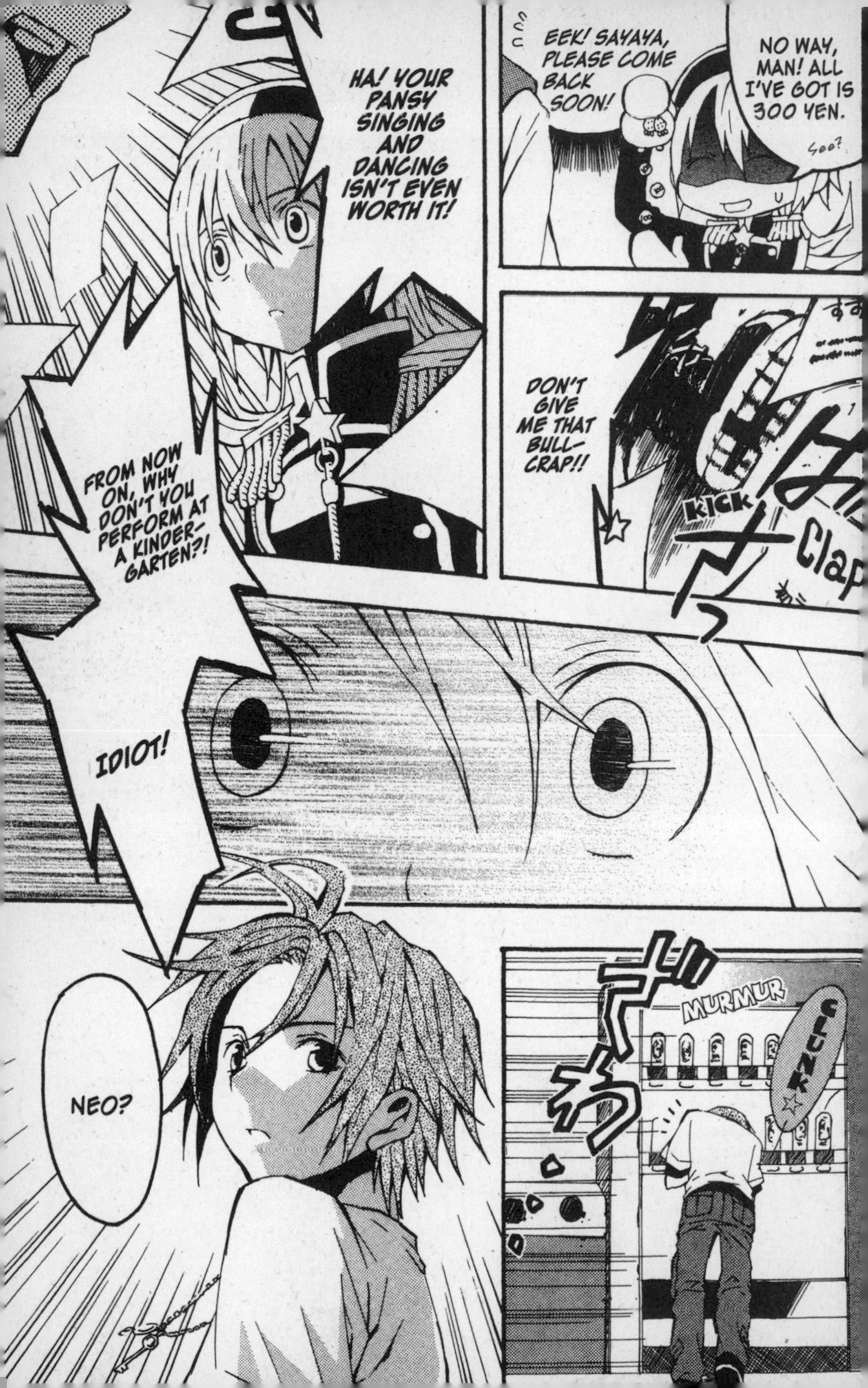
NO WAY, MAN! ALL I'VE GOT IS 300 YEN.
EEK! SAYAYA, PLEASE COME BACK SOON!
DON'T GIVE ME THAT BULL-CRAP!!
KICK
Clap
HA! YOUR PANSY SINGING AND DANCING ISN'T EVEN WORTH IT!
FROM NOW ON, WHY DON'T YOU PERFORM AT A KINDER-GARTEN?!
IDIOT!
MURMUR
CLUNK
NEO?

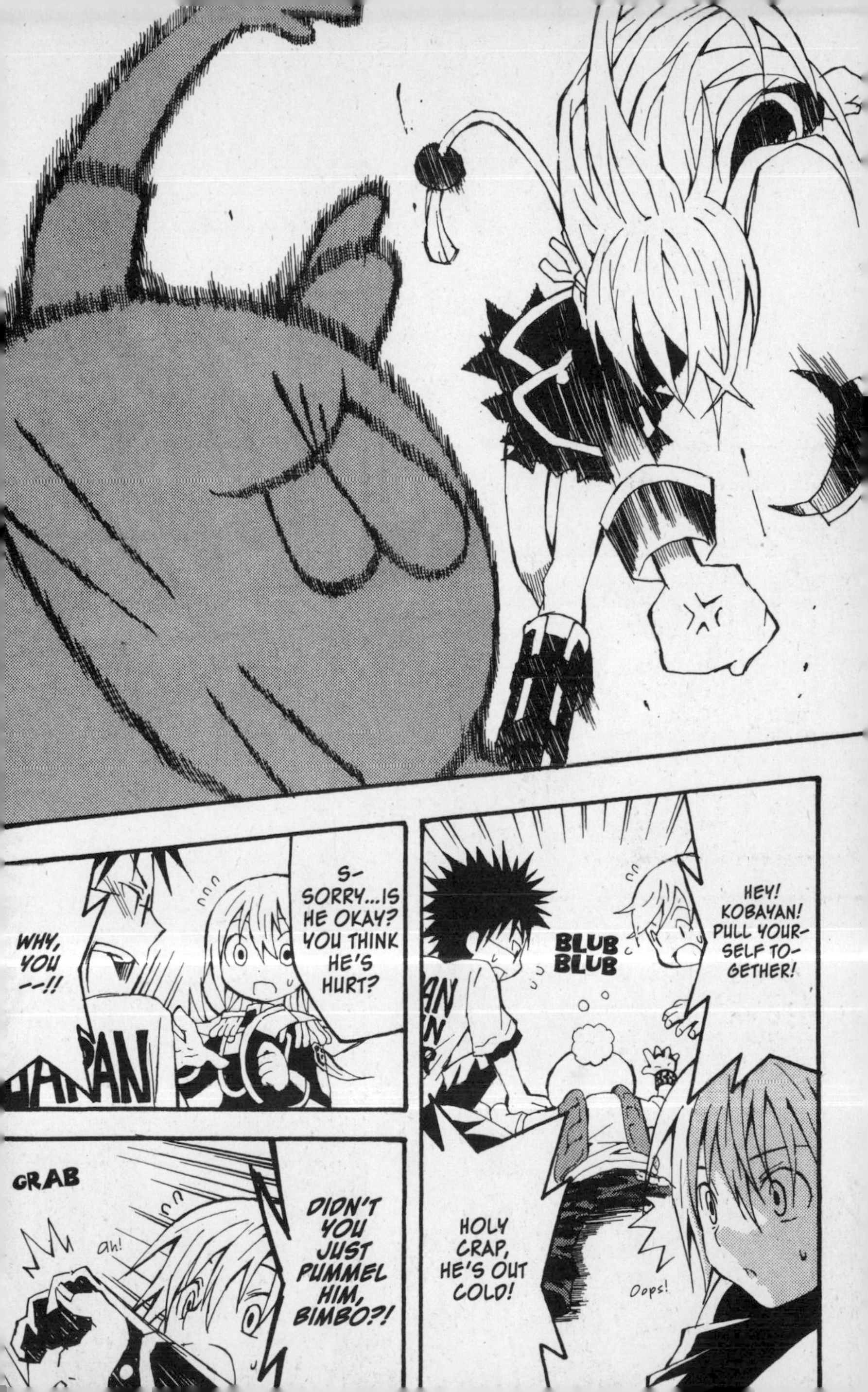
HEY! KOBAYAN! PULL YOURSELF TOGETHER!
BLUB BLUB
Oops!
HOLY CRAP, HE'S OUT COLD!
S-SORRY...IS HE OKAY? YOU THINK HE'S HURT?
WHY, YOU--!!
DIDN'T YOU JUST PUMMEL HIM, BIMBO?!
ah!
GRAB

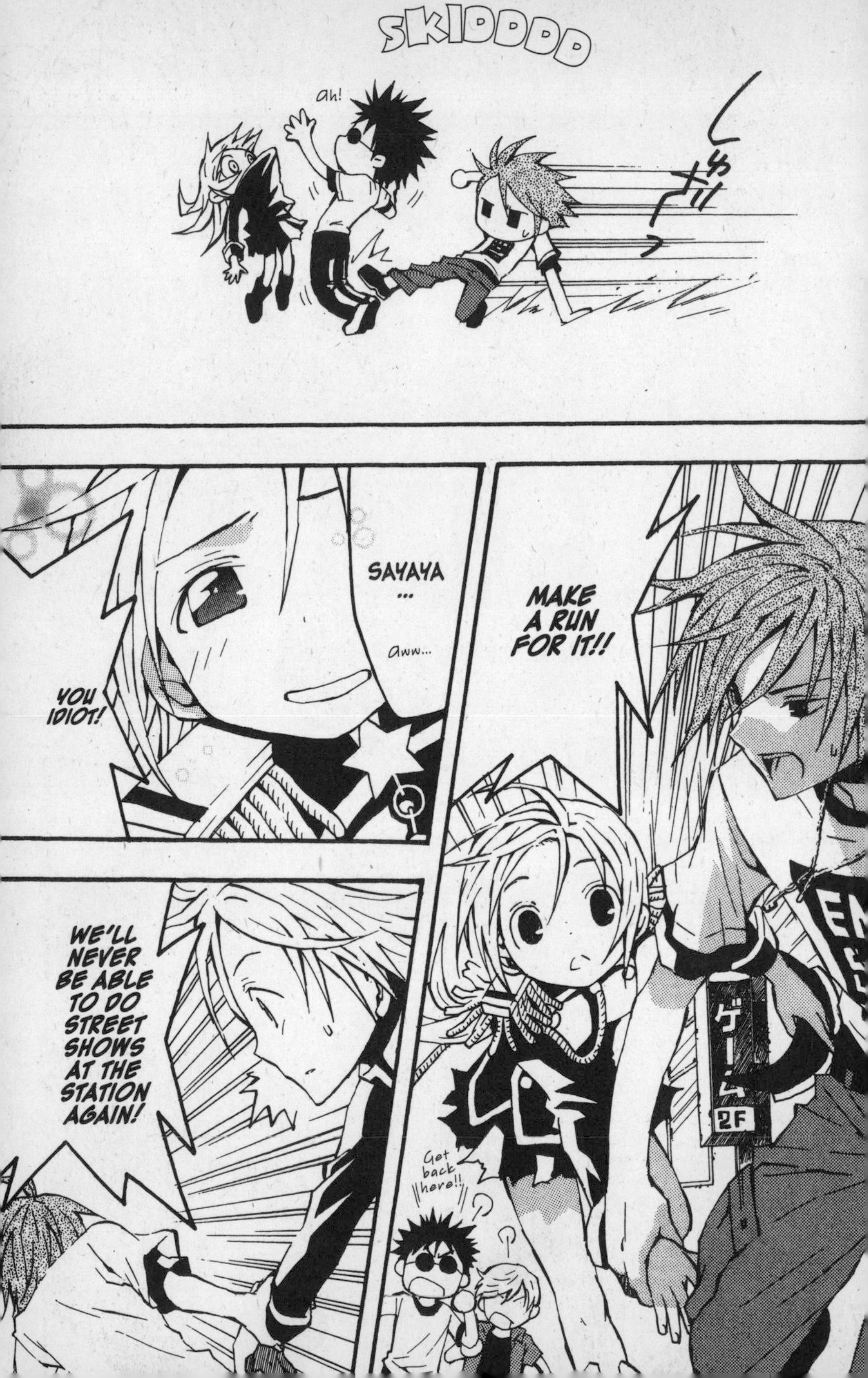
SKIDDDD
ah!
MAKE A RUN FOR IT!!
ゲーム 2F
Get back here!!
SAYAYA...
aww...
YOU IDIOT!
WE'LL NEVER BE ABLE TO DO STREET SHOWS AT THE STATION AGAIN!

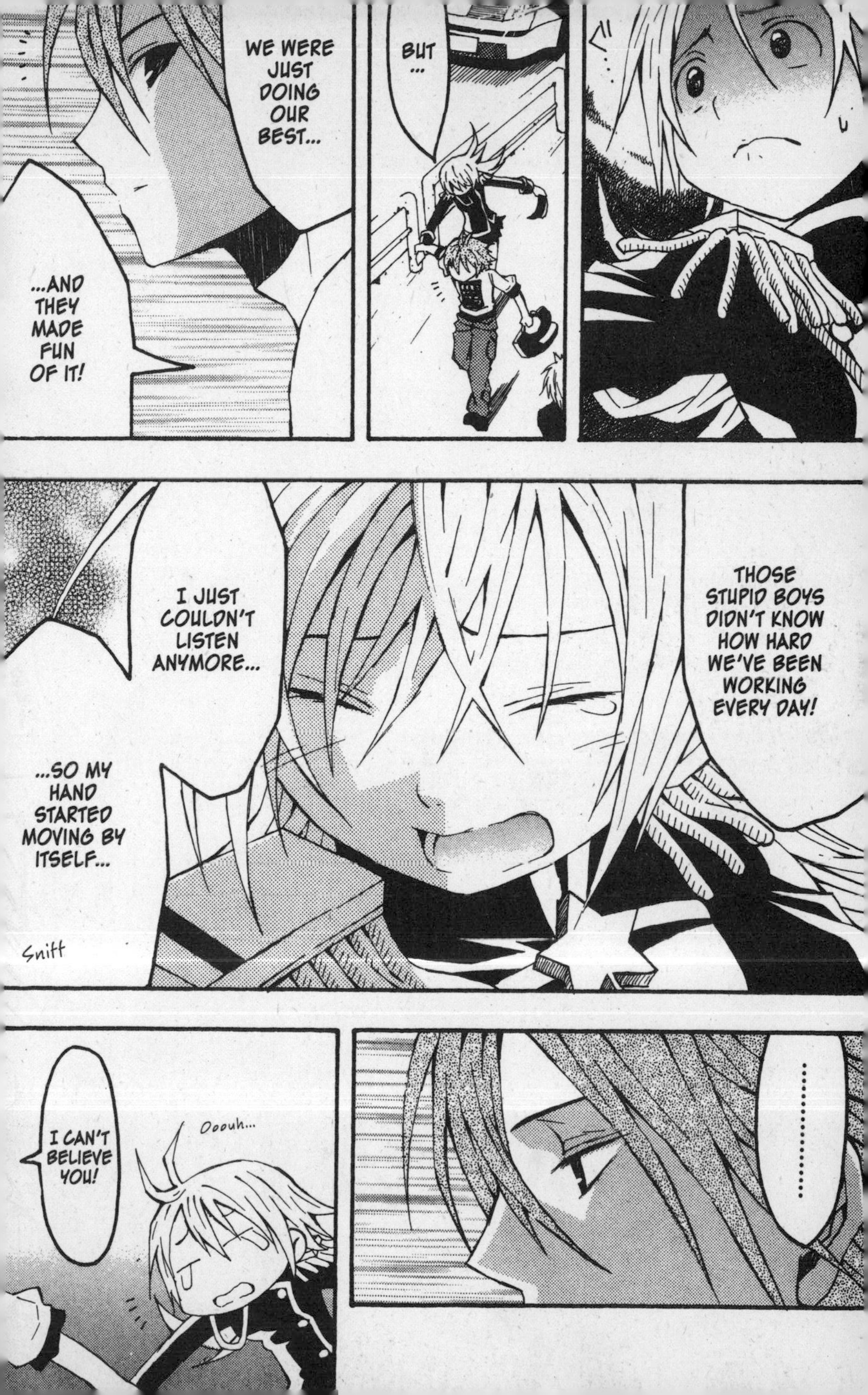
BUT ...
WE WERE JUST DOING OUR BEST...
...AND THEY MADE FUN OF IT!
THOSE STUPID BOYS DIDN'T KNOW HOW HARD WE'VE BEEN WORKING EVERY DAY!
I JUST COULDN'T LISTEN ANYMORE...
...SO MY HAND STARTED MOVING BY ITSELF...
Sniff
....
I CAN'T BELIEVE YOU!
Ooouh...

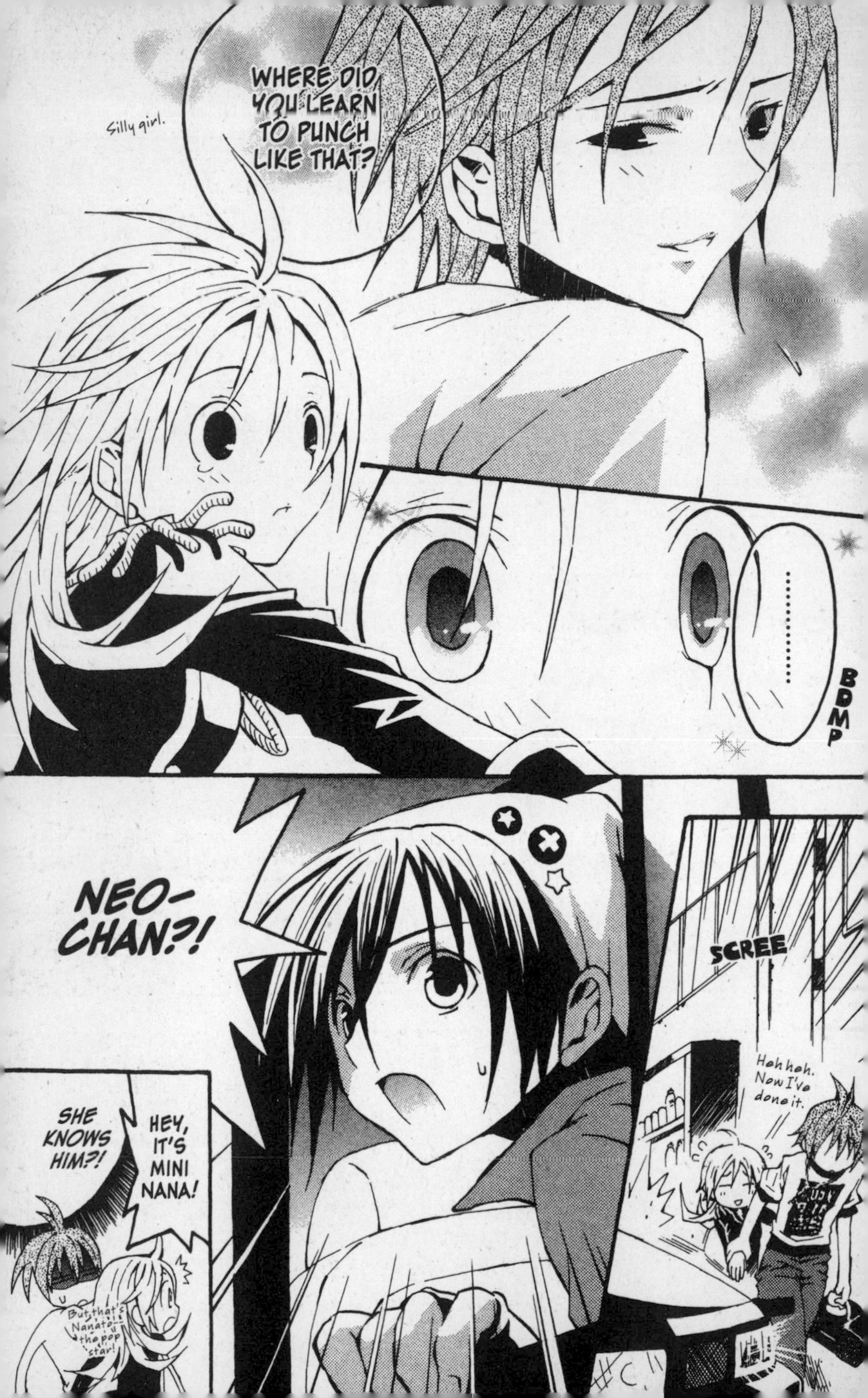
WHERE DID YOU LEARN TO PUNCH LIKE THAT?
Silly girl.
......
BDMP
SCREE
Heh heh. Now I've done it.
NEO-CHAN?!
HEY, IT'S MINI NANA!
SHE KNOWS HIM?!
But that's Nanato-- the pop star!

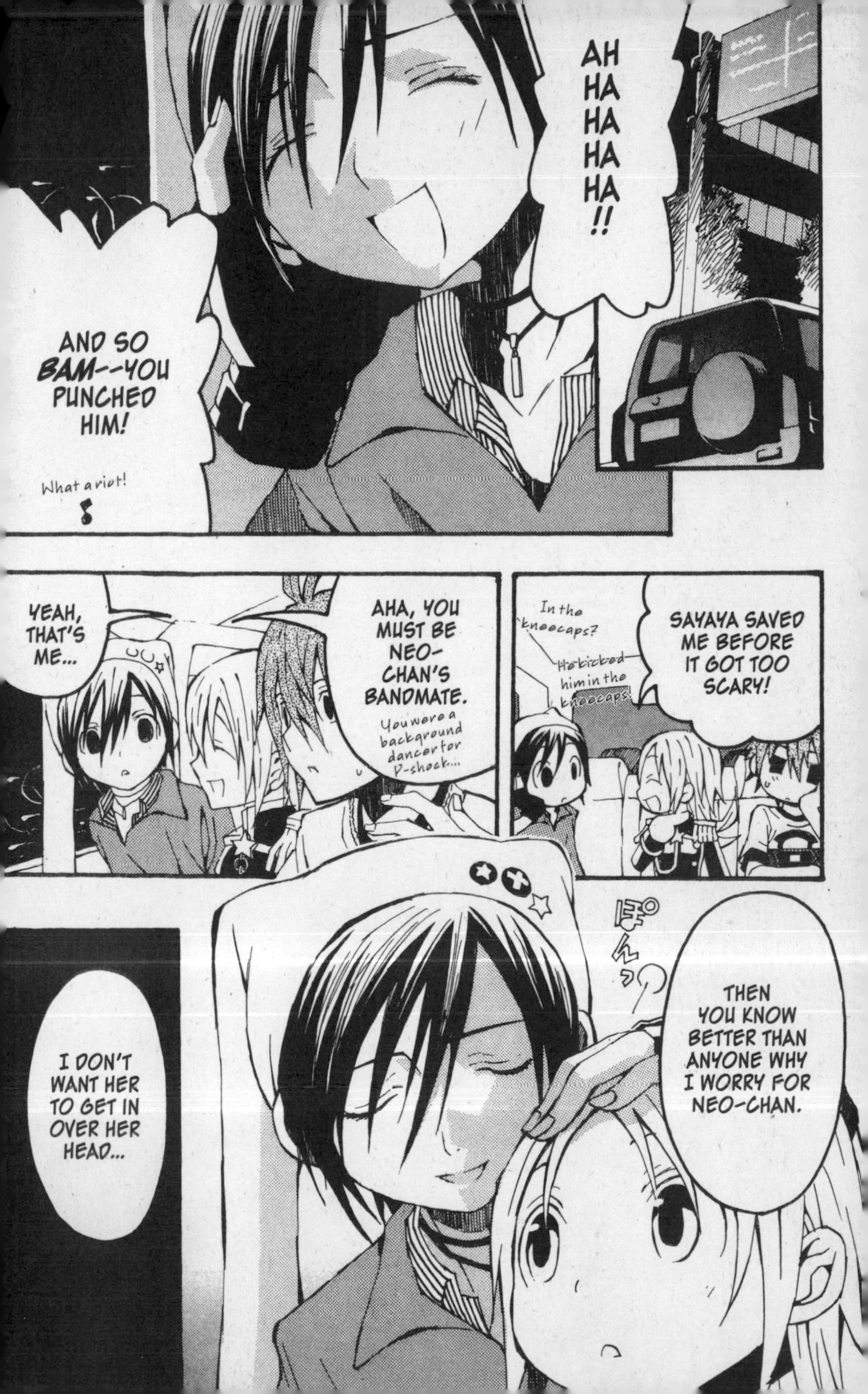
AH HA HA HA HA!!
AND SO BAM--YOU PUNCHED HIM!
What a riot!
SAYAYA SAVED ME BEFORE IT GOT TOO SCARY!
In the kneecaps?
He kicked him in the kneecaps.
AHA, YOU MUST BE NEO-CHAN'S BANDMATE.
You were a background dancer for P-shock...
YEAH, THAT'S ME...
ぽんっ
THEN YOU KNOW BETTER THAN ANYONE WHY I WORRY FOR NEO-CHAN.
I DON'T WANT HER TO GET IN OVER HER HEAD...

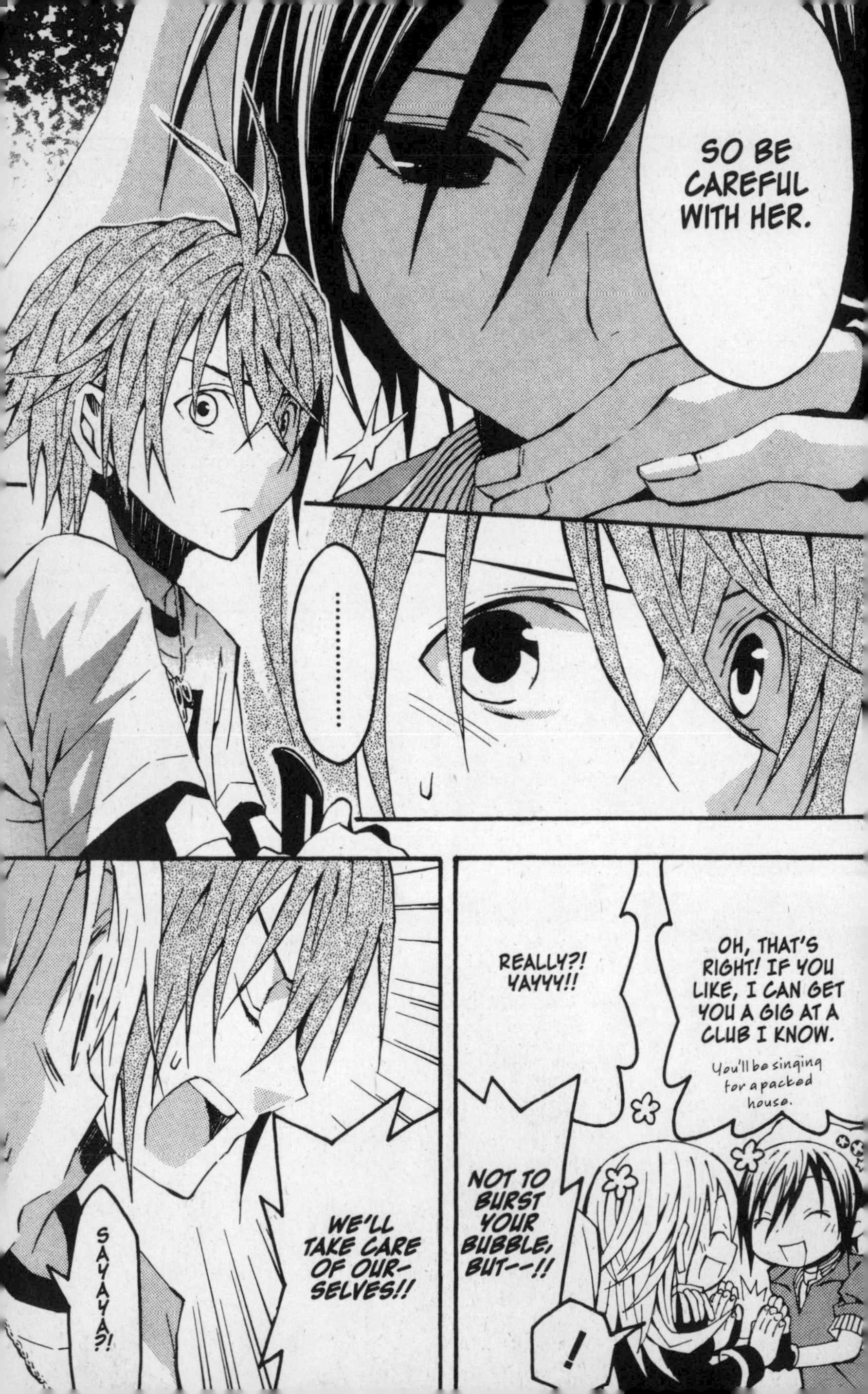
SO BE CAREFUL WITH HER.
......
OH, THAT'S RIGHT! IF YOU LIKE, I CAN GET YOU A GIG AT A CLUB I KNOW.
You'll be singing for a packed house.
REALLY?! YAYYY!!
NOT TO BURST YOUR BUBBLE, BUT--!!
!
WE'LL TAKE CARE OF OUR-SELVES!!
SAYAYAS!

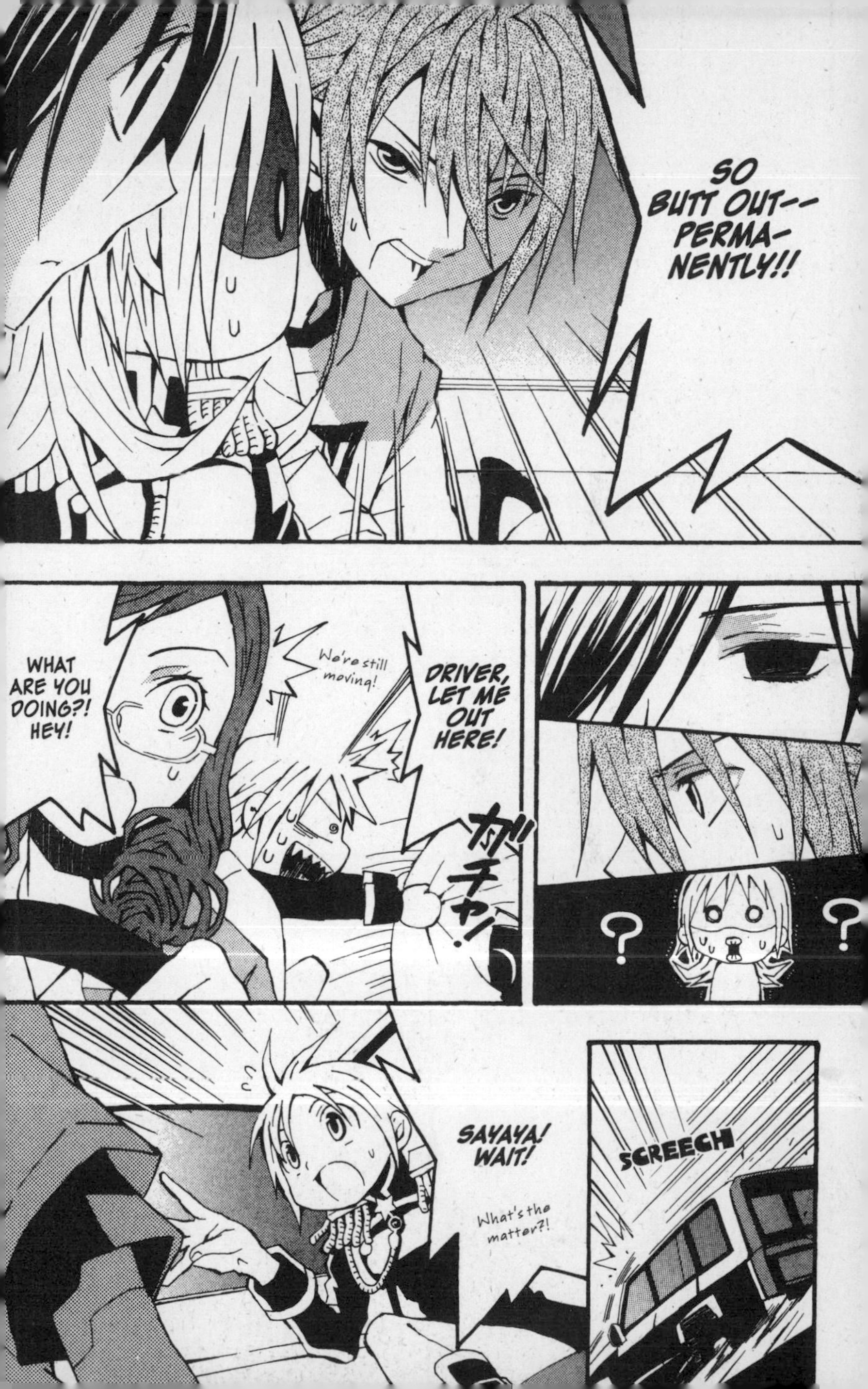
SO BUTT OUT--PERMA-NENTLY!!
DRIVER, LET ME OUT HERE!
We're still moving!
WHAT ARE YOU DOING?! HEY!
ガチャ!
SCREECH
SAYAYA! WAIT!
What's the matter?!

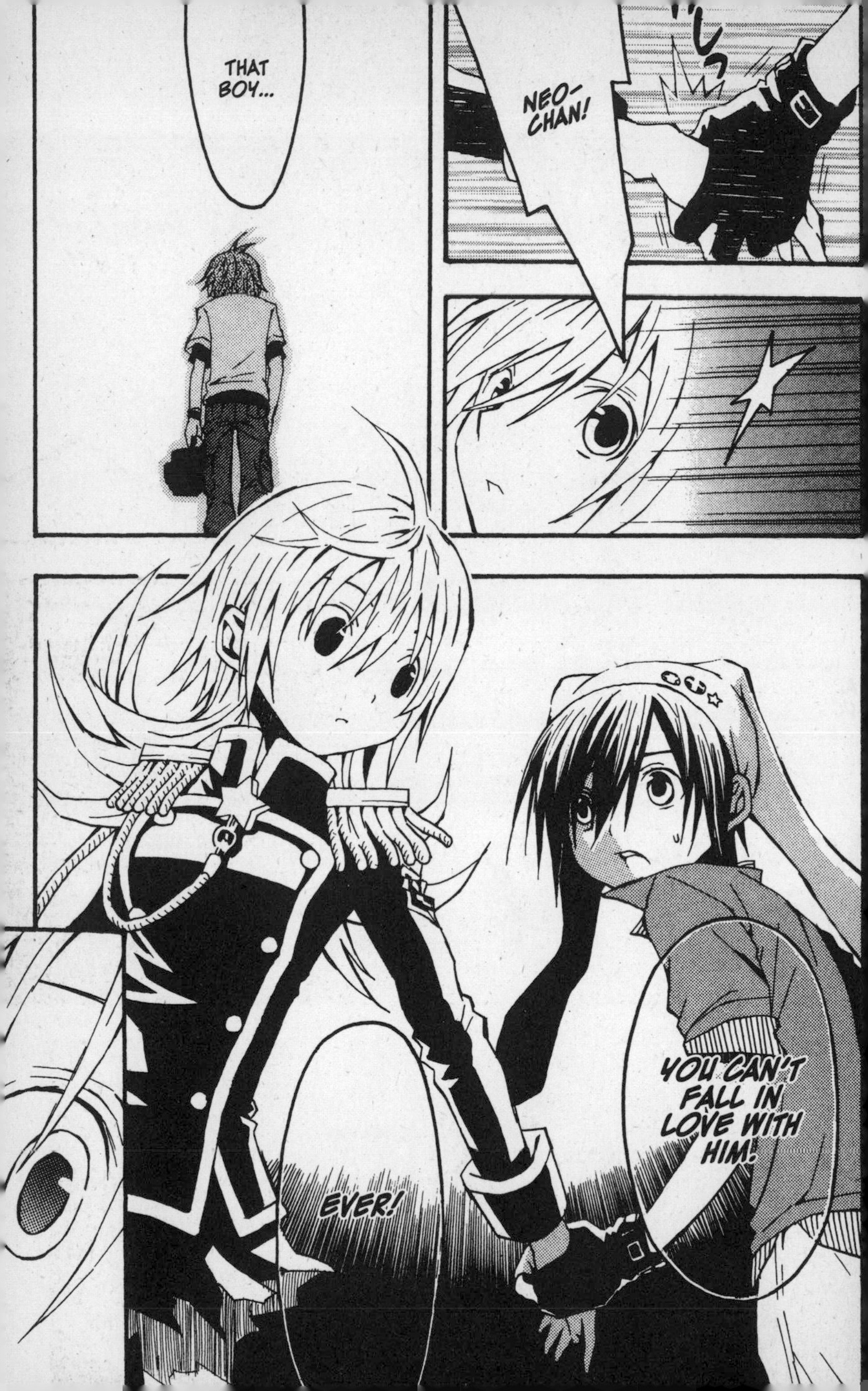
NEO-CHAN!
THAT BOY...
YOU CAN'T FALL IN LOVE WITH HIM!
EVER!

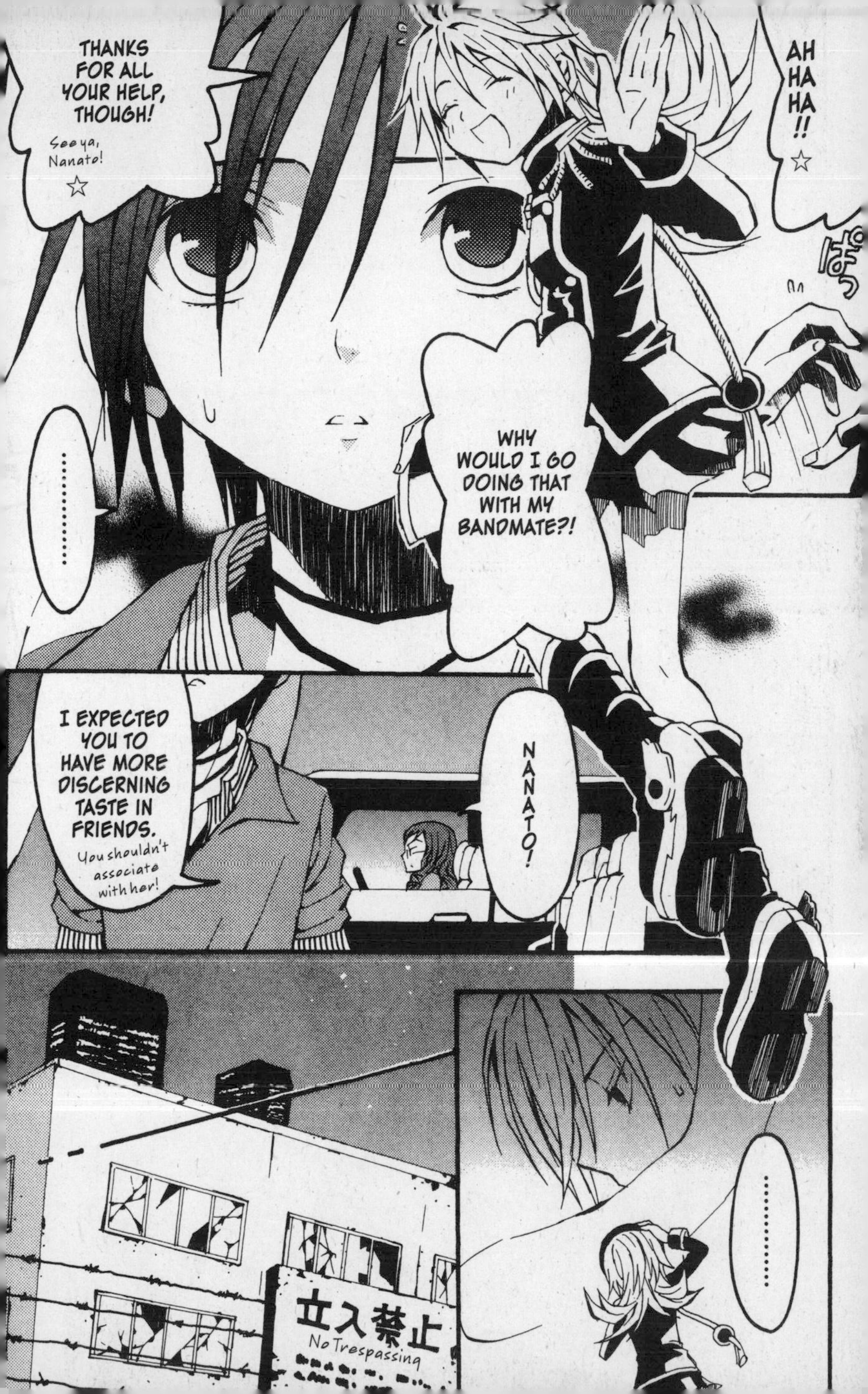

AH HA HA!! ☆
ぽっ
THANKS FOR ALL YOUR HELP, THOUGH!
See ya, Nanato! ☆
WHY WOULD I GO DOING THAT WITH MY BANDMATE?!
......
NANATO!
I EXPECTED YOU TO HAVE MORE DISCERNING TASTE IN FRIENDS.
You shouldn't associate with her!
......
立入禁止
No Trespassing

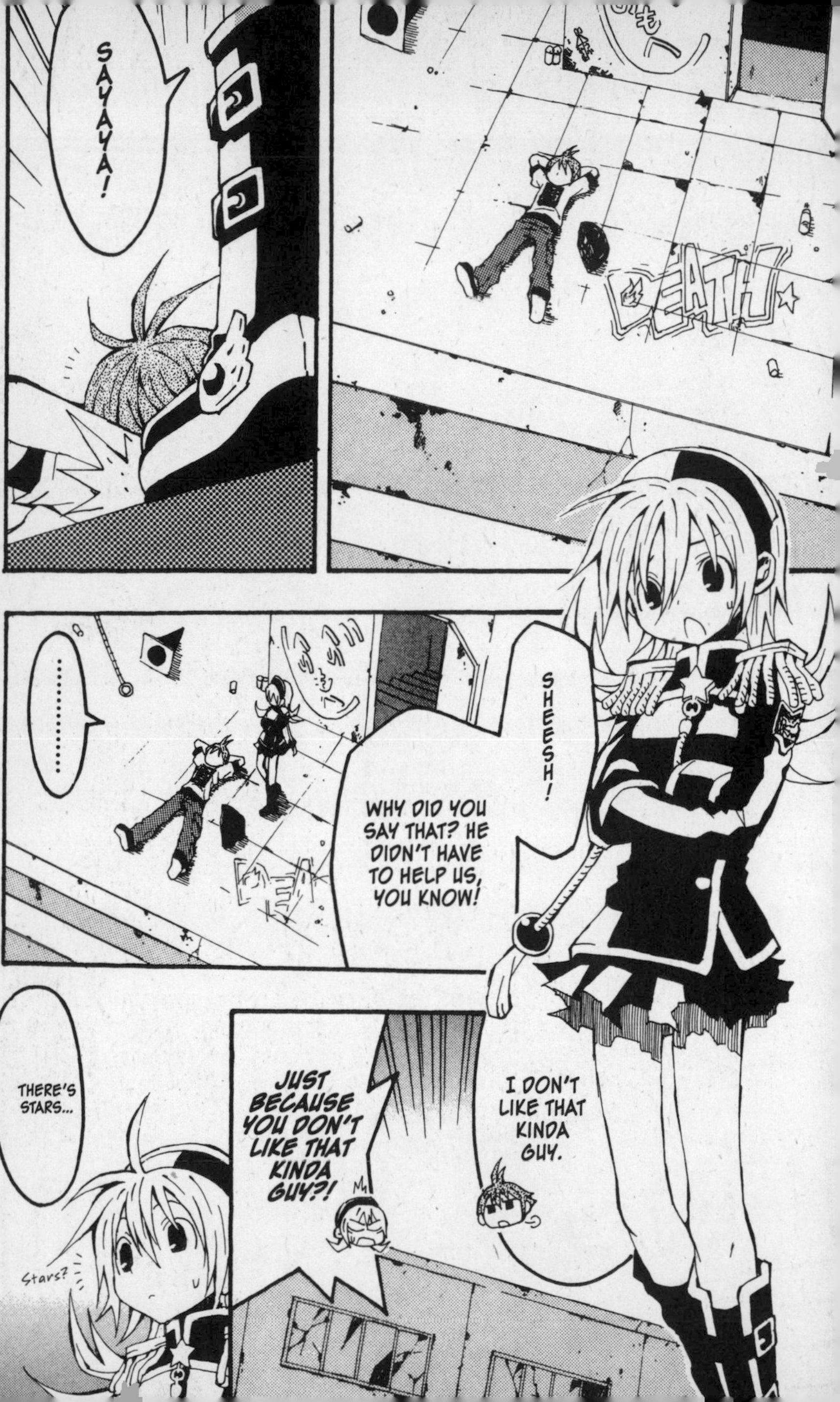
DEATH
SAYAYA!
SHEESH!
WHY DID YOU SAY THAT? HE DIDN'T HAVE TO HELP US, YOU KNOW!
I DON'T LIKE THAT KINDA GUY.
......
JUST BECAUSE YOU DON'T LIKE THAT KINDA GUY?!
THERE'S STARS...
Stars?

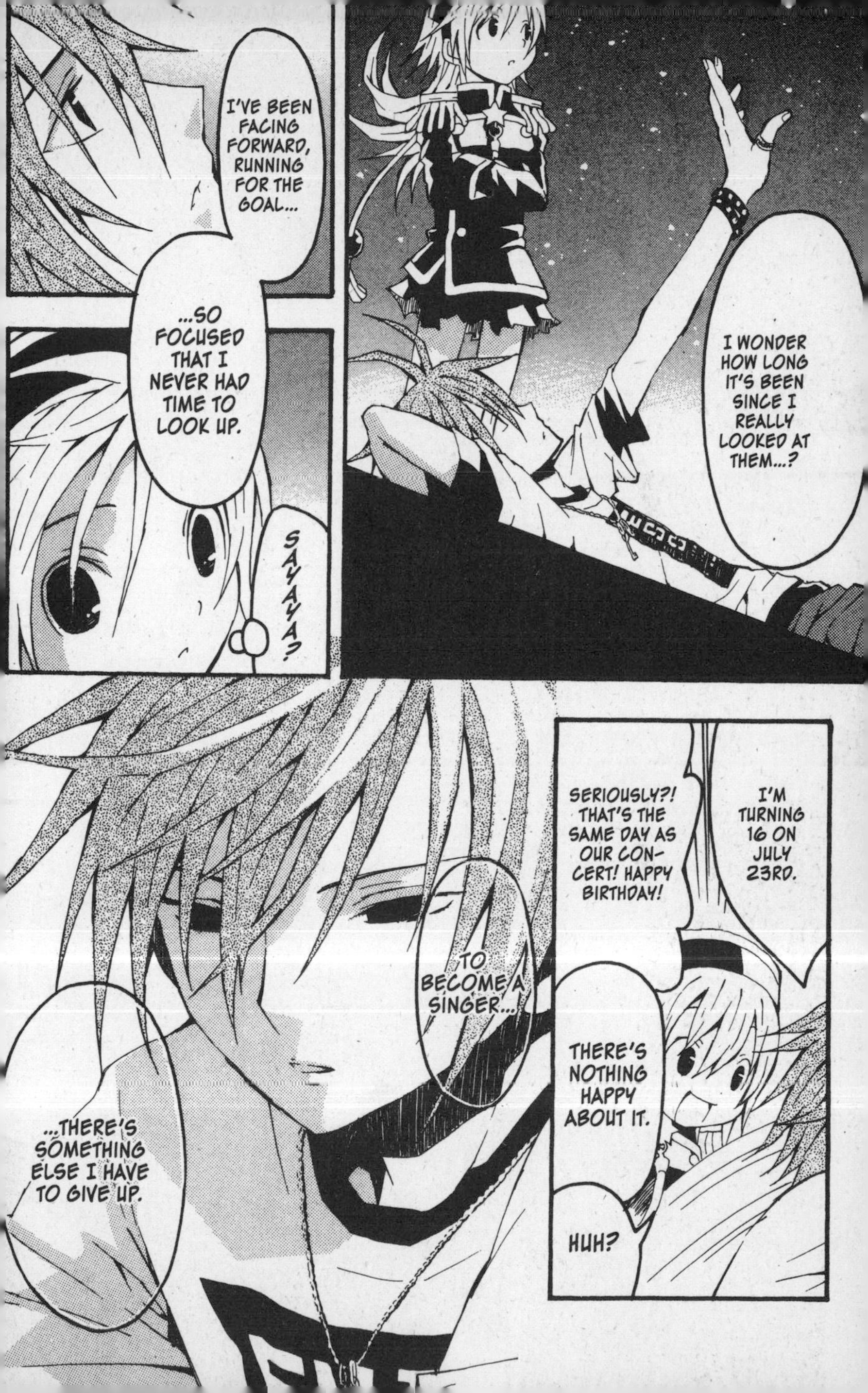
I WONDER HOW LONG IT'S BEEN SINCE I REALLY LOOKED AT THEM...?
I'VE BEEN FACING FORWARD, RUNNING FOR THE GOAL...
...SO FOCUSED THAT I NEVER HAD TIME TO LOOK UP.
SAYAYA?
I'M TURNING 16 ON JULY 23RD.
SERIOUSLY?! THAT'S THE SAME DAY AS OUR CON-CERT! HAPPY BIRTHDAY!
THERE'S NOTHING HAPPY ABOUT IT.
HUH?
TO BECOME A SINGER...
...THERE'S SOMETHING ELSE I HAVE TO GIVE UP.

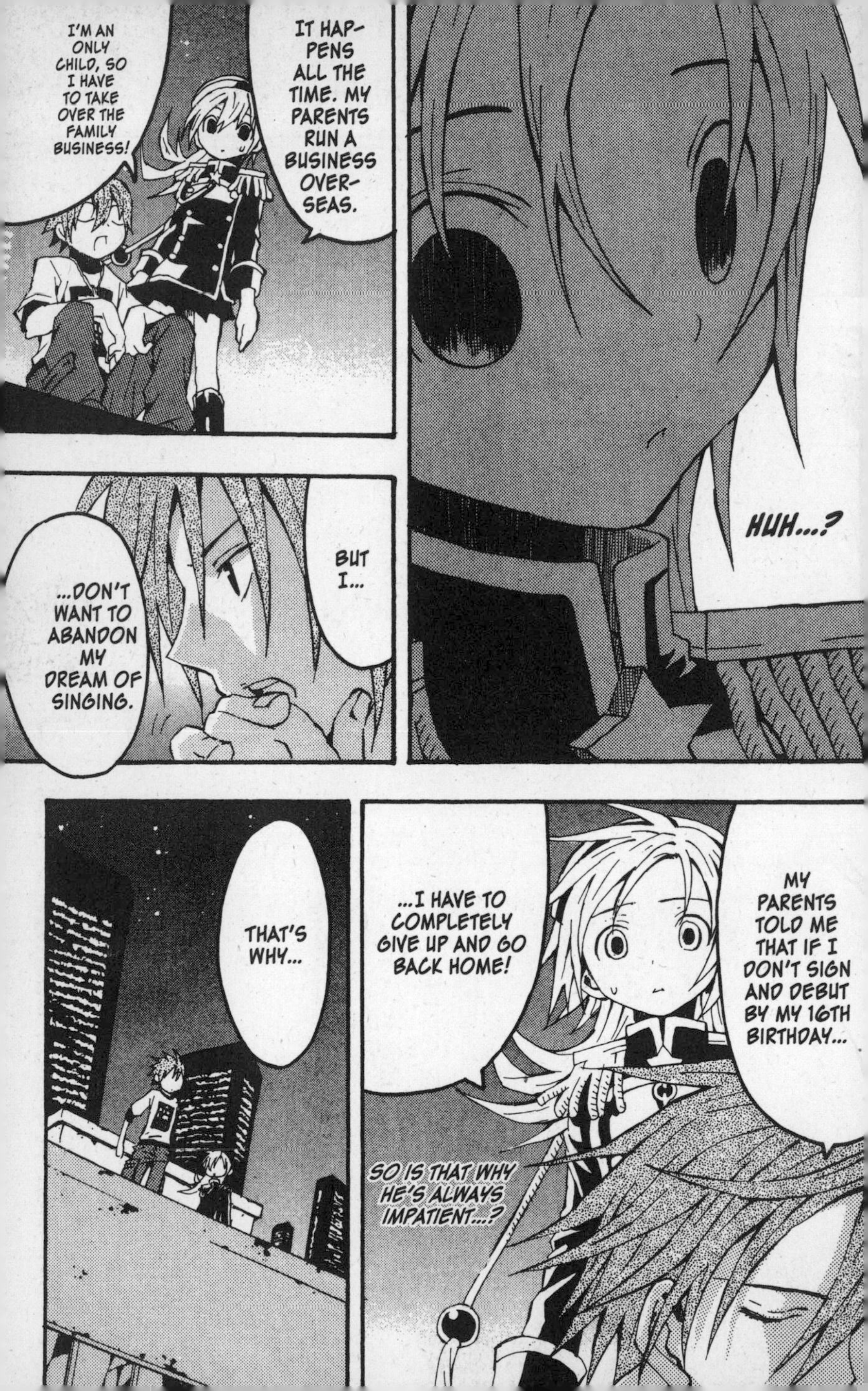
HUH...?
IT HAPPENS ALL THE TIME. MY PARENTS RUN A BUSINESS OVERSEAS.
I'M AN ONLY CHILD, SO I HAVE TO TAKE OVER THE FAMILY BUSINESS!
BUT I...
...DON'T WANT TO ABANDON MY DREAM OF SINGING.
MY PARENTS TOLD ME THAT IF I DON'T SIGN AND DEBUT BY MY 16TH BIRTHDAY...
...I HAVE TO COMPLETELY GIVE UP AND GO BACK HOME!
SO IS THAT WHY HE'S ALWAYS IMPATIENT...?
THAT'S WHY...

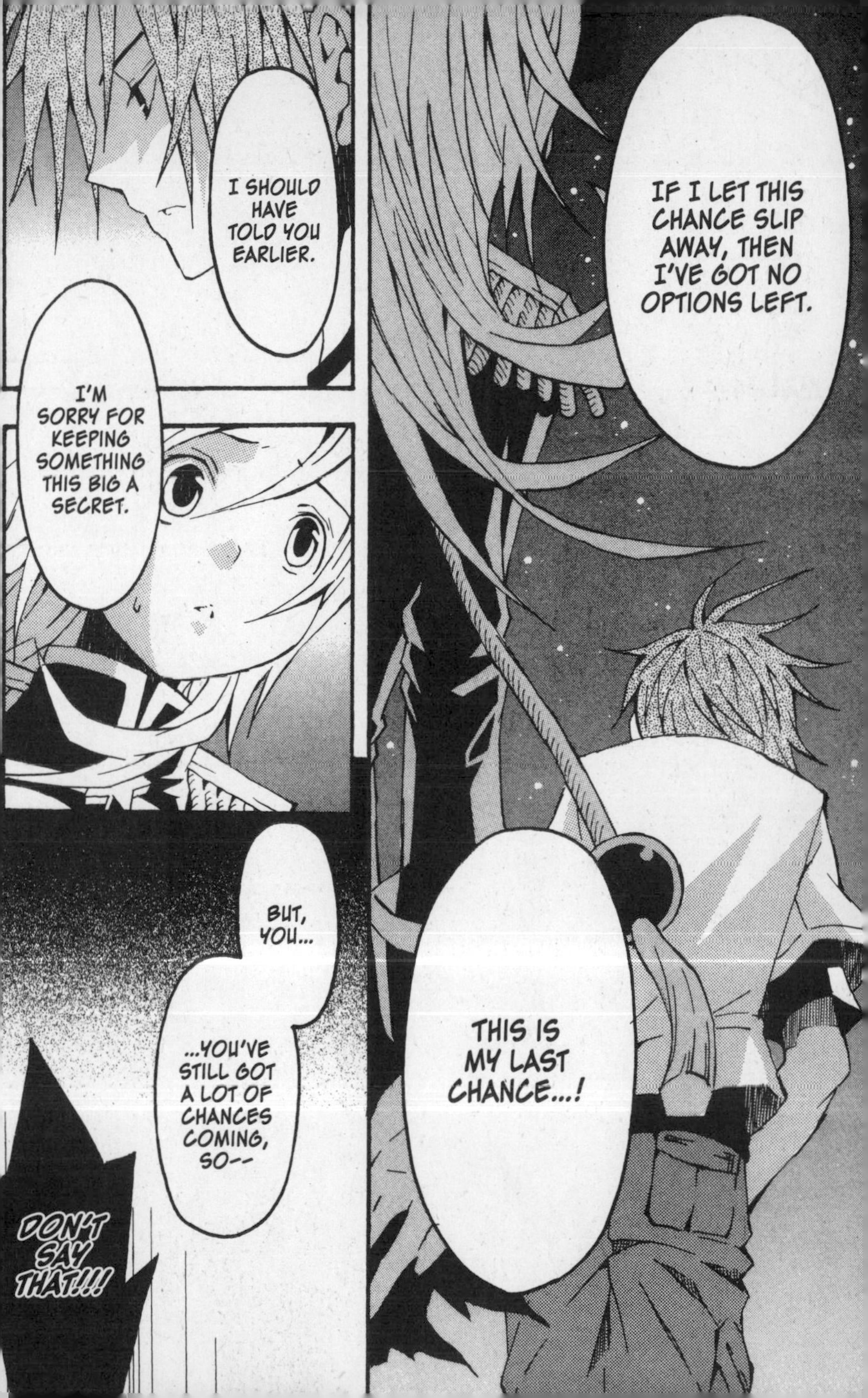
IF I LET THIS CHANCE SLIP AWAY, THEN I'VE GOT NO OPTIONS LEFT.
THIS IS MY LAST CHANCE...!
I SHOULD HAVE TOLD YOU EARLIER.
I'M SORRY FOR KEEPING SOMETHING THIS BIG A SECRET.
BUT, YOU...
...YOU'VE STILL GOT A LOT OF CHANCES COMING, SO--
DON'T SAY THAT!!!

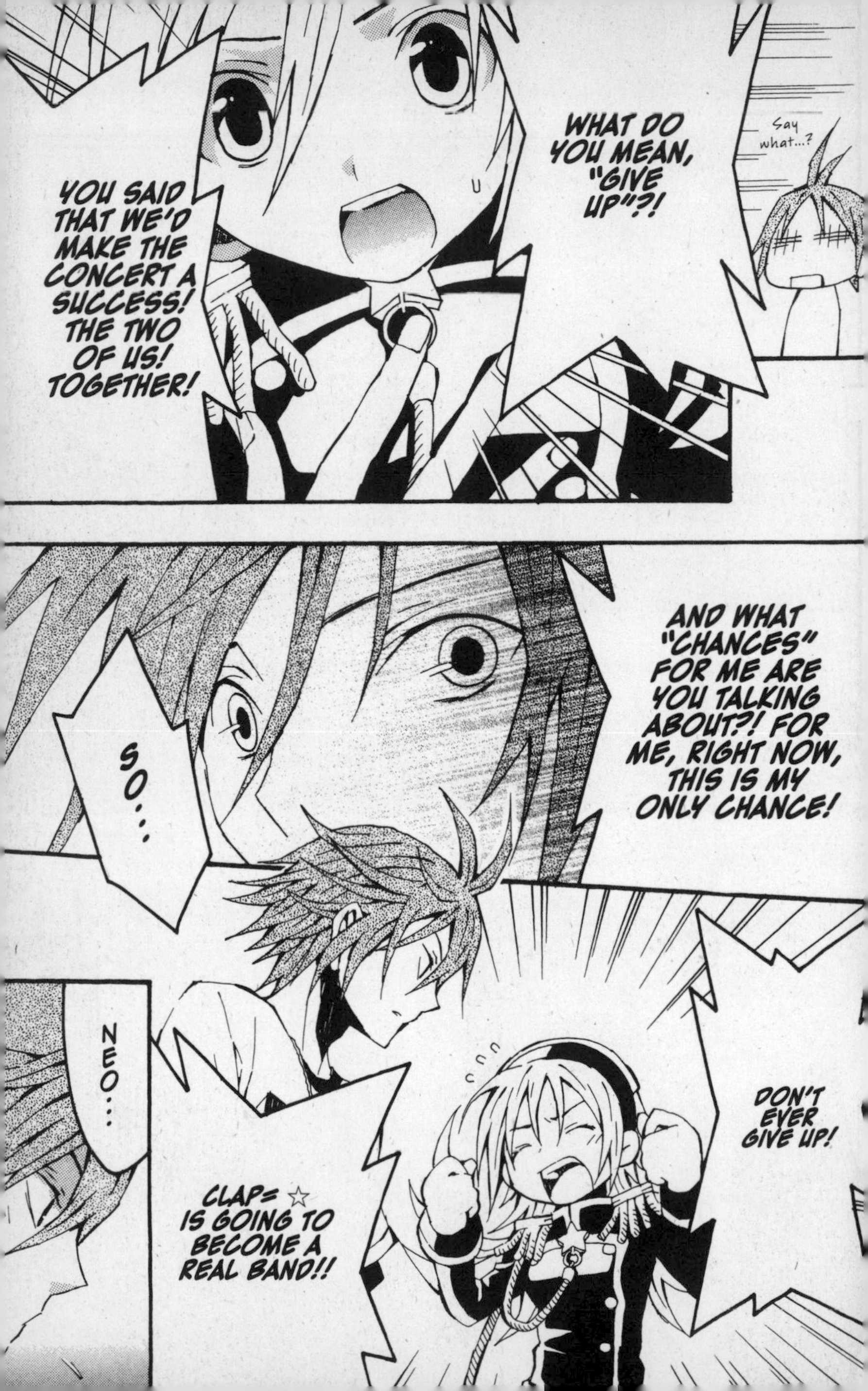
Say what...?
WHAT DO YOU MEAN, "GIVE UP"?!
YOU SAID THAT WE'D MAKE THE CONCERT A SUCCESS! THE TWO OF US! TOGETHER!
AND WHAT "CHANCES" FOR ME ARE YOU TALKING ABOUT?! FOR ME, RIGHT NOW, THIS IS MY ONLY CHANCE!
SO...
DON'T EVER GIVE UP!
CLAP= ☆ IS GOING TO BECOME A REAL BAND!!
NEO...

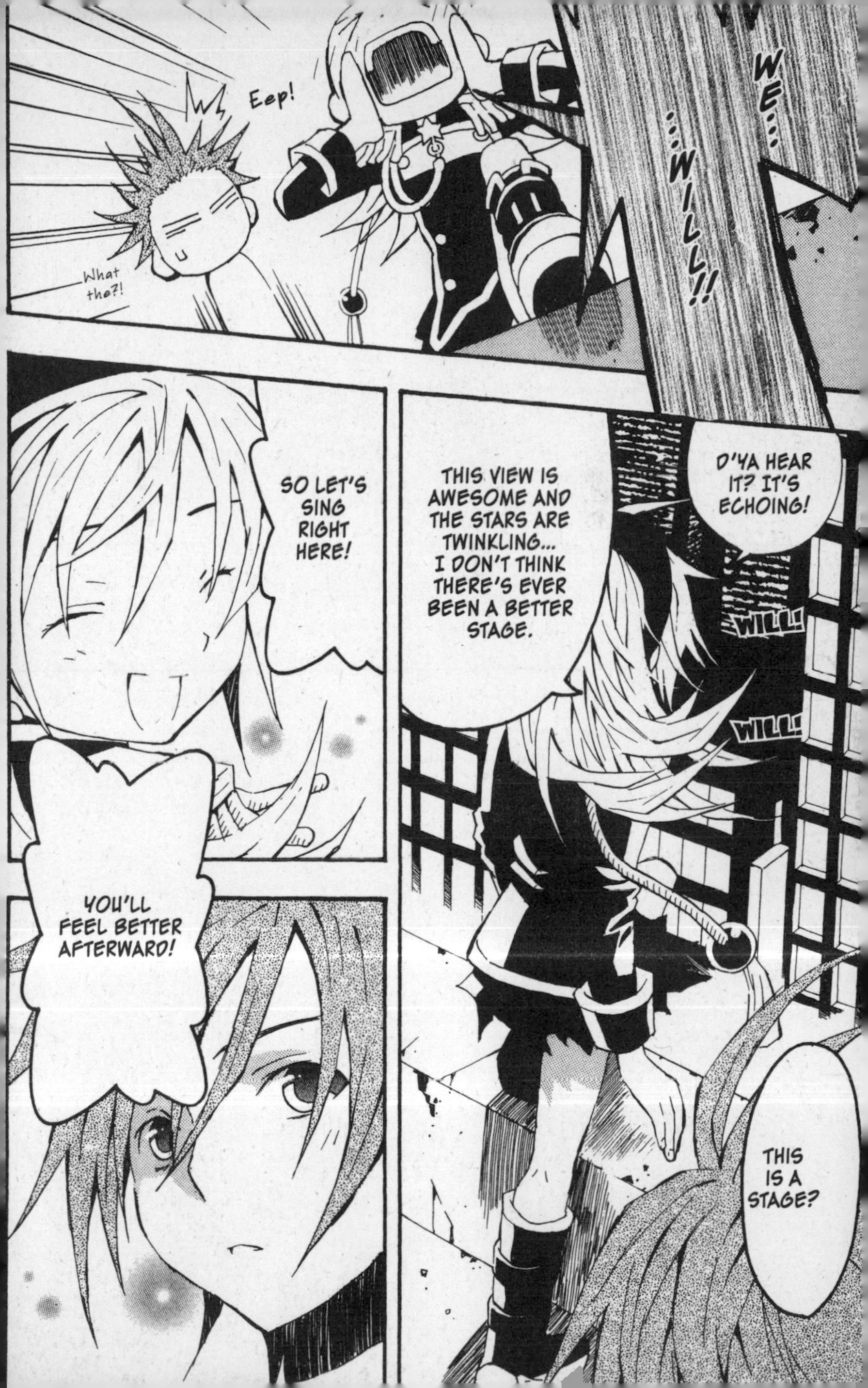
WE... ...WILL!!
Eep!
What the?!
D'YA HEAR IT? IT'S ECHOING!
THIS VIEW IS AWESOME AND THE STARS ARE TWINKLING... I DON'T THINK THERE'S EVER BEEN A BETTER STAGE.
WILL!
WILL!
THIS IS A STAGE?
SO LET'S SING RIGHT HERE!
YOU'LL FEEL BETTER AFTERWARD!

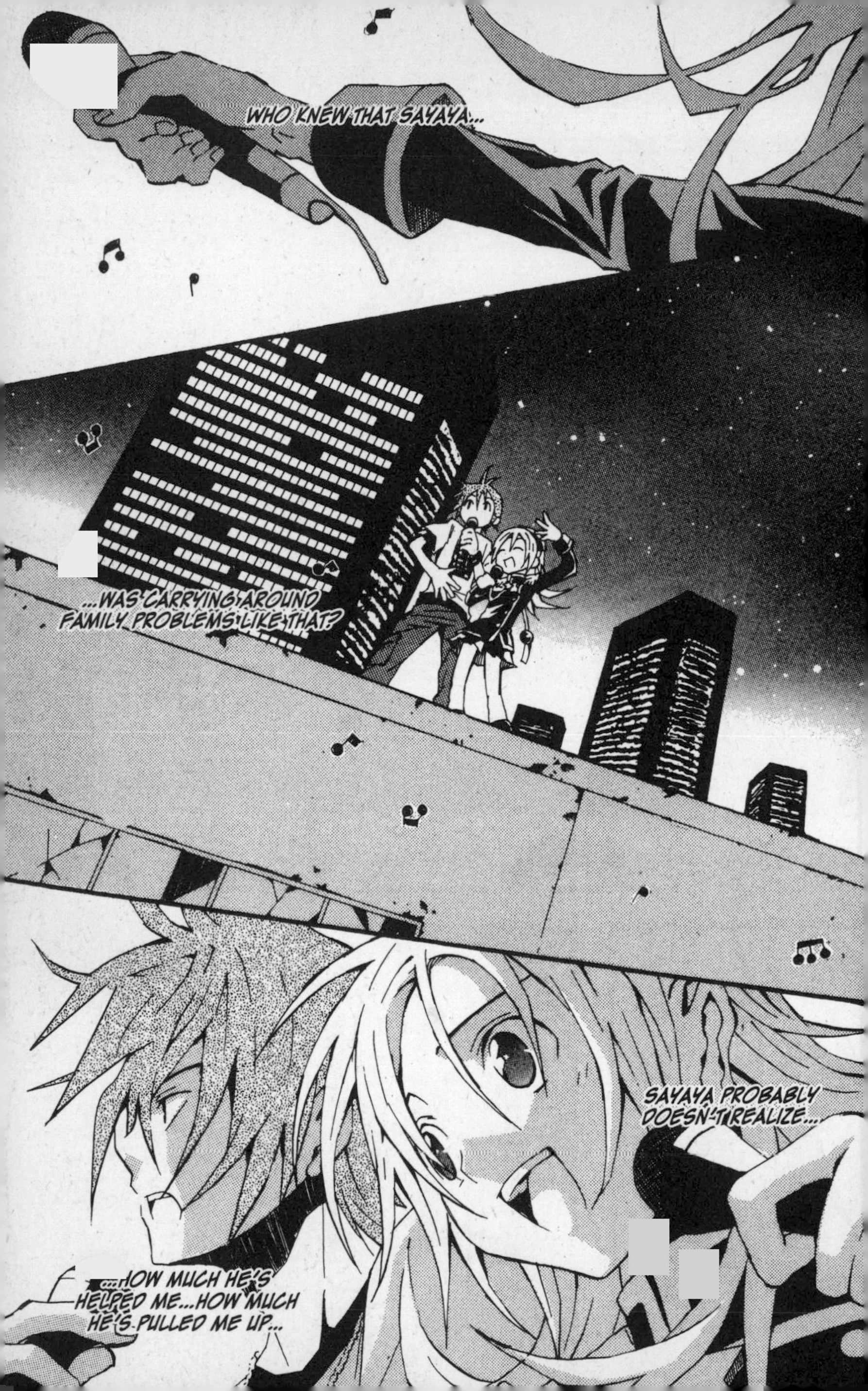
WHO KNEW THAT SAYAYA...
...WAS CARRYING AROUND FAMILY PROBLEMS LIKE THAT?
SAYAYA PROBABLY DOESN'T REALIZE...
...HOW MUCH HE'S HELPED ME...HOW MUCH HE'S PULLED ME UP...

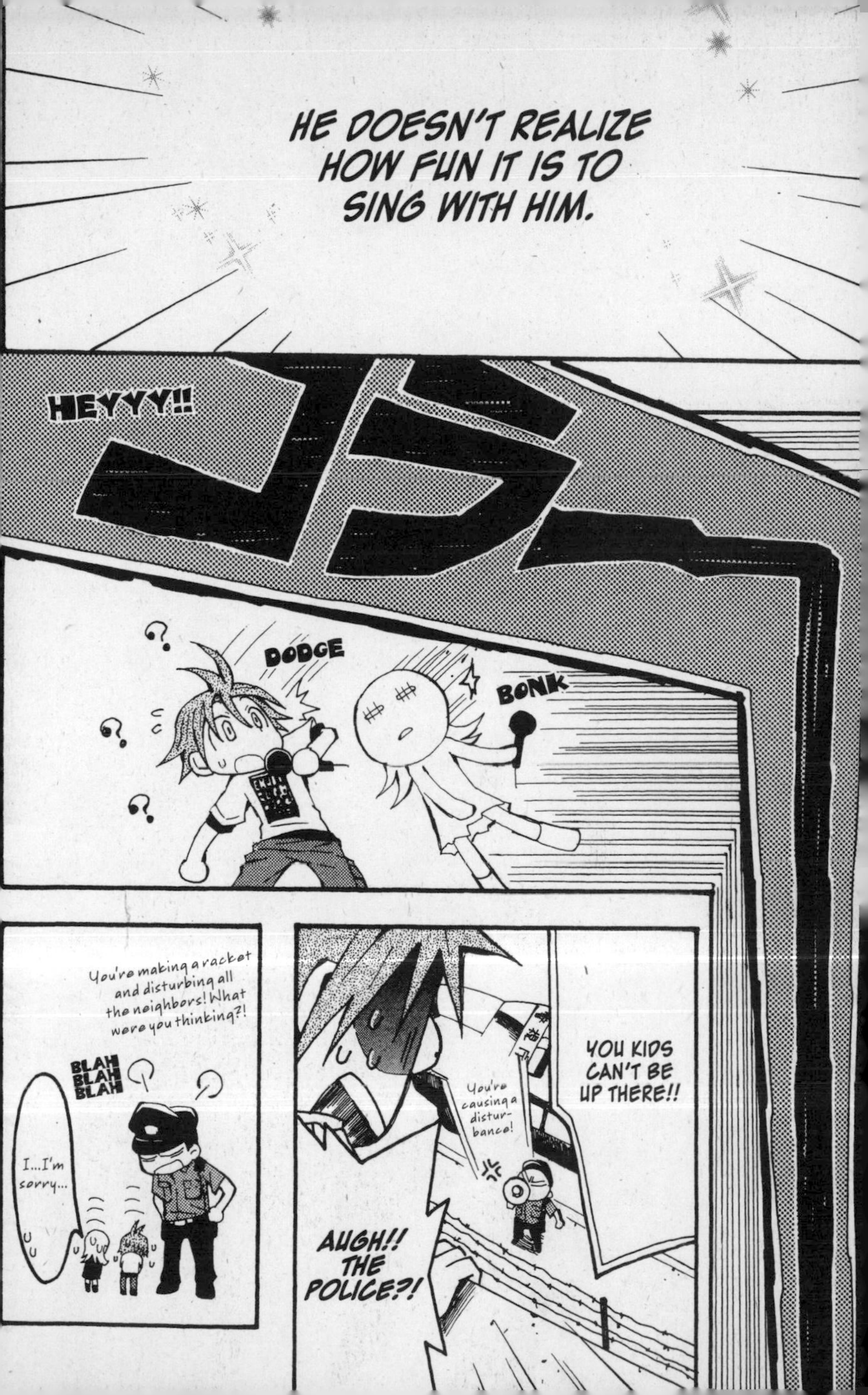
HE DOESN'T REALIZE HOW FUN IT IS TO SING WITH HIM.
HEYYY!!
コラー
DODGE
BONK
YOU KIDS CAN'T BE UP THERE!!
You're causing a distur-bance!
AUGH!! THE POLICE?!
You're making a racket and disturbing all the neighbors! What were you thinking?!
BLAH BLAH BLAH
I...I'm sorry...

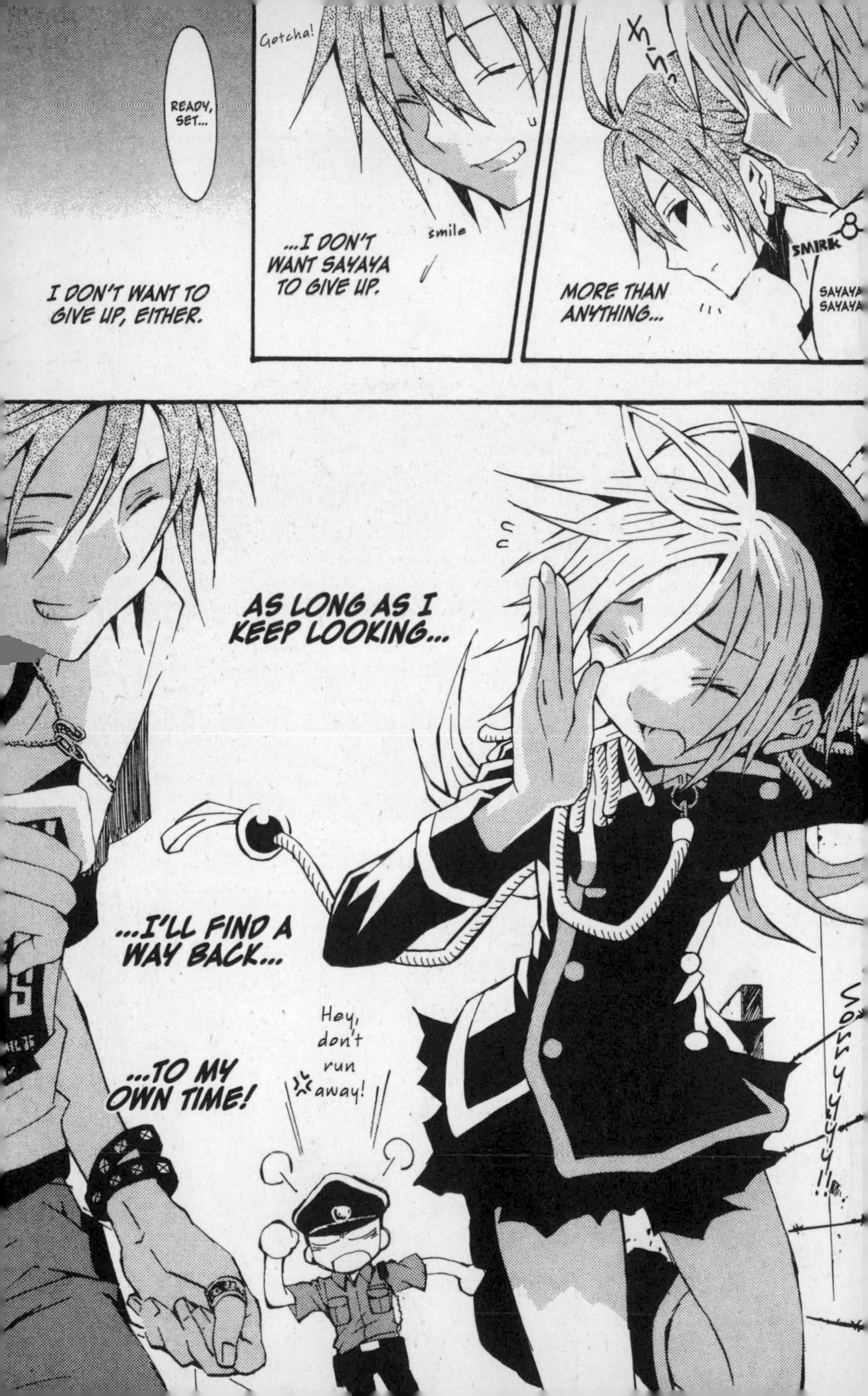
MORE THAN ANYTHING...
SMIRK
SAYAYA SAYAYA
Gotcha!
smile
...I DON'T WANT SAYAYA TO GIVE UP.
READY, SET...
I DON'T WANT TO GIVE UP, EITHER.
Sorryyyyyy!!
AS LONG AS I KEEP LOOKING...
...I'LL FIND A WAY BACK...
...TO MY OWN TIME!
Hey, don't run away!

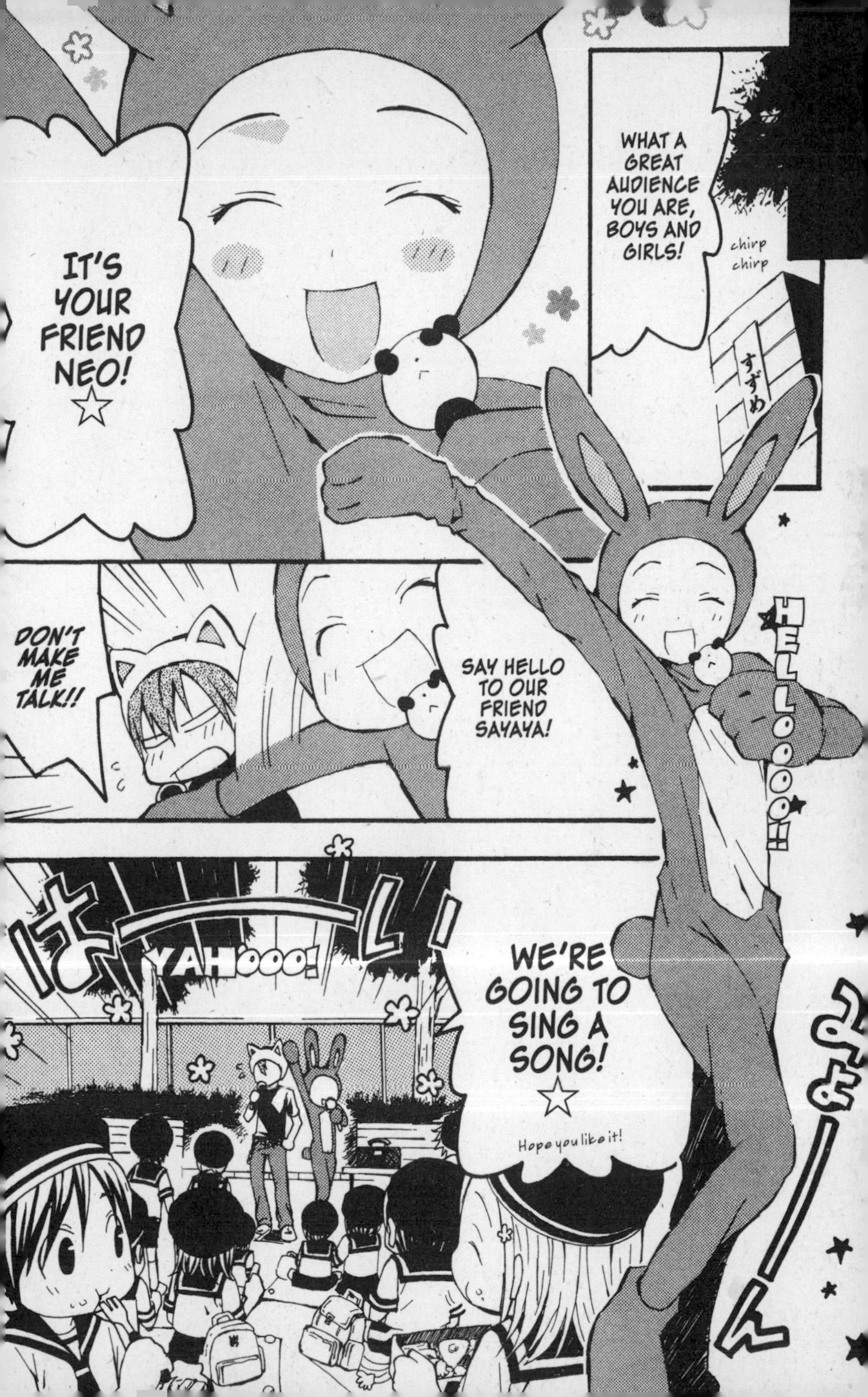
WHAT A GREAT AUDIENCE YOU ARE, BOYS AND GIRLS!
chirp chirp
すずめ
IT'S YOUR FRIEND NEO! ☆
SAY HELLO TO OUR FRIEND SAYAYA!
DON'T MAKE ME TALK!!
HELLOOOOO!!
WE'RE GOING TO SING A SONG! ☆
Hope you like it!
ぴょーん
はーーい
YAHOOOO!

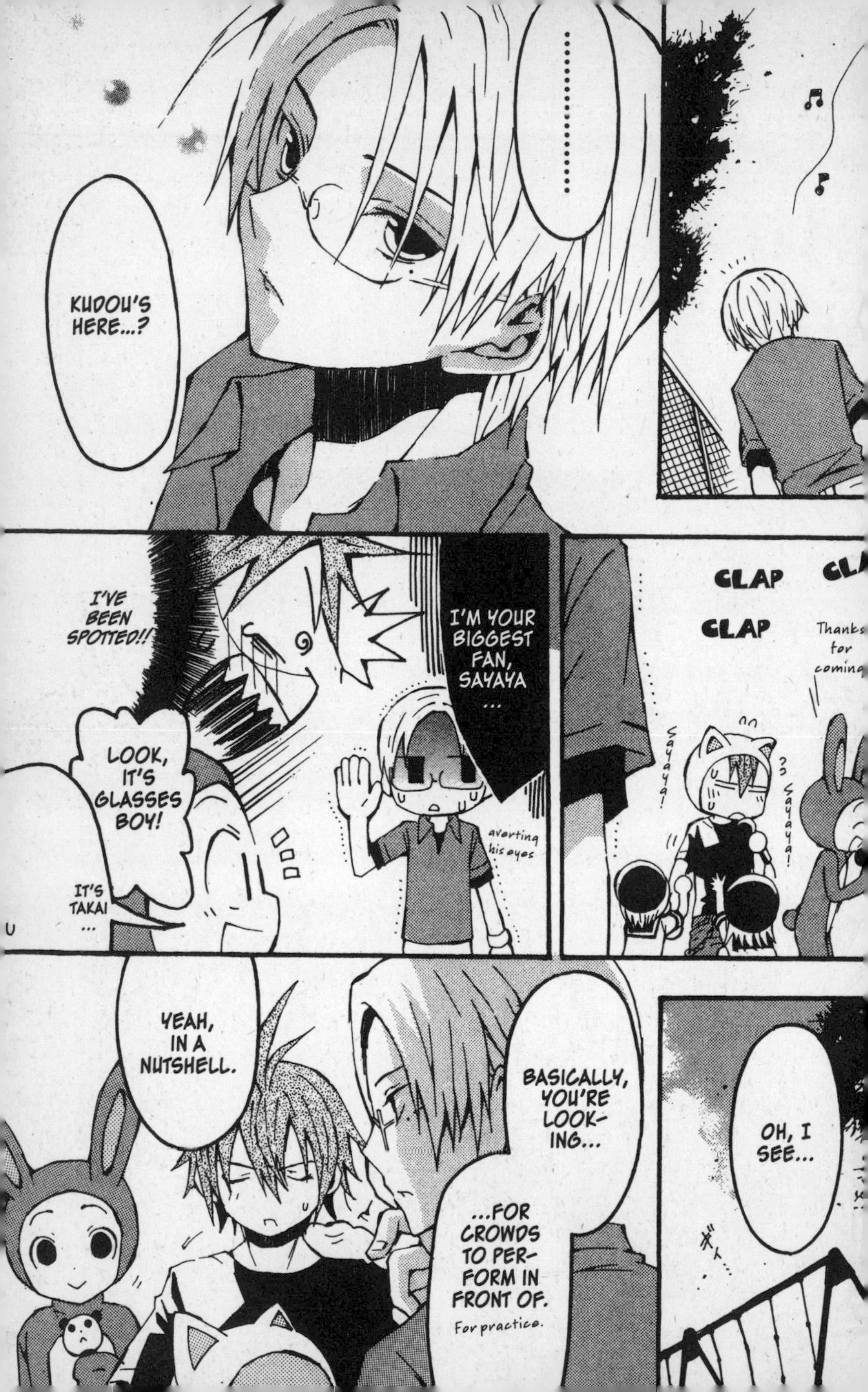
......
KUDOU'S HERE...?
CLAP
CLAP
Thanks for
Sayaya!
Sayaya!
I'M YOUR BIGGEST FAN, SAYAYA ...
I'VE BEEN SPOTTED!!
averting his eyes
LOOK, IT'S GLASSES BOY!
IT'S TAKAI ...
OH, I SEE...
BASICALLY, YOU'RE LOOKING...
...FOR CROWDS TO PERFORM IN FRONT OF.
For practice.
YEAH, IN A NUTSHELL.

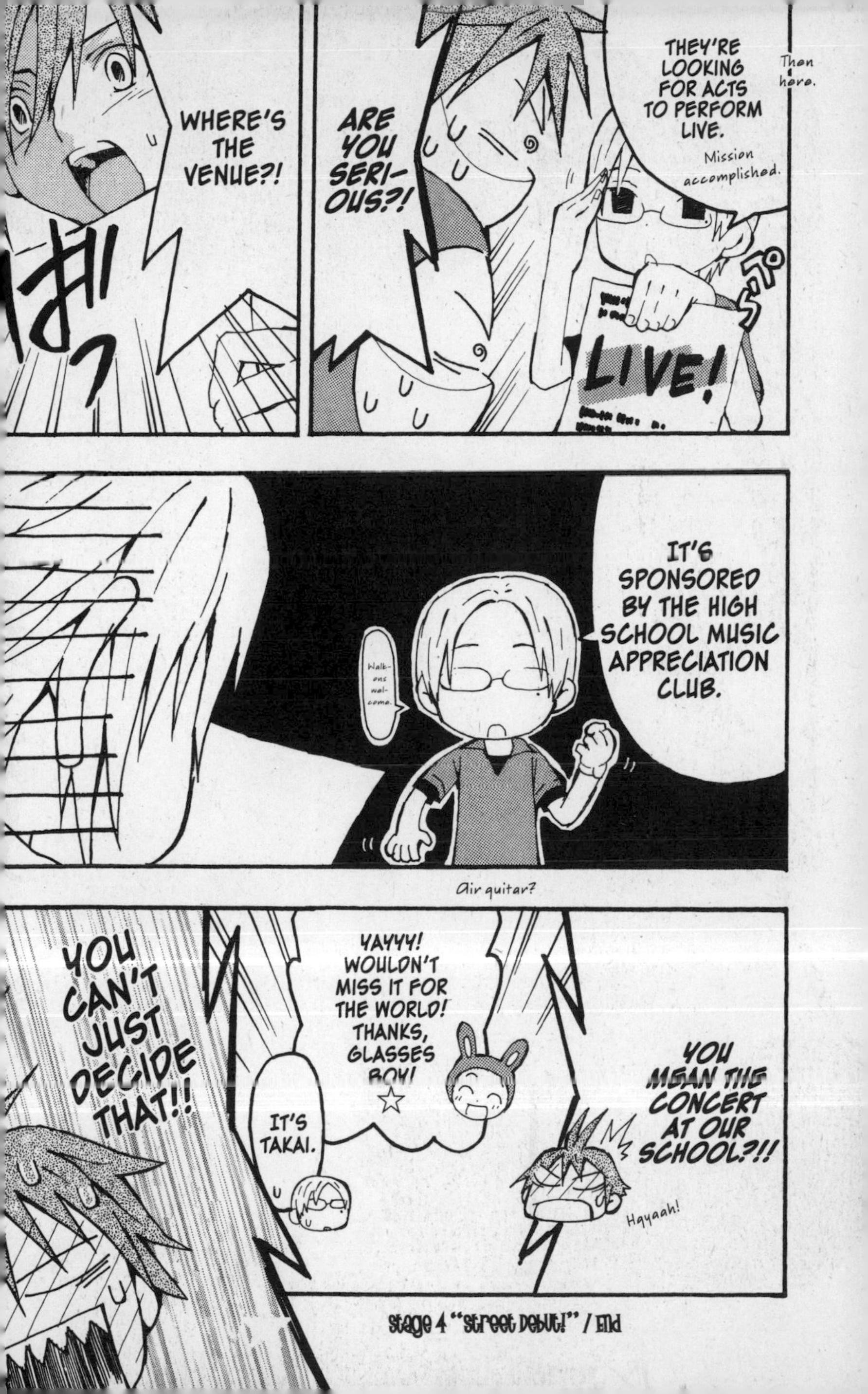
THEY'RE LOOKING FOR ACTS TO PERFORM LIVE.
Then here.
Mission accomplished.
ARE YOU SERI-OUS?!
WHERE'S THE VENUE?!
IT'S SPONSORED BY THE HIGH SCHOOL MUSIC APPRECIATION CLUB.
Walk-ons welcome.
Air guitar?
YOU MEAN THE CONCERT AT OUR SCHOOL?!!
Hayaah!
YAYYY! WOULDN'T MISS IT FOR THE WORLD! THANKS, GLASSES BOY! ☆
IT'S TAKAI.
YOU CAN'T JUST DECIDE THAT!!

Stage 4 "Street Debut!" / End

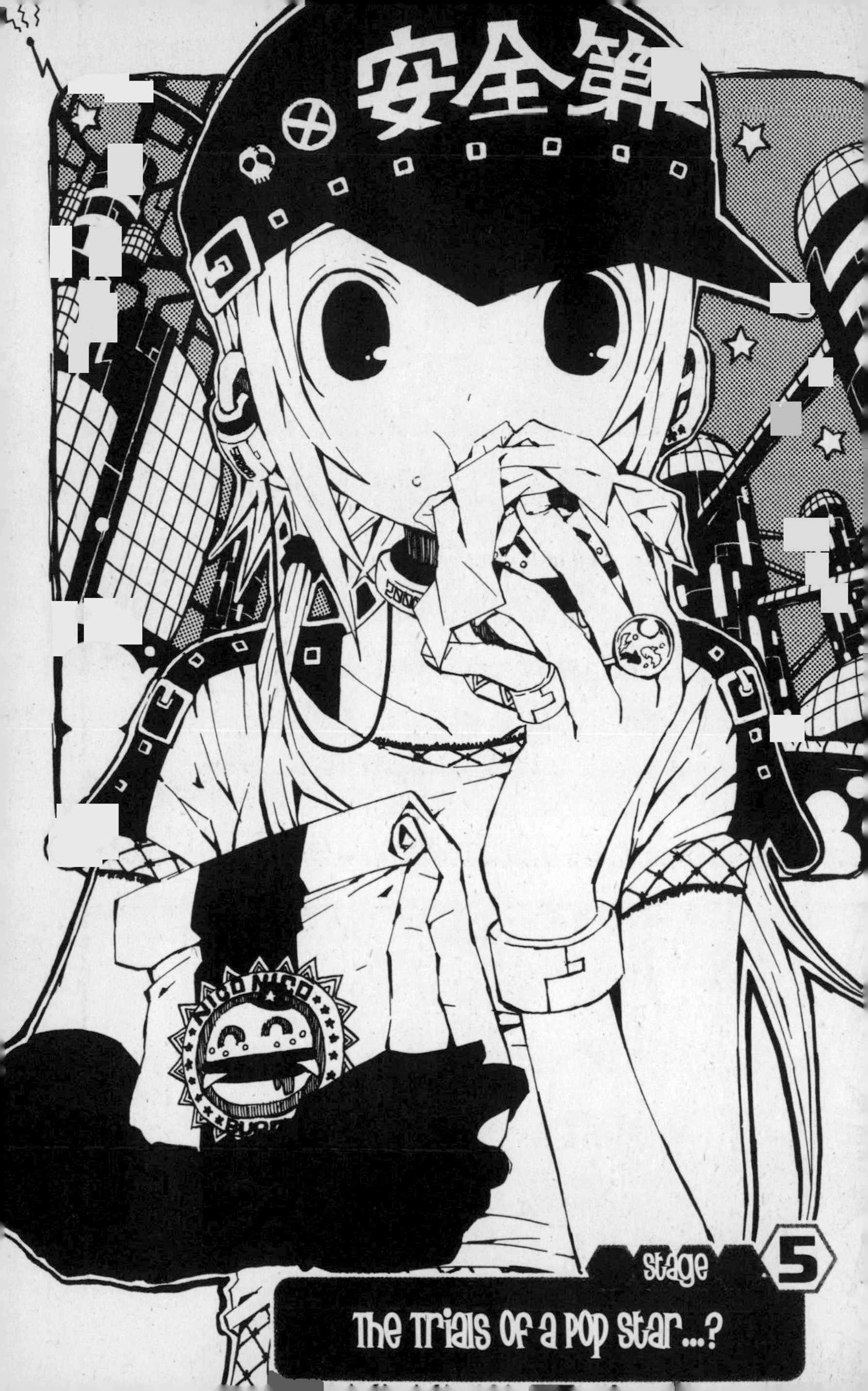
安全第
NICO NICO
stage 5
The Trials of a Pop Star...?

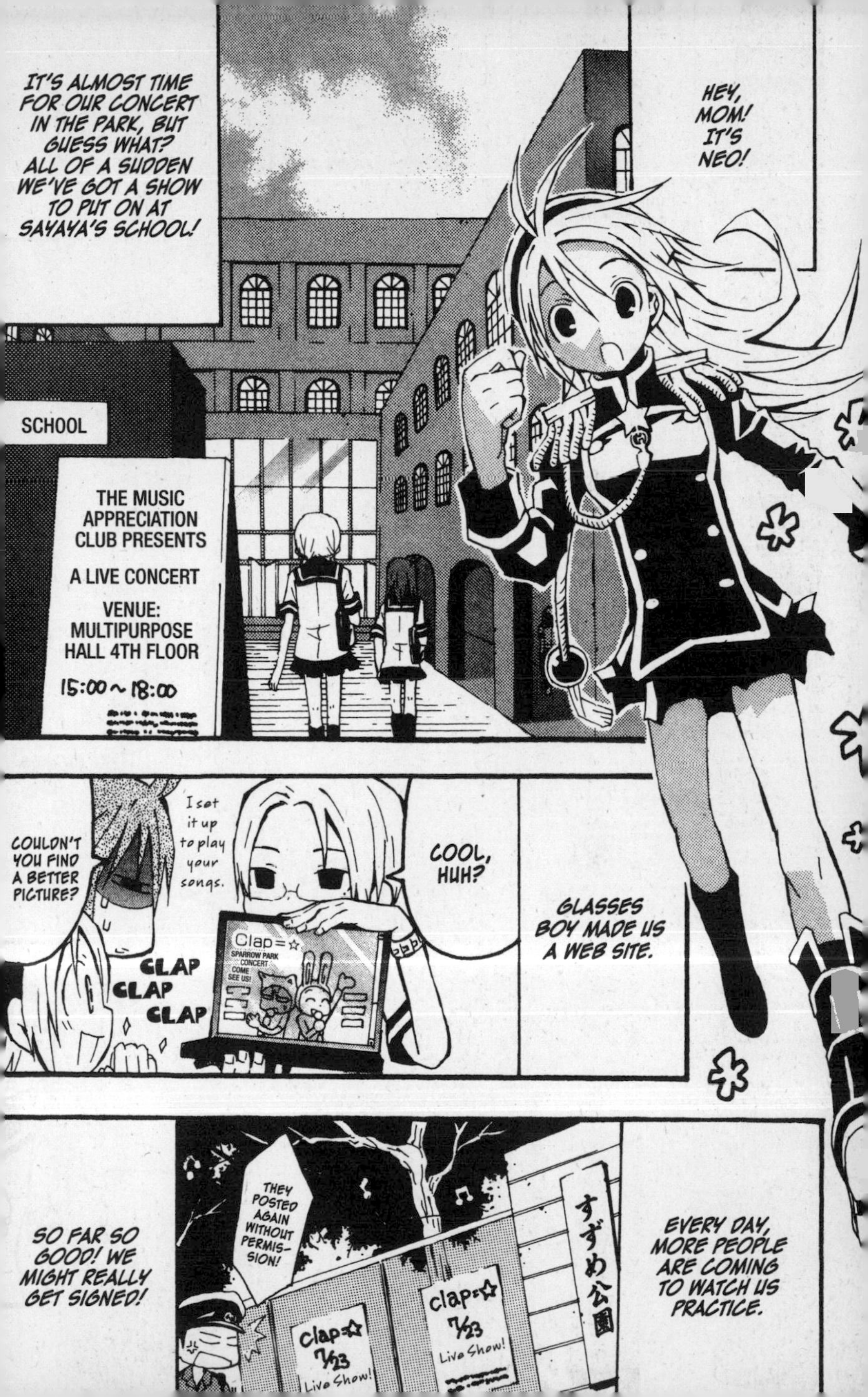
HEY, MOM! IT'S NEO!
IT'S ALMOST TIME FOR OUR CONCERT IN THE PARK, BUT GUESS WHAT? ALL OF A SUDDEN WE'VE GOT A SHOW TO PUT ON AT SAYAYA'S SCHOOL!
SCHOOL
THE MUSIC APPRECIATION CLUB PRESENTS
A LIVE CONCERT
VENUE: MULTIPURPOSE HALL 4TH FLOOR
15:00~18:00
GLASSES BOY MADE US A WEB SITE.
COOL, HUH?
I set it up to play your songs.
COULDN'T YOU FIND A BETTER PICTURE?
Clap=☆
SPARROW PARK CONCERT
COME SEE US!
CLAP
CLAP
CLAP
EVERY DAY, MORE PEOPLE ARE COMING TO WATCH US PRACTICE.
すずめ公園
clap=☆ 7/23 Live Show!
THEY POSTED AGAIN WITHOUT PERMIS-SION!
Clap=☆ 7/23 Live Show!
SO FAR SO GOOD! WE MIGHT REALLY GET SIGNED!

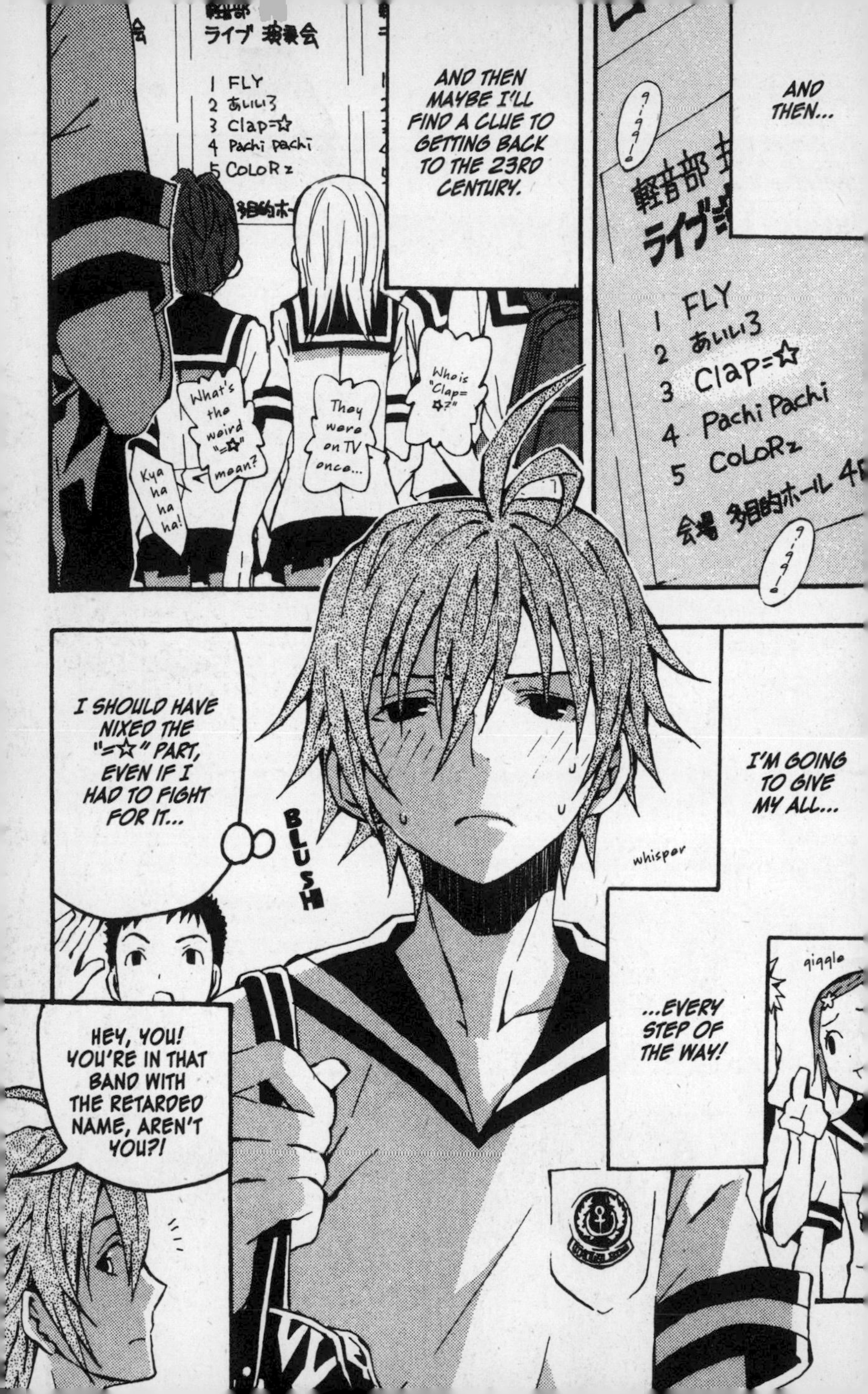
AND THEN...
軽音部
ライブ
1 FLY
2 あいい3
3 Clap=☆
4 Pachi Pachi
5 CoLoRz
会場 多目的ホール
AND THEN MAYBE I'LL FIND A CLUE TO GETTING BACK TO THE 23RD CENTURY.
ライブ 演奏会
1 FLY
2 あいい3
3 Clap=☆
4 Pachi pachi
5 CoLoRz
Who is "Clap=☆?"
They were on TV once...
What's the weird "=☆" mean?
Kya ha ha ha!
I'M GOING TO GIVE MY ALL...
whisper
BLUSH
I SHOULD HAVE NIXED THE "=☆" PART, EVEN IF I HAD TO FIGHT FOR IT...
giggle
...EVERY STEP OF THE WAY!
HEY, YOU! YOU'RE IN THAT BAND WITH THE RETARDED NAME, AREN'T YOU?!

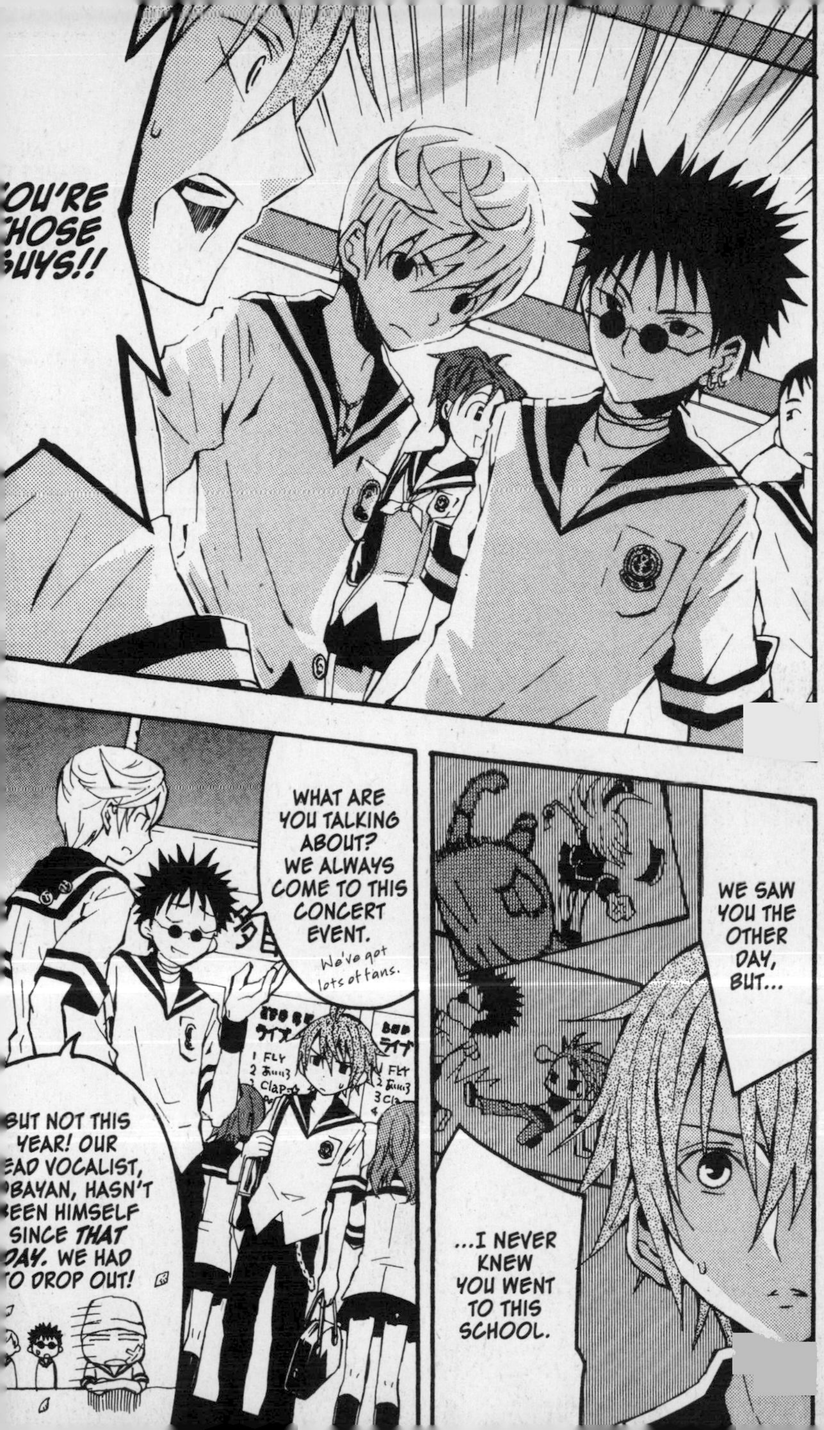

OU'RE HOSE UYS!!
WE SAW YOU THE OTHER DAY, BUT...
...I NEVER KNEW YOU WENT TO THIS SCHOOL.
WHAT ARE YOU TALKING ABOUT? WE ALWAYS COME TO THIS CONCERT EVENT.
We've got lots of fans.
BUT NOT THIS YEAR! OUR EAD VOCALIST, OBAYAN, HASN'T EEN HIMSELF SINCE THAT DAY. WE HAD O DROP OUT!

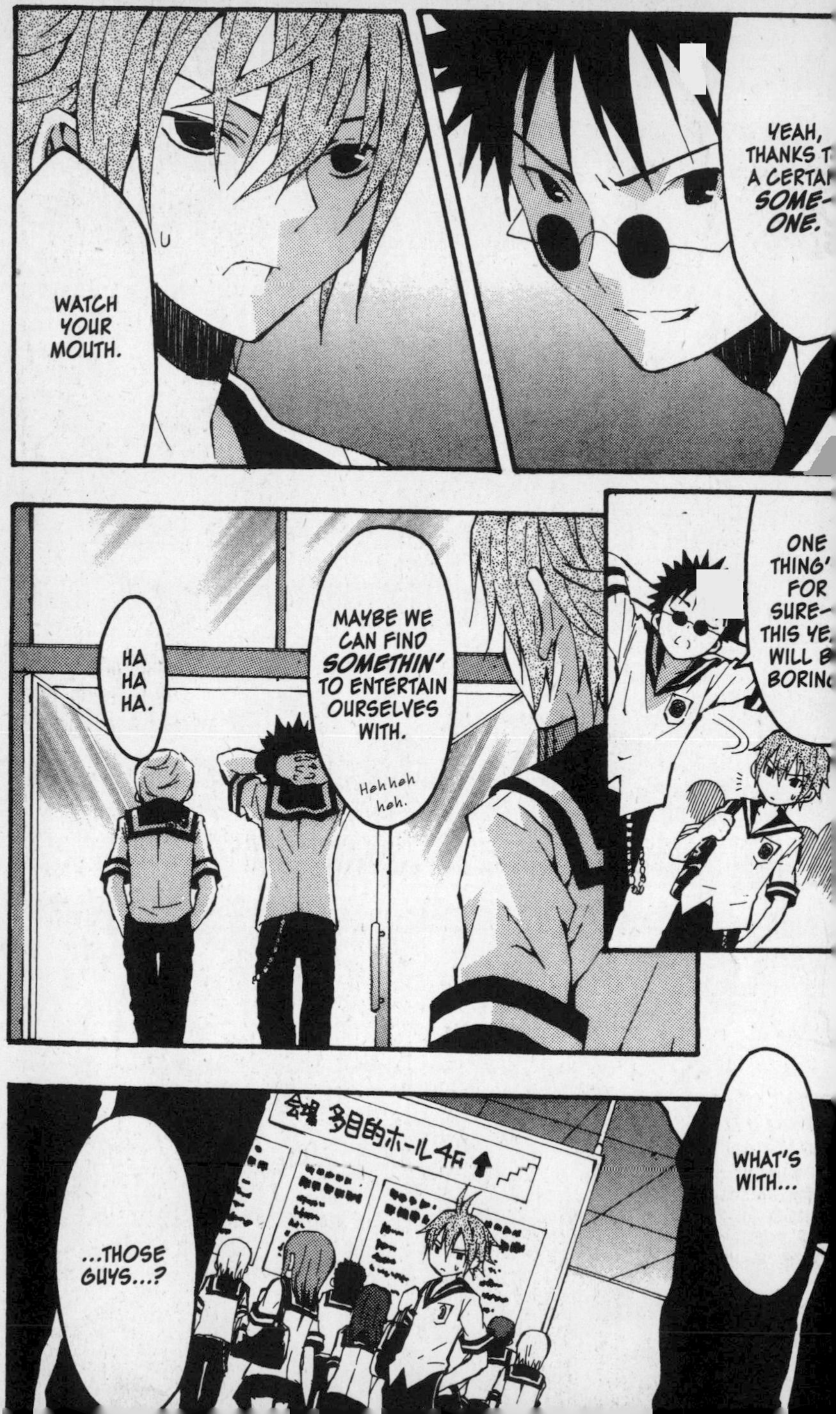
YEAH, THANKS T A CERTAI SOME-ONE.
WATCH YOUR MOUTH.
ONE THING' FOR SURE- THIS YE WILL B BORIN
MAYBE WE CAN FIND SOMETHIN' TO ENTERTAIN OURSELVES WITH.
Heh heh heh.
HA HA HA.
WHAT'S WITH...
会場 多目的ホール4F
...THOSE GUYS...?

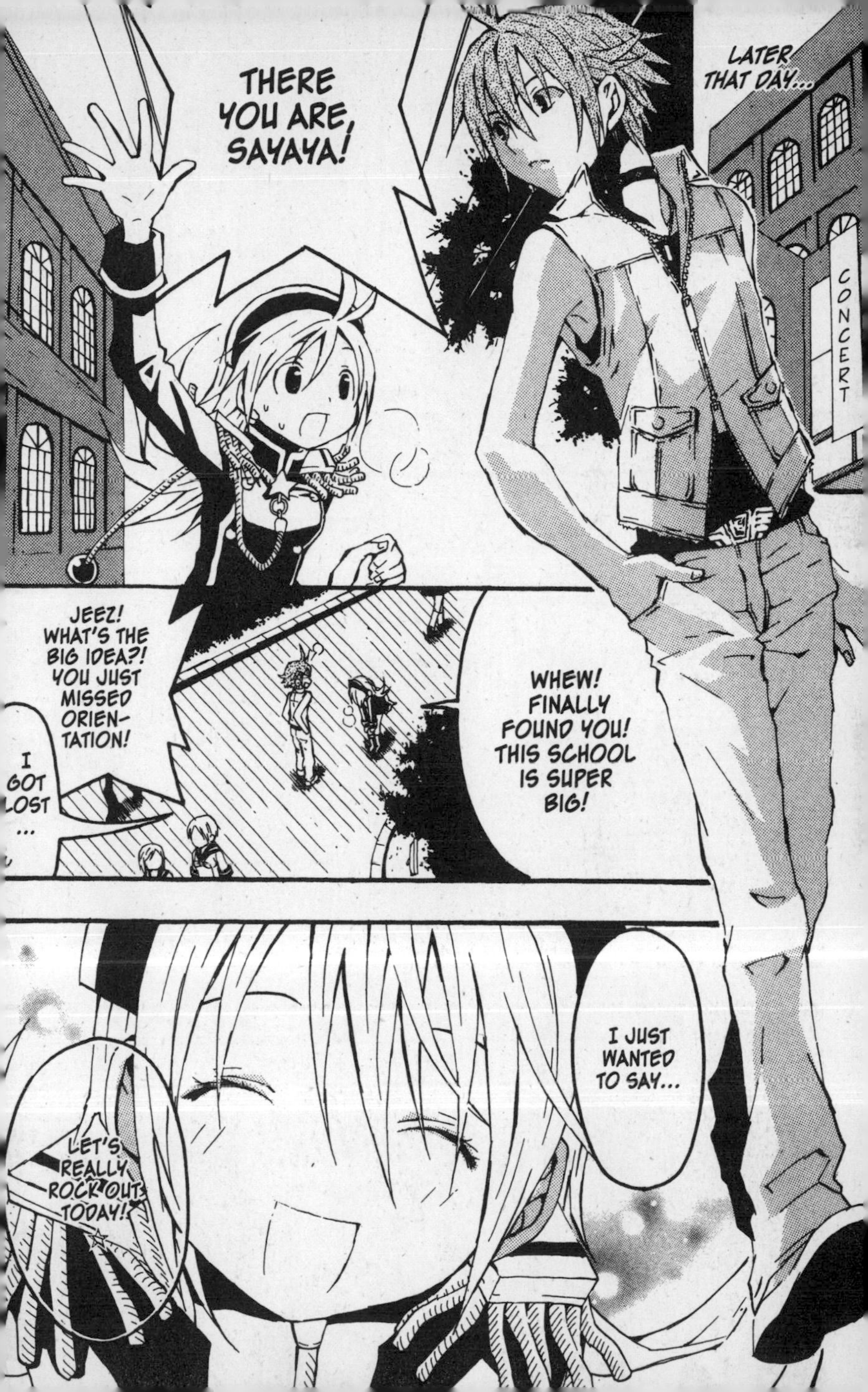
LATER THAT DAY...
CONCERT
THERE YOU ARE, SAYAYA!
WHEW! FINALLY FOUND YOU! THIS SCHOOL IS SUPER BIG!
JEEZ! WHAT'S THE BIG IDEA?! YOU JUST MISSED ORIEN- TATION!
I GOT LOST ...
I JUST WANTED TO SAY...
LET'S REALLY ROCK OUT TODAY!

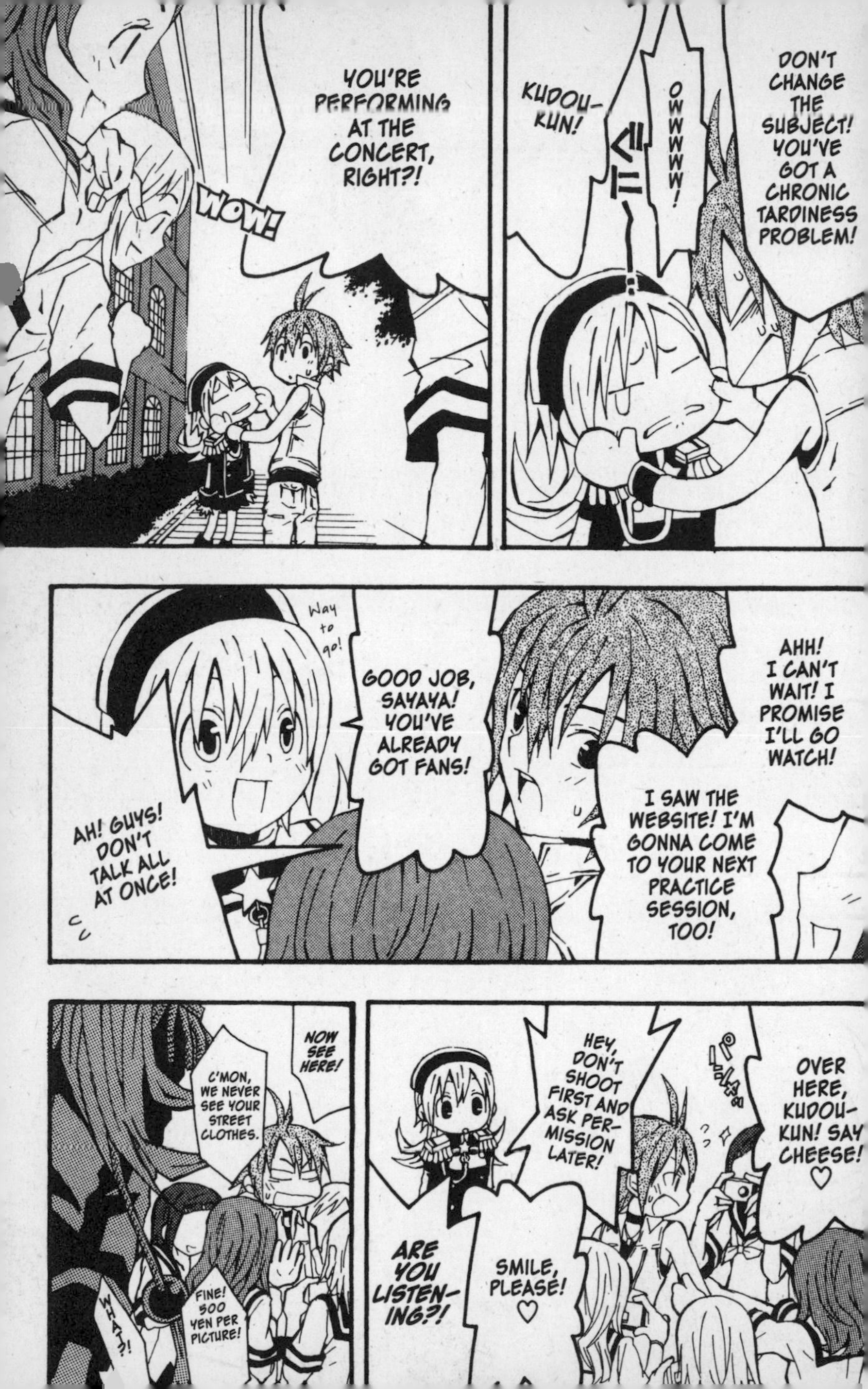
DON'T CHANGE THE SUBJECT! YOU'VE GOT A CHRONIC TARDINESS PROBLEM!
OWWWWWW!
KUDOU-KUN!
YOU'RE PERFORMING AT THE CONCERT, RIGHT?!
WOW!
AHH! I CAN'T WAIT! I PROMISE I'LL GO WATCH!
I SAW THE WEBSITE! I'M GONNA COME TO YOUR NEXT PRACTICE SESSION, TOO!
Way to go!
GOOD JOB, SAYAYA! YOU'VE ALREADY GOT FANS!
AH! GUYS! DON'T TALK ALL AT ONCE!
OVER HERE, KUDOU-KUN! SAY CHEESE! ♡
HEY, DON'T SHOOT FIRST AND ASK PER-MISSION LATER!
SMILE, PLEASE! ♡
ARE YOU LISTEN-ING?!
NOW SEE HERE!
C'MON, WE NEVER SEE YOUR STREET CLOTHES.
FINE! 500 YEN PER PICTURE!
WHAT?!

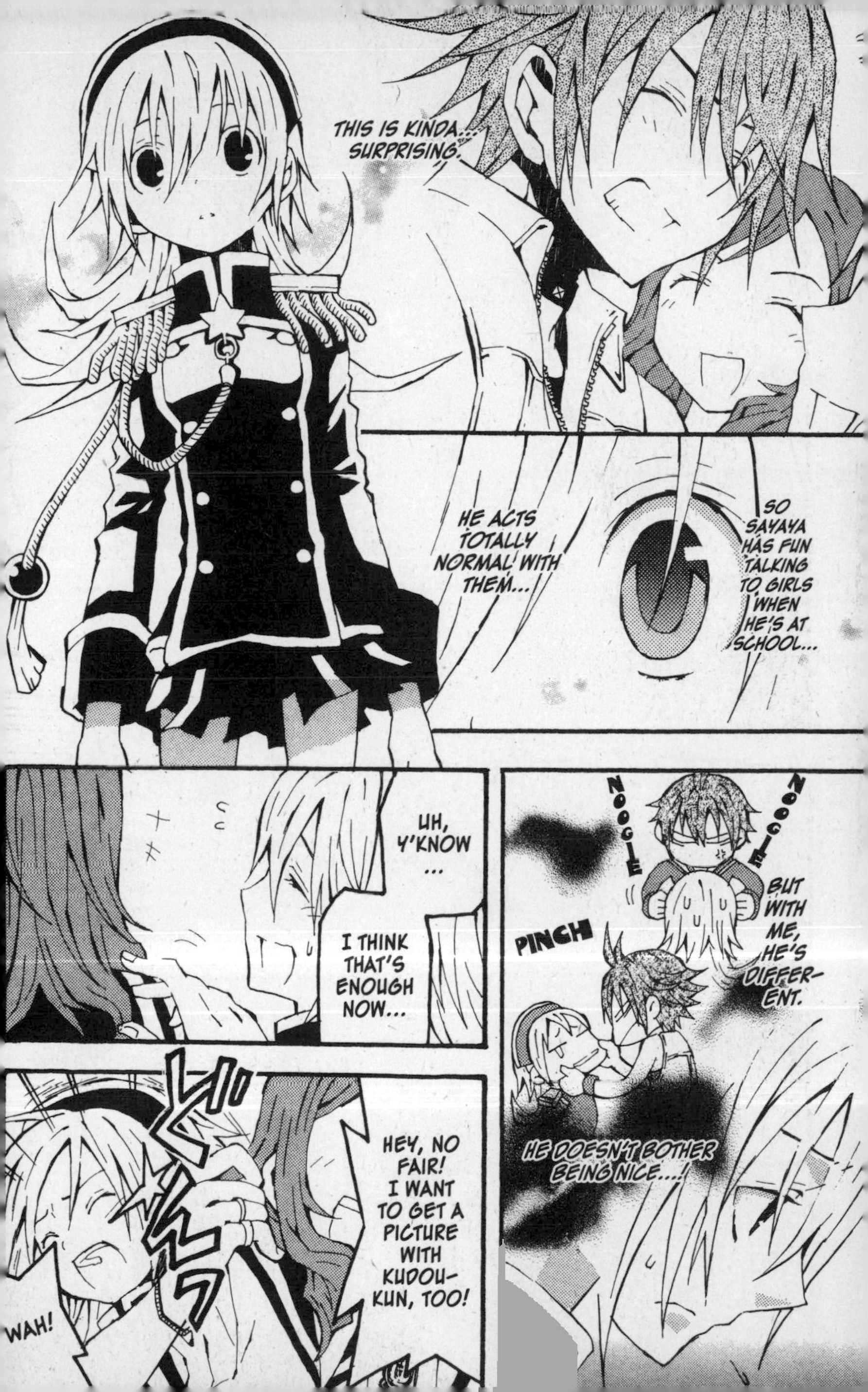
THIS IS KINDA... SURPRISING.
SO SAYAYA HAS FUN TALKING TO GIRLS WHEN HE'S AT SCHOOL...
HE ACTS TOTALLY NORMAL WITH THEM...
NOOGIE
NOOGIE
BUT WITH ME, HE'S DIFFER-ENT.
PINCH
HE DOESN'T BOTHER BEING NICE...!
UH, Y'KNOW ...
I THINK THAT'S ENOUGH NOW...
HEY, NO FAIR! I WANT TO GET A PICTURE WITH KUDOU-KUN, TOO!
WAH!

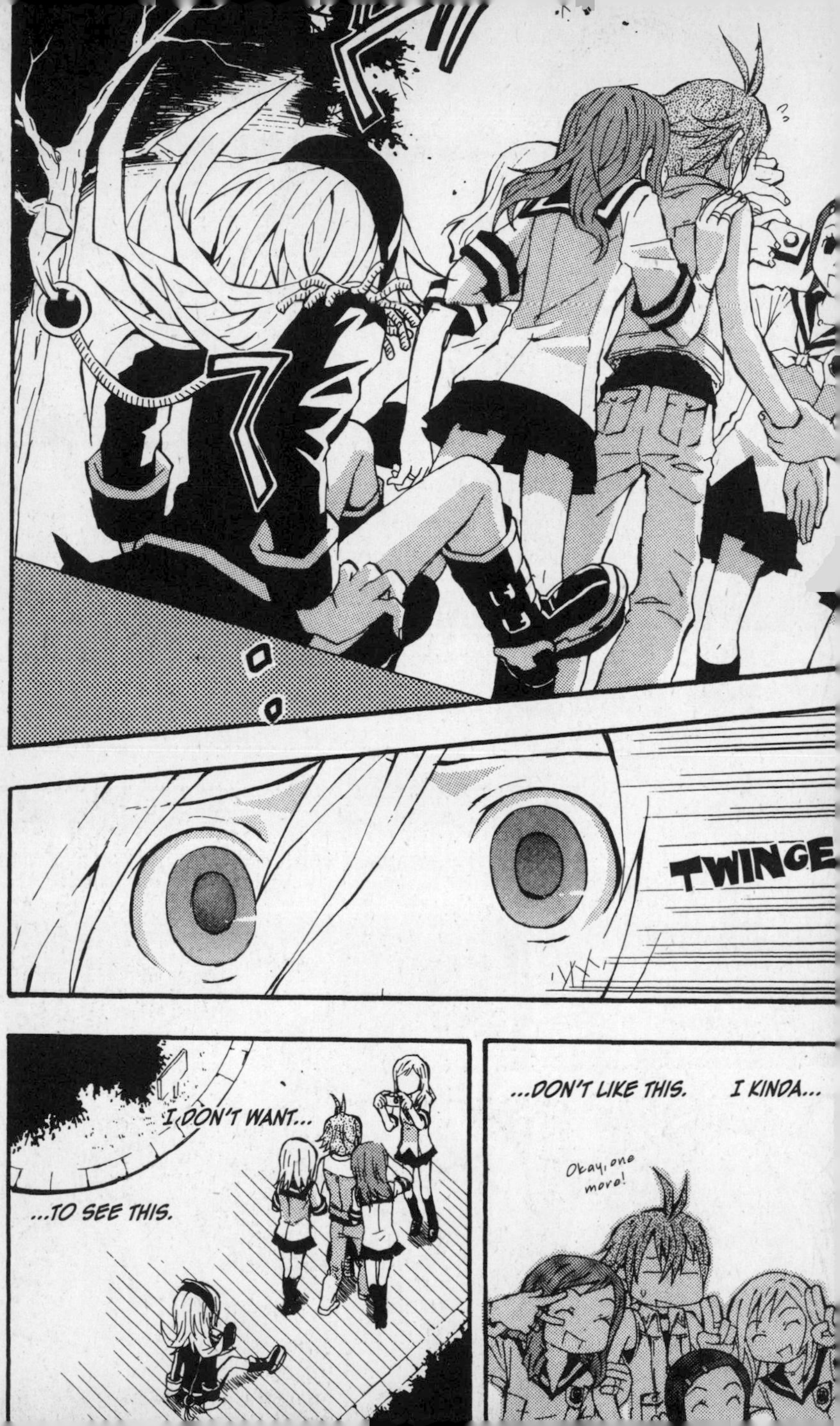
TWINGE
I KINDA...
...DON'T LIKE THIS.
Okay, one more!
I DON'T WANT...
...TO SEE THIS.

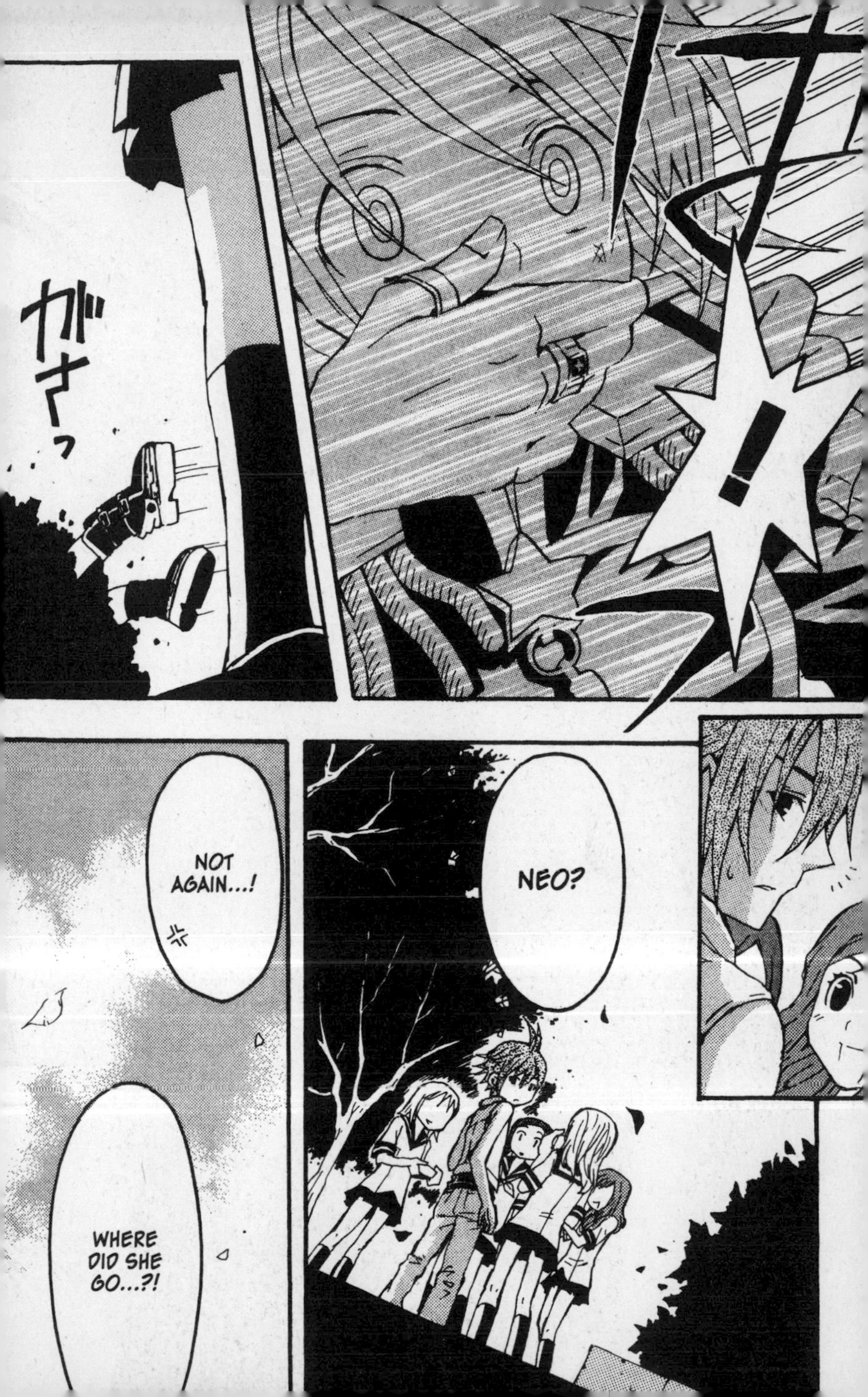
!
がさっ
NEO?
NOT AGAIN...!
WHERE DID SHE GO...?!

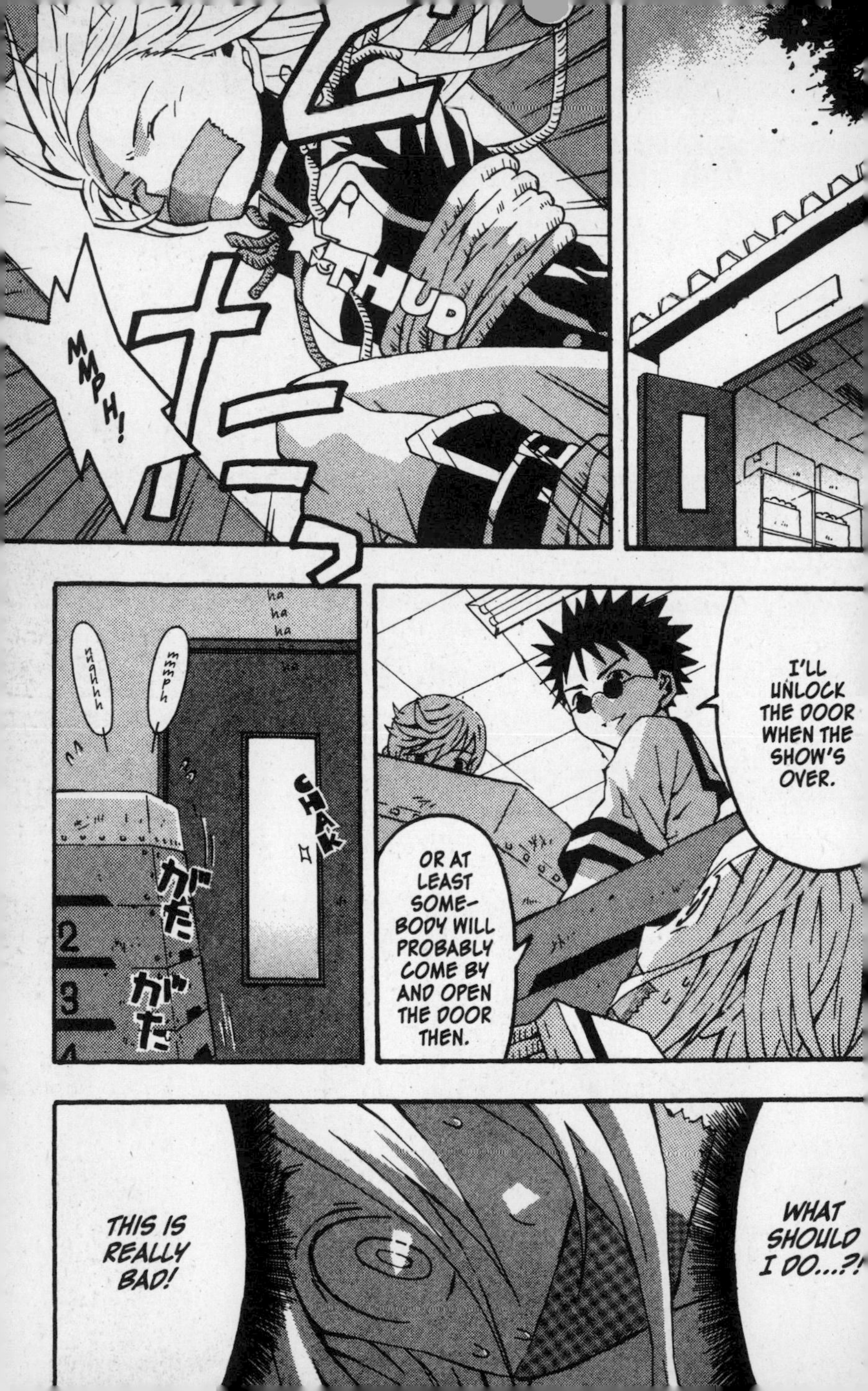
THUD
MMPH!
I'LL UNLOCK THE DOOR WHEN THE SHOW'S OVER.
OR AT LEAST SOMEBODY WILL PROBABLY COME BY AND OPEN THE DOOR THEN.
ha ha ha
mmmph
nghhh
CHAK
がたがた
WHAT SHOULD I DO...?!
THIS IS REALLY BAD!

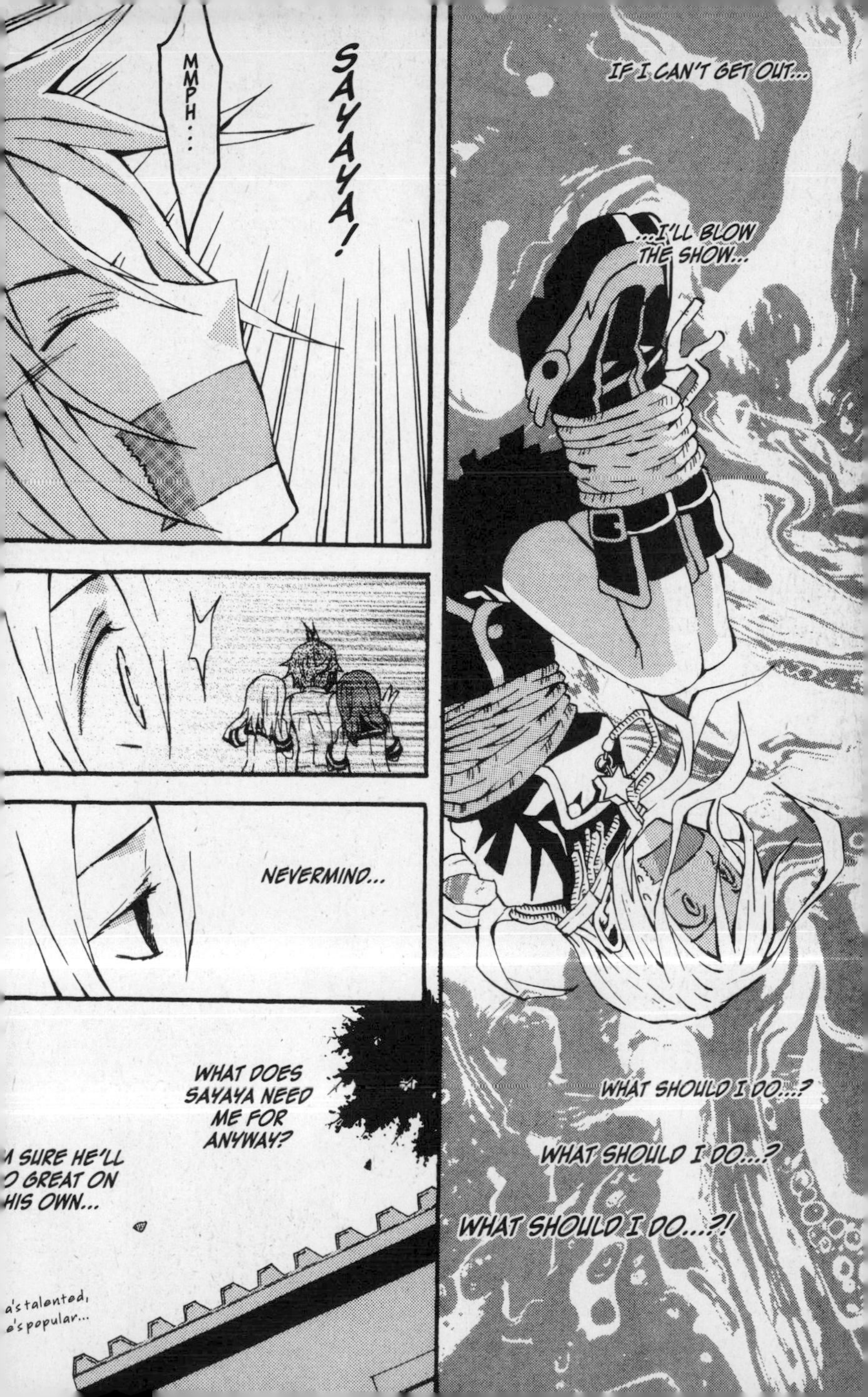
IF I CAN'T GET OUT...
...I'LL BLOW THE SHOW...
WHAT SHOULD I DO...?
WHAT SHOULD I DO...?
WHAT SHOULD I DO...?!
SAYAYA!
MMPH...
NEVERMIND...
WHAT DOES SAYAYA NEED ME FOR ANYWAY?
M SURE HE'LL O GREAT ON HIS OWN...
a's talented, e's popular...

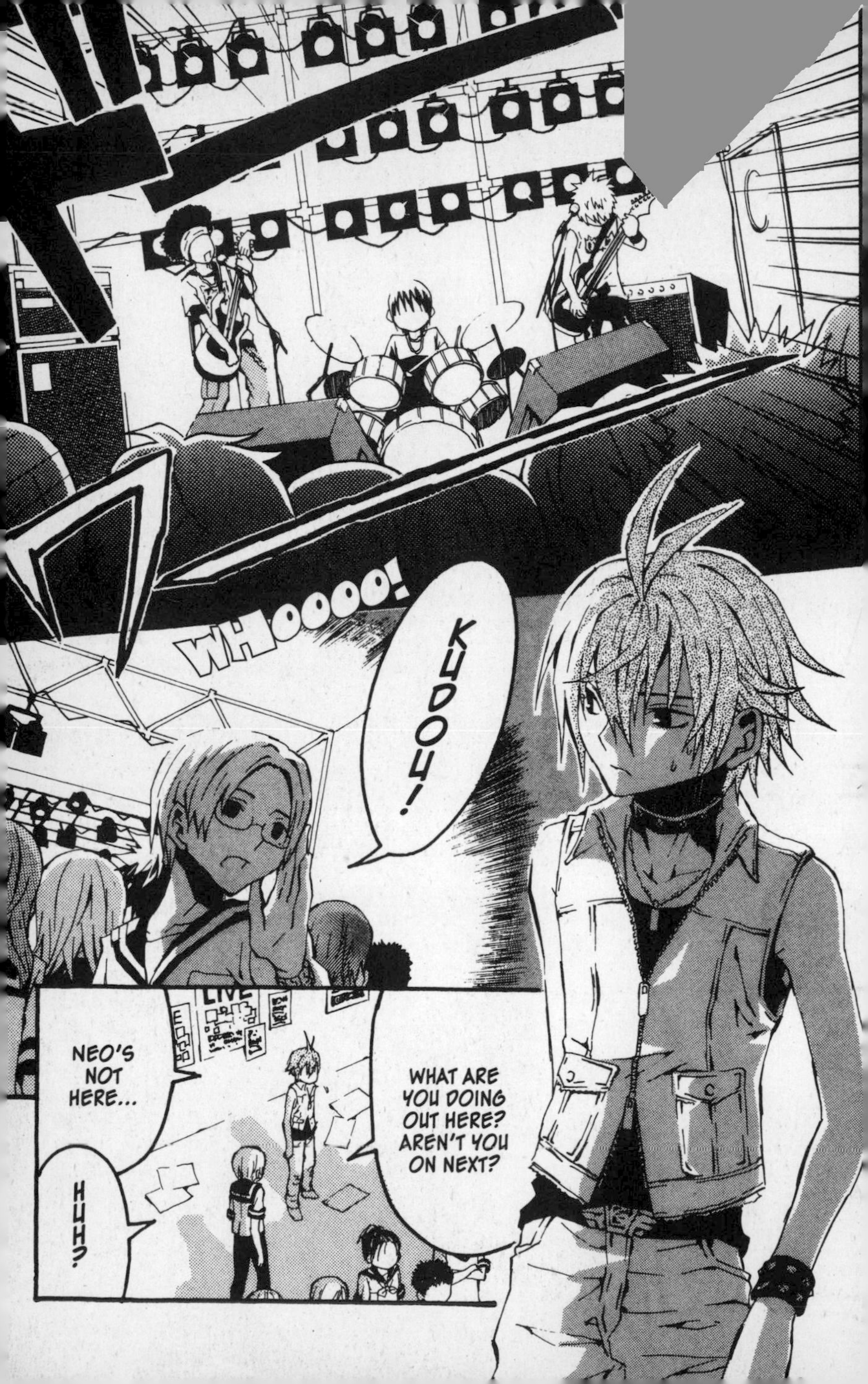
WHOOOOO!
KUDOOU!
WHAT ARE YOU DOING OUT HERE? AREN'T YOU ON NEXT?
NEO'S NOT HERE...
HUH?
LIVE

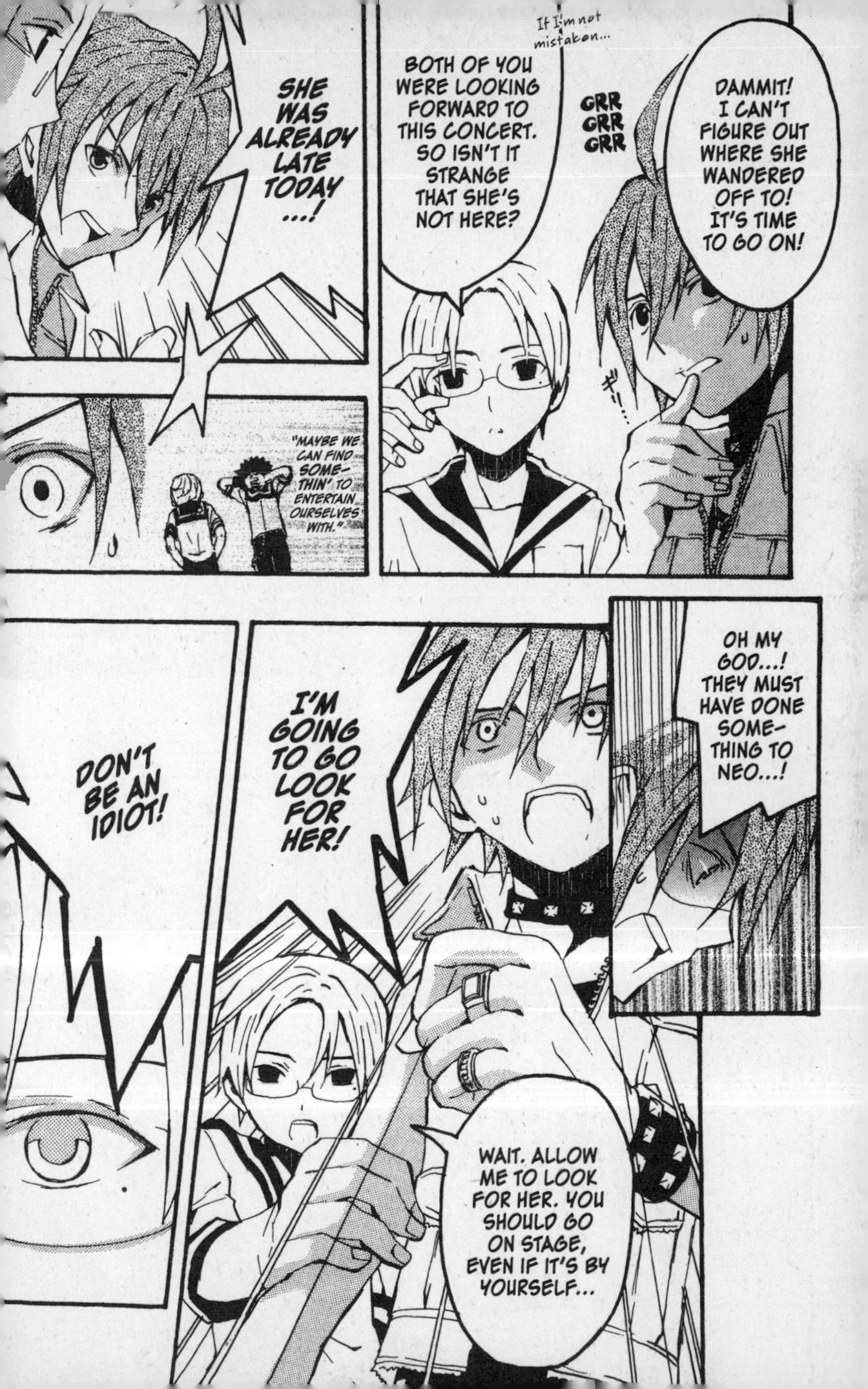
DAMMIT! I CAN'T FIGURE OUT WHERE SHE WANDERED OFF TO! IT'S TIME TO GO ON!
GRR GRR GRR
If I'm not mistaken...
BOTH OF YOU WERE LOOKING FORWARD TO THIS CONCERT. SO ISN'T IT STRANGE THAT SHE'S NOT HERE?
SHE WAS ALREADY LATE TODAY ...!
"MAYBE WE CAN FIND SOME-THIN' TO ENTERTAIN OURSELVES WITH."
OH MY GOD...! THEY MUST HAVE DONE SOME-THING TO NEO...!
I'M GOING TO GO LOOK FOR HER!
WAIT. ALLOW ME TO LOOK FOR HER. YOU SHOULD GO ON STAGE, EVEN IF IT'S BY YOURSELF...
DON'T BE AN IDIOT!

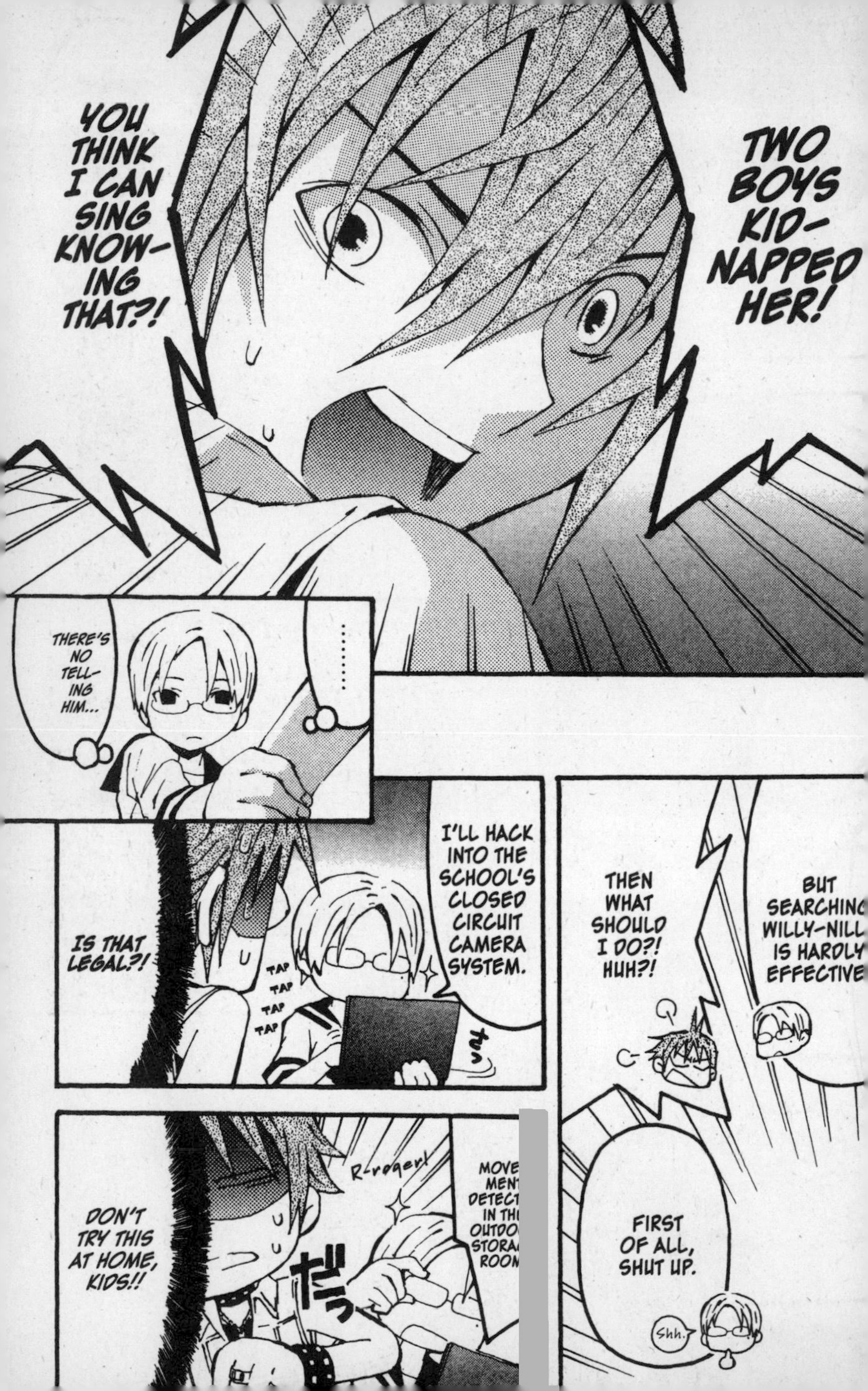
TWO BOYS KID-NAPPED HER!
YOU THINK I CAN SING KNOW-ING THAT?!
......
THERE'S NO TELLING HIM...
BUT SEARCHING WILLY-NILL IS HARDLY EFFECTIVE
THEN WHAT SHOULD I DO?! HUH?!
FIRST OF ALL, SHUT UP.
Shh.
I'LL HACK INTO THE SCHOOL'S CLOSED CIRCUIT CAMERA SYSTEM.
TAP TAP TAP TAP
IS THAT LEGAL?!
MOVE-MENT DETECT IN TH OUTDOO STORA ROOM
R-roger!
DON'T TRY THIS AT HOME, KIDS!!

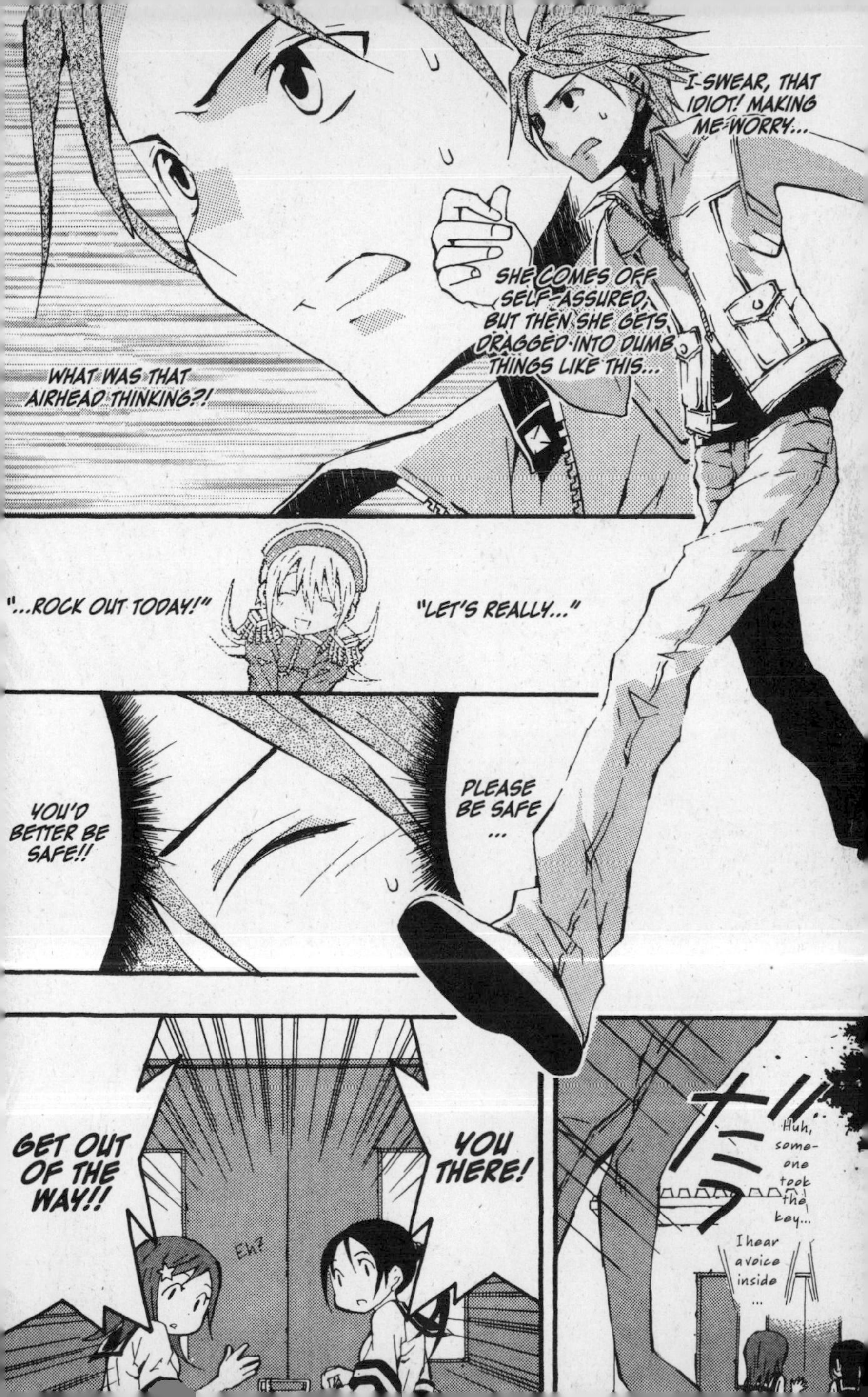
I SWEAR, THAT IDIOT! MAKING ME WORRY...
SHE COMES OFF SELF-ASSURED, BUT THEN SHE GETS DRAGGED INTO DUMB THINGS LIKE THIS...
WHAT WAS THAT AIRHEAD THINKING?!
"LET'S REALLY..."
"...ROCK OUT TODAY!"
PLEASE BE SAFE ...
YOU'D BETTER BE SAFE!!
Huh, someone took the key...
I hear a voice inside ...
YOU THERE!
GET OUT OF THE WAY!!
Eh?

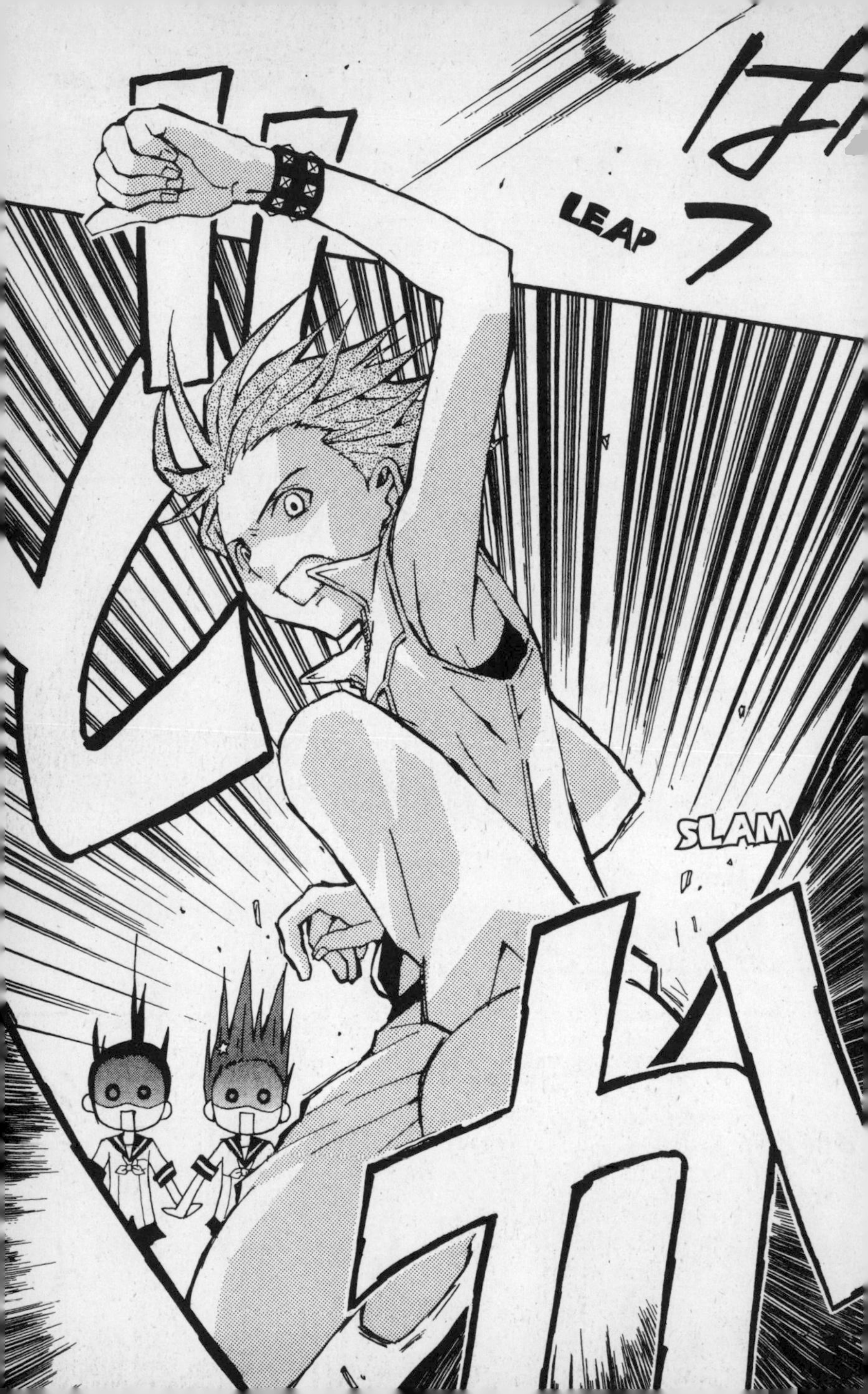
LEAP
SLAM

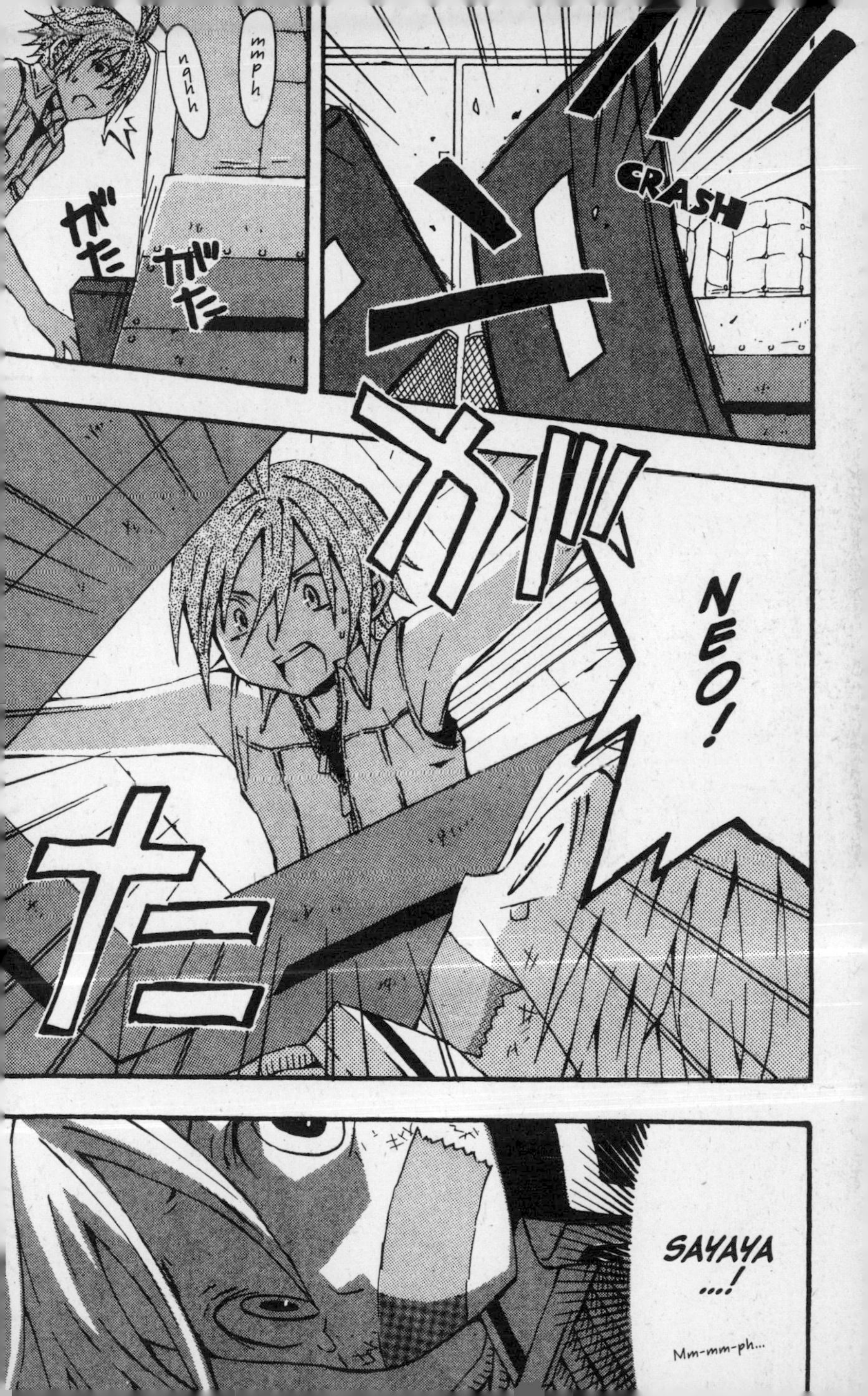
CRASH
mmph
nghh
がた
がた
NEO!
SAYAYA ...!
Mm-mm-ph...

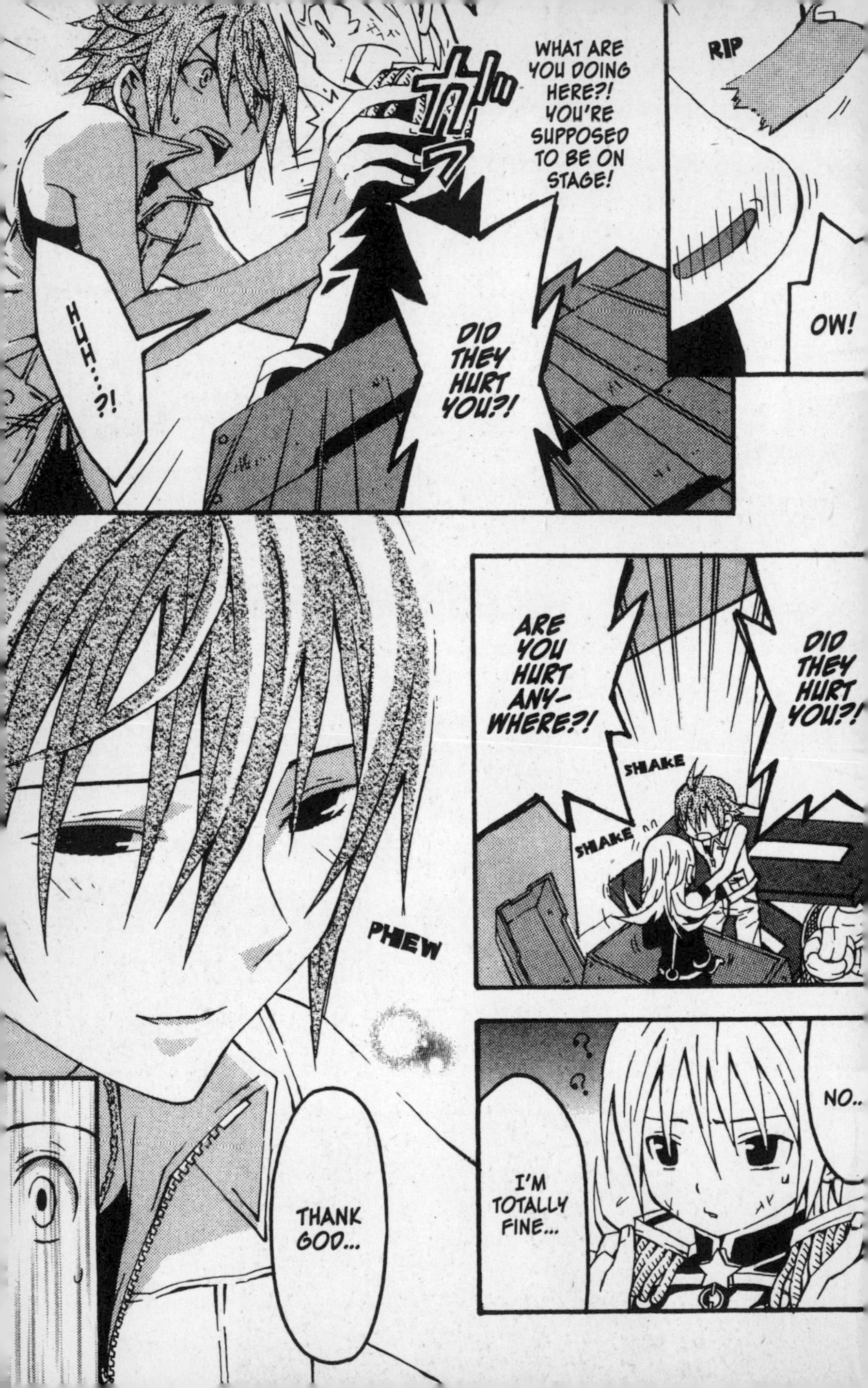
RIP
OW!
WHAT ARE YOU DOING HERE?! YOU'RE SUPPOSED TO BE ON STAGE!
DID THEY HURT YOU?!
HUH...?!
DID THEY HURT YOU?!
ARE YOU HURT ANY-WHERE?!
SHAKE
SHAKE
NO..
I'M TOTALLY FINE...
PHEW
THANK GOD...

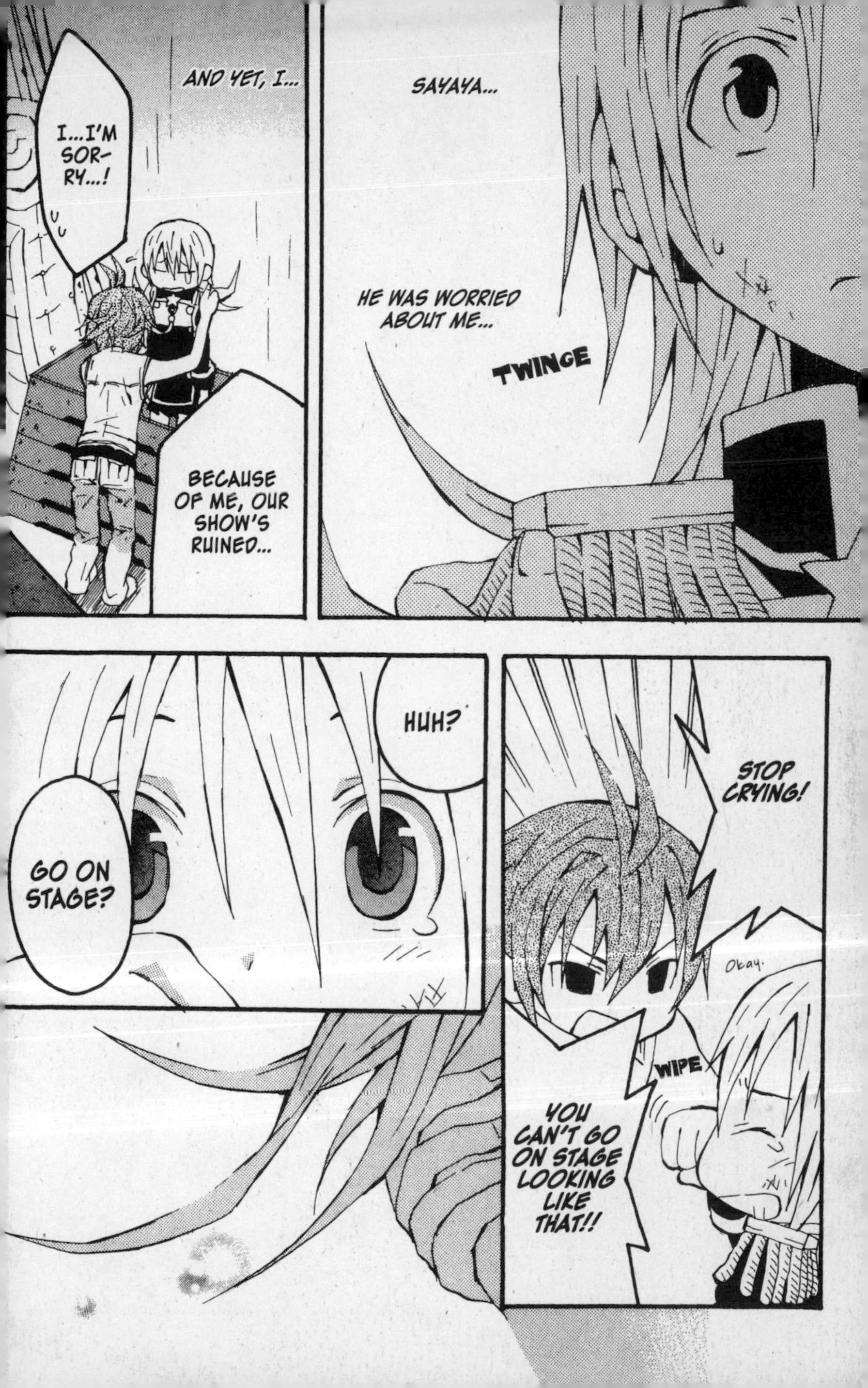
SAYAYA...
HE WAS WORRIED ABOUT ME...
TWINGE
AND YET, I...
I...I'M SOR-RY...!
BECAUSE OF ME, OUR SHOW'S RUINED...
STOP CRYING!
Okay.
WIPE
YOU CAN'T GO ON STAGE LOOKING LIKE THAT!!
HUH?
GO ON STAGE?

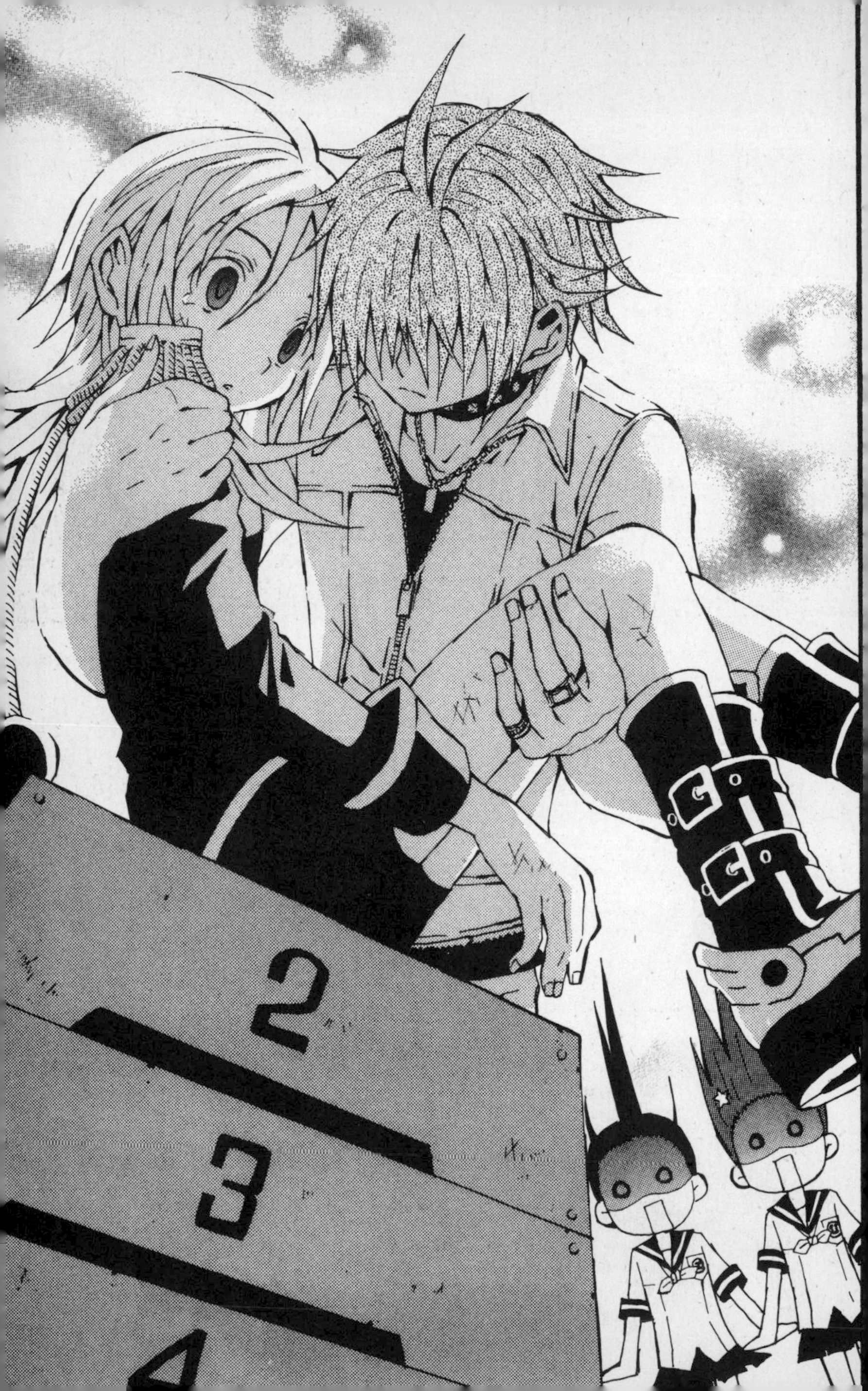
2
3
4

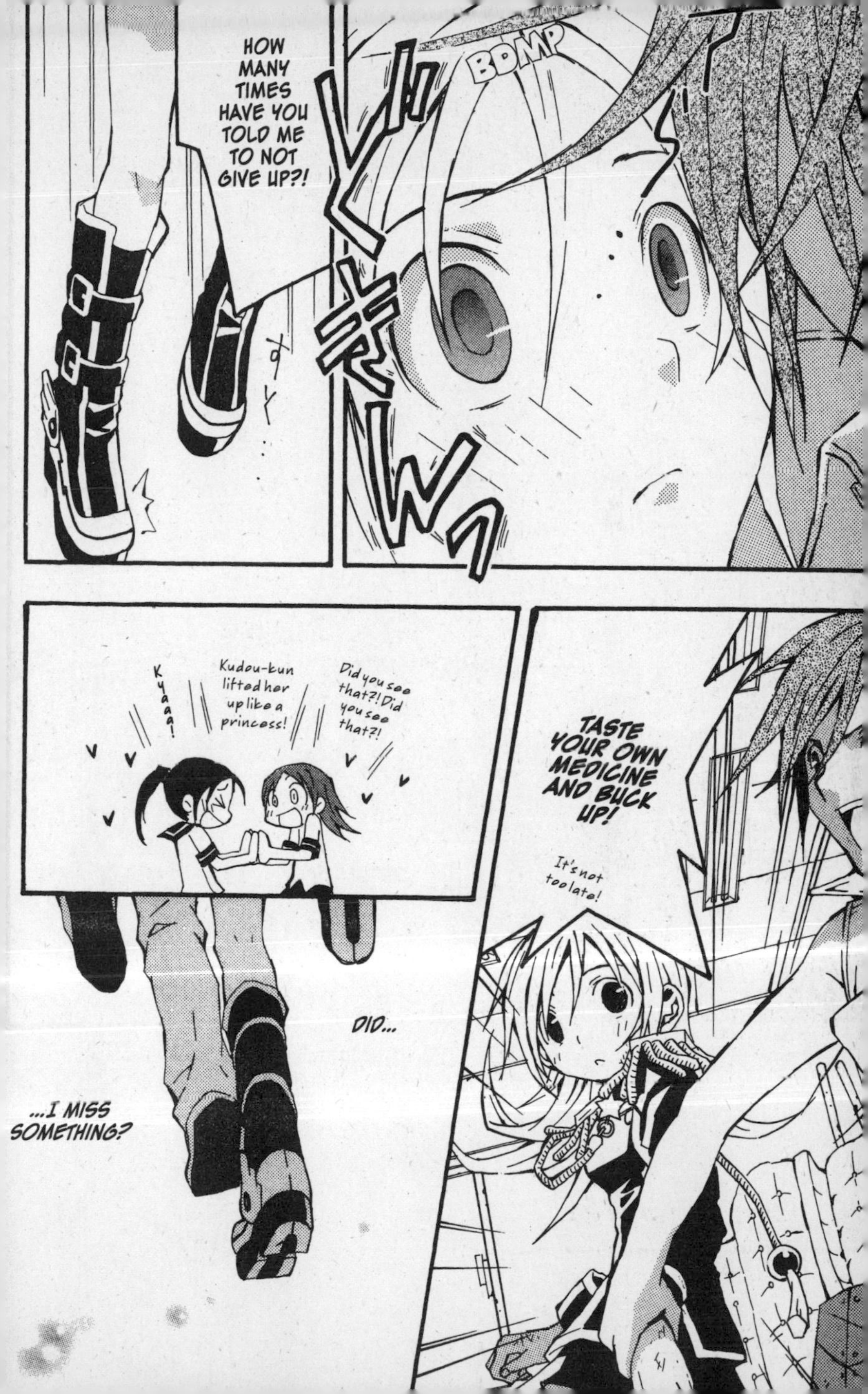
BDMP
HOW MANY TIMES HAVE YOU TOLD ME TO NOT GIVE UP?!
TASTE YOUR OWN MEDICINE AND BUCK UP!
It's not too late!
Did you see that?! Did you see that?!
Kudou-kun lifted her up like a princess!
Kyaaa!
DID...
...I MISS SOMETHING?

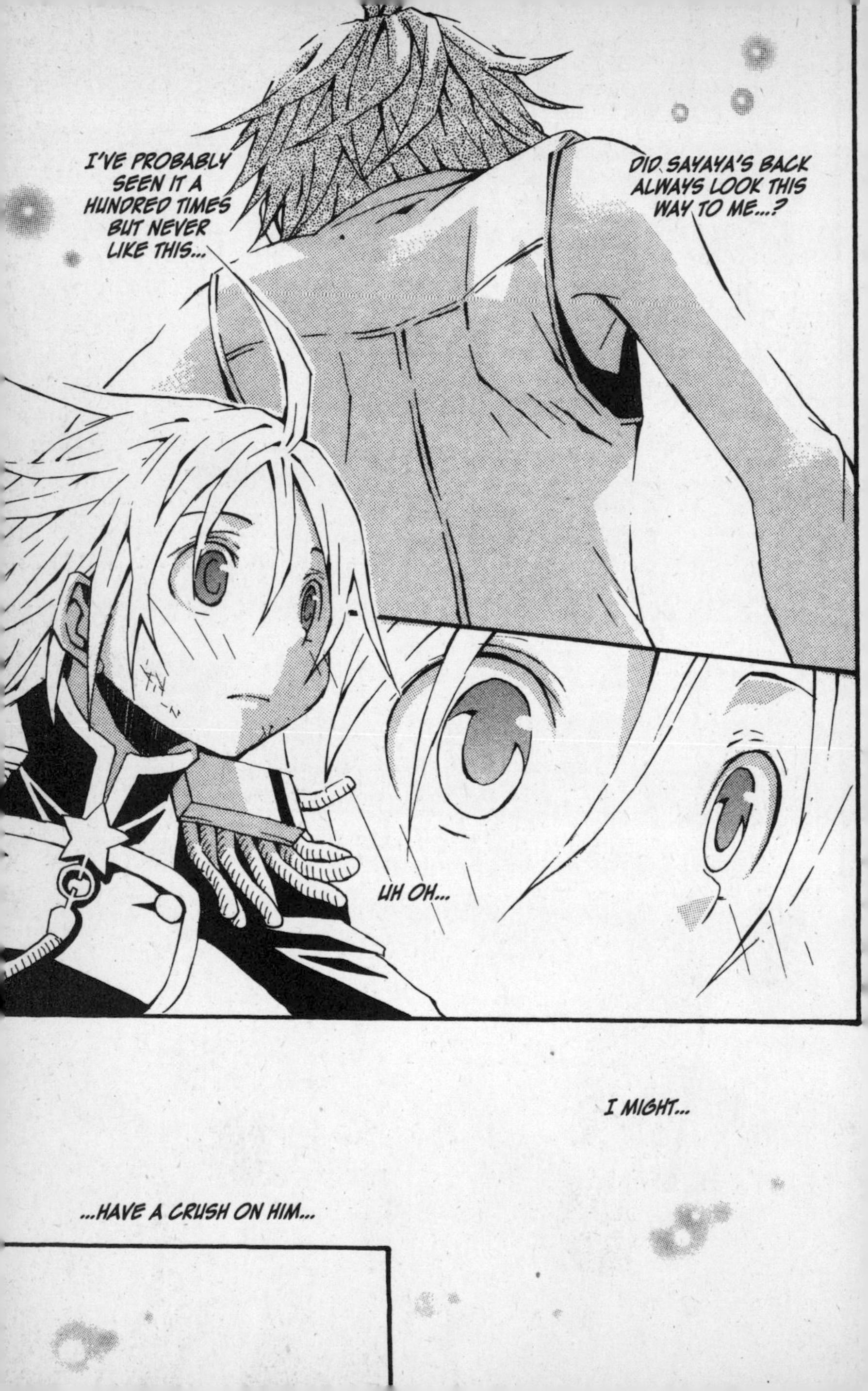
DID SAYAYA'S BACK ALWAYS LOOK THIS WAY TO ME...?
I'VE PROBABLY SEEN IT A HUNDRED TIMES BUT NEVER LIKE THIS...
UH OH...
I MIGHT...
...HAVE A CRUSH ON HIM...

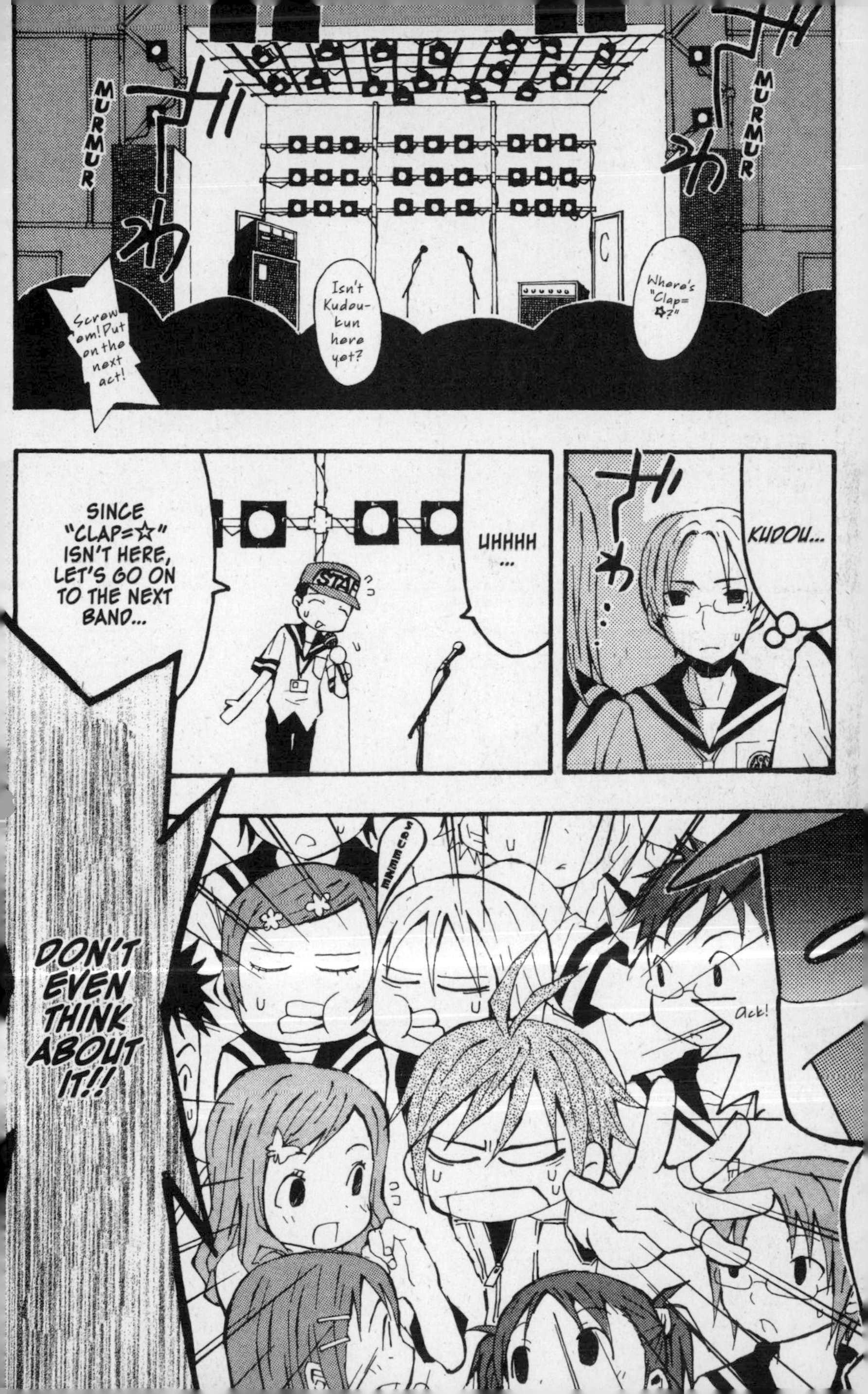
MURMUR
Where's "Clap=✿?"
Isn't Kudou-kun here yet?
Screw 'em! Put on the next act!
MURMUR
KUDOU...
UHHHH ...
SINCE "CLAP=☆" ISN'T HERE, LET'S GO ON TO THE NEXT BAND...
Ack!
DON'T EVEN THINK ABOUT IT!!

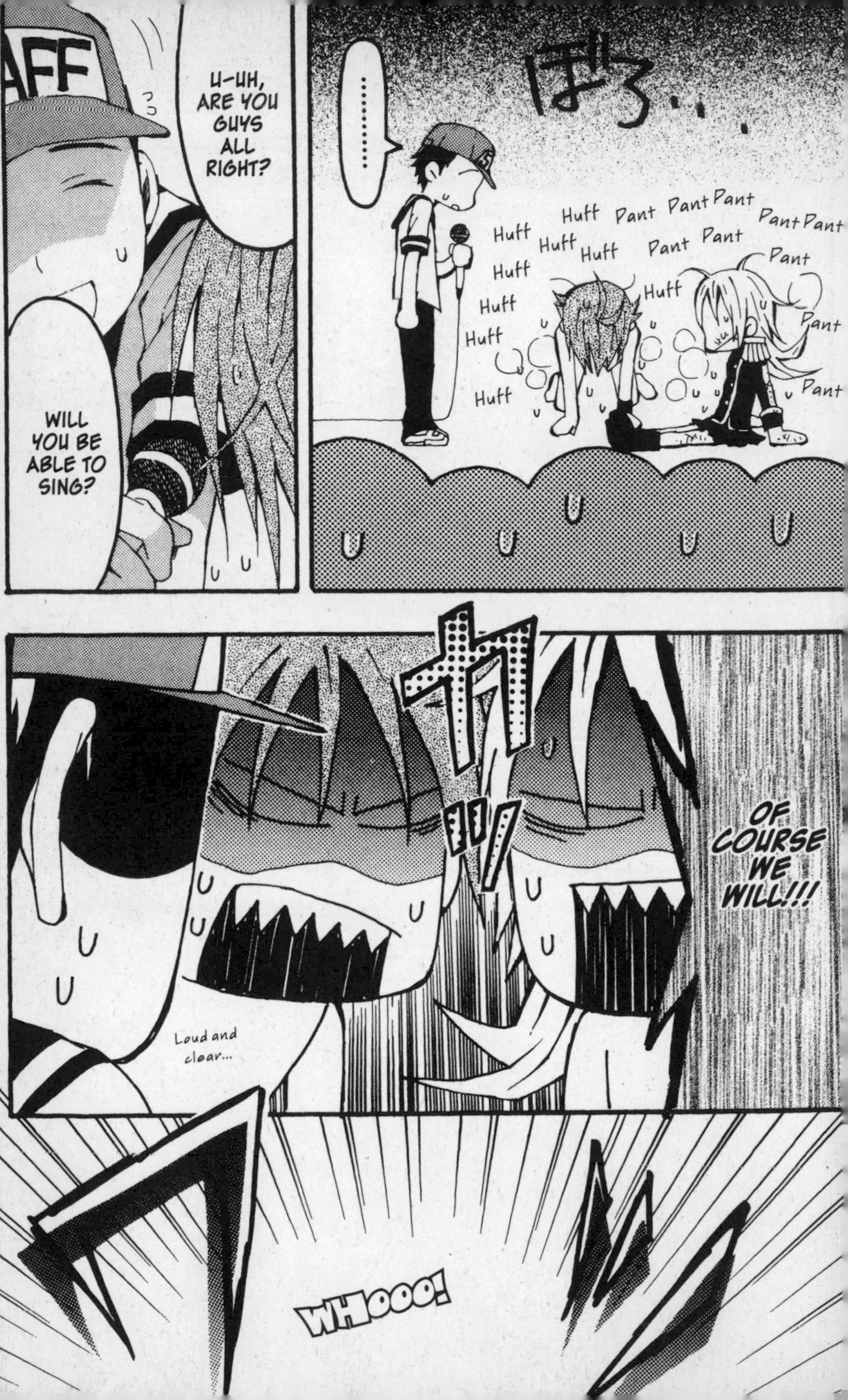

......
ぼろ...
Huff Huff Huff Huff Huff Huff Huff Huff Huff
Pant Pant Pant Pant Pant Pant Pant Pant Pant Pant
U-UH, ARE YOU GUYS ALL RIGHT?
WILL YOU BE ABLE TO SING?
OF COURSE WE WILL!!!
Loud and clear...
WHOOO!

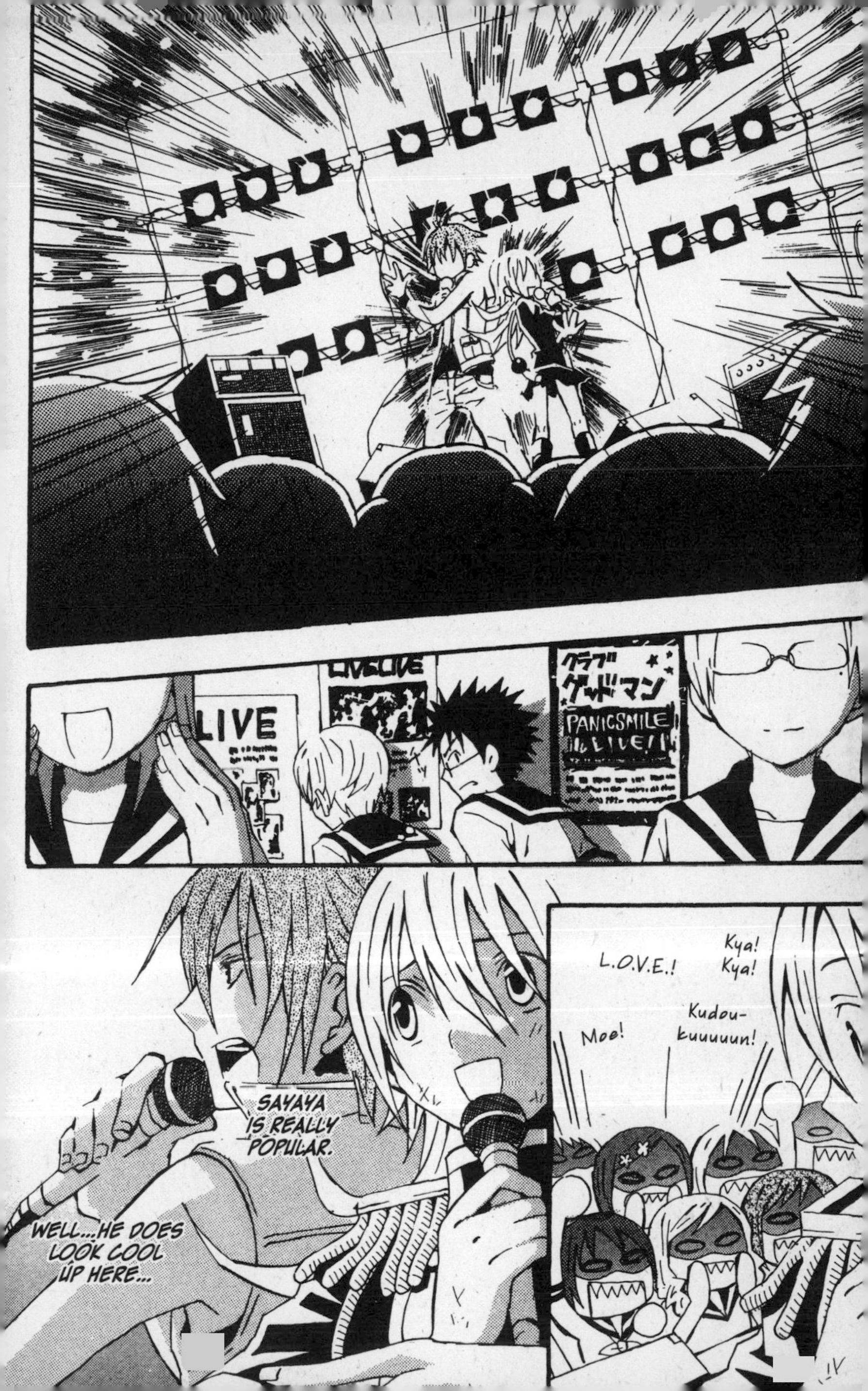
クラブ
グッドマン
PANICSMILE
LIVE!
LIVE LIVE
LIVE
Kya!
Kya!
L.O.V.E.!
Kudou-
kuuuuun!
Moe!
SAYAYA IS REALLY POPULAR.
WELL...HE DOES LOOK COOL UP HERE...

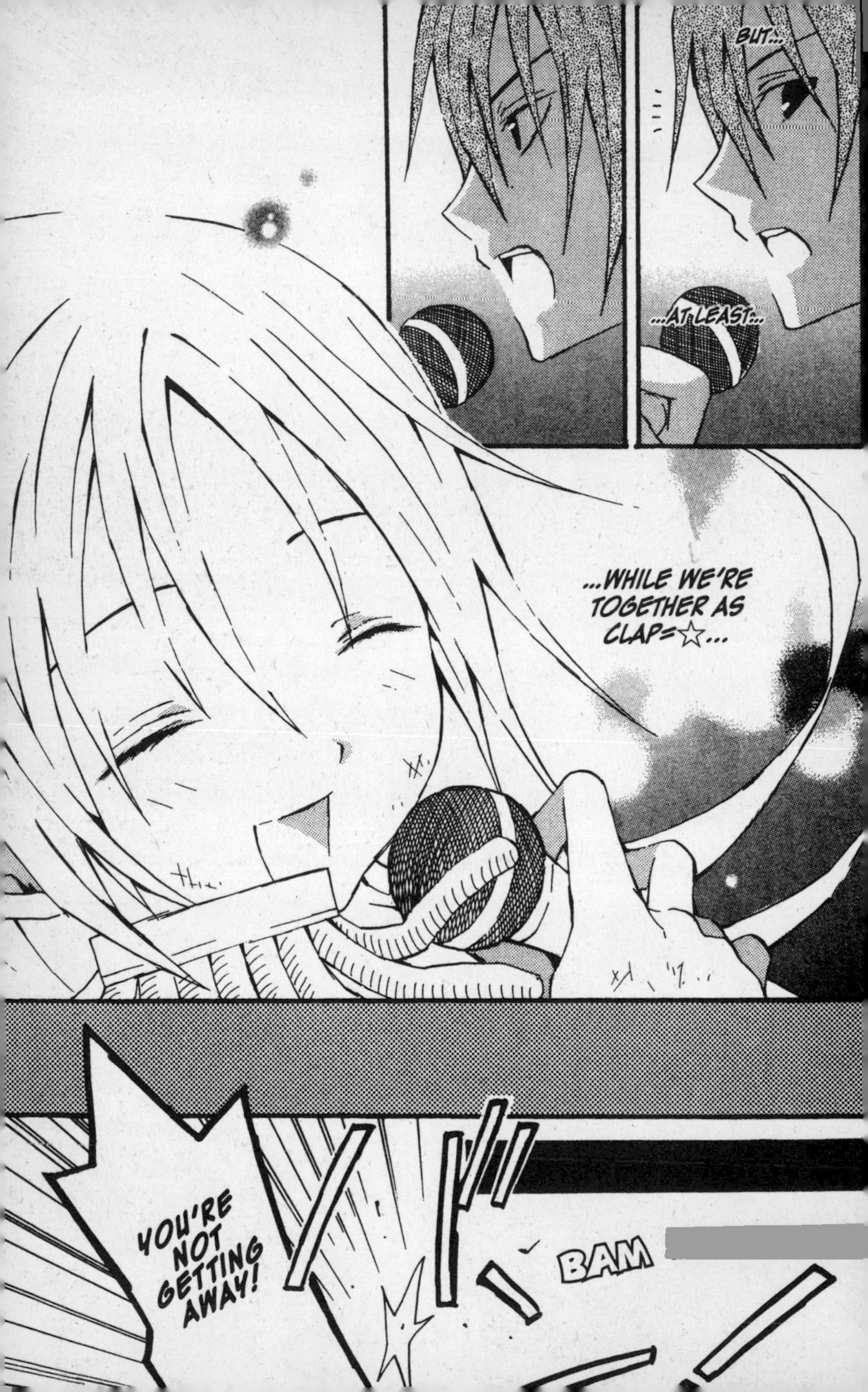
BUT...
...AT LEAST...
...WHILE WE'RE TOGETHER AS CLAP=☆...
BAM
YOU'RE NOT GETTING AWAY!

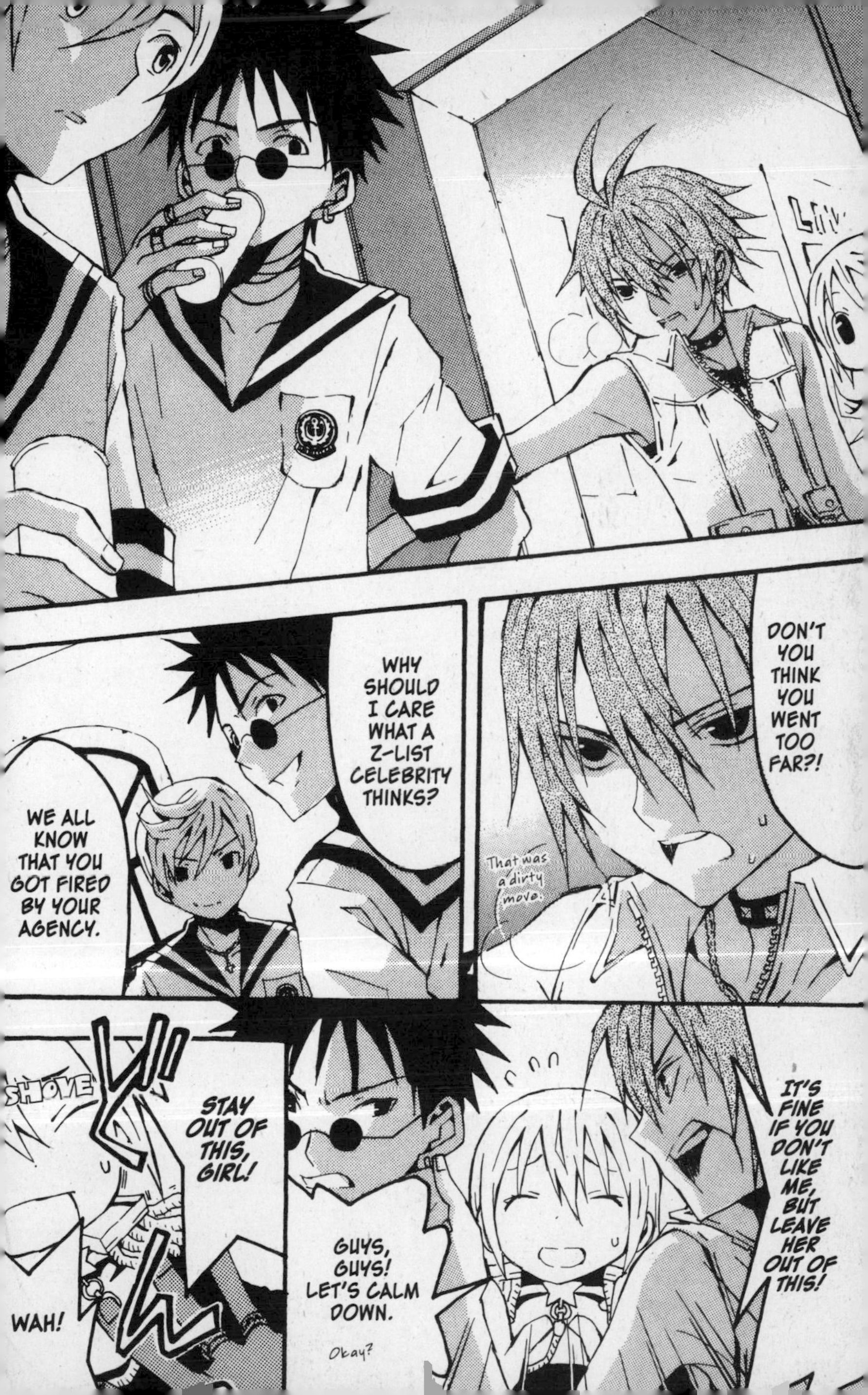
DON'T YOU THINK YOU WENT TOO FAR?!
That was a dirty move.
WHY SHOULD I CARE WHAT A Z-LIST CELEBRITY THINKS?
WE ALL KNOW THAT YOU GOT FIRED BY YOUR AGENCY.
IT'S FINE IF YOU DON'T LIKE ME, BUT LEAVE HER OUT OF THIS!
GUYS, GUYS! LET'S CALM DOWN.
Okay?
SHOVE
STAY OUT OF THIS, GIRL!
WAH!

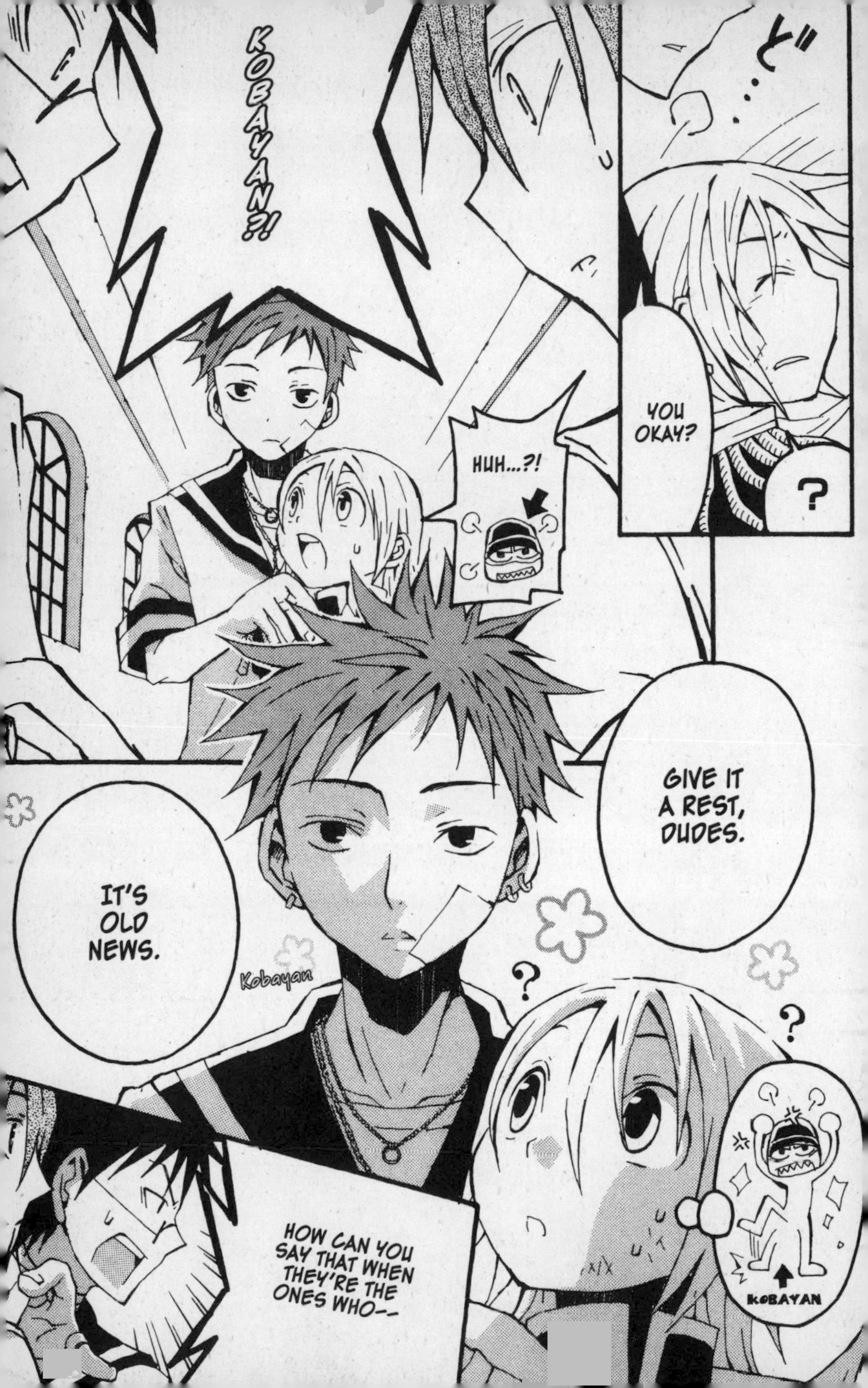
ど"
YOU OKAY?
?
KOBAYAN?!
HUH...?!
GIVE IT A REST, DUDES.
IT'S OLD NEWS.
Kobayan
?
?
KOBAYAN
HOW CAN YOU SAY THAT WHEN THEY'RE THE ONES WHO--

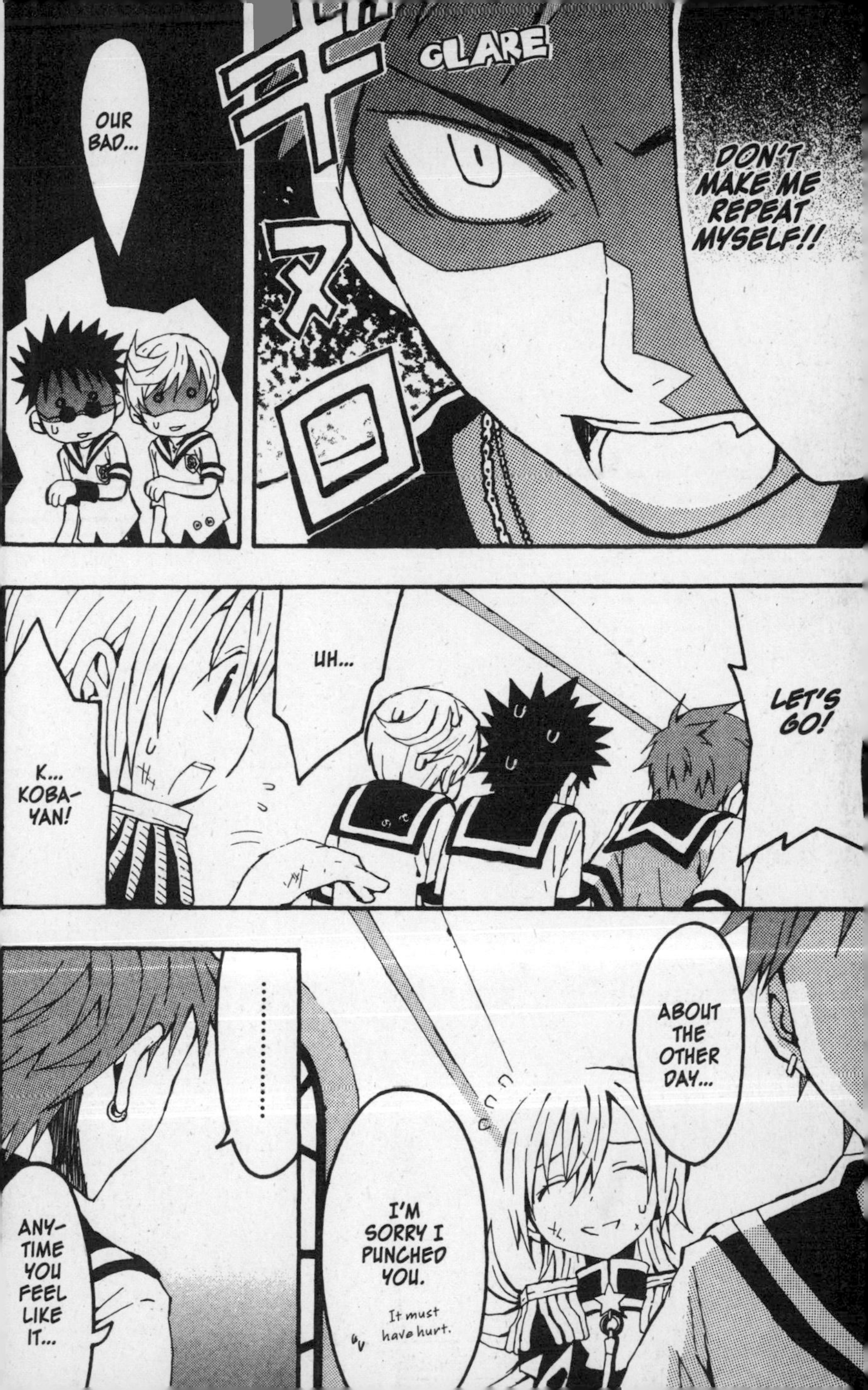
GLARE
DON'T MAKE ME REPEAT MYSELF!!
OUR BAD...
LET'S GO!
UH...
K... KOBA-YAN!
ABOUT THE OTHER DAY...
I'M SORRY I PUNCHED YOU.
It must have hurt.
......
ANY-TIME YOU FEEL LIKE IT...

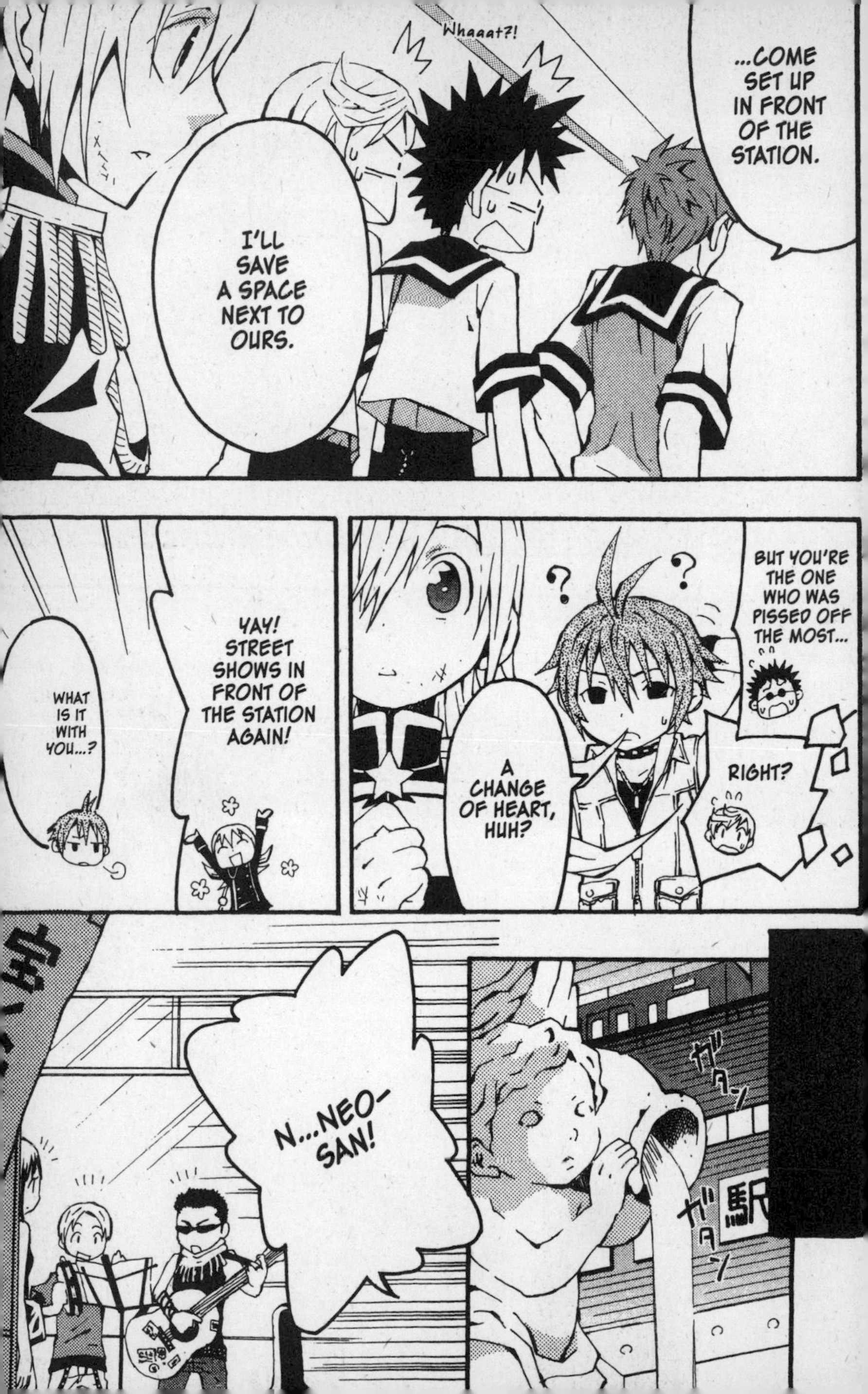
...COME SET UP IN FRONT OF THE STATION.
Whaaat?!
I'LL SAVE A SPACE NEXT TO OURS.
BUT YOU'RE THE ONE WHO WAS PISSED OFF THE MOST...
RIGHT?
A CHANGE OF HEART, HUH?
YAY! STREET SHOWS IN FRONT OF THE STATION AGAIN!
WHAT IS IT WITH YOU...?
ガタン
ガタン
駅
N...NEO-SAN!

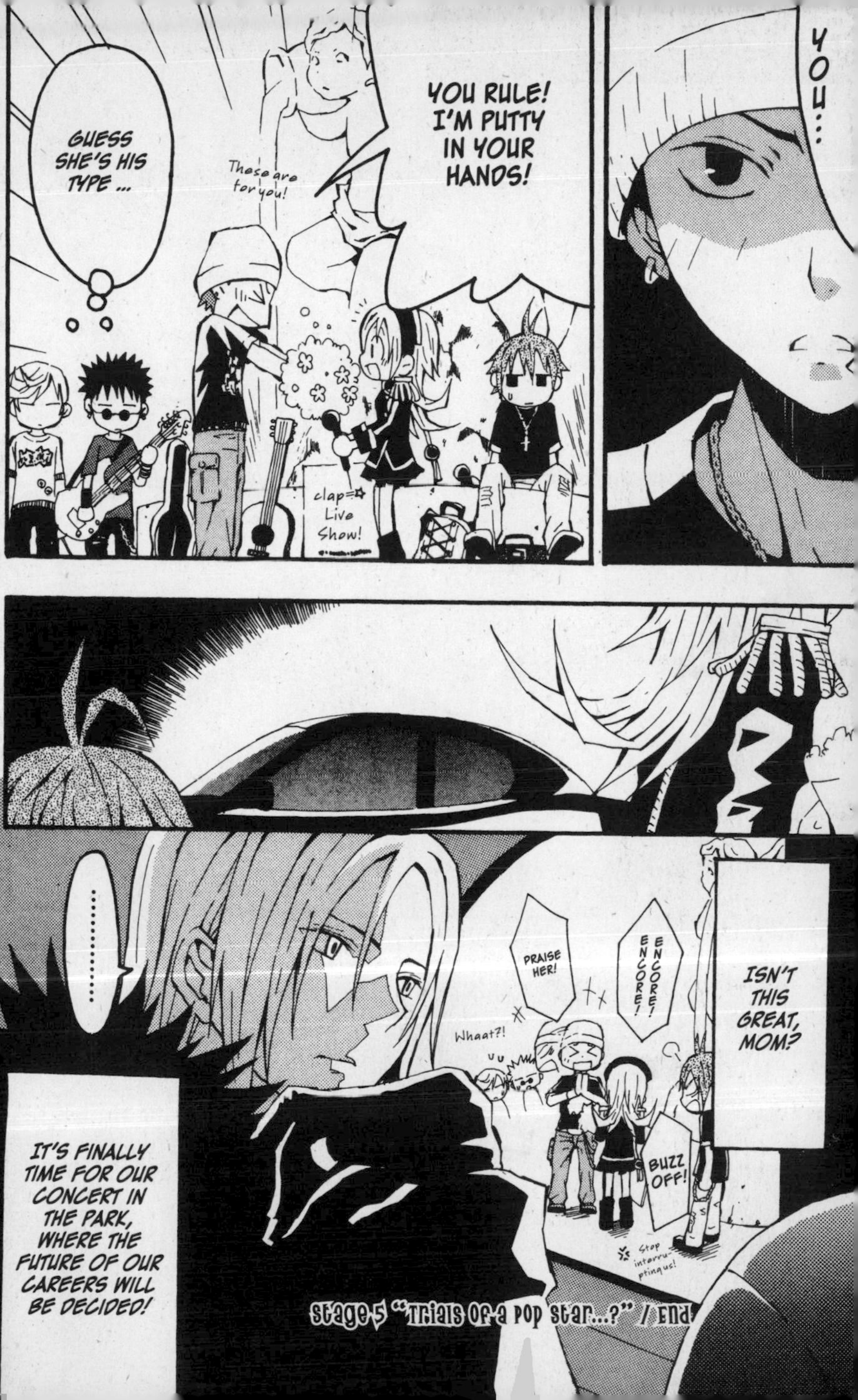
YOU...
YOU RULE! I'M PUTTY IN YOUR HANDS!
These are for you!
GUESS SHE'S HIS TYPE ...
clap Live Show!
ISN'T THIS GREAT, MOM?
ENCORE! ENCORE!
PRAISE HER!
Whaat?!
BUZZ OFF!
Stop interrupting us!
......
IT'S FINALLY TIME FOR OUR CONCERT IN THE PARK, WHERE THE FUTURE OF OUR CAREERS WILL BE DECIDED!

Stage 5 "Trials of a Pop Star...?" / End

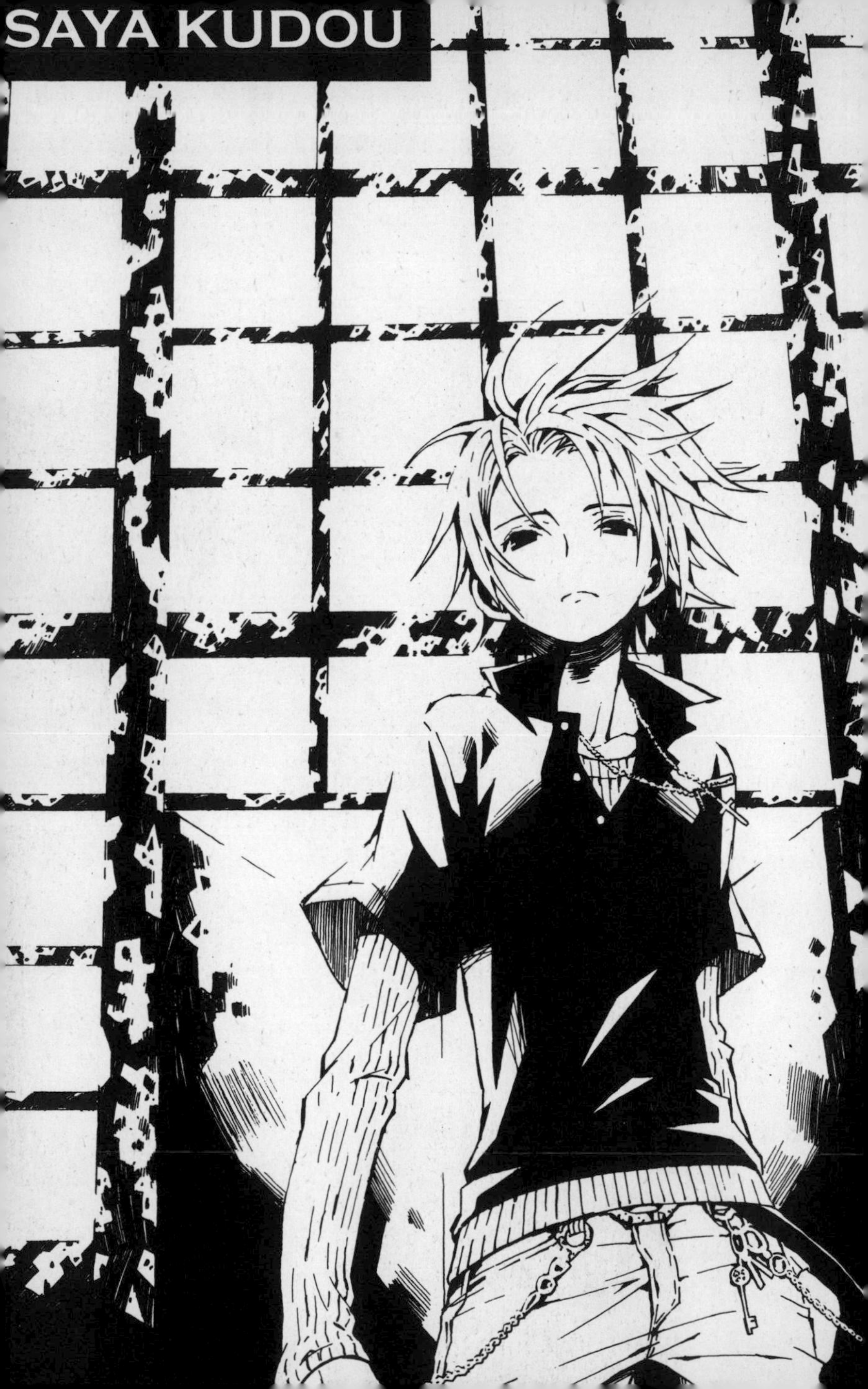
SAYA KUDOU

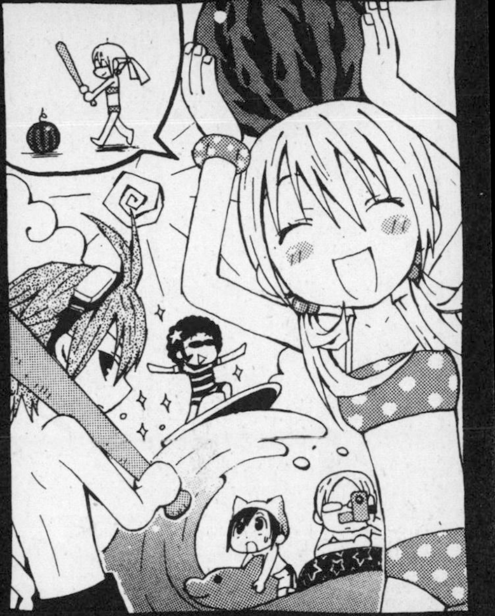

10 minutes later

↓

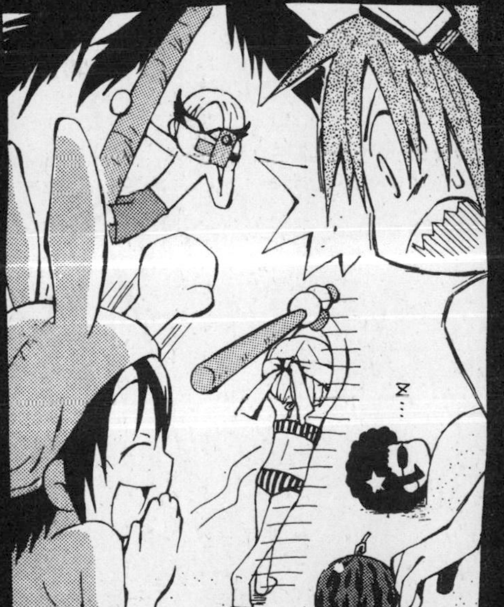

CAN YOU SPOT THE DIFFERENCES?

THIS "FIND THE DIFFERENCES" WAS ORIGINALLY PRINTED IN *ASUKA* MAGAZINE, WHERE THIS MANGA IS ERIALIZED. THE BOTTOM ILLUSTRATION EPICTS THE SCENE 10 MINUTES AFTER THE TOP ILLUSTRATION. CAN *YOU* FIND ALL THREE DIFFERENCES?

ON'T CHEAT! ANSWERS BELOW.

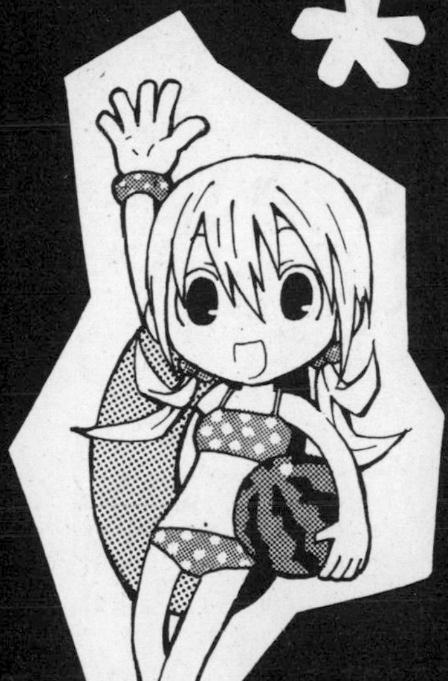

Answers: Neo's swimsuit, Nanato's hat, Takai-kun's glasses

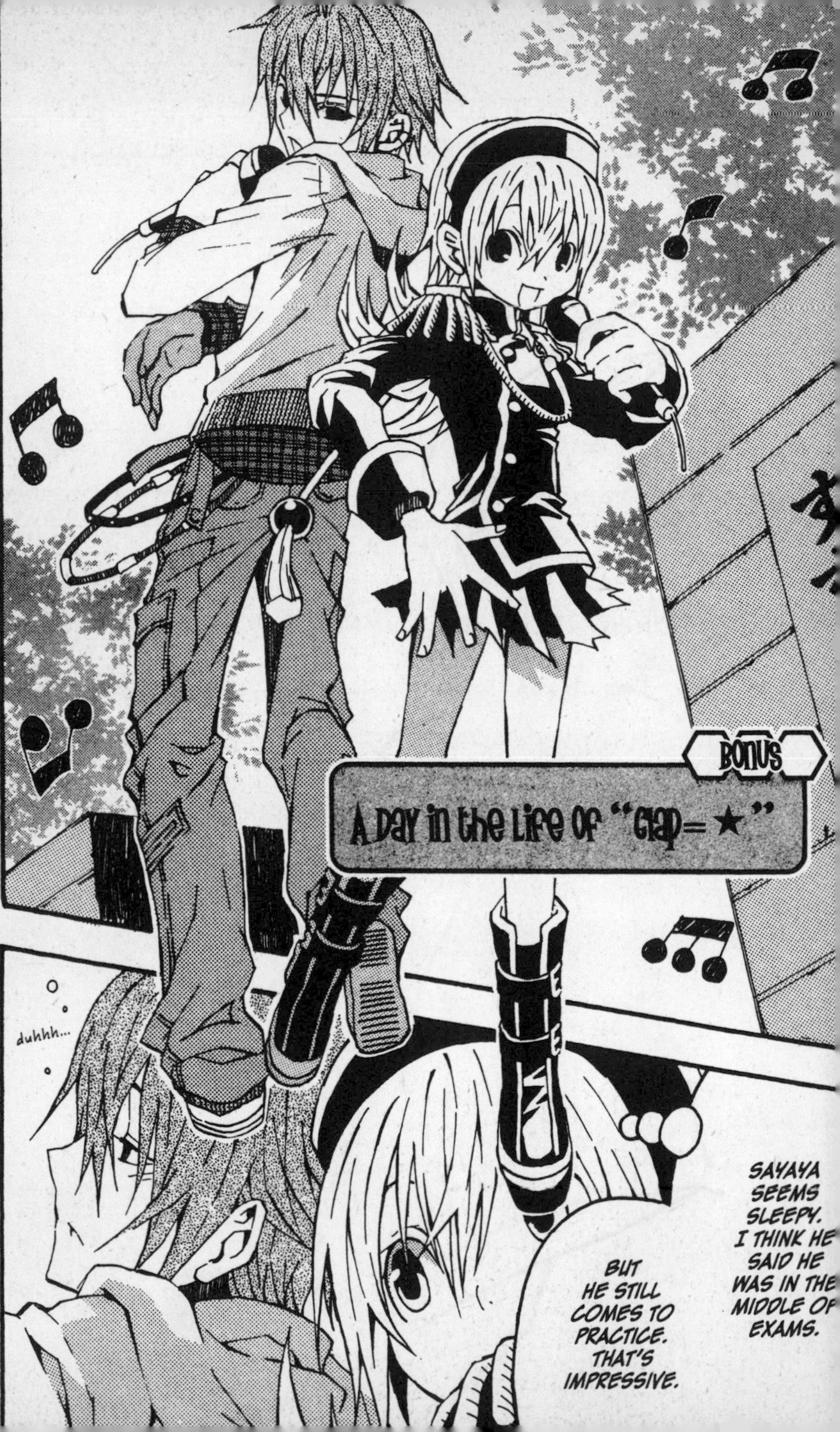
BONUS
A DAY IN THE LIFE OF "CLAP=★"
duhhh...
SAYAYA SEEMS SLEEPY. I THINK HE SAID HE WAS IN THE MIDDLE OF EXAMS.
BUT HE STILL COMES TO PRACTICE. THAT'S IMPRESSIVE.

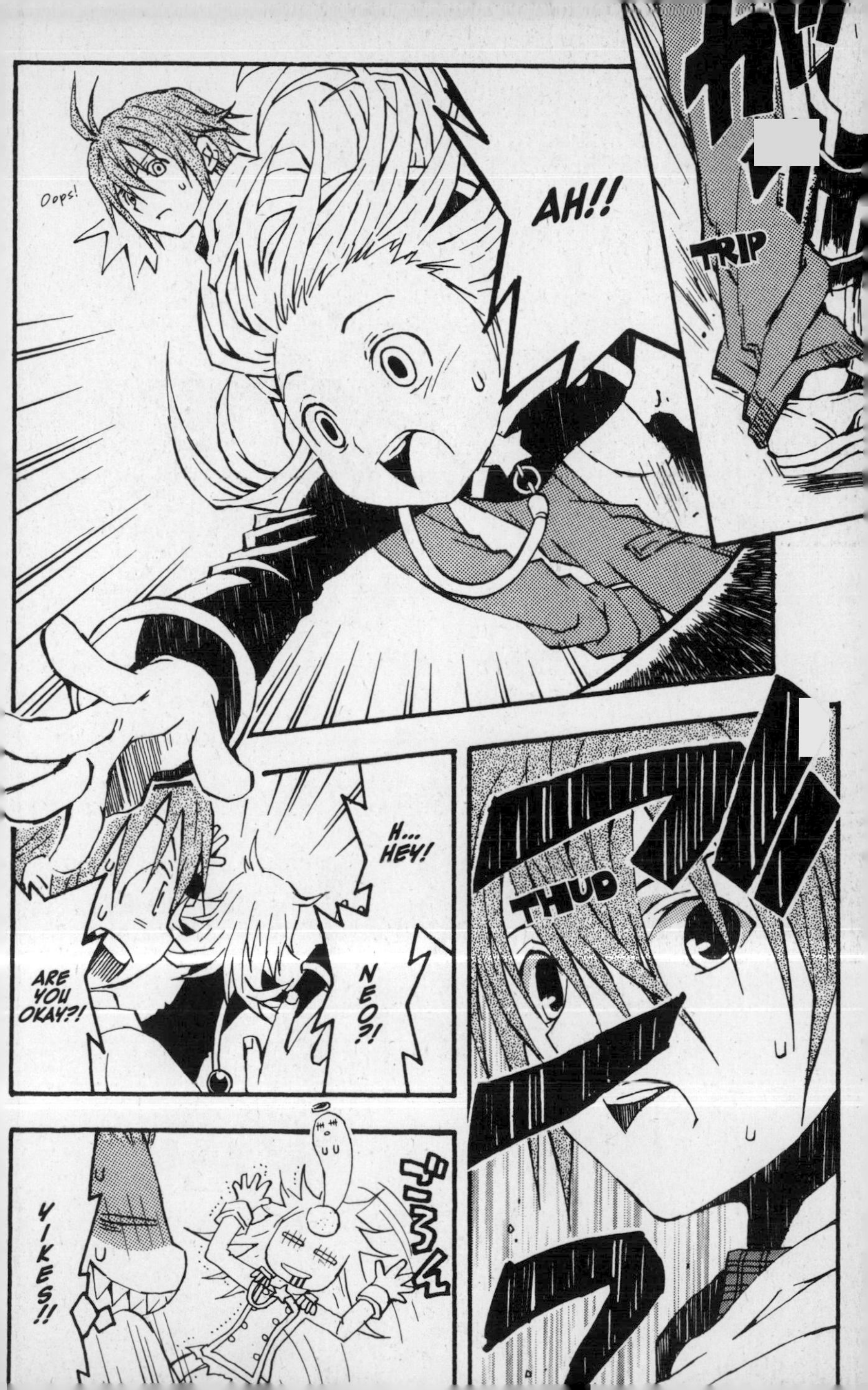
TRIP
AH!!
Oops!
THUD
H... HEY!
NEO?!
ARE YOU OKAY?!
YIKES!!

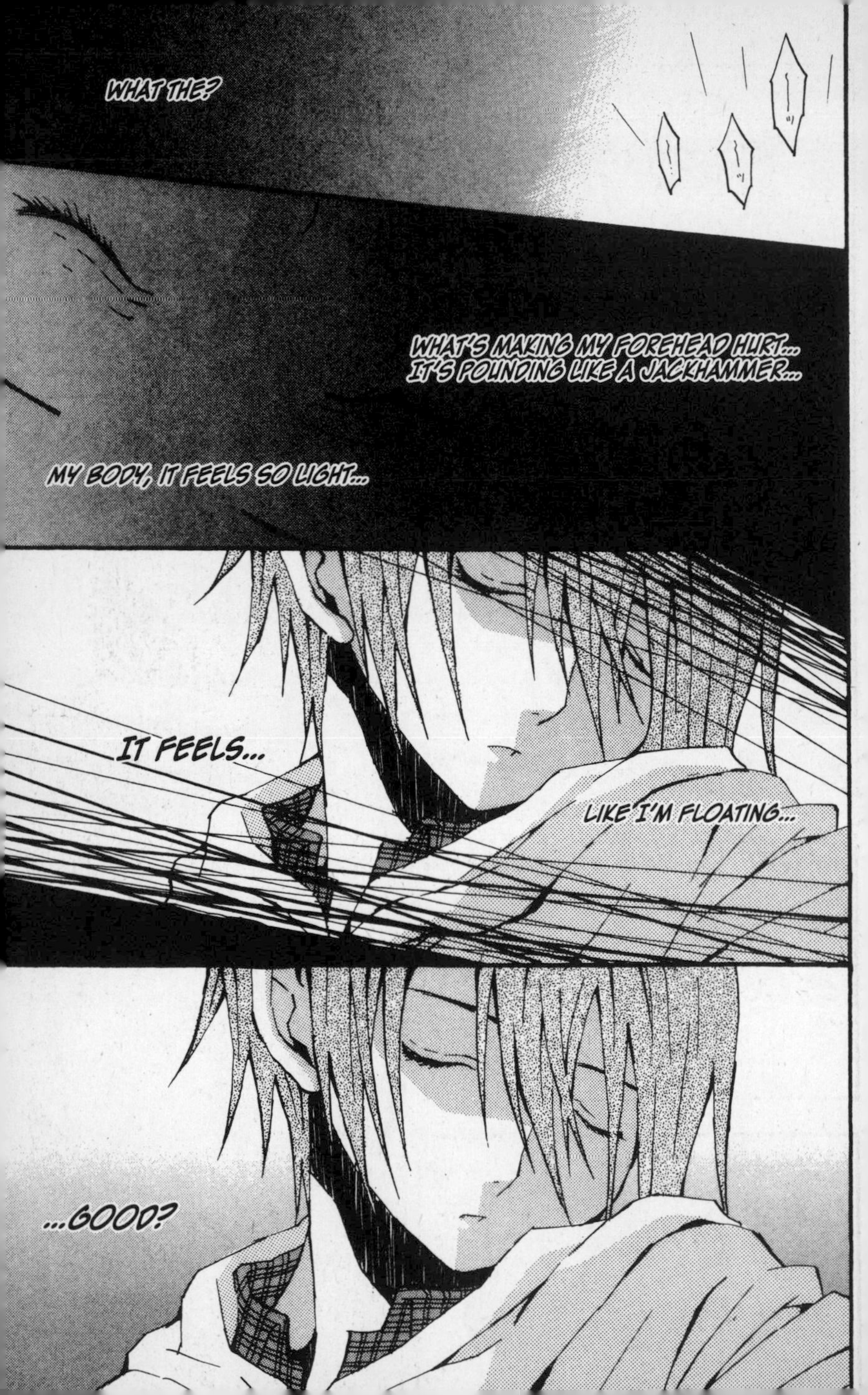
WHAT THE?
!!
!!
!!
WHAT'S MAKING MY FOREHEAD HURT... IT'S POUNDING LIKE A JACKHAMMER...
MY BODY, IT FEELS SO LIGHT...
IT FEELS...
LIKE I'M FLOATING...
...GOOD?

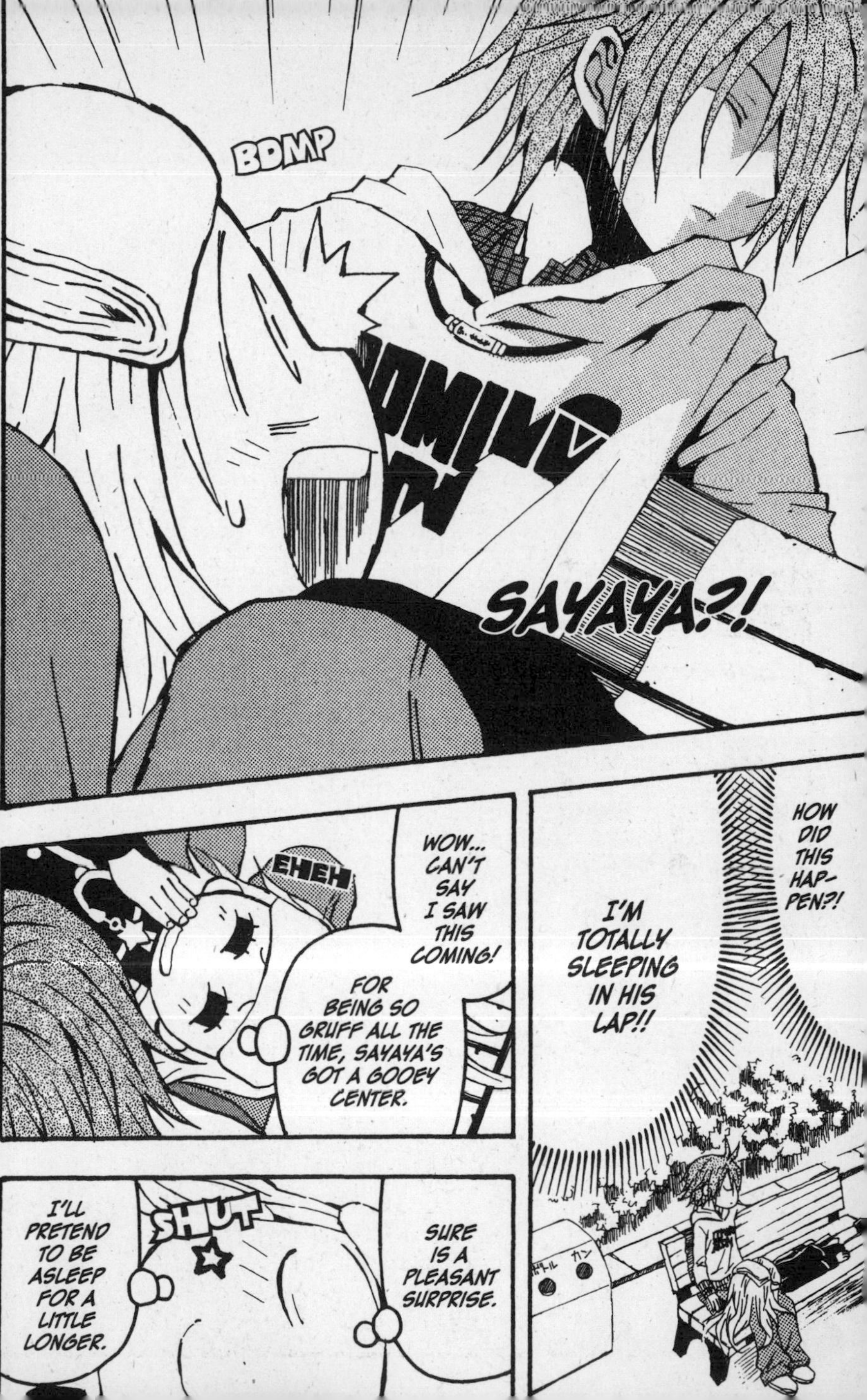
BDMP
SAYAYA?!
HOW DID THIS HAP-PEN?!
I'M TOTALLY SLEEPING IN HIS LAP!!
WOW... CAN'T SAY I SAW THIS COMING!
EHEH
FOR BEING SO GRUFF ALL THE TIME, SAYAYA'S GOT A GOOEY CENTER.
SURE IS A PLEASANT SURPRISE.
SHUT
I'LL PRETEND TO BE ASLEEP FOR A LITTLE LONGER.

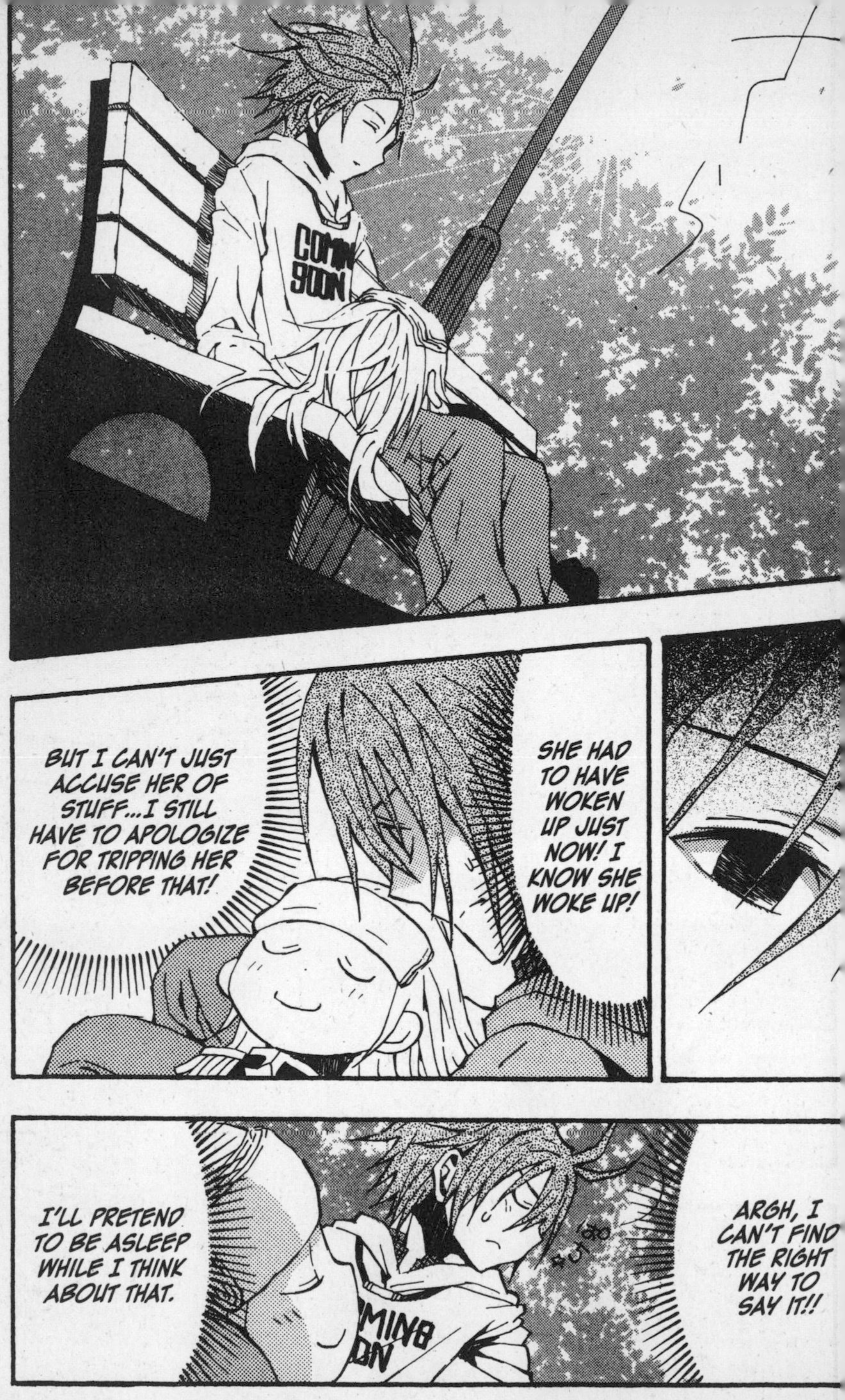
SHE HAD TO HAVE WOKEN UP JUST NOW! I KNOW SHE WOKE UP!
BUT I CAN'T JUST ACCUSE HER OF STUFF...I STILL HAVE TO APOLOGIZE FOR TRIPPING HER BEFORE THAT!
ARGH, I CAN'T FIND THE RIGHT WAY TO SAY IT!!
I'LL PRETEND TO BE ASLEEP WHILE I THINK ABOUT THAT.

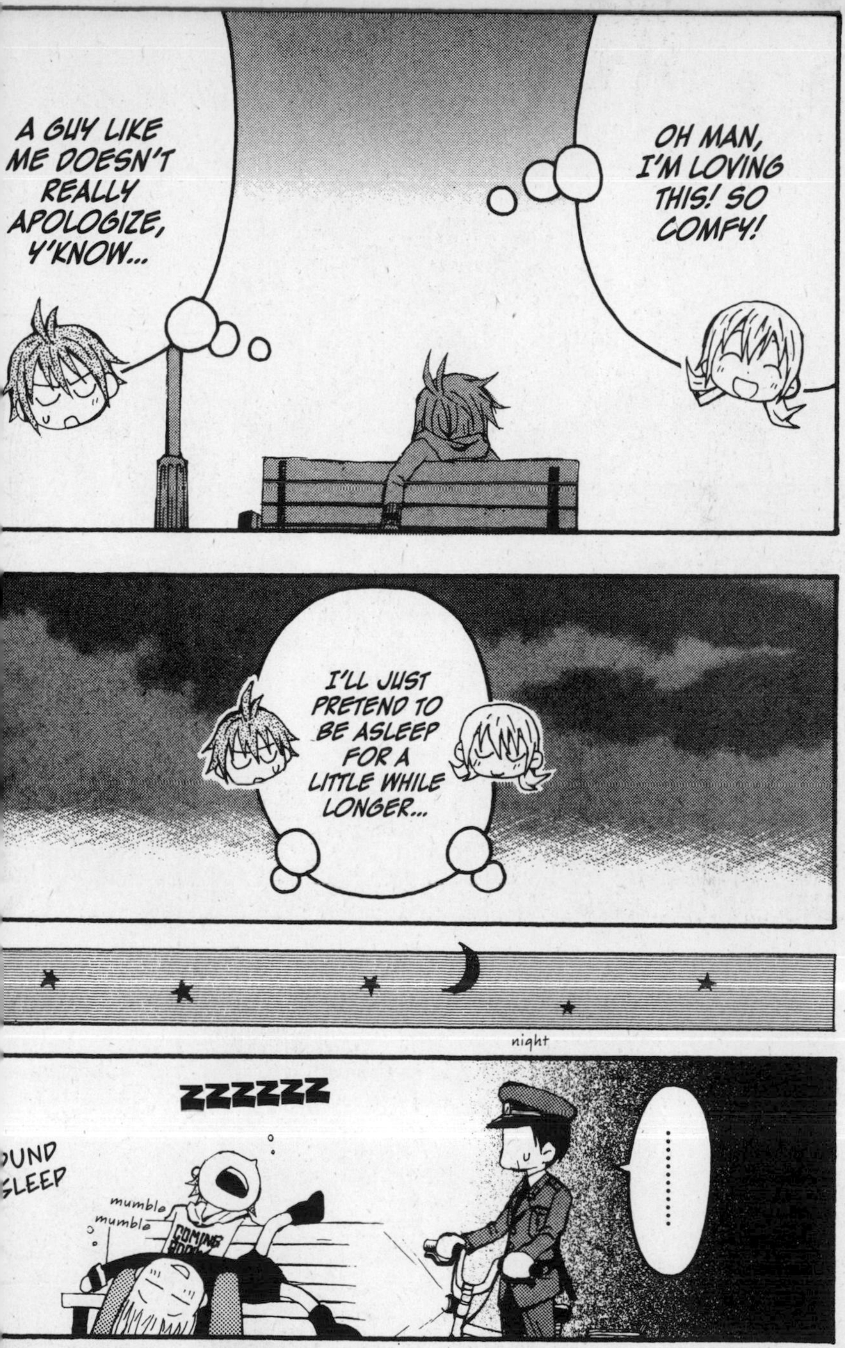
OH MAN, I'M LOVING THIS! SO COMFY!
A GUY LIKE ME DOESN'T REALLY APOLOGIZE, Y'KNOW...
I'LL JUST PRETEND TO BE ASLEEP FOR A LITTLE WHILE LONGER...
night
......
ZZZZZZ
mumble mumble

Bonus "A Day in the Life of "Clap=★" " / End

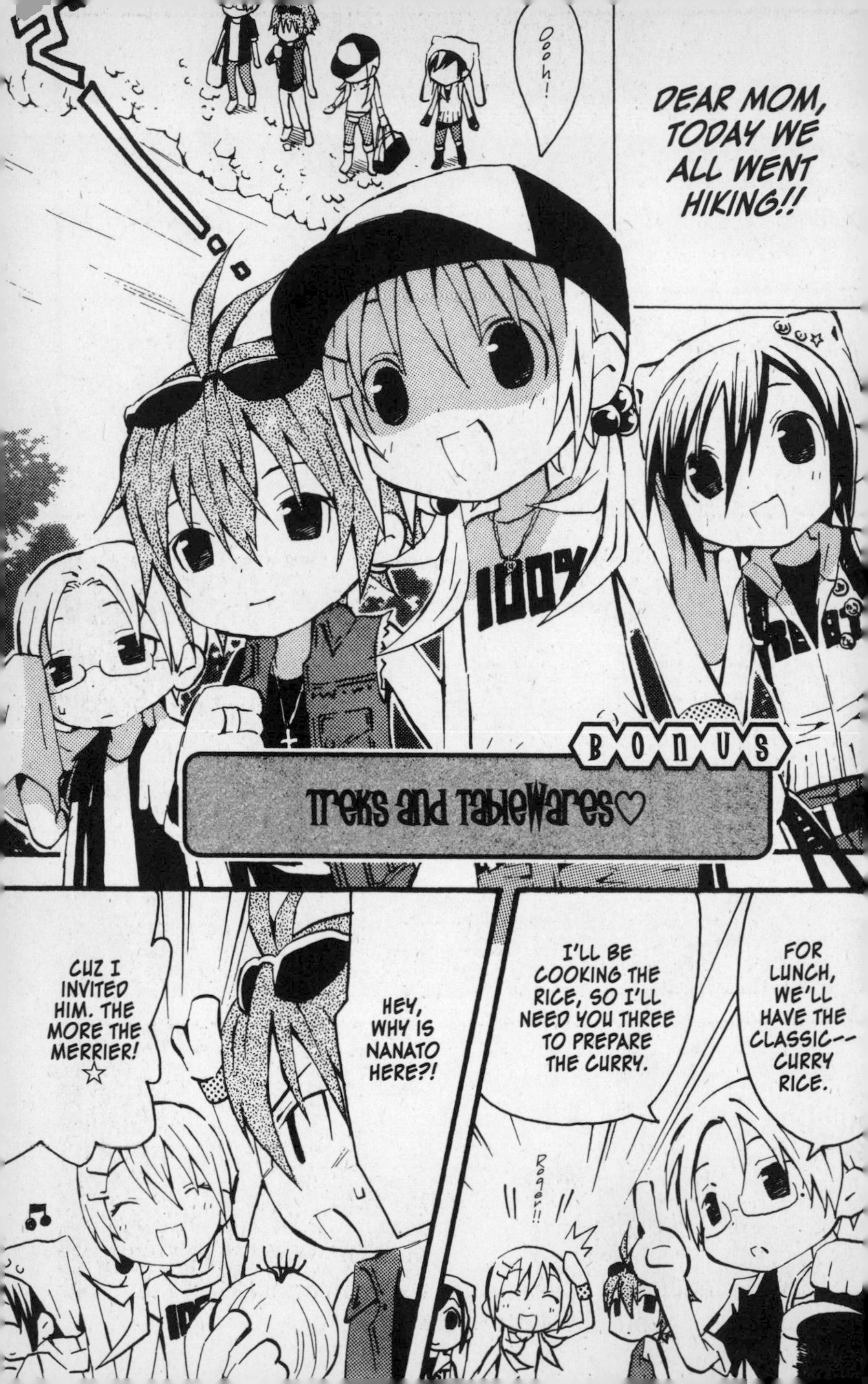
DEAR MOM, TODAY WE ALL WENT HIKING!!
Oooh!
BONUS
Treks and Tablewares♡
100%
FOR LUNCH, WE'LL HAVE THE CLASSIC--CURRY RICE.
I'LL BE COOKING THE RICE, SO I'LL NEED YOU THREE TO PREPARE THE CURRY.
Roger!!
HEY, WHY IS NANATO HERE?!
CUZ I INVITED HIM. THE MORE THE MERRIER! ☆

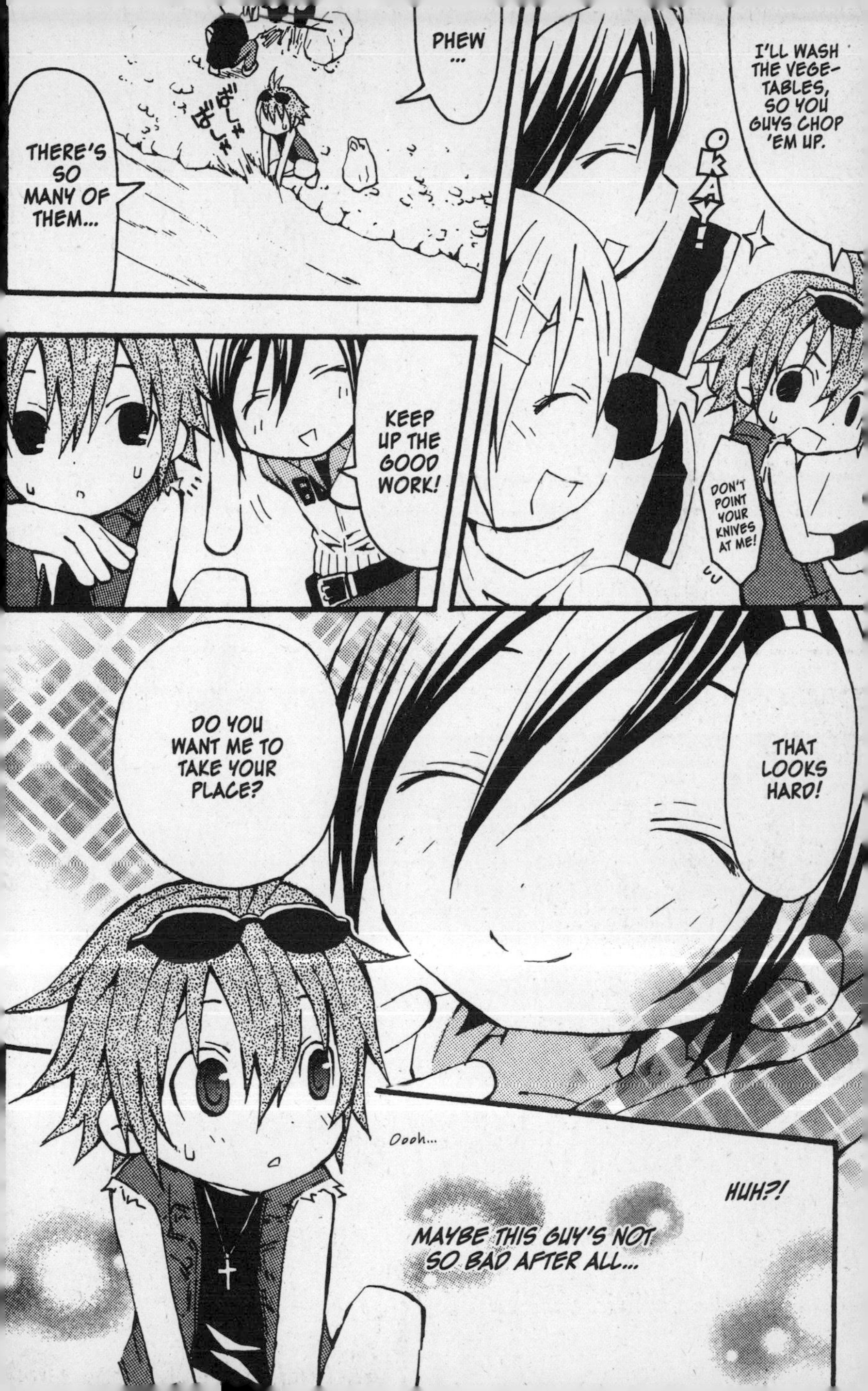
I'LL WASH THE VEGE-TABLES, SO YOU GUYS CHOP 'EM UP.
OKAY!
DON'T POINT YOUR KNIVES AT ME!
PHEW...
ばしゃばしゃ
THERE'S SO MANY OF THEM...
KEEP UP THE GOOD WORK!
THAT LOOKS HARD!
DO YOU WANT ME TO TAKE YOUR PLACE?
Oooh...
HUH?!
MAYBE THIS GUY'S NOT SO BAD AFTER ALL...

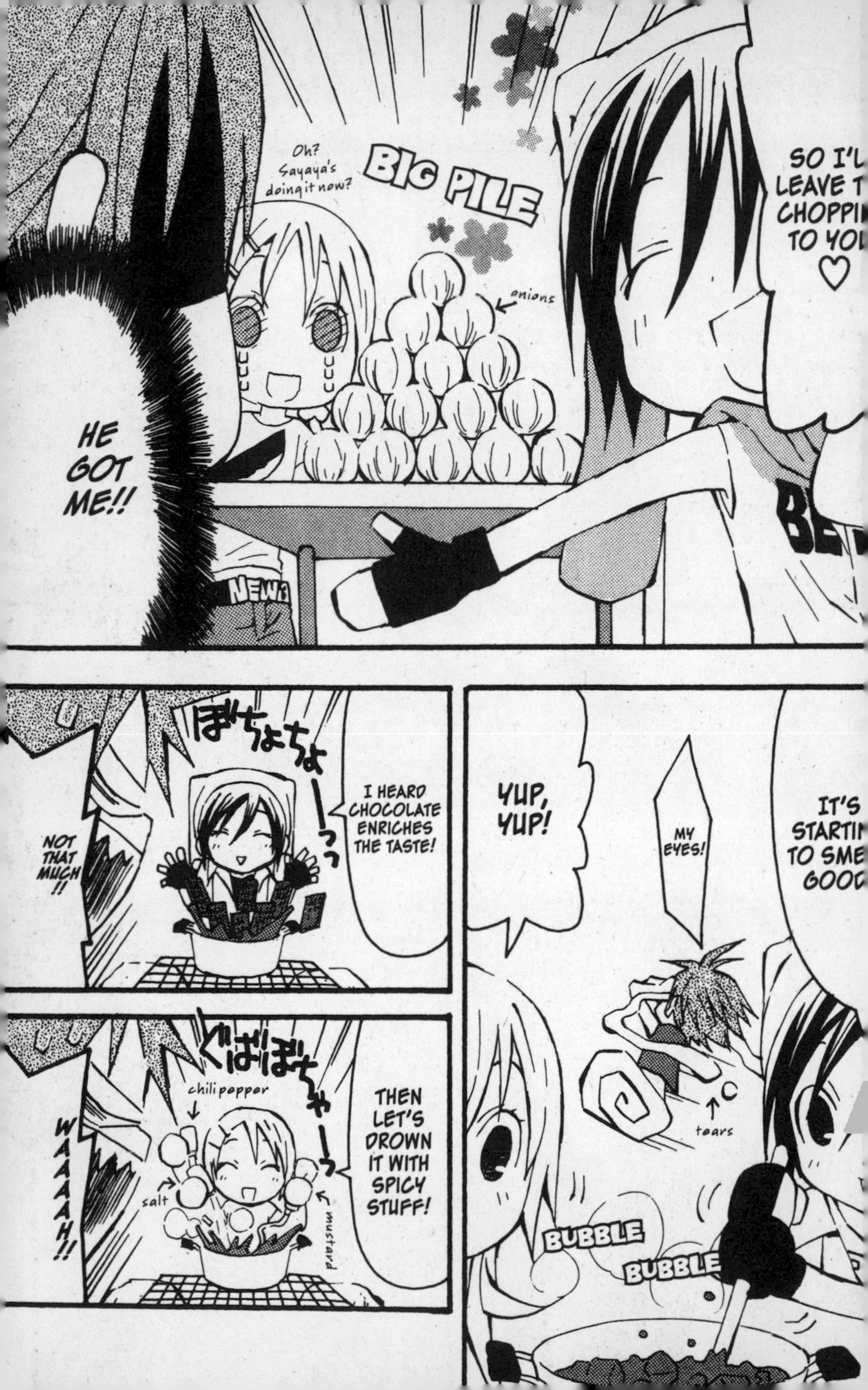
SO I'L
LEAVE T
CHOPPI
TO YO ♡
BIG PILE
Oh? Sayaya's doingit now?
onions
HE GOT ME!!
NEW
IT'S STARTI TO SME GOOD
MY EYES!
YUP, YUP!
tears
BUBBLE
BUBBLE
ぼちょちょーっ
I HEARD CHOCOLATE ENRICHES THE TASTE!
NOT THAT MUCH!!
ぐぱぼちゃーっ
THEN LET'S DROWN IT WITH SPICY STUFF!
chili pepper
mustard
salt
WAAAAH!!

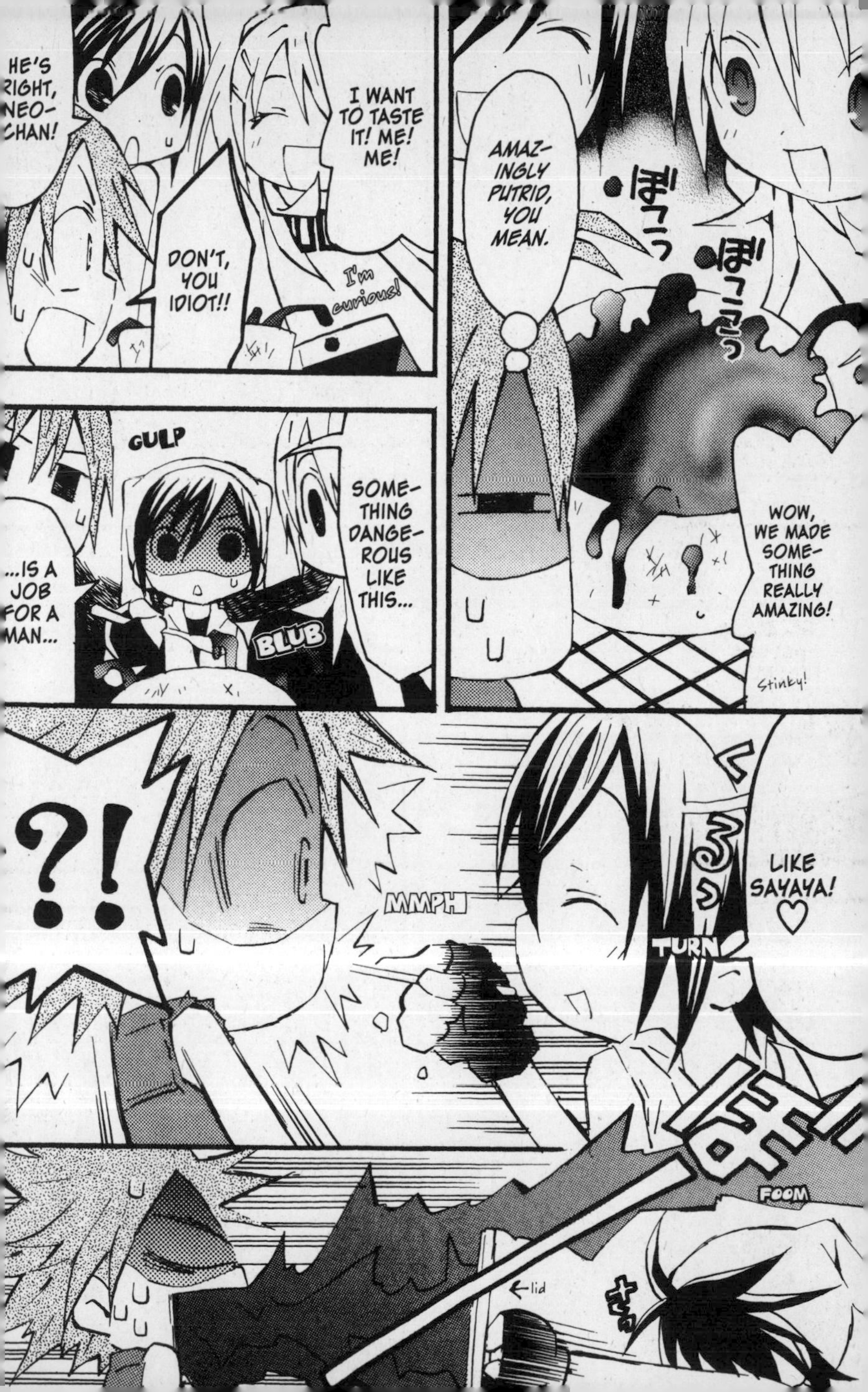

WOW, WE MADE SOMETHING REALLY AMAZING!
Stinky!
ぼこっ
ぼこっ
ぼこここっ
AMAZINGLY PUTRID, YOU MEAN.
I WANT TO TASTE IT! ME! ME!
I'm curious!
DON'T, YOU IDIOT!!
HE'S RIGHT, NEO-CHAN!
SOMETHING DANGEROUS LIKE THIS...
GULP
BLUB
...IS A JOB FOR A MAN...
LIKE SAYAYA! ♡
くるっ
TURN
MMPH
?!
FOOM
←lid

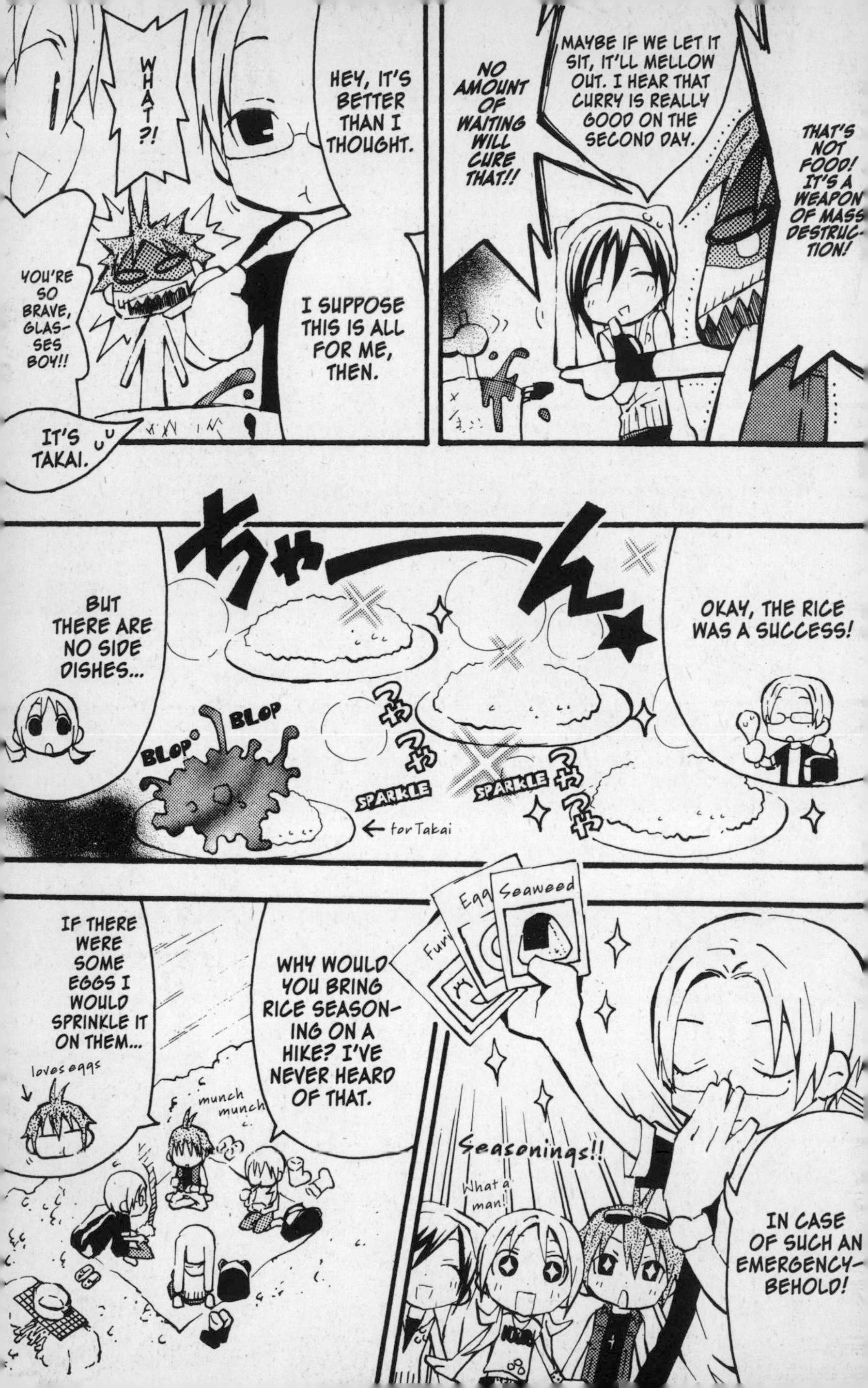
MAYBE IF WE LET IT SIT, IT'LL MELLOW OUT. I HEAR THAT CURRY IS REALLY GOOD ON THE SECOND DAY.
THAT'S NOT FOOD! IT'S A WEAPON OF MASS DESTRUCTION!
NO AMOUNT OF WAITING WILL CURE THAT!!
HEY, IT'S BETTER THAN I THOUGHT.
WHAT?!
I SUPPOSE THIS IS ALL FOR ME, THEN.
YOU'RE SO BRAVE, GLASSES BOY!!
IT'S TAKAI.
ちゃーん★
OKAY, THE RICE WAS A SUCCESS!
つやつや
SPARKLE
つやつや
SPARKLE
BLOP
BLOP
← for Takai
BUT THERE ARE NO SIDE DISHES...
IN CASE OF SUCH AN EMERGENCY—BEHOLD!
Seaweed
Seasonings!!
What a man!
WHY WOULD YOU BRING RICE SEASONING ON A HIKE? I'VE NEVER HEARD OF THAT.
munch munch
IF THERE WERE SOME EGGS I WOULD SPRINKLE IT ON THEM...
loves eggs

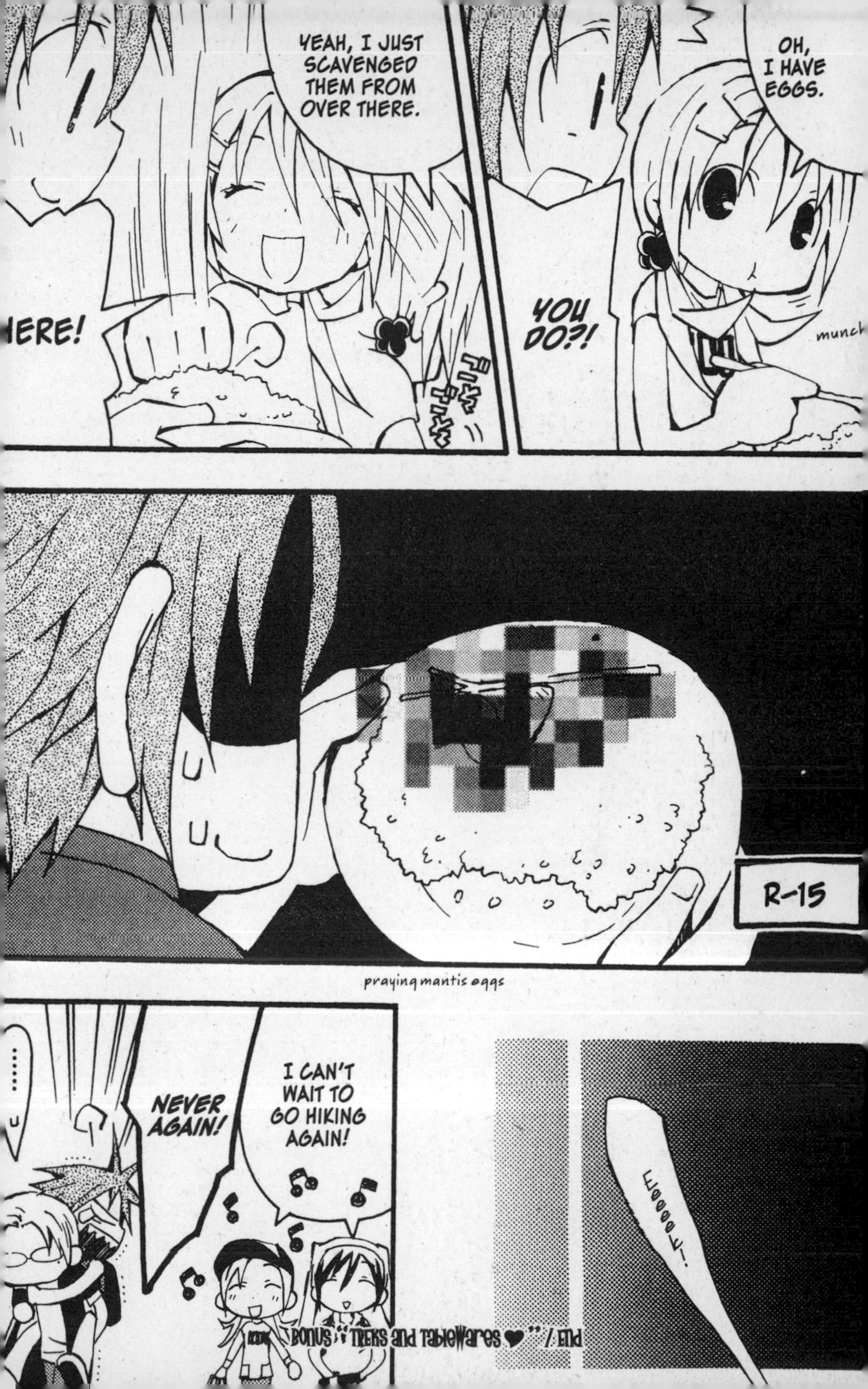
OH, I HAVE EGGS.
YOU DO?!
munch
YEAH, I JUST SCAVENGED THEM FROM OVER THERE.
HERE!
R-15
praying mantis eggs
Eeeeek!
I CAN'T WAIT TO GO HIKING AGAIN!
NEVER AGAIN!
......
Bonus "Treks and Tablewares ♥" / End

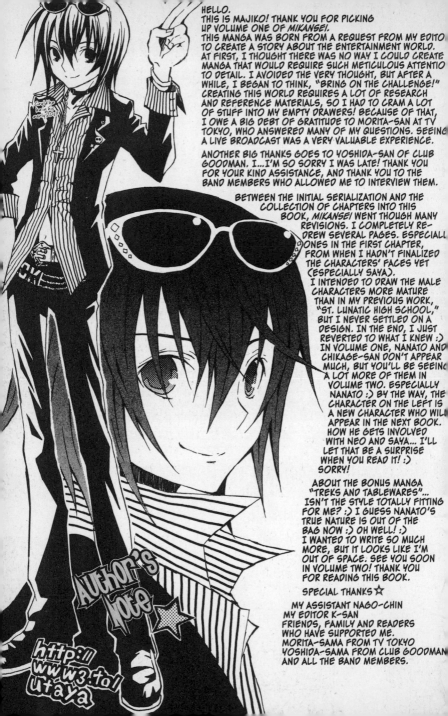

HELLO.
THIS IS MAJIKO! THANK YOU FOR PICKING UP VOLUME ONE OF *MIKANSEI*.
THIS MANGA WAS BORN FROM A REQUEST FROM MY EDITO TO CREATE A STORY ABOUT THE ENTERTAINMENT WORLD. AT FIRST, I THOUGHT THERE WAS NO WAY I COULD CREATE MANGA THAT WOULD REQUIRE SUCH METICULOUS ATTENTIO TO DETAIL. I AVOIDED THE VERY THOUGHT, BUT AFTER A WHILE, I BEGAN TO THINK, "BRING ON THE CHALLENGE!" CREATING THIS WORLD REQUIRES A LOT OF RESEARCH AND REFERENCE MATERIALS, SO I HAD TO CRAM A LOT OF STUFF INTO MY EMPTY DRAWERS! BECAUSE OF THAT, I OWE A BIG DEBT OF GRATITUDE TO MORITA-SAN AT TV TOKYO, WHO ANSWERED MANY OF MY QUESTIONS. SEEING A LIVE BROADCAST WAS A VERY VALUABLE EXPERIENCE.

ANOTHER BIG THANKS GOES TO YOSHIDA-SAN OF CLUB GOODMAN. I...I'M SO SORRY I WAS LATE! THANK YOU FOR YOUR KIND ASSISTANCE, AND THANK YOU TO THE BAND MEMBERS WHO ALLOWED ME TO INTERVIEW THEM.

BETWEEN THE INITIAL SERIALIZATION AND THE COLLECTION OF CHAPTERS INTO THIS BOOK, *MIKANSEI* WENT THOUGH MANY REVISIONS. I COMPLETELY RE-DREW SEVERAL PAGES. ESPECIALL ONES IN THE FIRST CHAPTER, FROM WHEN I HADN'T FINALIZED THE CHARACTERS' FACES YET (ESPECIALLY SAYA).
I INTENDED TO DRAW THE MALE CHARACTERS MORE MATURE THAN IN MY PREVIOUS WORK, "ST. LUNATIC HIGH SCHOOL," BUT I NEVER SETTLED ON A DESIGN. IN THE END, I JUST REVERTED TO WHAT I KNEW :) IN VOLUME ONE, NANATO AND CHIKAGE-SAN DON'T APPEAR MUCH, BUT YOU'LL BE SEEING A LOT MORE OF THEM IN VOLUME TWO. ESPECIALLY NANATO :) BY THE WAY, THE CHARACTER ON THE LEFT IS A NEW CHARACTER WHO WILL APPEAR IN THE NEXT BOOK. HOW HE GETS INVOLVED WITH NEO AND SAYA... I'LL LET THAT BE A SURPRISE WHEN YOU READ IT! :) SORRY!

ABOUT THE BONUS MANGA "TREKS AND TABLEWARES"... ISN'T THE STYLE TOTALLY FITTING FOR ME? :) I GUESS NANATO'S TRUE NATURE IS OUT OF THE BAG NOW :) OH WELL! :) I WANTED TO WRITE SO MUCH MORE, BUT IT LOOKS LIKE I'M OUT OF SPACE. SEE YOU SOON IN VOLUME TWO! THANK YOU FOR READING THIS BOOK.

SPECIAL THANKS ☆

MY ASSISTANT NAGO-CHIN
MY EDITOR K-SAN
FRIENDS, FAMILY AND READERS WHO HAVE SUPPORTED ME.
MORITA-SAMA FROM TV TOKYO
YOSHIDA-SAMA FROM CLUB GOODMAN
AND ALL THE BAND MEMBERS.

Could he be in his early 20s?

Author's Note

http://www3.to/ utaya

IN THE NEXT VOLUME OF

THE BOND BETWEEN NEO AND SAYA
STRENGTHEN AS THEY PREPARE FOR THE
HIGHLY ANTICIPATED CONCERT. WILL
"CLAP=☆" END IN BITTERSWEET GOODBYES
OR WILL THEY HAVE A STAR DEBUT AS
PROMISED? AND WHO REALLY IS NANATO,
AND WHY IS HE SO PROTECTIVE OF NEO?
MEANWHILE, THE 23RD CENTURY FINALLY
MAKES CONTACT WITH NEO BUT...

FIND OUT MORE IN VOLUME 2
OF MIKANSEI NO. 1!!

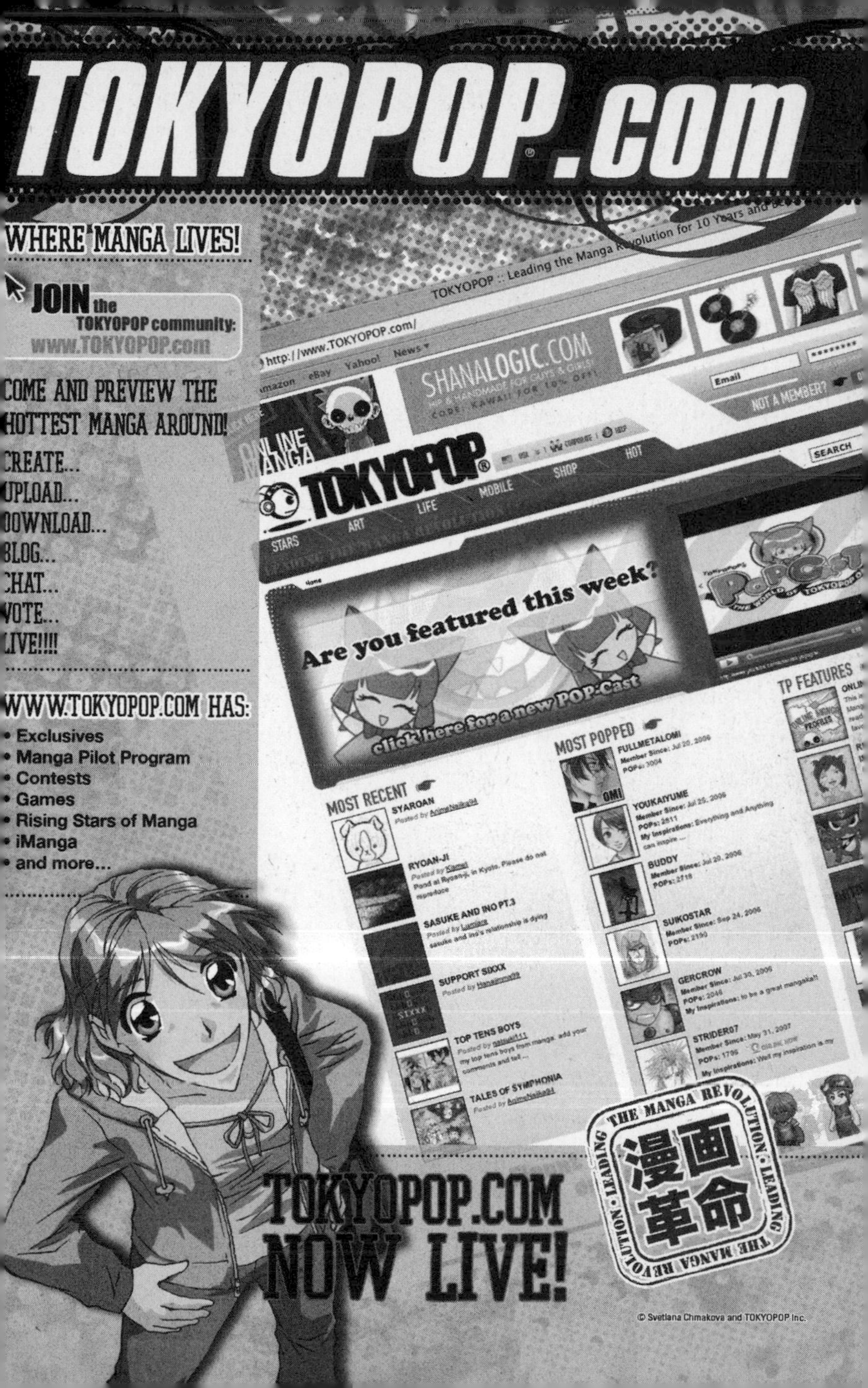
TOKYOPOP®.com
WHERE MANGA LIVES!
JOIN the TOKYOPOP community:
www.TOKYOPOP.com
COME AND PREVIEW THE HOTTEST MANGA AROUND!
CREATE...
UPLOAD...
DOWNLOAD...
BLOG...
CHAT...
VOTE...
LIVE!!!!
WWW.TOKYOPOP.COM HAS:
• Exclusives
• Manga Pilot Program
• Contests
• Games
• Rising Stars of Manga
• iManga
• and more...
TOKYOPOP :: Leading the Manga Revolution for 10 Years and Be
http://www.TOKYOPOP.com/
SHANALOGIC.COM
TOKYOPOP®
STARS
ART
LIFE
MOBILE
SHOP
HOT
SEARCH
NOT A MEMBER?
Are you featured this week?
click here for a new POP-Cast
MOST RECENT
MOST POPPED
TP FEATURES
SYAROAN
RYOAN-JI
SASUKE AND INO PT.3
SUPPORT SIXXX
TOP TENS BOYS
TALES OF SYMPHONIA
FULLMETALOMI
YOUKAIYUME
BUDDY
SUIKOSTAR
GERCROW
STRIDER07
TOKYOPOP.COM NOW LIVE!
THE MANGA REVOLUTION • LEADING
漫画革命
© Svetlana Chmakova and TOKYOPOP Inc.